CONSPIRACY ON CATO STREET

On the night of 23 February 1820 twenty-five impoverished craftsmen assembled in an obscure stable in Cato Street, London, with a plan to massacre the whole British cabinet at its monthly dinner. The Cato Street Conspiracy was the most sensational of all plots aimed at the British state since Guy Fawkes' Gunpowder Plot of 1605. It ended in betrayal, arrest, and trial, and with five conspirators publicly hanged and decapitated for treason. Their failure proved the state's physical strength, and ended hopes of revolution for a century. Vic Gatrell explores this dramatic yet neglected event in unprecedented detail through spy reports, trial interrogations, letters, speeches, songs, maps, and images. Attending to the 'real lives' and habitats of the men, women, and children involved, he throws fresh light on the troubled and tragic world of regency Britain, and on one of the most compelling and poignant episodes in British history.

Vic Gatrell is a professorial Life Fellow of Gonville and Caius College, who has taught for most of his career in the Cambridge Faculty of History. His previous books include *The Hanging Tree: Execution and the English People* (1997), which was awarded the Whitfield Prize of the Royal Historical Society; *City of Laughter: Sex and Satire in Eighteenth-Century London* (2009), which was awarded the Wolfson Prize for History and the PEN Hessell-Tiltman Prize; and *The First Bohemians: Life and Art in London's Golden Age* (2013), which was shortlisted for the PEN Hessell-Tiltman Prize.

CONSPIRACY ON CATO STREET

A Tale of Liberty and Revolution in Regency London

Vic Gatrell

CAMBRIDGE
UNIVERSITY PRESS

CAMBRIDGE
UNIVERSITY PRESS

University Printing House, Cambridge CB2 8BS, United Kingdom

One Liberty Plaza, 20th Floor, New York, NY 10006, USA

477 Williamstown Road, Port Melbourne, VIC 3207, Australia

314–321, 3rd Floor, Plot 3, Splendor Forum, Jasola District Centre,
New Delhi – 110025, India

103 Penang Road, #05–06/07, Visioncrest Commercial, Singapore 238467

Cambridge University Press is part of the University of Cambridge.

It furthers the University's mission by disseminating knowledge in the pursuit of
education, learning, and research at the highest international levels of excellence.

www.cambridge.org
Information on this title: www.cambridge.org/9781108838481
DOI: 10.1017/9781108974981

First published 2022

Printed in the United Kingdom by TJ Books Limited, Padstow Cornwall

A catalogue record for this publication is available from the British Library.

Library of Congress Cataloging-in-Publication Data
Names: Gatrell, Vic, 1941– author.
Title: Conspiracy on Cato Street : a tale of liberty and revolution in Regency London /
Vic Gatrell, University of Cambridge.
Other titles: Tale of liberty and revolution in Regency London
Description: Cambridge ; New York, NY : Cambridge University Press, 2022. |
Includes bibliographical references and index.
Identifiers: LCCN 2021049190 (print) | LCCN 2021049191 (ebook) |
ISBN 9781108838481 (hardback) | ISBN 9781108974981 (ebook)
Subjects: LCSH: Cato Street Conspiracy, 1820. | Revolutionaries – Great Britain –
History – 19th century. | Great Britain – History – George IV, 1820–1830. | Great
Britain – Politics and government – 1789–1820. | Thistlewood, Arthur, 1770–1820. |
Treason – England – London – History – 19th century. | Conspiracies – England –
London – History – 19th century. | BISAC: HISTORY / Europe / Great Britain / General
Classification: LCC DA537 .G38 2022 (print) | LCC DA537 (ebook) |
DDC 941.07/4–dc23/eng/20211102
LC record available at https://lccn.loc.gov/2021049190
LC ebook record available at https://lccn.loc.gov/2021049191

ISBN 978-1-108-83848-1 Hardback

Presently, passing to particular instances, we recalled the already old story of the attempt to blow up the Greenwich Observatory; a blood-stained inanity of so fatuous a kind that it was impossible to fathom its origin by any reasonable or even unreasonable process of thought. For perverse unreason has its own logical processes. But that outrage could not be laid hold of mentally in any sort of way, so that one remained faced by the fact of a man blown to bits for nothing even most remotely resembling an idea, anarchistic or other. As to the outer wall of the Observatory it did not show as much as the faintest crack. I pointed all this out to my friend who remained silent.

Joseph Conrad in 1920, on his novel, *The Secret Agent:
A Simple Tale of the Nineteenth Century* (1907)

When any man, or any set of men, place themselves above the laws of their country, there is no other means of bringing them to justice than through the arms [weapons] of a private individual. If the laws are not strong enough to prevent them from murdering the community, it becomes the duty of every member of that community to rid his country of its oppressors. . . . Insurrection then became a public duty.

Arthur Thistlewood's last speech, 28 April 1820

This, gentlemen, is not the way that kings are destroyed, and governments overthrown.

John Adolphus, defence counsel, 19 April 1820

Contents

PART FOUR ORDINARY BRITONS

PART FIVE THE EXECUTIONS

Illustrations and Maps

MAPS

ILLUSTRATIONS

Preface

Well over a century ago Joseph Conrad gave the most modest of subtitles to *The Secret Agent,* his novel about London's late-Victorian anarchists. *A Simple Tale of the Nineteenth Century,* he called it. On the face of it, the story told in this book about an earlier, non-fictional group of terrorists in regency London is a simple tale too. It takes us up close and personal to the conspirators who on the night of 23 February 1820 assembled in an obscure stable in Cato Street on the western edge of London in order to massacre the whole British government as it sat down to dinner in a Grosvenor Square mansion. This was the most sensational of all plots aimed at the state between the Gunpowder Plot of 1605 and the Irish Republican Army's Brighton bomb attack on Thatcher and her party in 1984. Had it succeeded, it would have changed our world utterly.

The conspiracy's exposure shook Britain profoundly. Optimists believed that it woke the nation from its long neglect and moved it towards reform. But the first parliamentary Reform Act lay a dozen years ahead, so it was truer to say that the conspirators' entrapment by government spies and their punishment afterwards marked the moments when the state's power was unchallengeably displayed and when hopes for revolution of the French kind were decisively flattened. Very few even of the Chartists in the 1840s envisaged root-and-branch revolution. Why Britain avoided a revolution in the following century is in good part explained by the Cato Street drama.

The men's elaborate trials in April aimed to dramatise the conspirators' violence in order to justify repressive laws and to expunge the stain of the Peterloo massacre the year before. The punishments that followed settled the question. Along with three weavers independently executed as traitors in Scotland for leading the so-called Scottish insurrection, five Cato Street men were the last in Britain to have their heads taken off for treason. They were also the last to be killed for treason until after the Irish Easter Rising in 1916, when fifteen men were executed by firing squad in Dublin and Roger Casement was hanged in Pentonville Prison.

What follows is the first book to explore this great moment by engaging with the conspirators' experiences, habitats, and mental world as intimately as is now possible. Innumerable spy reports, verbatim trial interrogations, and a vast range of newspapers, letters, speeches, songs, and images allow a rare degree of 'thick description'. When necessary, the humblest of these sources are quoted at length, since the misspelled and ill-punctuated writings of the half-literate in past times are seldom so accessible to their descendants. Probably no other episode in eighteenth- and nineteenth-century British history can be so fully accessed from the dialogues of the common people as this one.

Part I of the book tells the 'simple tale' first. It offers a straightforward narrative of the conspirators' entrapment and arrests, for, as every novel-ist knows, the devils lie in the details. Yet, like historians, novelists also know that simple tales can carry broad implications. The rest of the book broadens out therefore, to offer the forensic study that linear narratives can't deliver.

Part II discusses how past writers have interpreted the story and how we might today interpret it more sensitively. It notes the interests and powers of the rich men and aristocrats who kept the disfranchised in their place in regency Britain, and the equalising ideas that induced some of the disfranchised to inform the rich about their corruption and to demand redress, with violence if need be. It attends to the post-war conditions that poor craftsmen were up against: their impoverish-ment and declining craft status, the battered courtyards and lodgings they occupied, the taverns they frequented, and their own understand-ings of the cruel times they lived in: what and how did they think? One chapter addresses their habitats – and London itself – to provide the story with the topographical frame which historians so often bypass.

Part III provides a contextual narrative of radical protest in regency London by tracing the Cato Street leader Arthur Thistlewood's move-ment towards terrorist fantasy and violence. It notes the impact of the ultra-radicals' abortive insurrection after the Spa Fields meeting in 1816, and of the Peterloo massacre in Manchester in 1819, and it discusses the government spy and *agent provocateur* George Edwards's betrayal of the conspiracy's every detail to the Bow Street police and Lord Sidmouth's home office.

Part IV attends to the 'ordinary Britons' who got caught up in or who supported the conspiracy – their marriages, hardships, literacy or lack of it, and the racial and other prejudices that determined their life-chances. Most of the activists were under-employed shoemakers with wives and children to support. Two were black Jamaicans who had been born into slavery. One of them, Davidson, lost his head.

The book ends in Part V with the conspirators' trials and convictions and five of the leaders' hangings and decapitations. It notes the differing reactions to this horror on the part of the plebeian and the polite crowd respectively, and it finishes with an extraordinary drawing of the executions by the visiting French artist Théodore Géricault. His unfinished sketch hints at a shift in attitudes to the suffering of others that in these years began to reshape the contours of western sensibility.

A book of this kind can hardly help speaking to the present. Despite obvious changes, the inequalities and deprivations that moved the conspirators, and the privileged interests and powers that contained them, still operate. As William Faulkner once wrote, the past is not only never dead; it is not even past.

Acknowledgements

This book was conceived long ago in the 1980s when I was working in the National Archives on a quite different subject. One day curiosity moved me to order from the Treasury Solicitor's Papers a box intriguingly labelled 'pike-heads as exhibits'. Its contents had been used in evidence against a group of London radicals who were twice tried for treason – unsuccessfully in 1817 and successfully in 1820. Out of the box fell three heavy hand-tooled iron batons. Each measured some twelve inches in length and an inch or so across the middle, each had been beaten flat into the shape of a file, and each tapered to a point at both ends. One point was burred so that it could be securely jammed into a wooden staff; the other was smoothed so that it could be 'run into a fellow's guts', as the book's chief protagonist eloquently put it. Both in 1817 and in 1820 thousands of these things had been secretly manufactured and hidden about London. In 1820 two or three of them were meant to be inserted up the dripping necks of the most hated of the government ministers. Their heads were to be carried through London's streets to signal the advent of a long hoped-for British revolution.

My opening of that box and my encounter with the jaw-dropping materiality of its contents jolted me into several weeks' archival note-taking. The notes were put aside as other books and projects got in the way, but that encounter stayed with me. It alerted me to the truth, now more obvious than it was then, that our understandings of past times might be advanced not only through the study of surviving texts, but also through the study of localities, objects, and episodes which historians tend to ignore because of their apparent triviality and obviousness. In what follows I chart a story of considerable consequence not only through mountains of spy reports and semi-literate letters, but also through the accumulation of material, topographical, and incidental detail.

My immediate debts are to Jeremy Krikler, who first encouraged me to write about Cato Street; to Vivian Bickford Smith, Vyvyen Brendon, and Jerry White, who cheered me up in my more pessimistic moments; to Piers Brendon, a constant fount of advice who read through an early draft with a sharp eye for repetitions, misphrasings, and other failings; and to Mark Damazer, who read both an early and a late draft with a critical eye on the work's accessibility and potential. At the Press, Liz Friend-Smith, Natasha Whelan, and Hilary Hammond have been understanding and helpful. To all these people my warmest thanks.

My greatest debt is to Pam. As ever, she has been the *sine qua non* without whose warm support and readerly eye this would never have been written. I dedicate what follows to her, and also (again) to Freya, Harry, and Jack, and now also to Joe, who hadn't been born for the last one.

Abbreviations

BDMBR	*Biographical Dictionary of Modern British Radicals* (3 vols, 1979)
BM	British Museum
HC Deb	House of Commons Debates
HO	Home Office Papers, National Archives
LCS	London Corresponding Society
OBSP	*Old Bailey Sessions Papers* (www.oldbaileyonline.org)
ODNB	*Oxford Dictionary of National Biography*
TS	Treasury Solicitor's Papers, National Archives

Timeline

1792	Jan.	London Corresponding Society (LCS) established
	Dec.	Tom Paine convicted of seditious libel *in absentia*
1794		Habeas corpus suspended (to June 1795); treason trials of Hardy, Horne Tooke, and Thelwall result in acquittals in November
1795		Treason Act and Seditious Meetings Act passed after George III stoned on way to open parliament
1798		Habeas corpus suspended (to Feb. 1799; extended to May and again to Mar. 1800)
		LCS and United Irishmen arrests (including Evans, Spence, Despard)
1798–9	July–Feb.	Thistlewood an ensign in West Yorkshire militia
1803	*21 Feb.*	*Marcus Despard and six co-conspirators hanged and decapitated for treason*
	July–Sept.	Thistlewood in Lincolnshire militia
1804		Thistlewood marries heiress Jane Worsley in Lincoln; she dies in 1805
1806	3 Oct.	Julian Thistlewood, Arthur's son by Ann Thorn[el]ley, born in Horncastle
1808		Thistlewood marries Susan Wilkinson, daughter of Horncastle butcher
1811		Arthur, Susan, and Julian Thistlewood come to Edgware Road, London
	Mar.	Thistlewood on committee for United Irishman Peter Finnerty
		Prince of Wales becomes regent during George III's madness
1813	Feb.	Thistlewood offers to subsidise Margarot's visit to Bonaparte
		Thistlewood gambles away his brother's £900
1814	*Apr.*	*Napoleon abdicates*
		Thistlewood takes Thomas Evans's son to Paris
	Sept.	Death of Thomas Spence, agrarian socialist
		Thomas Evans establishes Society of Spencean Philanthropists
1815	*20 Mar.*	*Napoleon returns to Paris after escaping from Elba – start of Hundred Days*
	18 June	*Battle of Waterloo: Napoleon exiled on St Helena*
	20 Nov.	*Second Treaty of Paris ends French wars*
		Thistlewood's second visit to Paris
1816	2 Dec.	Spa Fields meeting addressed by Orator Hunt; 'Spa Fields insurrection'
		Thistlewood and 'young' Watson in hiding; 'young' Watson escapes to America
1817	Feb.	John Castle recruited as government spy
	9 Feb.	Thomas Evans and son imprisoned for a year
	4 Mar.	Habeas corpus suspended for a year to 1 March 1818
	10 Mar.	*March of the Lancashire 'Blanketeers'*

(continued)

	12 Mar.	John Cashman the sailor hanged for looting gun shops after Spa Fields
	17 Mar.	Treason Act renews 1795 Act against 'compassing, imagining, inventing, [etc.] death or destruction . . . of the heirs and successors of George III'
	25 Mar.	Seditious Meetings Act ('Gagging Act'); applied until July 1818 but renewed under Six Acts 1819; repealed 1824
	28 Apr.	Thistlewood arrested; held with 'old' Watson, Preston, and Hooper in Tower
	9–16 June	Watson, Thistlewood, Preston, and Hooper arraigned for treason; 'old' Watson acquitted when spy's role exposed; others' prosecutions collapse
	Sept.	Bartholomew Fair 'insurrection'
	7 Nov.	*Hanging and decapitation of Derbyshire luddites*
	Dec.	William Hone acquitted for blasphemous libels
1818	Jan.	Edwards starts reporting to Stafford, chief clerk at Bow Street police office
	3 Feb.	Thistlewood challenges home secretary Sidmouth to a duel
	1 May	Thistlewood imprisoned for a year in Horsham gaol as result (for 'breach of peace')
1819	Jan.	Richard Carlile opens radical bookshop at 55½ Fleet Street; Edwards the spy trades next door
	May	Thistlewood released from Horsham gaol
		Watson introduces Edwards to Thistlewood
	21 July	Smithfield reform meeting, addressed by Hunt and Watson
	16 Aug.	*Peterloo massacre, Manchester*
	13 Sept.	Hunt's triumphal entry into London; radicals quarrel at Crown and Anchor dinner
	Oct.	Richard Carlile sentenced to six years for blasphemous libel
	1 Nov.	Finsbury Market meeting a failure
	2 Nov.	Castlereagh introduces Sidmouth's Six Acts (passed 30 Dec.): against seditious meetings, blasphemous and seditious libels, unlawful drilling, unstamped newspapers, and restricting private possession of arms and bail conditions
	Nov.	Robert Wedderburn arrested for blasphemous libel
1820	*29 Jan.*	*Death of George III; prince regent becomes George IV*
	1 Feb.	Cabinet dinner cancelled in mourning
	16 Feb.	*George III's funeral in Windsor*
	23 Feb.	Conspirators arrested in Cato Street stable
	3 Mar.	Conspirators examined by privy council
	16 Mar.	Hunt (and others) tried for 'sedition' (at Peterloo); imprisoned for thirty months
	10 Apr.	Géricault visits London; returns to Paris in June (second visit Nov./Dec. 1820, for a year)
	15–28 Apr.	The Cato Street trials (Thistlewood's 17, 18, 19 April)
	28 Apr.	Friday: death sentences
	1 May	Monday: executions
	2, 9 May	Alderman Wood exposes the spy Edwards in the Commons; motion for committee to investigate rejected
	5 June	*Queen Caroline lands at Dover; George IV moves to divorce her*
1821	*19 July*	*George IV's coronation; Abbey doors locked against Queen Caroline*
	7 Aug.	*Caroline dies from 'constriction of the bowel'*

A Note on the Text

In citing the writings of the semi-literate, I retain misspellings and absent punctuations but omit '*sic*' for simplicity; I remove redundant capitals and insert extra spaces where stops are missing.

In the notes, trial reports are referenced by short title or abbreviation, and sometimes by column and sometimes by page (see 'The Trial Reports' for details).

All books listed in the Bibliography are published in London unless otherwise stated.

THE SIMPLE TALE

CHAPTER 1

The Cato Street Conspiracy: What Happened

In 1975 the London County Council added to its archive a photograph of a small workshop in the mews alley of Cato Street, just behind London's Edgware Road (Fig. 1.1). Built in 1803 as a gentleman's stable on the then western edge of built-up London, the building is now converted into a modern dwelling, but when the photograph was taken it looked battered and bruised after more than two centuries' use. Measuring eighteen feet wide and sixteen deep, it had a double-doored space on the left to admit a carriage, and a narrow stable door on the right that once opened onto three horse-stalls. At the rear a ladder led up to a hayloft furnished with a carpenter's bench and some hay boxes. Two small rooms opened off the loft, one a bedroom with a fireplace and a window over the street, the other a windowless room at the rear (Fig. 1.2). Even in 1820 the building had 'a mean and ruinous aspect'.

In 1819 the stable's owner, a military general named Watson, went to India and let it to one of his servants, named Firth. For a while Firth kept five cows in the stable while he dossed down upstairs; but after a time he gave up cow-keeping and sublet the building to an ex-soldier named John Harrison, charging him 'five shillings a week for six months certain'. Harrison said he wanted to keep his horse and cart there, but he was really looking for somewhere for his friends to meet before they ventured forth in order to change the course of history. That is how on the cold winter night of 23 February 1820, twenty-five or so impoverished men,

1.1. *The Cato Street Stable in 1975* (© City of London Corporation)

some of them hungry, assembled in the stable's loft in order to commit what we would now call a terrorist atrocity.

The plan was ambitious. From Cato Street, their leader Arthur Thistlewood would walk them a mile south through dimly gas-lit streets to Lord Harrowby's mansion in Grosvenor Square, where they believed the whole government cabinet would be dining (Map 1). The attackers would carry pistols, swords, and home-made hand grenades and pikes. There, according to the turncoat conspirator Robert Adams in court,

> Thistlewood himself was to rap at the door and give a note to the porter while the others rushed in and, presenting a pistol at the porter's head, should compel him to point out the room where the company were. [Then they would] secure the staircase and area to prevent the servants below from interfering, and if occasion should require be prepared with hand grenades to throw amongst them. ... Harrison and Adams being tall and swordsmen should first go into the room.

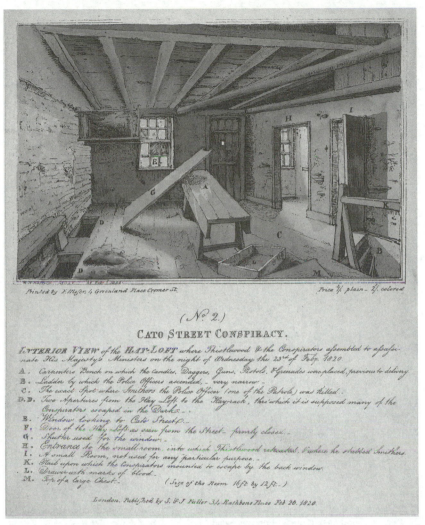

1.2. F. Moser, after W. H. Harriott, *Cato Street Conspiracy (No. 2): Interior View of the Hay-Loft* (26 February 1820) (© Yale Center for British Art)

... Two men were to be placed at the stairs, leading to the upper part of the house; one was to have fire arms, to be protected by another with a hand-grenade in his hand ... If any servants attempted to make any retreat from the lower part of the house, or from the upper part of the house, these men with the hand-grenades, were to clap fire to the hand-grenades, and fling it

1. Cato Street stable
2. Géricault's lodgings 1820, 39 Edgware Road
3. Adam Elmore, 3 John Street
4. Harrowby's mansion, 39 Grosvenor Square
5. King Street Life Guards stables
6. Portman Street Foot Guards barracks
7. Thistlewood's lodgings in 1811, 64 Edgware Road
8. Hazard's reading club, 54 Queen Street
9. Davidson and Wilson, Eliots Row, Lord's
10. Shaw Strange, Lisson Grove
11. Robert George, Chapel Street

Map 1. Cato Street to Grosvenor Square (from William Faden's 1813 edition of Richard Horwood's 1792–9 *PLAN of the Cities of LONDON and WESTMINSTER, the Borough of SOUTHWARK, and PARTS adjoining Shewing every HOUSE*) (London Topographical Society, 1985)

in amongst them altogether. Two men at the same time were to be placed at the area, one with a blunderbuss and another with a hand-grenade: if any body attempted to make their retreat from the lower part of the house that way, they were to have a hand-grenade thrown in amongst them there. ...

Into what part of the house did he [Thistlewood] *propose they should go?* – Where their lordships were.

And what to do? – To murder all they found in the room, good or bad.

After Harrison and Adams had completed the killing, Ings would 'cut off every head that was in the room, and the heads of lords Castlreagh [*sic*] and Sidmouth he would bring away in a bag, he would provide for the purpose two bags'. The heads would be stuck on pike-heads and paraded through London.[1]

While this was in progress, designated parties would create diversions by setting fire to the Portman Street barracks off Oxford Street, the Life Guards' horse barracks at King Street, an oil warehouse in Southwark, and Furnival's Inn in Holborn.[2] The Portman Street barracks were selected because the ex-soldier Harrison had once been billeted there and knew through which windows one could lob fire balls into the hayloft.[3] Small parties would also hijack cannon from the Finsbury Artillery barracks in the City and from the Light Horse barracks on upper Gray's Inn Lane – the notion being that the first 'they could easily get by killing a centinel [*sic*]', and the second 'they could get at very easily, by breaking in some small doors'.[4] Thus armed, they would attack the Bank of England, Newgate prison, and the Tower of London. They would then set up a provisional government in the Mansion House, and James Ings the butcher would be its secretary. The discontented populace would surely rise behind them, the royal family would be dealt with (though nobody said how), and the people would be given back the ancestral liberties which Norman aristocrats and their descendants had denied them for centuries. Nobody spoke overtly of 'revolution', but whatever ensued was set to match the French cataclysm of 1789.

The conspiracy had been a long time in the making. In December 1816 its leader Arthur Thistlewood and two of his associates, an apothecary called Dr James Watson and a shoemaker named Thomas Preston, had already planned to mount an insurrection after a great reform meeting in

Spa Fields in north London. Soldiers made sure that their plan failed miserably, and in 1817 they narrowly escaped execution for treason because of it. Thereafter London's ultra-radicals continued to meet, quarrel, and plot until they were re-energised in August 1819 by the Peterloo massacre. At a peaceful reform meeting on St Peter's Field in Manchester, dragoons and yeomanry killed seventeen unarmed men and women and one child in arms, and grievously injured 670 more. This horror was the Cato Street conspiracy's most immediate provocation and justification. Thistlewood made his way to Manchester and Leicester in October, and Mancunians in return visited Thistlewood. A national rising was in prospect. Floods of letters from northern magistrates and informers warned the home office that Lancashire, Yorkshire, and Clydeside were awaiting a London insurrection and would mount their own in sympathy. Trade and tavern clubs were ready for action. The London Irish were ready too, though less reliably since they mistrusted every one of the English, even poor ones.

Over the winter Thistlewood, Watson, and Preston gathered about them a hard core of supporters. It included two under-employed shoemakers, John Brunt and Richard Tidd, two ex-soldiers, John Harrison and Robert Adams (Adams had become yet another shoemaker), the butcher James Ings, a Jamaica-born cabinet-maker William Davidson, and an impoverished model maker called George Edwards. Alas for the conspirators, Edwards was the government spy and *agent provocateur* who achieved the conspiracy's downfall. Since early 1819 he had been reporting the ultra-radicals' every move to the home secretary Sidmouth and the Bow Street magistrate Richard Birnie. Under their guidance he lured the conspirators into a trap.

In December, Edwards reported that they were talking of massacring the House of Commons en masse but decided against it because they didn't have enough bullets and because Thistlewood said he wanted only to kill the ministers, not the innocent.[5] Then they planned to assassinate the ministers while they dined at Lord Westmorland's, only to find the house ringed by Bow Street officers. As they aimed to do the same on 1 February at a cabinet dinner at Lord Harrowby's, George III died inconveniently, so the dinner was cancelled. Next they plotted to murder ministers individually while soldiers and police were at Windsor for the king's funeral on 16 February, forgetting that the ministers would be in Windsor too. At last on Tuesday, 22 February Edwards arrived at the conspirators' meeting place in Fox Court off Gray's Inn Lane, to announce excitedly that he had just spotted this advertisement in the *New Times*: 'The Earl of Harrowby gives a Grand Cabinet Dinner to-morrow at his house, in Grosvenor-square'. Harrowby would host the dinner as lord president of the privy council. At last the whole cabinet offered itself as a sitting target.

Thistlewood should have been suspicious. The *New Times* was edited by a tory loyalist; and since the advert appeared in no other paper he might have guessed that Edwards and his masters had inserted it themselves. But past delays and disappointments had brought the group to fever pitch. They swallowed the bait. Ings announced that he looked forward to cutting Castlereagh's head off with his butcher's knife, and the shoemaker Brunt stamped about the room declaring that he'd be damned if he didn't believe in a God now, because for this one and only time in his life his prayers were answered. When someone questioned the wisdom of proceeding, 'Brunt put himself into a passion, and so did all of them, particularly Harrison, who walked about the room and threatened the first man that attempted to fling cold water upon the concern, he would run him through directly with a sword.'[6]

The privy councillors expected to attend the dinner were to include Lord Liverpool the prime minister, Lord Sidmouth the home secretary, Canning the president of the board of control, and the foreign secretary Lord Castlereagh.[7] None would be missed. Radicals thought Castlereagh the biggest villain. As Irish chief secretary he had helped to suppress the 1798 Irish rebellion mercilessly. 'Derry Down Triangle', the radical journalist William Hone called him, referring to the flogging triangle on which his disciplines were delivered. Killing him would bring the Irish to their side. This was also the Castlereagh who as foreign secretary favoured reactionary governments on the continent, who spied on and plotted against the regent's errant wife Caroline, and who introduced Sidmouth's repressive Six Acts in the Commons after the Peterloo massacre in August 1819. This last horror Castlereagh elaborately excused.

Castlereagh cut his own throat in 1822. Long-term syphilis might have been one reason for the suicide, blackmail over his intimacy with a transvestite another. But he and Sidmouth were also the most loathed men in Britain, a condition difficult to live with. After Peterloo the poet Shelley immortalised Castlereagh in his *Masque of Anarchy*:

> I met Murder on the way –
> He had a mask like Castlereagh –
> Very smooth he looked, yet grim;
> Seven bloodhounds followed him.
>
> . . .
>
> He tossed them human hearts to chew
> Which from his wide cloak he drew.

Byron got to the point more economically:

> Posterity will ne'er survey
> A nobler grave than this:
> Here lie the bones of Castlereagh:
> Stop, traveller, and piss.

It was a bonus that the duke of Wellington and the lord chancellor Eldon would also attend the dinner. Although the victor of Waterloo was hailed by loyalists as a national hero, radicals damned him. A powerful and now forgotten streak of anti-militarism moved a populace that had been fighting for twenty years and had paid an awful price. As one ditty put it in the thick of the wars:

> I hate that drum's discordant sound,
> Parading round, and round, and round;
> To me it talks of ravag'd plains,
> And burning towns, and ruin'd swains,
> And mangled limbs, and dying groans,
> And widows' tears, and orphans' moans,
> And all that misery's hand bestows,
> To swell the catalogue of human woes.[8]

After the peace Wellington was the master of the ordnance in a government that had levied 3,000 additional soldiers and marines to enforce domestic order. As post-war satirists attacked the costs of supporting a monstrous peacetime force of 150,000 men and an extravagant staff, Wellington stood for the 'standing army' that liberty-minded English people had deplored since the seventeenth century.[9]

Lord chancellor Eldon epitomised the crabbed and reactionary lawyer. Nobody had more strongly supported the repression of radical opinion in the 1790s, or had so energetically resisted the reform of criminal law and its punishments, the emancipation of Catholics, the abolition of slavery, and the regulation of child labour. In 1817 and 1819 he endorsed the suspension of habeas corpus and a renewal of the Treason and Seditious Meetings Acts, and in 1820 he thought that after hanging and decapitation the Cato Street men's bodies should be publicly butchered into quarters, even though the gruesome ritual was last performed in 1782. Eldon got his reward from Shelley as well:

> Next came Fraud, and he had on,
> Like Eldon, an ermined gown;
> His big tears, for he wept well,
> Turned to mill-stones as they fell.
> And the little children, who
> Round his feet played to and fro,
> Thinking every tear a gem,
> Had their brains knocked out by them.

The Harrowby mansion at 39 Grosvenor Square had been built around 1727 on the south side of London's grandest and second largest square. Of its forty-seven householders in 1790, thirty-one were titled. They included three dukes, six earls and a viscount, and the archbishop of York. Harrowby, a baron, had bought the house in 1804 when he was appointed Pitt's foreign secretary of state. He got his earldom in 1809 and became lord president of the privy council under Liverpool. He favoured Catholic emancipation and the abolition of the slave trade, but he was of peevish temperament and defended repressive measures and harsh punishment at home as zealously as the worst of them. His mansion was externally plain but internally rich in Turkey carpets, gilded mirrors, and marble side tables, and its mahogany dining-room table seated eighteen. The vast paintings over the main staircase were by John Laguerre, emulating those in Kensington Palace.[10]

In this never-never land his majesty's ministers would supposedly be sitting down to their halibut, mutton, and gooseberry tart, all ripe for the killing, and into this company the conspirators would irrupt with the odours of their own insanitary dwellings and bodies heavy upon them and mass murder in mind. In the event the cabinet sensibly dined at Liverpool's in Whitehall, but they took care to leave Harrowby's staff cooking and preparing as if the dinner was proceeding. Nobody warned the staff that hand grenades might soon be heading their way. Dinner was set for seven o'clock; only at eight did Harrowby send a note to cancel the preparations.[11] As it happened, the archbishop of York lived next door to Harrowby, and that same evening his household was preparing to entertain the new king George IV and the king's two brothers. Canning later joked that if things had gone wrong the royal family might have been wiped out by mistake. The bustle of their carriages would persuade Thistlewood's watchers that a great assemblage was gathering at Harrowby's.

On Tuesday, 22 February, Thistlewood and friends had a day to get ready. They met in the bare room they had rented in Fox Court to agree on their plan and bring their weapons from their hiding places. As the spy reported,

> Davidson brought in a great many musket balls and a hand saw, and Thistlewood directed that three or four rounds of powder should be prepared for the cannon to serve for the moment, what more [was] wanting to be procured at the time by rushing into the oil shops. Ings drew a long knife from his pocket declaring it was for the purpose of cutting Lord Castlereagh's head off and that he would bring it away in a bag.

John Shaw Strange started flinting pistols in Brunt's front workroom, but had to be sent to the back room because the people opposite could see him.

The fateful morning of Wednesday, 23 February was spent in mobilising their supporters across town. Thistlewood managed to pen three copies of a placard to post on walls: 'Your tyrants are destroyed – the provisional government is now sitting'. To this he added an address to urge soldiers to join the Friends of Liberty. Any who did so 'should have their discharge with full pay for life and twenty pounds to take them home'. Paying them would be no problem once the Bank was raided and its coffers emptied. Men were sent in shifts to watch Harrowby's house to ensure that no Bow Street officers were smuggled in to ambush them. 'If any soldiers or officers should be seen going in there [they must] be reported to the committee, if not, the plans go on.'[12] The watchers were easily distracted. At one point they supped on bread, cheese, and porter (a form of stout) in the Rising Sun in Charles Street, round the corner from Harrowby's. A local servant later testified that he played dominos with 'that short man with a brown coat on' (Brunt) and his tall companion (Adams). At one point Adams was caught short, lavatorially speaking: '*Did you walk in the square?* – Yes. I walked some time till I got ashamed of myself, and I walked to the back of the square, and met [Brunt] on the other side of it.'

Mustering followers for the attack that night wasn't entirely successful. Nearly half of the forty or so who were expected to turn up in Cato Street failed to do so. The cow keeper Thomas Hiden told 'Black' Davidson that he had to collect some cream before he went to Cato Street. 'Come, you dog, come,' Davidson rebuked him, 'it will be the best thing you were ever in in your life'. But Hiden went off nonetheless, and betrayed them. Waylaying Lord Harrowby in Hyde Park, he humbly gave him a note for Castlereagh. Dated 21 February, its script was shaky and not fully legible, but it blew the plot sky-high. Although ministers already knew exactly what was intended, reference to this letter in court would conceal their dependence on Edwards:

> My Lord this ... [?] ... I have sent to you to save your lives and to save the government of my contary as the plan is ... to take your lives and all things is redy that when the Cabbinet Councell is at Dinner these villings ar goain to enter in to the house with Great things [grenades] they нае made of gun powder and other things of tin ... They have for the purpose of these ... things [f]or to be thrown in the room a ... [and?] with fuse and what is not killed with these things is to be killed with the soard and spikes [pikes] my lord I ham sory that it is out of my power to in form you the very man [?]

But think the spikes may be found in Gees Court of Oxford Street [Dwyer's lodging] or in the Cottagess behind Jinckins nursry New Road Marele Bon [Davidson's lodging] my lord they mean to after slaughter to set fuer your house and Lord ... duke of Willighton Bishop of London and Lord Sedmouth My Lord I have heard that your Bigest inemy is Thissellwood and Prestin my lord My lord I have given you every Informaschon that I can my lord my life is at stake for whith these words to you I for ever [will be] known by the villings [villains] My lords and gentlemen I have writ this as well as Could My lord if I should be [killed] by these [. . . ?] I hope you will think of my family.[13]

Another absentee turncoat was the Irish bricklayer, John Dwyer. Dwyer later testified that he had met Davidson on 4 February while both men, in penury, worked at the parish mill in Marylebone. Dwyer, however, found some work at Elmore's stables in John Street opposite the Cato Street entry, and Davidson brought Thistlewood to visit him there. Under pressure Dwyer promised the support of twenty-seven or so Irishmen from his own Irish rookery in Gee's Court off Oxford Street. On 22 February he took fright, and wrote to Sidmouth in good copperplate script to 'make a very serous communication respectting a conspiracy against the government and state that is carrying on in this Metropoliss'. He was interviewed and corralled as a prosecution witness. On that very last day in their hideout in Fox Court, Thistlewood was still telling his committee that Dwyer would bring fifty armed Irishmen that 'the whole of the Irish men & women will be ready half an hour after the beginning'.[14] No such luck. The defence later proved in court that Dwyer was 'one of those horrible characters who are in the habit of extorting money from respectable persons, by a false accusation of an unnatural crime, and actually has boasted of finding this a good way for making money'. He gave evidence against Thistlewood but was thought too tainted to be used in the other men's trials.[15]

Many who did turn up in the stable were strangers to each other. Unsure where Cato Street was and what to do when they got there, they had been told to go to the Tyburn turnpike at the foot of the Edgware Road where a man would be waiting for them under the gaslight. To him

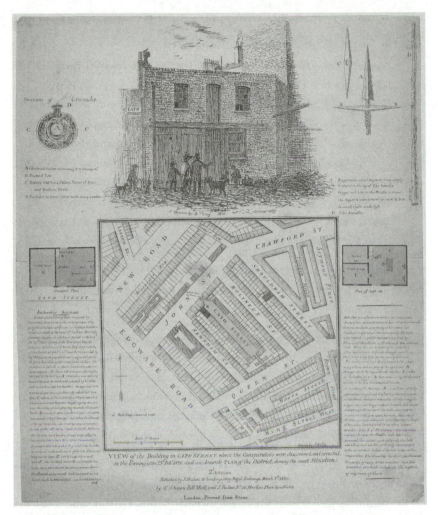

1.3. J. Wylde, after B. King, *View of the Building in Cato Street where the Conspirators were Discovered*, with map and depictions of hand grenade and pike-head (2 March 1820) (© Yale Center for British Art)

they should whisper the password 'b', 'u' and 't'; to which he would respond with 't', 'o', and 'n' and then lead them north to the stable (Fig. 1.3).

Once someone was told that a plot was under way he could hardly be allowed out of it, so some intimidation was called for. John Monument and Adams described this vividly after they turned king's evidence. Monument:

> *You had joined in this plan to assassinate his majesty's ministers?* – Unwillingly.
> *You did join it?* – Through fear.
> *How through fear?* – I was afraid if I did not join it, it would be the worse for me; for when Brunt came on the 22nd of February, he said, that any one that was any ways concerned with them, and did not go, would be destroyed. . . . I was forced to join it, I could not get away.
> *What forced you to Tidd's, and forced you along the streets [with him]?* – Fear.
> *You told us just now, that a man in a brown coat was told he might retire; why did not you retire?* – I should have been loath to take him at his word.
> *It was fear brought you into it, and fear kept you in it?* – Yes, it was.[16]

Adams likewise. Between 13 and 30 January he had been in Whitecross Street debtors' prison, and so missed much of the planning, but he had to explain why on his release he had failed to leave the group:

> *Then if your intention was against it, how came you to join them again?* – I joined upon them in this way, gentlemen of the jury; there had been threatening language several times held out by Brunt, if any man that belonged to the party concerned, withdrew himself from it, he would take care that that man should be marked out; what could I do then?
> *Then it was fear made you join them?* – It was fear that kept me to them.

Adams added that he was scared of Ings because 'when anything occurred his whole blood and soul boiled for murder.'[17]

Revolutionary zeal was unevenly spread. James Wilson, an ex-soldier turned milkman, told Thistlewood that he first had to deliver milk to a customer, and Monument told Brunt that he first had to finish off some shoes, though he did turn up later. Those who did turn up included two or three 'mere boys' who had little idea what they had let themselves in for. One innocent, an unemployed 33-year-old cobbler from Dundee called James Gilchrist, joined the group because he was starving. As he addressed the court, he burst into tears:

> I knew nothing of it [the plot] till about four o'clock in the afternoon; I was going to look for work; I had neither money nor bread, so I met with a man

who told me to come to the Horse and Groom [in Cato Street], that they were going to have a supper there. I was not a man that suffered myself to be among radicals, but I had nothing to eat, and absent from my friends, and none to help me. . . . I went to the place at six o'clock at night, and met four or five men whom I did not know . . . I borrowed a halfpenny, and bought some bread at a shop; . . . I followed them on, not knowing what I was going about; . . . and when I went up stairs, in a very little time came in bread and cheese; I took an old sword and hacked it down; the men came round seemingly as hungry as I was, and I never asked . . . the meaning of those arms.

Gilchrist had no illusions about his lowly place in the world. When a police officer suddenly appeared on the loft ladder, 'I knew by his neckcloth, and the appearance of a gentleman, that it was my duty to surrender myself. . . . I served my king and my country twelve years, and this is the recompense; O God!' he sobbed, 'I have nothing more to say.' He was the only convicted conspirator whose account of himself the judge believed. His death sentence was respited, but he was allowed to walk free without compensation only after eight months in gaol, to a future that was bleak beyond imagining.[18]

THE ARTS OF KILLING

The Cato Street conspirators were ordinary Britons and many were humble shoemakers, but they bore a distinction peculiar to their times. Although only Harrison and Adams might have seen battle, all of them had been touched by the biggest military mobilisation in British history to that date, so they knew a good deal about the arts of killing. In 1805 over a quarter of a million of the British males capable of carrying arms were or had been in the army, and a half of that again in the navy. A further 385,000 were in the volunteers, 30,000 in the naval home guard, and 60,000 in supplementary militias. Across the years 1798–1810 about one in five adult males were under arms. Only a third of the regulars were normally garrisoned outside the country, so uniforms were visible on every British street and tavern – as they had been throughout the war-battered eighteenth century.[19]

It was no surprise that the conspirators turned to violence when their generation had been so well taught how to use it. While Gilchrist had served king and country for twelve years, Thistlewood had learned his swordsmanship in the West Yorkshire militia in 1798–9 and in the 3rd Lincolnshire militia in 1803.[20] 'Black' Davidson claimed twice to have been impressed into the navy, and spoke of having several times risked his life for his adopted country: 'I have not had the honour to wear the red jacket but have fought in a blue [naval] one,' he boasted to a radical meeting in December 1819.[21] Richard Tidd had enlisted in several regiments under false names, absconding from each as soon as he was paid his bounty for joining it.[22] John Palin, who escaped arrest until November 1820, had been a corporal in the East London Militia. John Brunt's father had been killed while serving in the American war, whereafter his mother and her four children had become paupers chargeable to the parish of St James. In 1816 Brunt mended soldiers' boots in Cambrai in northern France, the headquarters of Wellington's army of occupation. There he had fallen in with Robert Adams and had tutored him in shoemaking. Adams had been a private in the Horse Guards for five years between 1797 and 1802 and recruited to the conspiracy as a trained swordsman. John Harrison had served with the Life Guards for ten and a half years before his discharge in August 1814. He became a journeyman baker, but in the grim winter of 1818/19 he had allegedly staved off starvation by stealing sheep. Since May 1819 he had survived by cleaning shoes and by turning a Mrs Reeves's mangle in Little Park Street. As a Life Guard he had been posted in the King Street barracks, which was why he could tell Thistlewood how to set the building alight with fire balls.[23]

Their expertise was orchestrated by the apothecary Dr James Watson, at fifty-four the oldest of the conspirators. Watson was in debtors' prison when the conspiracy erupted so he escaped arrest and trial; but in 1817 he, Thistlewood, and the shoemaker Preston had been jointly arraigned for treason after the abortive Spa Fields insurrection of the previous December, and their relationship remained close though fractious. Watson seems not to have seen military service, but he combined martial ingenuity with childlike inventiveness – and with a habit of writing everything down. Thistlewood told him that he wrote 'too many papers' and that this led to 'a discovery of plots'.[24]

Watson's habit explains how we know that in 1816 he had invented the letter-bomb – 'a chemical preparation', the informer Castle told the home office, 'composed of pulverised silver, steel filings and pounded flint which is so liable to explosion that if a little of it is put into a letter the mere opening of the Letter would cause it to explode'. In 1816 Watson reinvented a very ancient instrument 'for acting against the horse, a sort of carriage on 4 wheels with scythes projecting from it on each side and in the front so that three or four men might drive it before them and clear a street while those behind might be firing over them'. And as 'a man of better education and more scientific profession than the others', he undertook to prepare 'the medicaments which were to kill whole barracks full of soldiers' – namely smoke-bombs.[25]

He was at it again in January 1820. The slip of paper on which he then wrote out his recipe for fire balls has a cheerful domesticity about it: 'mutton suit' mixed with horse turpentine, hog's lard, and saltpetre, with twists of brown paper for the fuses (Fig. 1.4). And it was Watson again who drafted a coded exhortation to soldiers to join the insurrection:[26]

> Brave Soldiers, the Tyrants are no more! Make common cause with the people! Think of your fathers mothers and friends! Be just to the miseries they have long endured! Be just to your selves! Be brave and be free!!! Join the people; to be the freest nation on earth then you will be the most prosperous and happy. Wait for instructions from the Provisional Government it is engaged in projecting measures to reward you ~~for your services~~ [*crossed out*] Your condition will be made happy. Obey the provisional decrees. You are brave be just to your countries wrongs. ~~Fate demand~~ [*crossed out*] justice demands protection of the Rights of man. A great reward is your Right.

These words were to be broken up and individually transcribed on six vertical strips of paper that had to be placed in the correct order to be readable. Each strip was headed by a cipher: BN, EA, JT, UU, SR, and TE, and one remembered the sequence by reordering every second letter to read 'Be just [to] nature'. The mystery could be cracked in minutes (Fig 1.5). Signing it 'G.E', Edwards sent it to Bow Street.

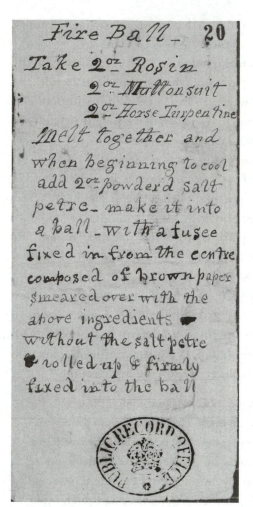

1.4. Dr Watson's recipe for a fire ball (© National Archives)

Although Watson's inventions might have been playful if not simply thick-headed, enthusiasms and skills of these kinds bore fruit in the preparations Thistlewood and friends made both for the 1816 Spa Fields insurrection and for the killings intended in 1820. In each case they made and stockpiled weapons over months, mainly at Thistlewood's expense. In 1816 he paid a journeyman blacksmith £4 15s to make 250 pike-heads to jam into the ends of staves and broomsticks. Two hundred of these were later recovered from their hiding place in Watson's privy in Hyde Street, and three (now cleaned) are preserved as evidence in the

1.5. Dr Watson's coded address to the soldiers (© National Archives)

treasury solicitor's papers.[27] In 1819 the group covertly sold pikes to willing customers at 1s 3d each, and stored them in a makeshift arms depot in Spitalfields.[28] In preparation for Cato Street, Thistlewood employed a typefounder named Harris to cast over a thousand ball cartridges from lead and pewter while his followers made incendiary fire balls from Watson's recipe and Harrison taught them how to make hand grenades.

The grenades were made with 'fiendish ingenuity'. From the centre of a small tin box containing two or three ounces of gunpowder rose a narrow tube two and a half inches long, filled with damped powder as a fuse. The whole was wrapped in rope steeped in tar, then surrounded by the pieces of iron, then further wrapped in a seven-inch ball of rope yarn. The grenades could propel the spikes, nails, files, and bits of sheet iron inside them a hundred yards 'with the force of a musket'. A Bow Street constable described them as 'covered with tarpaulin, and bound round with cords, filled full of nails and other things, ... some made of tin, which were very strong indeed ... If they were set fire to, and put under the walls of the houses in the street where we were walking, they would lift them up.' One 'was nearly as big as my hat'.[29] These horrid creations were 'nothing like our artillery grenades', an artillery sergeant testified. The army's grenades were packed with pistol balls, but these contained nails that would 'fly about killing and wounding the persons in the room' (the last thing artillery sergeants would think of doing). The new king had one sent to him for inspection.[30]

The outcome of these efforts was first listed in Edwards's spy report of 22 February:

> [at Tidd's lodging] 24 hand grenades; one large ditto; 48 pike shafts; 20 ditto blades; several old files for pikes; 4 lb of powder; 2 lb of ditto; 1800 rounds of ball cartridge; 20 ditto. ... At the type manufactory Type Street Finsbury belonging to Harris 9 swords – 3 pike blades several files for pikes and a musket &c; also about one cwt. of cast iron to make into shot. Cook has pikes & fire arms for 5 or 6 persons and 30 or 40 other persons are well armed.[31]

Later, the court was told that the weapons recovered in the Cato Street loft were:

> thirty-eight ball cartridges, firelock and bayonet, one powder flask, three pistols and one sword, with six bayonet spikes and cloth belt, one blunderbuss, pistol, fourteen bayonet spikes and three pointed files, one bayonet, one bayonet spike and one sword scabbard, one carbine and bayonet, two swords, one bullet, ten hand-grenades, two fire balls, one

large grenade and bayonet, a rope ladder, one sword stick, forty ball cartridges, one bayonet and three loose balls, these were all found in the loft.

Further arms were found on individuals:

in the pocket of Bradburn, six ball cartridges, three balls, and some string put round him to act as a belt; the pistol which it is alleged Tidd fired, the pistol which it is alleged Wilson attempted to fire, a blunderbuss, sword belt and scabbard; in the stable, two pistols, one sword, twelve sticks with ferrules; in the pocket of Tidd, two ball cartridges, and round him a leathern belt; two ball cartridges facing the stable, and ten ditto in Newnham-street; one musket cut down and one sword from Davidson; one haversack, cross belts, one pricker, bayonet, scabbard, cartouche box and a belt round his body; two haversacks, one belt and tin powder case, from Ings; four pistol balls, one pistol key and a knife case, from Ings; one haversack containing seventeen ball cartridges, three balls, one pistol flint, one pricker, one worm for drawing cartridges, one knife and a turnscrew, one stick cut to receive a bayonet, left in the public-house.[32]

CATO STREET

On the western side of the lower Edgware Road in 1820 the fields of Paddington were lightly dotted with houses and labourers' makeshift huts. Its eastern side was lined with recently built four-storey terraces with back gardens, and behind these lay (and lie) modest streets and mews built for labourers and artisans. Scattered among them were a few unlovely alleys of one-up-one-down or two-up-two-down terraced dwellings. Of these Cato Street was the unloveliest. Its freehold ground rents and house 'carcases' were first advertised for sale in 1805.[33]

The street was aptly though coincidentally named since Cato the Younger's resistance to Julius Caesar's tyranny had given him a place in the radical pantheon. It also offered escape routes across or up the Edgware Road into countryside, with fields and hedges to hide in. (On Thistlewood's first arrival in London he and his family had lodged on the Edgware Road a block away from Cato Street, so he knew the territory.)

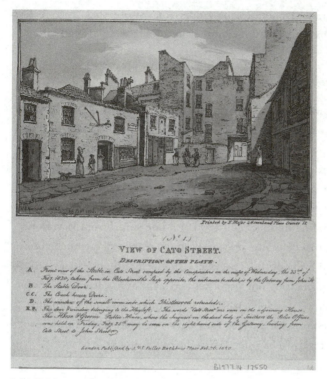

1.6. F. Moser, after W. H. Harriott, *Cato Street Conspiracy (No. 1): View of Cato Street* (26 February 1820) (© Yale Center for British Art)

Its disadvantage was that Harrowby's Grosvenor Square mansion was twenty minutes' fast walk to the south, and the Portman Street barracks were along the route. Even in dimly lit streets, twenty-odd men walking fast and carrying pikes, pistols, and hand grenades might just be noticed.

A lithograph published three days after the arrests shows Cato Street's aspect (Fig. 1.6). It exaggerates its width but fairly conveys the simplicity of its cottages, and it shows the stable's location in the northern corner (centre frame, with sightseers outside it). The built-over exit at the northern end led into John Street (now Crawford Place); the Horse and Groom pub was accessed under it. A similar exit at the southern end led into Queen Street (now Harrowby Street). Cato Street's surface seems unpaved, but the house next to the stable carries a gaslight. Today everything in the street has gone except the Grade II listed stable. Later in the nineteenth century the Cato Street cottages gave way to plain three-storey terrace houses and lodgings, and in the 1970s most of these were replaced by low-rise apartment blocks. In early 2021 the house converted from the stable was on sale for £1.4 million.

By an extraordinary fluke we know who lived in the street. The national census schedules for 1821 are now lost, but a fragment survives in the Westminster Archives, and, as luck would have it, it covers part of Marylebone parish and Cato Street itself. In forty-five dwellings in a lane 150 metres long lived 124 families and 383 individuals – or 8.5 people per dwelling. Of these 246 were male and 137 female. Of the females, 93 were aged under fifteen; the older ones were probably away in service. The excess of men suggests a high proportion of unmarried lodgers. Many were Irishmen employed on Paddington's new building developments or on the transport hub at the recently completed Paddington canal basin. The Horse and Groom was a rough-house that watered them copiously. A very few years later twenty Irishmen were brought before the Marylebone magistrate after a Saturday night punch-up outside the pub. A group of canal navvies had disagreed with a party of Cato Street Irishmen, tempers had risen, watchmen arrived to order the navvies home, and the Irish called out fifty of their countrymen to attack the watchmen. A picket of soldiers had to be called from Portman Street to disperse them. By the 1830s Cato Street was said to be full of the 'lowest class' of Irish; the poverty investigator Charles Booth found them still there in the 1890s.[34]

Comings and goings in such a place were closely observed. Five Cato Street neighbours were later enlisted as prosecution witnesses to testify to the conspirators' presence, though only three were called. They had all noticed the black cabinet-maker William Davidson. His appearance certainly surprised Mrs Elizabeth Weston, the wife of a plumber and glazier who lived next door to the stable. She was watching her little boys playing in the street when she saw someone (Harrison) unlock and enter the stable with a bag on his shoulder. Then at six o'clock 'a man of colour' came to her door to ask her 'to give him a light if I pleased. I said "Yes, to be sure"; . . . I gave him a light, and he took his hat off his head and put [it] over it, and I leant out of my door and saw him go into the stable door; . . . that is all I know about it.' She said 'oh dear' and had been 'very ill ever since'. Richard Munday, a labourer at number 3, testified that 'at watering-time, three o'clock, when I came home to water' (to drink water? – men passed it anywhere), he had seen a man covering the stable windows with sacking. Going later to the Horse and Groom for beer he saw the black man under the archway with two fluttering candles in his hand. His coat flew open and revealed pistols and a sword stuck through a belt. 'In the name of God!' Munday exclaimed, Irishman as he was. He went home 'and mentioned it to my wife immediately'. The couple bolted their door and went to bed.[35]

As the men assembled in the loft, bread, cheese, and porter were handed round and pistols were loaded. Tidd was late, though Brunt said he'd be along shortly. Tensions ran high. Too few had arrived, and some were reluctant to go further. Ings began to stamp and swear and tear at his hair 'as if he was mad'. 'Damn my eyes,' he shouted: 'If you drop the concern now, I will cut my throat or shoot myself.' 'My good fellows,' Thistlewood said, 'for God's sake don't think of dropping the object we met here for, if we drop the thing now it will turn out another Despard's job.' (Marcus Despard and six of his associates had been hanged and decapitated for treason in February 1803.) Brunt reassured the doubters: 'They had things ready which would destroy the buggers in a very short time for they could blow up the house over their heads'. Thistlewood added that 'there were plenty of them, and that the servants, supposing them to amount to sixteen, would be struck with surprise, and before that was over they might enter the room and kill them all, and that it would not occupy more than ten minutes'. He then arranged the order of attack. Brunt, Ings, Hall, Thistlewood, Davidson, Strange, Bradburn, Harrison, and Adams were to make up the dining-room party.[36]

Then reality struck. From the bottom of the loft ladder someone called out 'halloo, show a light'. The Bow Street constables had arrived, and soldiers followed soon after. The conspiracy was busted.

CHAPTER 2

Arrests and Reactions

ARRESTS

On the morning of Wednesday, 23 April a magistrate at the Bow Street police office signed a warrant for the arrest of fourteen men, each of whom had featured in spy reports in the weeks and months past. The home office's own conspiracy was about to bear fruit. The name of Edwards the spy was included to give him cover:

> To all constables of the county of Middlesex. These are to require you and every [one] of you to take and bring before me or some other of his majesty's justice of the peace for the said county, the bodies of *Arthur Thistlewood* and thirteen other persons named: *Brunt, Hall, Ings, Potter, Palin, Edwards, Strange, Adams, Tidd, Wilson, Davidson, Harrison and Cook* of whom you shall have notice. The said parties being charged before me upon the oath of Henry Hobhouse, magistrate, on suspicion of feloniously assembling with intent to set fire to divers houses and to commit murder upon divers of his majesty's subjects. Whereof fail not. Given under my hand and seal the 23rd day of February 1820. Robert Baker. One of his majesty's justices for the said county.[1]

Late that afternoon the Bow Street constable George Ruthven installed himself in disguise in the Horse and Groom on Cato Street's corner to monitor arrivals in the stable opposite. A detachment of Coldstream Guards should have led the charge on the stable, but they were led by an incompetent royal bastard, Lieutenant Frederick Fitzclarence, and got lost on the short way from the Portman Street barracks because they 'were not clearly directed, or they did not understand where the place was, as they were at the contrary end of [Cato] street when the assassins

27

commenced their murderous attack upon the officers, and it was only by the discharge of pistols that they found out where the building was'.[2] A dozen Bow Street men had to do the job for them.

At eight o'clock, with the plebeian conspirators assembled in the stable, constable Ruthven signalled for the attack, and an almighty fracas ensued. On the ground floor the officers first encountered Davidson the Jamaican. He had 'belts, musket or fuses on his shoulder and a sword by his side'. He dodged them and ran off down the street, waving a cutlass in one hand and a blunderbuss in the other. Constable Ellis chased and caught him. Handcuffed, Davidson shouted 'Blast and damn the eyes of all who would not die for liberty', and wildly sang 'Scots, wha' ha' wi Wallace bled / ... Welcome tai your gory bed / Or to victorie'.[3] Constables Ruthven, Ellis, and Smithers then stormed bravely up the stable ladder. At the top Thistlewood and several others faced them with pistols, swords, and cutlasses. As Smithers rushed forward to seize him, Thistlewood lunged at him with his sword. It went straight to the heart. 'Poor Smithers fell into the arms of his brother-officer, Ellis, exclaiming – "Oh, God! I am ..." – and in the next instant was a corpse.' George Cruikshank the caricaturist depicted this moment in dramatic chiaroscuro, claiming that he had sketched the interior on the spot and had faithfully etched his scene from Ruthven's description. A dozen similar images were published, but none matched the ambition or size of this one. To this day it remains the conspiracy's iconic representation. Everyone, it seems, wore top hats (Fig. 2.1).

A candle-lit battle ensued. Bullets whizzed, powder fizzed, smoke billowed, and someone shouted, 'Kill the buggers; throw them down stairs!' As the candles were extinguished a rush of escaping men forced the constables back down the ladder. Several escaped through a small window high in the loft's back wall which led to an exit through the passage of Mrs Weston's house. She and her husband gave the alarm, and several men were captured that way.

Downstairs, Constable Westmacoatt confronted butcher Ings. As Ings drew his knife Westmacoatt hit him hard on the right eye with his staff. Ings later testified that his head 'swelled tremendously'. At that point Westmacoatt saw Thistlewood rushing down the ladder. He let Ings go

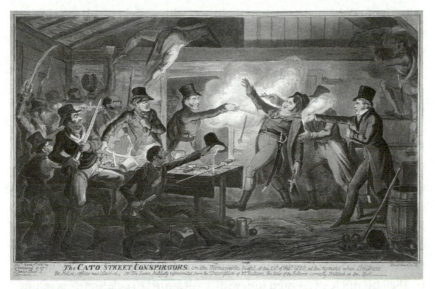

2.1. George Cruikshank, *The Cato Street Conspirators* (Humphrey, 9 March 1820) (Guildhall Library & Art Gallery/Heritage Images/Getty Images)

and Ings ran for it. A hysterical shoot-out followed. As Westmacoatt testified next day, Thistlewood

> fired right down as he was descending and when he reached the bottom he turned round and presented a pistol at this deponent's head and fired. He then made a cut at this deponent with a sword – upon which this deponent made a spring at him under the sword and at this instant deponent was knocked down by some person unknown to him and the light was put out. This deponent saw Thistlewood rush out at the door of the stable it being moonlight.[4]

Ruthven thought that twenty to thirty shots were fired altogether. A ball passed under constable Surman's scalp and exited above his ear (he recovered). Another ball grazed Westmacoatt's head, and a further constable got three bullet holes in his hat and one through his coat-sleeve. Constable Wright was saved from a sword-thrust by the thickness of his braces.

Men vanished into the night, Thistlewood and Ings among them. In the Edgware Road, Ings was chased by constable Brooks. Ings fired at him and put a ball through his coat and grazed the top of his shoulder. Then, as Ings stated, he 'met a man in the street with a stick, he hit me violently over the head. . . . I got round that man, and a watchman came and hit me with his stick.' He collapsed. The constable found seven or eight bullets in his pockets, some gunpowder in a tin flask, and 'a kind of belt on each side for pistols'. In poor shape, Ings was handcuffed and taken with others to the Marylebone watchhouse.[5]

When the Guards did arrive at last, Tidd aimed his pistol at Lieutenant Fitzclarence. Before he could shoot, Sergeant Legg wrestled him down into the stable's dungheap and handcuffed him. Fitzclarence had a small sword-fight or two and got his uniform torn and a leg bruised, but otherwise achieved little. Nonetheless newspapers later had to refer to him as 'gallant'. This was because he was the eldest of the duke of Clarence's ten illegitimate children by Mrs Jordan the actress, while his uncle by blood was George IV, and his father became William IV in 1830. In 1820 his uncle presented him with a gilt sword to celebrate his valour.[6] The remaining conspirators did surrender at last. 'Do not hurt me, do not kill me, and I will tell you all,' cried one – probably Monument.

It was an undistinguished police operation, though a brave one. A little less rushing up the ladder and face-to-face battling, a little more patience, persuasion, and prior surrounding of the stable, not to mention more competent leadership of the soldiers, would have served the case better. The officers agreed that they had had twenty-four or twenty-five men trapped in the stable. Fifteen or sixteen escaped, including the leader, and only nine were arrested. The next day's newspapers listed them:

> James Ings, butcher
> James Wilson, tailor
> Richard Bradburn, carpenter
> James Gilchrist, shoemaker
> Charles Cooper, bootmaker
> Richard Tidd, bootmaker
> John Monument, shoemaker
> John Shaw Strange, shoemaker
> William Davidson, cabinet-maker[7]

These were handcuffed and taken two to a coach down the Edgware Road and along Oxford Street to the tall Georgian house in Bow Street that accommodated the chief magistrate and the police office. Each coach carried two soldiers on the box and two behind and was backed by soldiers with fixed bayonets. The newspapers said that the 'vast concourse' that followed them was 'mostly in good humour'. 'Mostly' meant that some weren't at all in good humour.

At Bow Street, soldiers surrounded the police office, their arms gleaming in the light of flaring torches and giving what someone described as an un-English complexion to the night. Inside, the men were interrogated by the police magistrate and then brought out to be taken to Cold Bath Fields prison in Clerkenwell. Reporters scrutinised them closely. Davidson was noticed as 'a man of colour, and a worthy coadjutor of Messrs. Watson, Thistlewood, and Co. upon many occasions.' Ings glared as fiercely as his injured eye allowed; the others were 'men of short stature, mean exterior, and unmarked physiognomy'. The *Morning Chronicle* reported that all were filthy. It was 'as if their faces and hands had not been washed for a week; in fact, they were disgustingly dirty, so that it was extremely disagreeable to approach them'. They were 'disgusting, ill-favoured, ... vulgar, ferocious, and malignant. The only clean man among them was William Davidson, the tawney'.[8]

That night, according to one of Castlereagh's private letters, the constables learned that the escaping Thistlewood had hastened to Grosvenor Square 'with the sword in his hand bloody with which he had murdered the constable', but had retreated when he found sentinels guarding Harrowby's house. To prevent his escape, word was sent to close the ports at Dover and Harwich, and a reward of £1,000 was offered for information leading to his capture. He didn't get far. Next morning Edwards the spy directed the constables to 8 White Street, Little Moorfields, the lodging of one Harris, a typefounder who worked for Caslon & Catherwood in Chiswell Street. On Wednesday morning Thistlewood had rented from Mrs Harris 'half a bed', to be shared with her nephew. On Thursday morning the officers found him in the bed, clothed and wearing his breeches and stockings. 'Our information did not fail us,' Castlereagh added smugly: 'The constable who first entered the room suddenly threw himself upon him, and thus fettered his exertions until he was secured. The naked sword was by his side in bed under the clothes. He is a most desperate dog.' With a pistol to his head the dog surrendered meekly. Bullets and flints were found in his pockets.

This was the moment when Thistlewood realised that he had been betrayed by Edwards, the 'one man in London who knew where he was to be found'. He forgot that Harris knew where he was too. Although Harris had featured in Edwards's earlier reports as a manufacturer of the conspirators' bullets and pike-heads, he might also have been in government pay. Allegedly it was thanks to Mrs Harris's quick wits in tipping him off that Harris escaped as the officers arrested Thistlewood, but he was unlikely to have been left untouched if he was a real conspirator. A warrant was issued for his arrest, but he then disappears from the record. No attempt was made to arrest him before Thistlewood's capture; and he wasn't mentioned in the trials except in relation to his wife's giving Thistlewood a bed.[9]

Bow Street's officers were better at surveillance, detecting, and arresting than at defusing an explosive bunch of terrorists in a hayloft. Brunt, Adams, Harrison, and Hall had also escaped from the stable by climbing through the loft's back window. The fugitives were rounded up in the days following; and Hall and Adams gave the statements that saved them from prosecution. Brunt was arrested the next day in his Fox Court lodging off Gray's Inn Lane. His young apprentice Joseph Hale testified that his master had arrived home at nine o'clock last night in a state of confusion:[10]

> *Did you hear him [Brunt] say any thing to his wife of what had happened?* – I heard him say to his wife it was all up, or words to that effect.
> *What else did he say?* – He said that where he had been a great many officers had come in.
> *Anything else?* – Just as he spoke these words a man came in.
> *Did he say anything about himself before the man came in?* – He said he had saved his life, and that was all.
> ... *What did Brunt say to him upon his coming in?* – He shook hands with him, and asked him, when he came in, if he knew who had informed.

What answer did the man give? – He said, 'No'.

Did the man say whether any thing had happened to him? – Yes; he said he had a dreadful blow on the side, and was knocked down.

Did Brunt say anything more? – Yes.

What did he say? – He said, 'there is some thing to be done yet'. . . . They went away together.

After their departure Hale and Mrs Brunt investigated the back room in their Fox Court tenement which the conspirators had rented as their last secret meeting place. There they found a pike pole, an iron pot containing tar, several rolls of tarred brown paper, and papers twisted up with strings around them 'as big as two fists'. Hale again:

What do you understand them to be? – I have heard since they are hand-grenades.

At about what time did your master come home again? – On the Wednesday evening about eleven o'clock.

Did he give you any directions before he went to bed? Yes.

What? – He told me to get up in the morning as soon as I could, and to clean his boots. . . . They were very dirty.

The next morning did you get up early? – He called me about half past six.

What did he say to you? – He asked me if I knew the Borough [south of the Thames]. I told him, yes.

Did he ask you as to any particular part of the Borough? – He asked me if I knew Snow's Fields, I told him no.

After this, did he and you go into the back room? – Yes.

What directions did he give you? – He told me to bring a basket in out of his room and put in the things out of the cupboard.

Did you and he put any things into the basket? – Yes.

Was there one basket or two? – Two baskets.

Were the things out of the cupboard put into those baskets? – Yes, they were.

Did he tell you who lived at Snow's Fields that they were going to? – Yes.

Who? – Potter.

. . . – We went into Brunt's room to look for something to tie the other basket in, and two officers came up.

Did they take your master into custody? – Yes.

The officer who next day swore to Brunt's arrest was the splendidly named Samuel Hercules Taunton, a veteran Bow Street man who had arrested some of Despard's men in 1802. After capturing Brunt, Taunton went to Tidd's nearby lodging in Hole-in-the-Wall Passage. It was now nine in the morning. His wife and children watched helplessly as the officer uncovered 1,500 ball cartridges, ten grenades, eleven bags of gunpowder, and twenty-seven pike handles 'with sockets at the ends for pikes'.[11] As Adams testified later:

> *Were all the arms kept in the room [i.e. the Fox Court meeting room]?* – No, they were not.
>
> *Where were the rest kept?* – The dépôt was at Tidd's.
>
> *Do you know where Tidd lived?* – Yes.
>
> *Where was it?* – In the next room adjoining to myself.
>
> *That was in Hole-in-the-Wall Passage?* – Yes. ....
>
> *Was that the place where the greater part [of the weapons] was kept?* – ... That was the place appointed to take in things. Thistlewood was always in a hurry when there was any thing in readiness to be taken there; he called it the dépôt.[12]

On information received, two officers found Adams in his room next to Tidd's on 25 February.

Bow Street spent the next weeks hunting down others who had escaped. Robert George, for example, wasn't named in the arrest warrant, but he was known as a member of Thistlewood's committee. At some point in the week following 23 February a young lad lost a marble while playing behind a row of cottages in Chapel Street, Paddington, a couple of blocks north of Cato Street. Hunting for it, the boy entered a yard and found there an outdoor privy containing firearms. He reported this to a couple of soldiers he met outside, and they told a Bow Street man named Perry who was attending the coroner's inquest on Smithers in the Fox and Hounds. Hastening to the spot, Perry found that the house belonged to a haberdasher and tailor named George, and that the privy door had been nailed shut since the boy had peeked inside it – though only, lied Mrs George, to stop it blowing in the wind. As that lady was required to prise the door open, the daughter of the house wrung her hands in distress as she watched. Inside they found a musket, bayonet, pistol, sword, and powder and balls.[13]

Mr and Mrs George denied knowledge of the weapons, but admitted that their son Robert might have left them there, and that he lodged across the street. Perry found that Robert had absconded from across the street on the 23rd and that he might be hiding in a house in Goswell Street. There, constables Ruthven and Salmon learned that Robert was a seafaring man and might be found at the Dundee Arms in Wapping, from which he intended to take the ferry for Gravesend to join an East Indiaman due to sail on 5 March. The constables hastened to the Dundee Arms. At seven that evening George turned up, only to learn that the Gravesend ferry had already sailed. He called for a consoling brandy and water. What he got instead was Constable Salmon rushing up and putting a pistol to his head. 'If you offer to stir I will fire,' Salmon exclaimed. Ruthven and Salmon handcuffed him and took him in a hackney coach to the Covent Garden watch-house. They learned that Robert's brother John, a known Spencean, had rented a hidey-hole for Robert in Earl Street, a few blocks from where they found Thistlewood. Searching John's lodging, they found a stick which Robert had given him, 'at the bottom of which was a thick iron ferrule about two inches long, hollowed at one end to receive a pike-head or dagger'. After interrogation by Birnie, Robert George was committed on a charge of high treason and sent to join his friends in Cold Bath Fields. He later escaped trial by giving information.

While the more marginal players were imprisoned in Tothill Fields house of correction in Westminster, the lead prisoners were first locked up in Cold Bath Fields prison in north London. This grim fortress wasn't the least instrument in the government's chamber of horrors. It was the harshest gaol in London (Fig. 2.2). Rebuilt in 1794 as a so-called model prison, it became the prime destination for those sentenced to imprisonment since Newgate was increasingly choked by prisoners awaiting trial in the Old Bailey. Its cruellest disciplines – the treadmill and the 'silent system' – were introduced well after Cato Street; and further cells were added then too, until by mid-century it covered nine acres and was the

2.2. *Cold Bath Fields Prison* (Ackermann, 1814) (Guildhall Library & Art Gallery/Heritage Images/Getty Images)

largest prison in Britain and perhaps the world. But its earlier condition was also appalling, as radicals of the 1790s and 1800s knew to their cost. In 1799 the poet Coleridge summarised the Devil's appreciation of the place as he swaggered on his Devil's Walk through London:

> As he went thro' Cold Bath Fields he look'd
> At a solitary cell;
> And the Devil was pleas'd, for it gave him a hint
> For improving the prisons in hell.[14]

Here the lead men stayed for over a week while the police collected evidence and put the fear of God into them in the hope of turning them into crown witnesses. On 3 March, as the ministers debated whom to prosecute and for what, the prisoners were taken to Whitehall for further cross-examination by the privy council whom they had so keenly hoped to murder. Thistlewood, Monument, Wilson, Davidson, Tidd, Gilchrist, Ings, Bradburn, Shaw, Cooper, and Brunt had to wait while handcuffed to each other. They were joined by others implicated in the case who were brought from Tothill Fields house of correction – Preston, Simmons, Harrison, Hall, and Firth, handcuffed similarly. Newspapers added that the men were hooted and groaned at by the crowd outside. 'Groaning', once a universal expression of disapproval, was replaced by booing in modern times.

The men's behaviour was observed closely. 'The appearance of the whole was wretched in the extreme, and one or two of them seemed mere boys. Thistlewood appeared quite downcast, his features every day undergoing an alteration for the worse.' His gentlemanly mien had evaporated. The *Morning Chronicle* reported that he wore a threadbare black coat and waistcoat, old corduroy trousers and old worsted stockings. 'His features had a sallow and squalid aspect, the bones seemed to be not only staring through his cheeks but his limbs seemed equally bare of flesh.' Wilkinson, compiler of the conspiracy's *Authentic History*, reported that his complexion was jaundiced and that he seemed nerveless and emaciated. 'In the council's antechamber he occasionally gazed with indifference upon the strangers who thronged the room, but mostly fixed his eyes on the ground.'

Ings, meanwhile, was defiant. After his interrogation he returned to the others exclaiming in anger,

> It is want of food which has brought us here. Death would be a pleasure to me – I would sooner be hanged this instant, than turned into the street there; for I should not know where to get a bit of bread for my family; and if I had fifty necks, I'd rather have them all broken, one after the other, than see my children starve!

When a few patricians were admitted to peruse the men, 'Wilson, Davidson, and Tidd, who were linked together, ... laughed in derision'. Monument and Simmons were the last to be interrogated, and did not return for nearly half an hour. 'It appears that they, at this time, endeavoured to make their peace by a disclosure of what they knew.'[15]

The mistreatments that helped turn some men into crown witnesses are hidden from us, but the use of physical and emotional force is certain. Even the ageing William Hazard was bullied. He had run a radical reading club in Queen Street around the corner from Cato Street, and had offered his house as a gathering place for the conspirators if needed. To a fellow freemason, he explained how the privy council had conducted his interrogation: 'There were about 24 or more of them, ... I was like a hare among a pack of hounds, one snaping then another &c you must suppose my state having been there four nights in a cold prison, and not a mortal to speak to, but all seem'd and was my enemies.'[16] The grand jury found no true bill against him and he had to be discharged at last, though not before spending eleven miserable weeks in Tothill Fields prison. In neat copperplate script he then wrote to Sidmouth to explain that his imprisonment had impoverished him: 'My school by which I have thirty three years maintained my family comfortably, is all gone, and I at the age of sixty years am destitute, my wife through my arrest is afflicted with insanity, whereas if she was well might have rendered assistance to me.' He asked Sidmouth for compensation to save him from perishing from want – 'and also that your Lordship would order all my papers etc. to be restored to me with the handkerchief that encloses them'. A handkerchief had value then. Nobody replied to his letter.[17]

The more culpable parties would have been handled more harshly. Brought to Bow Street in a hackney coach, Adams was already 'greatly agitated, and said he was willing to disclose all he knew'. He was put into Cold Bath Fields for safekeeping. On Sunday, 27 February, the privy council and the crown's law officers examined him for an hour and a half in the home office. For reasons unexplained, Adams was soon labouring 'under severe indisposition'. Whatever terror they put into him in the prison converted him into the prosecution's most important witness.

Monument, Hiden, and Simmons also agreed to testify against their fellows. Hiden was 'examined with all the strictness in my power', the treasury solicitor wrote to the home office; he was very alarmed about giving evidence, but knew more than he had admitted to.[18] Simmons's statement was 'reluctantly given', Birnie wrote: 'I am sure he knows more.'[19] Monument was 'very uneasy' when brought from the Tower for his cross-examination. He was kept in a private room in the Old Bailey, attended by yeomen of the guard with swords drawn. Pale and dejected, he seemed 'by no means a willing witness', even though he was a late recruit to the conspiracy and marginal to it.

Bradburn, Strange, Firth, Gilchrist, Hall, and Cooper,were now returned to Cold Bath Fields, while Thistlewood, Ings, Harrison, Davidson, Wilson, Brunt, Tidd, and Monument were committed to the Tower of London as state prisoners on charges of murder and treason. Their coaches were escorted by Life Guards and followed by 'an immense throng of people'. At the Tower, the warders were increased from ten to sixty. Two armed warders were locked into each prisoner's cell and armed sentinels outside each door were ordered to ensure that no inside guard should leave the room except for 'occasional purposes'. Ings and Davidson were put in separate cells in St Thomas's Tower, Brunt in the Byeward Tower, Tidd in the Seven Gun Battery, Monument in a prison behind the horse armoury, and Thistlewood in the Bloody Tower, where he had a day room and a 'dark, low, and old' bedroom, with access to the Tower's roof for exercise and air. It was here that the two boy princes had supposedly been murdered by order of their uncle, Richard III, and Tudor queens had languished before losing their heads. By the regency years imprisonment in the Tower was unusual. Sir Francis Burdett had been put there for breach of parliamentary privilege in 1810, and Watson, Thistlewood, Preston, and Hooper were imprisoned there in 1817 as they awaited their treason trial for the Spa Fields insurrection. Otherwise no state prisoners had been detained there since 1799, and none were again until Roger Casement in 1916 and Rudolf Hess in 1941.[20]

What of the Bow Street constables who had achieved the arrests? Poor Gilchrist had been cowed by their gentlemanly appearance as they came up the Cato Street ladder: they wore neckcloths and top hats. In fact they were little regarded and poorly treated. Their guinea a week wage meant that some survived by corruption. The government did pay for Smithers' funeral and burial, and a generous £100 a year was settled on his widow. But a public subscription had to be opened for others. Ruthven and Ellis, first up the ladder, topped the list; Birnie of Bow Street pencilled '£100' against Ruthven's name and '£50' against Ellis's. The more modest rewards of the rest left them open to old temptations. John Wright, who in Cato Street owed his life to the thickness of his braces, was sentenced to death at the Old Bailey in 1823 for involvement in a burglary in Great Newport Street. The death sentence was respited, but he spent the next eight years in Newgate. In 1828 a petition for mercy explained that his Cato Street reward had 'led him into idle habits'. He had to wait another two years before his release.[21]

REACTIONS

'All England rung with astonishment and horror at this dreadful instance of atrocious depravity, and at the scandal and infamy which it had brought upon the national character.' Who 'all England' were was clarified when Lord Sidmouth explained to Earl De la Warr that 'even the most hardened incredulity was staggered by it, and party feelings appeared to be absorbed in those of indignation'. The lower orders were also shocked, he added as an afterthought.[22]

The Cato Street stable turned overnight into London's prime tourist attraction. Despite horrible weather, people of the first respectability went in carriages to view the rendezvous of the hellish conspiracy. Captain Fitzclarence walked two friends up and down Cato Street to show them the holes of bullets he had gallantly dodged, though he wouldn't have mentioned that his soldiers arrived too late to fire a shot.[23] A few days later the police allowed access to the stable, and 'several thousand of the highest rank' visited it. An enterprising local made them pay a shilling each to be shown round it. Wellington, Prince Esterhazy, Lord and Lady Hertford, she lately the regent's mistress, Lord Grosvenor and his son, and other 'persons of the highest consideration' flocked there.[24] Shown around by constable Lee, Grosvenor was 'shocked at the visible appearance of the unfortunate Smithers upon the carpenter's bench'. His blood had stained the floor too, and visitors stepped round it delicately. They included 'several of the fair sex, who braved the inconvenience of the difficult ascent to the loft for the gratification of their curiosity'.[25] Artists visited the stable – not only Cruikshank, Wivell, and opportunistic lithographers, but the major artists Géricault and David Wilkie also.[26]

The news echoed round Europe. In Paris the *Journal des débats politiques et littéraires*, the most widely read of the restoration newspapers, reported the case in detail (after a delay occasioned by the duke de Berry's assassination at the Opéra). The publisher Pierre Langlumé published an ill-informed lithograph, *Arthur Thistlewood, chef de la conspiration*, that illustrated the arrests above a 25–line explanation in French: it was one of several such.[27] It is possible that these reports encouraged Géricault to come to London and to sketch the executions (see Chapter 18). When the news reached the duchess of Devonshire in Rome, she congratulated her sister for being with Lady Liverpool when the 'tremendous plot was discovered: you must have been of such comfort and support to her'. 'One must learn to bear with the loss of all feelings of security. ... We were scarcely recovering from the feel of horror which the Duc de Berri's assassination had given us when this news from England really threw us into consternation.' She added that her existence in Rome was 'delightfull', but even her friend the cardinal had been threatened anonymously: 'Is it not shocking to see every country in this state of ferment!'[28]

Lord Byron heard the news far away in Ravenna where he was gallivanting as Teresa Guiccioli's *cavalier servente*. Soon he would be supporting the Carbonari in their battle for an Italian republic. 'The king times are fast finishing,' he wrote to John Cam Hobhouse in London: 'There will be blood shed like water, and tears like mist; but the peoples will conquer in the end.' But if romantic Italian revolutionaries were desirable, home-grown insurrectionists were another matter entirely. He was, he wrote, 'born an aristocrat, and naturally one by temper, with the greatest part of my property in the funds, [so] what have *I* to gain by a revolution?'[29] And though he loathed Castlereagh, he conceded that 'a gentleman scoundrel is always preferable to a vulgar one'. The Cato Street men were beneath contempt. 'What a set of desperate fools,' he exclaimed: 'As if in London after the disarming acts [Sidmouth's Six Act], or indeed at any time a secret could have been kept among thirty or forty'. Whereupon Byron's noble rot revealed itself:

> And if they had killed poor Harrowby – in whose house I have been five
> hundred times – at dinners and parties – his wife is one of 'the Exquisites' –
> and t'other fellows [in the cabinet] – what end would it have answered? ...
> really if these sort of awkward butchers are to get the upper hand – ... such
> fellows as these, who will never go to the gallows with any credit ... make
> one doubt of the virtue of any principle or politics which can be embraced
> by similar ragamuffins. I know that revolutions are not to be made with

rose water, but though some blood may & must be shed on such occasions, there is no reason it should be clotted – in short the Radicals seem to be no better than Jack Cade or Wat Tyler, and [ought] to be dealt with accordingly.[30]

Byron's disgust was the norm in the high cultural world. Walter Scott was in London and attended the last day 'of that bloody dog Thistlewood's trial'. He too thought the conspiracy 'as foolish as it was bloodthirsty and horrible':

> they had coaxed themselves into a firm belief that all the lower orders were possessed by the same demon which agitated themselves. Thistlewood declared every man a traitor who possessed above £10, and that the shopkeepers were all aristocrats ... Ings the butcher was to have the heads and plucks [entrails] of Lords Castlereagh and Sidmouth for his fee, and he had his bags ready to carry them off in, and a large knife to amputate them.

Scott was so appalled that back home in Melrose he asked his gentry neighbours to join a corps of marksmen, which he would lead against local malcontents.[31] The poet laureate Robert Southey was also delighted by the arrests – and by the fact that habeas corpus wasn't still suspended: had suspension still applied, 'these miscreants would (most of them) have been in confinement, & the Whigs lamenting over them & promoting subscriptions for them as the victims of oppression. The gallows will now have its due ... A highly civilized society seems to be within reach, if the devils who are got into the swinish multitude can be cast out.'[32]

In the London salons the shock was immediate. 'Since the Gunpowder Plot there has been nothing so terrible,' the countess of Caledon exclaimed: 'Seven thousand persons were ready that night to act on the signal being given. ... Had all taken place that was in contemplation, we should never have escaped a revolution.'[33] 'What a horrible thing, a general massacre of the entire cabinet! What a monstrous idea!' – so wrote the Russian ambassador's wife Princess Lieven on 25 February. Lady Harrowby had called at the Russian embassy in Harley Street to tell her about it. The details 'are so revolting, that one can scarcely believe that human beings like ourselves, with head and hands and feet, conceived such an abominable project. . . . I feel cold from head to foot, thinking of those men.' Lieven was no fool, but she spent a good part of her time waltzing and gossiping at Almack's and consorting with men like the regent, breathing such refined air that the news of the conspiracy made London suddenly and unpleasantly smell like Paris. But she was soon less worried about Cato Street than by the fact that a week after the arrests her Harley Street bedroom chimney blew down in a storm. She wondered 'how these wretched London houses stand up'.[34] A fortnight after the arrests, the American ambassador reported that the conspiracy still dominated conversation, 'so foul was its nature, and so near did it appear to have advanced to success'.[35]

In high tory circles it was common knowledge that the government had manipulated the conspirators. As early as 5 January, Sidmouth had told Wellington that a lethal plot was in progress. After the arrests Harrowby told the diarist Charles Greville that the government had been 'perfectly well informed' about the plot, knew just how to disarm it, and regarded the mob as 'quite inefficient for a regular operation'.[36] Castlereagh wrote cheerfully to his half-brother, the ambassador in Vienna:

> The whole has been arranged without a fault; and if you consider that we ministers have been for months the deliberate objects of these desperate concerts, planning our destruction, sometimes collectively, sometimes in detail, but always intent upon the project, and with our own complete knowledge, you will allow that we are tolerably cool troops, and that we have not manoeuvred amiss to bring it to a final catastrophe, in which they are not only all caught in their own net, but that we can carry into a court of justice a state conspiracy, which will be proved beyond the possibility of cavil, and which [will] form no inconsiderable feature in the *causes célèbres* of treasonable and revolutionary transactions.[37]

Ministers still had to pose as victims, however. They attended grand services to thank the Almighty for their preservation, certain that that entity would be on their side even if he felt uneasy about their hypocrisy. In the Lords, Sidmouth announced that 'the constitution of England [sic] was in greater danger than it had been in at any other time since the accession of the house of Brunswick to the throne'. Most newspapers agreed. Only the *Observer* defied the judges' ruling that the trials should not be reported until sentences had been passed, lest ongoing news of the trial inflame poorer people. For contempt of court its publisher William Clement was fined £500, but he refused to pay and so made his own contribution to press freedom. His Cato Street reporting, complete with woodcuts, doubled the *Observer*'s circulation to over 20,000, not counting illicit unstamped copies in addition.

PREPARING THE TRIALS

In March the government prepared sledgehammer prosecutions to crack these nuts. The privy council first had to decide whether to prosecute for murder rather than for treason, or whether to prosecute Thistlewood for treason and the others for murder – bearing in mind 'the difficulty of convicting a traitor, and the comparative ease of proving guilt upon a murderer'. In the event the convenience of prosecuting for murder was outweighed by the fact that that 'would exclude all evidence of the treasonable conspiracy, which it was highly expedient to develope to the public'. In any case murder trials might net only Thistlewood, Smithers's active killer. So they went for treason as the first count and for murder and felonious shooting as the second.[38]

By 5 April, 160 people had been told to hold themselves available as crown witnesses. Wellington charged the home office with gross misman-agement when it omitted the informer Abel Hall's name from the witness list, since his testimony would have lessened the need to call the spy Edwards. In fact Edwards's evidence could be dispensed with anyway, thanks to Hiden's letter to Castlereagh and Adams's and Monument's agreement to testify against their fellows. But extra care had to be taken to pick the right juries. The treasury solicitor Maule wrote to Hobhouse in the home office that in Tidd's and Davidson's trials 'too frequent a repetition of the same facts' (after Thistlewood's trial) might create 'a sort of reaction in men's minds in favour of the prisoners, particularly as the proof against the individuals as we go on will weaken'.[39] The govern-ment had been several times disappointed by juries in the past.

By referring to the Middlesex parliamentary poll-book, which listed how electors had voted in March, constables were able to mark the balloted jury lists with 'O' for 'loyal subjects', 'GG' for 'very loyal' and 'X' for 'friends of the prisoners'. On a sheet of thirty-nine names from Islington and Clerkenwell, 'X' was marked against an upholsterer, a silversmith, a jeweller, a printer, a bookseller, a founder, a silversmith and a stockbroker. A leather cutter was ruled out as 'XX': 'very bad a Radical' was written against him. The defence committee played the same game. On 12 April a spy reported that the prisoners' friends were assembling every other evening at the Nags Head, Shoe Lane. On their jury lists they marked 'O' for loyalists, 'X' for 'good' friends or 'XX' for 'strong'. They also gathered witnesses ready to testify that Edwards was the plot's principal instigator. Eventually some fifty jury challenges from prosecution and defence alike were allowed before Thistlewood's trial. The prosecution was pleased to achieve a jury for Thistlewood of six gentlemen or esquires and six tradesmen 'of good standing and opinion'.[40]

The prosecutions cost some £6,500 altogether – around £600,000 in today's values. This would be a puny total for a modern state trial with its security and bureaucratic costs and inflated fees, but it was unprecedented then. The reward for Thistlewood's capture accounted for £1,000 of the total (who it went to is unrecorded), and the reward for Palin's capture £200. Eighty-two prosecution witnesses shared £265 for attendance and £391 for tavern expenses. The crown didn't pay for defence witnesses. Prisoners' accommodation and food in the Tower, Cold Bath Fields, and Newgate cost £783. Further emoluments were enjoyed by this or that flunkey: the court was thick with criers, train-bearers, bell-ringers, and tipstaffs. A Mr Webb, surgeon of Cold Bath Fields prison, was paid £25 7s 6d. Was he the masked man who hacked the heads off five hanged bodies with a surgeon's knife?[41]

The aldermanic sheriff Rothwell of the City of London got the biggest emolument: £780 for 'expenses'. He had to pay the hangman and his assistant and attend the scaffold, where the crowd usually hooted him. Worse, he had to support the sessions dinners for the judges and their entourage. By custom the City aldermen, recorder, common serjeant, Newgate ordinary (chaplain), and pleaders and barristers joined in for the pleasure of it. Across three Old Bailey sessions dinners over nineteen days in 1807–8 the company downed 145 *dozen* bottles of wine costing £450. Even in the reform-minded 1830s

> marrow puddings always formed a part of [the first course]; the second never varied, and consisted exclusively of beefsteaks. The custom was to serve two dinners (exact duplicates) a day, the first at three o'clock, the second at five. As the judges relieved each other it was impracticable for them to partake of both; but the aldermen often did so, and the chaplain, whose duty it was to preside at the lower end of the table, was never absent from his post.

If the jury insisted on a long deliberation, the beefsteaks were renewed and conviviality was extended. Mr Adolphus might be asked to tell some of his best stories, and the ordinary might be challenged for a song. Then the judge would be called, and he staggered out to pass judgement.[42]

The Cato Street leaders had nearly a month in the Tower to ponder the fates of their illustrious predecessors. At the end of March grand juries returned true bills for charges of high treason against eleven of them: Thistlewood, Davidson, Ings, Brunt, Tidd, Wilson, Harrison, Bradburn, Strange, Gilchrist, and Cooper. For Smithers's murder, true bills were returned against Thistlewood, Brunt, Tidd, Wilson, Harrison, and Strange. Additional charges were laid for shooting at constables and soldiers, but the weightier charges eclipsed them.

THE FREED MEN

On Saturday 6 May, after the central drama was over and the men chosen for killing or for transportation had been finally dealt with, Abbott dismissed for lack of evidence against them the shoemaker Thomas Preston, the footman William Simmons, the tailor Abel Hall, the seaman arrested at Wapping, Robert George, the cow-man William Firth, and the schoolmaster William Hazard – even though they were known members either of the radical Marylebone reading club or of Thistlewood's committee in late 1819.[43] Simmons said he had done little more than give the conspirators 'information respecting the transactions of the higher orders', as a footman might, and now he had given information to the privy council as well.[44] Cross-examinations and spy reports had shown that Hall was as guilty as any of his fellow conspirators, but he had been turned while in prison and became one of the leading home office spies from then on to the 1830s.[45] Robert George made a 'statement' on 3 March,[46] while, as we have seen, Monument, Dwyer, and Hiden gave information and testified for the prosecution, and Robert Adams gave king's evidence before being returned to Whitecross Street debtors' prison.

The most prominent of those who got away with it was Preston. His complicity in the conspiracy was exposed by dozens of spy reports of his high visibility in meetings, but he avoided direct involvement in the fatal gathering on 23 February. He was lame and walked with a stick, so he had a real excuse for his absence. In December Thistlewood had himself proposed that Preston should 'be at home while the first job is doing and that his daughter and son and other persons that would swore well [sic] should be there to prove an alibi'. Edwards's report of 23 February duly stated that Preston had left his house in the afternoon of that day but 'was too late for the meeting'.[47]

Preston was the smartest and cockiest of the conspirators, and confident enough to tease authority. Before constables came to search his rooms, he destroyed every scrap of incriminating evidence. The constables found him pretending to be 'industriously engaged in mending a shoe, with his family about him'. He affected surprise at the visit, but accepted it 'with cheerfulness, not unaccompanied by an apparent sense of his own importance. His daughters were highly indignant at this intrusion on their domestic privacy.' Taken under guard to the Marquis of Anglesea pub in Bow Street to await interrogation, he sat with pipe and pot before the fire and boasted that 'the farce would not be complete till he was taken'. After spending the night in the Covent Garden watch-house, he asked the grandees who interrogated him next day 'what they meant by sending for him to disturb his peace of mind, and to disturb the economy of the family, alluding to his three daughters binding shoes, and himself making them'. After a half-hour interrogation he had to wait in a passage while his committal to gaol was drawn up. As Castlereagh passed by he observed loudly, 'Aye, there he goes! His lordship will remember what I have said to him as long as he lives. I have talked more treason, as they call it, today, than ever I did in my whole life before.' To a group of gentlemen he bowed, smiled, and said 'God bless you all.'

Then, on no evidence except his past record and Edwards's information, off to Tothill Fields prison Preston was sent, there with easy insolence to protest to Sidmouth that the governor read his letters. Citing the Bill of Rights and Magna Carta, he added: 'My Lord when I applyed to your Lordship for the yauce [use] of pen ink and paper which you was pleased to grant me ... I thought I had my mind no ways shaded with doute but I should enjoy the free privellege of communicating with my friends.'[48] When dismissed in court, the other discharged men bowed respectfully and departed, but Preston tried to make a speech and had to be silenced. He was released nine weeks later. He petitioned both Sidmouth and the king for compensation for wrongful imprisonment and for the return of his property. No replies are recorded. According to Abel Hall, after he left prison Preston had no work and got drunk 'with any shoemaker who will treat him'. Embittered and impoverished, he was relatively inactive in the 1820s, though he remarried and had a son; in the Chartist years he occasionally lectured. He died in great poverty in 1850 in a Field Lane slum, but his fame remained such that his burial in Bunhill Fields in 1850 was financed by well-wishers and attended by over 400 people.[49]

That left John Palin. He had several times been identified as one of Thistlewood's intimates, and had sided with Thistlewood against Henry Hunt in the radical quarrels in 1819. Aged about forty and once a corporal in the East London militia, he was 'a tall thin man, of meagre aspect and bilious complexion, shabbily dressed'; he was now a child's chair-maker, though lately arrested for debt, as so many were. When his lodgings was searched, at 'Mrs Privett's at Mrs Stedman's No. 1 Vine Yard Blackman St. Borough' (south of the Thames), a list of weapons was found in his breeches' lining. A £200 reward elicited the information that he was hiding in a 'hovel' in Battle Bridge at the top of Gray's Inn Lane. There the Bow Street officers were stalled for five minutes before they entered the cottage. Inside they found three men and a woman in one room, 'and only one bed in it'. Two of them were melting lead in a frying pan, but they had to be discharged as individuals unknown. In the bed lay a man who claimed to be unwell. The officers made him get up, found him fully clothed, and forced him to strip to see if he carried bruises from the Cato Street fracas. He didn't. No sign of Palin, however. They decided that he had escaped through St Chad's Wells at the back.[50]

Nine months later information led constables Ruthven, Ellis, and Westmacoatt to a house in Drury Lane, where they found him. During a lengthy examination by the privy council Palin admitted his involvement in the conspiracy, though he claimed that he had tried to persuade the conspirators to give up their plan. The council discharged him on a bond to keep the peace for seven years. Perhaps he offered future services as an informer, or else evidence against him might by then have been difficult to recover. Probably the privy council felt it was impolitic to reopen the case since any hint of jury resistance in Palin's case would remind the world of its doubts about the earlier convictions. Anyway, the crown's victory was secure. In September Sidmouth had reported to the king that most of those 'most active & successful in perverting and inflaming the minds of the labouring classes are either imprisoned, transported, or fled the country'.[51]

Sidmouth might have added 'decapitated'. But that outcome we'll leave to Part V, and turn now to another form of discussion – to the large question of interpretation.

PART TWO

TAKING ITS MEASURE

CHAPTER 3

Interpreting the Conspiracy

Many decades after the conspiracy, the social investigator Charles Masterman imagined poor Londoners addressing posterity in these words:

> We are very silent, so silent that no one to this hour knows what we think on any subject, or why we think it. . . . We cease to be children before we have ever known childhood. We take up the burden of silent work through long years of silent endurance. We rear up others to compete against us in a similar life. At length, at the closing of the day, we pass to a silent grave. Of the meaning of this dim, silent life existence we have no power to ascertain.[1]

The conspirators might have said this too – except that their voices are uniquely audible to those who listen. This is because their meetings, plots, and opinions were spied on and reported with uncommon efficiency, and because we also hear them noisily as they faced their accusers in court. A couple of wives speak as well, though faintly, since that was the way of the records then.

Thanks to the advancing wonder of shorthand reporting, Howell's *State Trials* gives us a verbatim record of everything said over the fourteen days of the Cato Street trials. It amounts to some 350,000 words of question-and-answer evidence and speeches by counsel and judges. Several other reports were of similar size and ambition. The earlier treason trial and arraignments in 1817 for Thistlewood's and others' abortive Spa Fields insurrection add a further 130,000 words to the quota. The word counts swell uncontrollably if one adds the reports in the London newspapers. Most of these deplored radicals as leaders or members of the 'mob' and 'rabble', but they reported their doings and trials in page after page of tiny print in order to expose the radicals' wickedness and justify their own contempt.

Most remarkable is the great stockpile of secret government papers. The Cato Street spy reports in the home office records are among the richest surveillance material in the whole nineteenth-century archive. They fully expose the role of the spies whose exist-ence was so indignantly denied in parliament, which means that we know more about the shifty business that went on behind the scenes than contemporaries did. Not all informers were crooked. George Edwards was one of nature's chancers, but others were incidental observers who didn't need to be paid to support the established order. Their clandestine scribbles generally corroborate each other, and most of the details they supplied were too commonplace and circumstantially convincing to have been fabricated. The official papers thickly describe these matters over the several months during which the Cato Street plot matured, as well as more patchily over the several years before it. Together, they convey every last particular of the conspirators' habitats and habits, and so facilitate one of our purposes now – to establish a sense of human connection with those poor people.

William Hazlitt once observed that Hogarth's pictures 'breathe a certain close, greasy, tavern air'. The same will be true of this book. It examines where it was possible to meet and where it wasn't, disputes in the camp and the liquor bought to woo recruits, how points of view were expressed and received through thickets of oaths, of how and where hand grenades and pike-heads were made and stockpiled – and all this by men who plotted in poor back rooms with perhaps a single chair to sit on, or in public-house club rooms that were lit rather than warmed by a few flickering flames during bitter winter nights. It tells us about their crowded single-room lodgings and the decaying alleys in which they were situated, about their illnesses, dropsies, limps, and insanities, their infi-delities and wives' desperation. We read their intimate letters, with erratic handwriting and cockneyfied spelling – 'I *ham*' for 'I am', as like as not. The story also reveals unexpected wonders: that Thistlewood had an artist grandson who in Paris worked with Degas, Pissarro, and Monet, of all people, and that the conspirators' hanging outside Newgate was sketched by the visiting French artist Théodore Géricault, again of all people.

In the whole of the eighteenth and nineteenth centuries no insur-rectionists – no plebeian groups – are more richly documented than these. In these senses the Cato Street voices are buried rather than lost voices. They bring that past to life and move both imagination and compassion.

This book's close focus on events in London means that it can only hint at the story's international and provincial connections. It must take as read the vast impact on British politics and culture of the French revolution and French wars, the Bourbon restoration of 1815 and revolutions in Spain, Naples, and South America. It must also take as read the northern, midland, and Scottish turbulence that often alarmed the government more than London's did. Provincial, Scottish, and metropolitan radical-ism was interlinked and London's Irish were chronically rebellious. And advanced radicals read and talked about all these connections.[2]

By covering large time spans and territories, however, surveys that deal with these wider matters pay their own price. They curtail lived detail and tend to present events like 'Cato Street' (or 'Peterloo') merely as short-hand signifiers in the vast pattern of events, rather than as complex realities fully reimagined. They likewise attend to the ideas of canonical Enlightenment writers more closely than they do to the muddled atti-tudes, slogans, and resentments that moved most people. The cost is a certain desiccation. Individual character is bypassed, and hungry and war-torn communities of wives, single mothers, widows, and children, of rat-infested timber-framed houses, of tiny one-family shops and work-shops, and of odorous streets, alleys, and tenements are downplayed. Moreover, 'histories of labour which are cast largely in terms of leaders and followers, of faceless ideologies, or equally faceless aggregates of workers ... [devalue] the numbers unlimited whose talents, energies and fortitude constituted the spine of radical leadership. Most have no memorial'.[3] From most studies we learn next to nothing about the protagonists' marriages or origins, or how they laboured or didn't labour, or hoped to make their lives bearable. Poverty always features in these large accounts, but we are not told otherwise why, as individuals, *they did it.*

This evasion has been encouraged by the contempt felt for the Cato Street conspirators at both ends of the political spectrum.[4] What, after all, did they have going for them? They weren't even the first British terrorists. Guy Fawkes and his colleagues and the civil war stand in the way of that. Irish insurgents were called terrorists in 1806; and English jacobins like Colonel Marcus Despard, executed in 1803, anticipated the Cato Street men as well. Edmund Burke had already referred to the Parisian jacobins as 'those hell hounds called terrorists', and the word 'terrorist' was defined in the dictionary published by the Académie française in 1798.

The story's powerful and comfortable victors and their successors believed that the conspirators were wicked, stupid, or both. One late-Victorian historian dismissed them as 'a very limited number of half-crazy creatures' and their conspiracy as 'the insane and fantastic plot of a handful of men, wholly unsupported by any following worth mentioning, in an obscure corner of London'.[5] Later they were dismissed as 'ruffianly guttersnipes' or as 'psychopaths' driven by 'personal neuroses'. Today a literary historian includes 'Cato Street' in his title but dismisses its protagonists as a 'band of feckless absurdly inefficient co-conspirators', and leaves it at that.[6] Others may think that the grim facts of life that hemmed in the underdogs fill enough miserabilist histories already, and that England's dignity is better served by stressing its achievements. An ultra-conservative survey that purports to be about *English Society 1668–1832* refers dismissively to the cut-and-slash massacre of seventeen unarmed men and women and one child by amateur cavalry and professional hussars at Peterloo in Manchester as 'the St Peter's Field incident' and omits it from its index; it does, however, four times index 'Peterhouse', its author's Cambridge college. Cato Street it doesn't mention. Hilton's *Oxford History of England 1783–1846* allows Cato Street two sentences in all its 784 pages.[7]

Historians on the left haven't been impressed either. Even as Thistlewood's head was being sawn off, the radical freethinker and bookseller Richard Carlile thought Thistlewood insane. His associates, he added, were 'laughed at, from the contemptibility of their characters, and their known want of courage; as pot-valiants only' – and laughed at above all as dupes of the ministers and Edwards their spy.[8] When later radicals recalled Cato Street in the 1840s it was in pity for 'Thistlewood, Ings the butcher, and some half-dozen plebeians besides, [who] were hung up in a string, like so many herrings, without the slightest ceremony'.[9]

In more recent times leftish historians have also consigned the conspiracy to the dustbin of history. It had no casualties other than the conspirators' own persons and families, and a constable who got in the way of Thistlewood's sword. Ending grimly on the scaffold, it led nowhere – least of all to the onward and upward March of Labour or the supposed Making of the English working class. Labour history has had undoubted achievements to its credit. In the 1960s and '70s it taught the necessity of writing history from the bottom up. Even so, in the long term its grip stifled the territory with its own conventions and righteousness, and its energy has faded. In history syllabi today, the study of popular radicalism is eclipsed by the fashion for global history, gender history, and so on.

A tale of deprivation and governmental malignity, guilt, and panic, Cato Street offers underdog history at its purest. As plebeian infidels, and failures at that, the Cato Street men had no chance of commemoration. Guy Fawkes's attempt to blow up parliament in 1605 also failed; yet it was a gentlemen's plot and about religious faith. The politer breeds of historian favour stories of that high kind, and protestant triumphalism guaranteed the fifth of November its continuing place in the calendar anyway. Comparatively speaking, the Cato Street men's lowly standing and vulgarity mean that the consequences for its memory have been bleak.

For a while, the plot shook the world. William Cobbett believed that it woke the nation from its long neglect: 'From that day the tone of the sons of corruption became less insolent and audacious. Everybody observed this, and every one said it to his neighbour.'[10] And it did teach some younger whigs that continued indifference to the disfranchised was dangerous. Even the conservative William Wilberforce felt that the parliamentary classes should 'rescue the multitude out of the hands of the Hunts and Thistlewoods' by making small concessions to reform.[11] This flash of awareness didn't last long, however. Interest in reform was soon dissipated in the feud between Queen Caroline and the obese narcissist who as king wanted to divorce her. (George III had died on 29 January.) The queen's landing at Dover on 5 June to claim her crown and George IV's efforts to deny her both that and marriage unleashed wide hostility to the new and deeply loathed monarch, so riots and turbulence continued, but on this very different subject. The queen 'was the only question I ever knew that excited a thorough popular feeling', William Hazlitt wrote; 'it took possession of every house or cottage in the kingdom; man, woman, and child took part in it, as if it had been their own concern'.[12] Although Hazlitt took the sourest view of radicals and demagogues who turned themselves into 'queenites' and went to 'worship the very rags of royalty' and bow to 'hereditary imbecility', the comic drama mobilised one of the great populist forces of the decade and distracted attention from radicalism's recent humiliation as well as its ambitions. It took another twelve years before parliament reformed itself, somewhat. As trade revived, the insurrectionary thrust wilted in Britain until depression revived it in the late 1830s and Chartist 1840s.

So it is that the conspiracy's chief memorial was achieved backhandedly by conservative landlords and functionaries of a tory London County Council (LCC). They changed the street names! When Cato Street was laid out in 1803–5, the landowner named it after the Roman orator, but in 1827 it was thought proper to disguise its infamy by renaming it 'Horace Street' after the Roman poet. Nearly a century later, in 1920, the LCC changed 'Queen' Street (round the corner from Cato Street) into 'Harrowby' Street, to show appreciation of that nobleman's readiness to put his Grosvenor Square mansion at risk of Thistlewood's hand grenades. The parallel cul-de-sac of Moore Street became 'Castlereagh Street' to honour that great man. This political point-scoring was reversed in 1937 when Herbert Morrison's Labour LCC restored Cato Street's original name. The blue plaque over the stable was placed there just before the Labour Party lost the 1977 Greater London Council election. It can only have been as a waggish tory riposte to these moves that the modern apartment block built in Cato Street to the south of the stable has been named Sidmouth House, after the home secretary whose manoeuvres destroyed the conspirators. And that's it.

Neither conservative nor leftish historians like anticlimaxes of the Cato Street kind. They prefer subjects that give the illusion of pointing forwards and that lead to change. As a result, both camps have treated this apparent dead end with something of the contempt felt by the ministers who masterminded it. Today this attitude seems myopic and dated. In recent decades our techniques and understandings have been enriched by histories of images and artefacts, topographies and mentalities, gender, women, and children, sociability, sensibility, and emotion, race and slavery, crime and punishment, and humour and satire – as well as by psycho-histories and micro-histories that offer thick descriptions of 'the small pieces of large puzzles'. Embracing not only the supposed heroes of 'labour' but also hitherto unregarded people, this enterprise has transformed our view of the past. That is why, despite the conspirators' failures, we can now see that their ineptitude was a historical creation after all, and that, despite its unreliable narrators and dangling subplots and characters, their story tells us a great deal about their London, their deprivations, and their very human condition. That's more than enough to be going on with. The history of this episode is a true tale with the depths of a novel.

The Cato Street men's intention to chop off aristocratic heads was undoubtedly futile, ignorant, and vicious. It may invite Joseph Conrad's indictment of his fictional anarchists when he noted in his comment on his *The Secret Agent* 'the criminal futility of the whole thing' and their 'half-crazy pose as of a brazen cheat exploiting the poignant miseries and passionate credulities of a mankind always so tragically eager for self-destruction'. 'The ultra reformers of this country,' the *Morning Post* announced after Peterloo, 'have all the headlong and cruel characteristics of a rabble, mixed up with the cunning of conspirators, and heightened by a keen abhorrence of what has been considered most valuable and glorious in society . . . Ascendancy they will inevitably acquire, if they are not crushed as a political body, and that promptly by the vigilance and energy of the ministers of the law.'[13]

Yet this wasn't how everyone saw it. If Richard Carlile thought Thistlewood insane, he also thought the conspirators were heroes whose executions 'would stamp their names as patriots, and [as] men who had nothing but their country's weal at heart'.[14] William Cobbett, too, recalled that in court the conspirators had 'scorned to disguise their intention, and insisted that their intention was just':

> They discovered not the least symptom of fear; spoke of their approaching death as a thing certain; asked for no mitigation of punishment of any description; and seemed anxious about nothing but the consequences which their death might produce to their country. At the place of their execution ... they showed the same intrepidity ... Braver men never died since man was first created.[15]

The mid-Victorian novelist George Borrow went further, though less sure of the facts. He described the conspirators 'as honest and brave as either Brutus or Sidney, and as willing to die for their principles'. 'There was no humbug' in them, he wrote:

> Thistlewood and Ings say to twenty ragged individuals [that] Liverpool and Castlereagh are two satellites of despotism; it would be highly desirable to put them out of the way. And a certain number of ragged individuals are surprised in a stable in Cato Street, making preparations to put Castlereagh and Liverpool out of the way, and are fired upon with muskets by Grenadiers, and are hacked at with cutlasses by Bow Street runners. ... The very first to confront the Guards and runners are Thistlewood and Ings; Thistlewood whips his long thin rapier through [constable] Smithers' lungs, and Ings makes a dash at [Colonel] Fitzclarence with his butcher's knife. Oh, there was something in those fellows! – honesty and courage!

Over a century later E. P. Thompson wrote admiringly that 'not many men who had been arraigned once for high treason were willing to put their heads in the noose a second and a third time, as Thistlewood did in 1817–18 and again in 1820'. (A first and second time certainly, but a third time was Thompson's invention.)[16]

Courage, no doubt, but what about witlessness? Thompson failed to notice that few men would let themselves be duped twice by government spies as Thistlewood did. Every informed radical knew that spies had decimated radical movements for decades. The hanging and beheading of Colonel Despard and six associates in 1803 proved that spies and judges could wantonly kill men. Thistlewood's own narrow escape from the axe should have given warning enough too, since he and his colleagues were entrapped by the spy and *agent provocateur* John Castle and arraigned for the abortive Spa Fields insurrection of December 1816. Thereafter the records show that at least three spies reported on Thistlewood's doings before George Edwards took over full time.[17] Again, in a small blizzard of paranoid accusations in late 1819, Thistlewood, 'Orator' Henry Hunt, and William Cobbett charged each other with being in government pay. Altogether, then, it was either insane or suicidal of Thistlewood in 1820 not to realise that he was being nudged towards his doom by government *provocateurs*. As for Borrow's approval: it could be applied to the most callous of modern terrorists. Does the conspirators' courage outweigh the murder of a policeman and the many more murders that were intended? Some will prefer to follow William Hazlitt, a man of liberal judgement. He took a sourer view of the matter when he thought of ultra-radicals as men 'with no centre of gravity', but as 'a collection of atoms whirled about in space by their own levity'.[18]

All that said, however, there are excuses for the conspirators that speak to their era. Leigh Hunt's *Examiner* delivered the gentlest verdict just before the trials: the Cato Street men were only 'paupers driven to desperation in unconstitutional times', he wrote; and this 'should hinder us from denouncing them ... as a set of atrocious scoundrels not to be mentioned in company with the rich and corrupt'.[19] Beyond that, in that unyielding and unequal polity, their ambition might have been futile but it wasn't irrational. Carlile again:

> By whatever means they were seduced into the fatal snare, their moving springs of action were *good*. They are a sample of the millions who wait for nothing but judicious leaders in whom they can place confidence. Let those who survive them, beware how they suffer themselves to be acted

upon by the spies and agents of that Government whose religion is to starve, massacre, and hang.[20]

Enlightenment values directed the conspirators as well as hardship, and their plots expressed a hope of collective improvement. Like everyone else, they had the guillotining of the French king fresh in mind, and that *had* changed the world. Their watchwords were liberty and justice and their aims mass enfranchisement and equality (for women too, in some cases). This they voiced with courage. 'I am satisfied nothing can be done in this country if men are afraid of their lives,' Brunt told the court in his last speech before dying: 'I was willing to do even murder in liberty's cause; and I would have died there upon the spot, if my lord Sidmouth and lord Castlereagh had come to take me, they should not have had me.' An anonymous letter to Thistlewood two days before the executions encouraged him thus:

Be of good cheer tho the tyrants may destroy the body they cannot annihilate your spirit which animates thousands of your fellow countrymen who will cherish your memory with gratitude. Remember that the cause [in] which you were engaged was the cause of [liberty?] and that had not success been defeated by the basest of perfidy your name would at this moment have been applauded as the savir [*sic*] of England.[21]

So the questions we should ask about these men should be sharper. When, if at all, might an assassin's motives excuse him? What abuses might he and his family have endured in their lives, and for what larger good did he believe he acted? Do the men's poverty, disfranchisement, impotence, and democratising intent mitigate their rush to desperate and bloody violence? Was it mad of Thistlewood to ponder the Roman virtue of tyrannicide, or to hope that a new Brutus, Cassius, or Cato would bring republican virtues to Britain? To which add the question, was it an act of justice that five of the conspirators were hanged and decapitated for treason, or are they better seen as cynically manipulated victims who were sacrificed to the interests of an insecure, frightened, and misgoverned aristocratic state?

After the discovery of the conspiracy a whig grandee announced that he was certain that 'there was nothing in the character or conduct of the criminals ... to raise either sympathy or curiosity'. A well-connected political lady knew better. Although Mrs Arbuthnot had no pity for the conspirators, she foresaw that 'Jacobin' opinion-makers would one day 'write away the abhorrence now felt for the crime by dwelling upon the poverty & wretchedness of the conspirators'.[22] Even as she wrote, William Cobbett was advising posterity not to present the conspirators as monsters, but rather to 'speak *truth* of the dead – setting them forth and sending them down to posterity in their *true* light', and to allow them a dignity hitherto denied them.[23] It's in that spirit that this book extends more warmth to the conspirators than it does to the privileged aristocrats who provoked and then killed them.

With some exceptions, these last weren't more particularly wicked or insane than most of Britain's master classes have been and are. Trapped in their own time, role, and class, their failings reflected their self-interest, their complacency about their own ascendancy and entitlement, and their unbridgeable distance from those they ruled. In their understandings, too, the French revolution, initially welcomed in much of the country, was transformed by Louis XVI's killing into a godless atrocity. The reaction to it and the declaration of war with France in 1793 unleashed a reactionary barrage that laid radical reformers low. An unbroken succession of tory-loyalist governments stretched from the younger Pitt's administrations (1783–1801 and 1804–6), through Addington's (1801–4), Spencer Perceval's (1809–12), and Liverpool's (1812–26). Addington turned into 'Lord Sidmouth' and became a key figure in this story. As Liverpool's home secretary between 1812 and 1822, he orchestrated the most extensive spy network the country had seen since Walsingham's under Elizabeth I. Canning said in tribute to his long career that he was like the smallpox: 'Everyone is obliged to have him once in their lives'. His later portrait conveys something of his charm (Fig. 3.1).[24] Each of these men was convinced that if government failed to suppress protest their social order would be as doomed as the French one. The self-justifications they had to hand were timeless:

> If the idea of the needy and vulgar undertaking to legislate for a country famed all over the world for its wealth, knowledge, and fame, did not fill the mind with terrible forebodings, it would afford an inexhaustible

3.1. E. Scriven, after George Richmond, *Henry Addington, 1st Viscount Sidmouth* (1833) (Hulton Archive/Getty Images)

source of ridicule.... In an instant titles and distinctions, as alleged badges of corruption, would disappear; the next objects to be pounded in the mortar of the Reformer would be the whole body of the dignified clergy; then the shears of the leveller would be applied to royalty.... We should as soon confide in the tender mercies of a half-famished hyaena, as in the humanity of an English Jacobin. We would as soon trust to the gentleness of a lioness, who had been just robbed of her young, as to the compassion of a leveller.[25]

All that said, however, an excess of justice has already been done to these people by generation after generation of privileged historians, so there's no need to do more of it here. They are not our subject. At issue, rather, is the awakening of new understandings among opinionated commoners, along with the fact that if the regency poor viscerally hated these high men, it was for the soundest of reasons. In contemplating the men's brutal executions one might say further: so much for the refined sensibilities and good taste of the age of Jane Austen. So much also for our own sensibility, that aristocratic violence in that era is normalised and its agents are celebrated as *elegant*. Five ignorant but liberty-minded men were first publicly hanged and then had their heads hacked off and held up dripping to an audience of many thousands. It explains why in the end what we may chiefly feel is pity.

CHAPTER 4

What They Were Up Against

LOYALISM OR SUBMISSION?

It would be foolish to underestimate the strength of wartime loyalism among the British people in the regency years, or to forget that by continental standards there was some cause to celebrate the British rule of law and parliament's check on monarchical despotism, however compromised they were. The decades-long tory domination of parliament rested on a deeply engrained anti-radical opinion. This was no surprise when the parliamentary vote in 1820 was public, corrupted, bribed, and enjoyed by 350,000 of the most comfortable adult males in the kingdom and by no more than 123,000 in the English boroughs. Exceptionally, a large number of shopkeepers and artisans could vote in the Westminster constituency. But the labouring masses were marginalised in the nation's affairs. What defined 'politics' in high people's opinion was self-referential. It meant that in the 1818 general election the tories under Lord Liverpool won a national majority of some 90 seats (mostly in the countryside), while in the same election in Westminster the radical candidates Hunt and Cartwright were humiliatingly rejected with 107 votes combined as against the 10,577 for the liberal whigs Burdett and Romilly. In the 1820 election just after Cato Street, Liverpool beat the whigs by 341 seats to 215.

With or without the vote, middling folk displayed their own interest in order. They joined loyalist volunteers and militias to resist French invasion – as young Arthur Thistlewood himself did, twice. Most of the humble derided radicals as 'rabble'. Since the satirists depended on these people's shillings, for every pro-reform and anti-corruption print in these years, dozens portrayed radicals as comic grotesques. Only the tiniest minorities would have voted for revolution, and in rural England deference was reflexive. Even the Cato Street men said that their conspiracy wasn't meant to harm the king, only the ministers. After the Cato Street executions the ex-LCS man John Thelwall observed that the English people were peace-loving: 'the bruising matches [fights] of the street vulgar have had always a sort of chivalrous honour and generosity in them'. During the Gordon riots of 1780, he recalled, 'not an assassination was perpetrated' by the rioters, even when hundreds of them were killed themselves.[1] Thelwall didn't notice, however, that at this level the crowd's generosity was hardly optional or freely chosen.

A conservative breed of historians hasn't noticed this either. It has primarily seen the regency's popular cultures as expressions of the 'church-and-king' and 'flag-saluting, foreigner-hating, peer-respecting side of the plebeian mind',[2] and assumed that acquiescence in the social hierarchy was 'natural'. Thus order was valued in Britain, we are told, and great machines and artworks were made under it, and an empire was extended and a global war won, and the world was blessed by Britain's might, and most Britons were glad to be British. It was also a sensitive, high-minded, deep-feeling culture, better than all others. These rosy views have infected the national culture like a curse. As I write, Amazon UK lists 30,898 book titles under the category 'regency romance' and 16,564 titles under 'Jane Austen', while Google Books lists 25,000 references to the exhausted phrase, 'regency elegance'. Because the era's military history is thought to have been glorious as well, Amazon adds 7,939 celebratory titles under 'Waterloo'. 'Regency radicalism' earns six entries, and 'regency poverty' or 'inequality' aren't recognised at all.

The truth is that populous and complex societies are fissiparous and multilayered rather than organically or mystically bonded. Contrary realities always coexist, and which we emphasise reflects our purposes, interests, and insights. That's why it shouldn't be expunged from memory that Britain was a chronically unsettled country. After the 1815 Peace, local outbreaks of group violence were reported almost every month or week, and it wasn't always radicals who led them. They were part of the timeless conversation between the powerful and powerless, for in tense places people were as querulous as they might be bovine elsewhere. In London, riots accompanied the passage of the Corn Laws in 1815, and a year later there were hunger riots in Ely and nearby Littleport. In a quick skim of the *Times* for 1816, we find Bermondsey journeymen tanners in April marching to a tanners' yard with drums and fifes playing and flags flying – the languages of war still in mind – to threaten death to the employers and demand their men's turnout. A working tanner was dragged to a pump to be 'pumped' under the water, then to be beaten up and nearly killed; a passing woman, pregnant, was mistaken for the master's wife and abused. In August, Newgate saw a riot of 140 convicts sentenced to transportation, and a month later the Whitecross Street debtors' prison erupted when imprisoned sailors pumped a fellow prisoner, attacked the turnkeys, broke windows and gas lamps, and blocked prison keyholes to stop guards entering.[3] To contradict John Thelwall, reaching for violence was all but reflexive. Go to the youthful fountainheads of aristocracy and you find Winchester College boys in 1818 protesting at their headmaster's spying methods by building barricades from the courtyard paving and pelting and locking up the masters; the head was held hostage by boys armed with axes. Soldiers and constables had to bring them to heel, and floggings and expulsions followed; but that didn't stop Eton boys in similar mode from revolting shortly after. Eton experienced six full-scale revolts between the 1770s and 1830s and Rugby five, including one in 1797 in which boys took prisoners at sword-point.[4] And so English life proceeded.

The wisest among contemporary elites knew that the regency was an unlovely era for the humble, and that it was sustained by the exploitation of poor people and the worse enslavement of black ones. One didn't have to be a radical to recognise that the inequalities endorsed by frightened or obscurantist governments were grotesque, and that the deprivations endured by the poor were in good part wilfully imposed. The Cato Street conspirators' and like people's narrow histories were moulded by their era's vast political and economic denials and provocations.

The *Independent Whig* newspaper calculated that at the start of the regency the civil list allowed £1,700,000 'to support a profligate prince and his concubines'. That meant that the cost of the regent's household broke down as follows:

£1,700,000   *Weight (in gold) Fifteen tons, twelve cwt., three quarters, seventeen pounds, six ounces and two pennyweights*
The daily pay to His Royal Highness is –
£4,657. 10. 8
Each hour, drunk or sober
£194. 8. 0
Each minute, asleep or awake
£3. 4. 8½.[5]

In fact the regent had his fat fingers only on most, not all, of this loot, but no thinking reader would have mistaken the point. A few minutes' walk away from the regent's Trumpishly glitzy Carlton House in Pall Mall, an artisan in work might have to live on £40 a year to keep his family if they worked with him, while a shopkeeping family of the middling sort might hope for £100. But plebeian income was unstable, and it was made more so for craftsmen as the obsolescence and repeal of the Elizabethan apprenticeship laws allowed unapprenticed labour to swamp old crafts like shoemaking.

Meanwhile, the financial and landowning interests, already fat from West Indian plantation profits and wartime demand, benefited from the ending of wartime income tax, even as the common folk continued to pay heavy taxes on everything from candles and malt to soap and salt. They paid for bread most cruelly. The grain harvest of 1816 was a disaster, yet the 1815 Corn Laws defended landed income by taxing foreign corn and by passing the costs to consumers. Not for nothing did the home secretary Lord Sidmouth announce that he wanted to be remembered as 'the country gentlemen's secretary of state'.[6] As the bloodiest war in memory ended at Waterloo in 1815, trade failures were worsened by national debt, paper inflation, and the ubiquity of sinecures and ceaseless expansion of the Civil List. The trades and industries that had done well out of the French wars stalled in 1816–17, and stalled again in 1819. Public debt amounted to nearly a thousand million pounds sterling.

The suffering that ensued from this polity wasn't all man-made. It was worsened by the peculiarly bitter winters of a little ice age. The worst winter in recent memory had been in 1794/5, when minus 21 °C was recorded in London on 25 January. The Thames froze over again in 1813/14; on it a 'frost fair' was set up, and an elephant was led across the river at Blackfriars. A year later the volcanic eruption of Mount Tambora in Indonesia, one of the greatest ever recorded, dispersed enough ash across the globe to lower British temperatures for a year, so that 1816 was a year 'without summer'. The following years were bitter, the winter of 1819/20 devastatingly so. This was the hardest winter since 1813/14, some said since 1795, and it was an inauspicious time for conspiracy. The once-in-a-lifetime appearance of the aurora borealis in London would have seemed ominous.

On New Year's Day 1820 the temperature in Westminster fell to minus 9°C, and the following three weeks saw deep snow across the south-eastern counties. The frost continued until the 23rd of the month. The non-tidal Thames froze as far downstream as Kew; through the metropolis it was 'full of floating ice, of great thickness'. In Kent, minus 15 °C was registered. Smog was semi-permanent. Late February 1820 saw a thaw, but on nine days in that month temperatures fell well below freezing. At eleven o'clock on the Sunday morning before the Cato Street assembling the snow fell so thickly that pedestrians could barely see their way, and the conspirators in Fox Court met in near darkness: 'I made towards the fire-place, but it was so dark I could scarcely tell who they were till one spoke to me; that was Tidd: he said, "How do you do, Adams?" – I said, "Is that you, Tidd?"'[7]

The weather swelled the number of 'disorders of the pulmonary organs'. As the cold killed off the destitute, newspapers published heart-rending stories. In January one John Masters and his wife were found dead on the floor in their 'little back-room' in Round Court near the Scotch Arms; neighbours had heard their 'groans and moans, shocking to hear'. The coroner decided that they didn't starve to death because there was some bread and butter in the room and a shilling in the man's pocket; 'but not having clothing, bed, nor fire, they perished of cold. – Verdict to that effect.' The same page of the *Morning Post* reported an inquest in St Giles's on the body of a woman called Hatchett (her first name is unknown): 'a more loathsome object cannot be described – a heap of bones, covered with rags and filth'. She had begged a cellar dweller off Drury Lane to take her in on that bitter night, even though the charitable woman herself slept on bare floorboards. Next morning she found Hatchett dead from want of food and clothes and cold, as she decided. Several of the jury thought she couldn't have died of hunger because the night before her death she had eaten a piece of herring.[8]

Charitable subscriptions to relieve the destitute and to shelter the 'houseless' peaked in this month. For a day or two, newspapers' pages filled with the lists of charitable donors that testified to some several hundred pitying hearts in that great city (no great number, in other words). The lord mayor's fund raised £6,405 mainly from one- to five-guinea subscriptions; chilly eminences like chief justice Abbott and the attorney general each gave ten guineas.[9] The total was too small to stop London's beggars multiplying, their numbers swollen by the discharge of some half-million soldiers and sailors. National poor relief rose from £2 million in 1792 to £8 million in 1818. In 1820 a parliamentary committee calculated that there were 15,000 beggars on London's streets. One of London's biggest buildings was the prison-like workhouse that housed the derelict poor at the foot of St Martin's Lane, behind the present National Gallery. It took up twice the area of the regent's Carlton House and twice the area of Newgate prison, and almost as much ground as Leicester Square.

In these conditions, only obscurantists denied that underdog deference and patriotism were sustained less by a natural gratitude than by top-down religious, political, and economic conditioning by the monied, the armed, and the pious. Most licensed newspapers and pamphleteers, churches and chapels, hymn books and chapbooks worked hard to induce consent. Evangelicals' advice that the humble should turn their other cheeks never once stopped sounding out in these fraught decades, and a so-called 'reformation of manners' led by the godly and the sexually continent duly established a firmer buttress for what became Victorian order.

Altogether, then, one has to add some obvious identifiers to the regency schedule. It wasn't just a prettily dressed era or one supportive of elegant young lovers with fetching cleavages and torsos. Inequality, exploitation, disfranchisement, enclosure, factories, slavery, war, hunger, beggary, hangings, transportation, floggings, bullets, sabres – and governmental repression: these were what guaranteed regency order and enabled the privileged to cavort so stylishly. Behind its elegant masks it was a cruel and oppressive era for common people, and polarisation was stark. The poet Southey wrote in November 1819: 'It is no longer a question between Ins and Outs, nor between Whigs and Tories. It is between those who have something to lose, and those who have everything to gain by a dissolution of society.'[10]

REVOLUTION?

Many decades ago the historian E. P. Thompson thought Britain was heading for a revolution in 1819–20. 'The government was isolated, and there were sharp differences within the ruling class', and the authorities were 'in a curious way' powerless. 'The government met in a hostile London, where juries had refused to convict Wooler and Hone, where grotesque prints and lampoons were displayed in the windows, and where publications which were, in the eyes of the authorities, seditious atrocities, were disseminated with impunity'. And as they were forced to release them from prison, the reformers perplexingly came forward 'in the role of constitutionalists'. Thompson heard anxious magistrates ask, 'at what point would this stop?'[11]

Thompson's view (1963) reflected his belief in the deepening crisis and class militancy of the time. He didn't cite Lenin overtly and was no Leninist himself, but he doubtless knew Lenin's three conditions of a revolutionary situation: that there must be a crisis among the upper classes that leads to a 'fissure' through which the discontent of the oppressed bursts forth; that the suffering and want of the oppressed should be more acute than usual; and that as a result there should be 'a considerable increase in the activity of the masses'. 'It is only when the lower classes do not want to live in the old way and the upper classes cannot carry on in the old way that revolution can triumph,' said Lenin in his *Collapse of the Second International.* Thompson implied these conditions were close to fulfilment. The ruling class's dilemmas were acute, he wrote, because '*no one supposed that the structure of power rested upon Pitt's barracks alone*'. The sentence is italicised because it begs the question we come to shortly.

In an age unable to forget the French revolutionary example, there is no question that in 1819 London and parts of the midlands and north were insurrectionary tinderboxes, though not everyone in high places could admit it. As Wellington put it, in turbulent times comfortable people always deceive themselves that the storm won't reach them and go on with their lives until it 'breaks in upon them by force'. Wellington's truism was cited by the diarist Robert Plumer Ward whose own sanguine views confirmed it. As Wellington's second in command in the ordnance office, he helped his master organise the country's military supplies, fortifications, and transport. In the tense winter months after Peterloo he recorded ministers' and his own reactions closely, and in a single invaluable chapter conveyed the panicky mood that led to the Six Acts.[12]

Ward was one of the comfortable people who looked on the bright side. He thought it a happy omen that when the regent was driven round Hyde Park more people cheered than hissed him, and women waved their handkerchiefs. Everyone at polite dinner parties assured him that radicalism was weaker in London than in the north, and that Sidmouth was more afraid of the Scotch mob than of the English. The radicals, he learned, couldn't count on more than a thousand men in the capital, and 'the lower orders wished not an invasion of property by fellows with no property.' He noted that on Lord Mayor's Day a rough crowd threw abuse and brickbats at the lord mayor, stopped carriages on their way to the Guildhall, and forced occupants to open their windows and say who they were. On giving his name, Wellington's brother was greeted with 'then you are a damned rascal, and ought to be ashamed to show your face among an honest public', while the duke of York was abused for his £10,000 a year allowance. In the event the crowd was easily evaded. When it stopped Wellington, the hero complimented it on its courtesy and drove on. And when Lord Harrowby was asked if he was ashamed of himself, he replied 'not at all' and drove on also.

Again, after the opening of parliament on 23 November, the regent was insulted as he returned through the Park, but Ward was more impressed by the number of people who applauded him. And when George III died in January 1820 Ward thought there was 'but one opinion and one feeling about him from the peer to the lowest tradesman. After all there is a great deal of loyalty innate in the nation, which will,

I trust, always keep it right.' 'How ridiculously eager we all are,' he wrote comfortably, 'about a thing which we all affect to despise, and which is in reality despicable.' By this he meant low public opinion, the opinion of what he called the 'fond many'.

Even so, Ward had to admit that those in the know took a darker view. When local radicals surveyed the duke of Hamilton's Lanarkshire estate and declared it big enough to give local weavers nine acres each, Hamilton armed Glasgow by mobilising a volunteer force of 5,000 men, 3,000 of whom were already 'regimented'. Almost every day reports arrived at the home office about preparations for revolt in the north and midlands. In Manchester men were drilling in large numbers and shouting 'Hunt and Liberty for ever', and trade in Manchester and district was at a standstill: 'It never was known so bad, nor are there any hopes of its amendment until the spring,' a magistrate reported. Ward couldn't see it. After touring the northern military depots in October, he told Sidmouth that he had found the north 'very peaceable, and even civil, and very anti-Radical'. At this Sidmouth 'shook his head, and pointing to volumes of papers, said, if I knew their contents I would not say so, for the pictures were frightful'.

Lord Mulgrave also warned Ward that 'things were critical', and that the country wouldn't survive a moment were disaffection better organised. He lamented that the peacetime army had been cut, and hoped for a volunteer force that would display 'a military spirit on the right side': that 'would alone save the country'. Robert Peel told Ward that Wellington also 'took a very gloomy view of things', and that the duke had expected 'great rioting in London' after the regent's speech, once the terms of the Six Acts were known. By early December Wellington was anticipating an uprising in Glasgow and Paisley. If suppression were needed, he said, it would have to be forceful and would cause more discontent even than Peterloo. When Ward travelled with Wellington to hear the Speech, the duke locked his coach doors against 'a very radical-looking mob' in Pall Mall and advised Ward to lean back into his seat if attacked, since 'you may fight a window better than a parapet wall'; he then mimed how to do it. At the Lords, Ward found that the crowd looked at the hero with interest but without cheering. After the Speech Ward suggested that the government's measures against free speech and assembly would deliver radicalism its death blow. '*Do* you?' Wellington replied with meaningful emphasis. Many were secretly 'frightened out of their wits', he added. He told Ward that he was thankful that the radicals had no access to arms, but he worried that if they got hold of a piece of cannon or 1,500 stand of arms 'it would go far to produce a revolution at once'. He thought that strong measures were useless when the public wouldn't support them – 'when one says, I am for them, but don't touch the liberty of the press; another, don't pretend to keep people from meeting'.

Castlereagh's anxieties about the 'mob' were just as acute, though he concealed them. When rioters besieged St James's Square in protest at the Corn Laws in 1815, thousands of 'the lowest of the London rabble' broke the windows of its houses. Life Guards on patrol were pelted by stones and mud amid cries of 'Down with the Piccadilly butchers!' (in reference to their brutality during the Burdett riots in 1810). As Castlereagh watched with soldiers reassuringly round the corner, he told his companion that 'the mob is not so dangerous as you think' and seemed unruffled by the abuse.[13] He displayed the same poise when he joined a shooting party in Norfolk in mid-January 1820 for what he, if not the birds, called a fortnight's 'relaxation'. As he travelled to that simple county he was pleased to think that parliament's 'more manly and determined tone' had returned the country to good order: he had the Six Acts in mind. 'Radical stock is very low indeed at the present moment,' he wrote to a friend, 'and the loyal have resumed their superiority and confidence.'

Castlereagh's poise was as fragile as Wellington's, however. For a year or two spies had been telling him and his fellow ministers of plots to kill them. In January 1820 T. J. Wooler of the *Black Dwarf* was cheerfully envisaging a future for his head:

> Yes – this is the noddle that humbles to none,
> That laughs at the freedom our ancestors won.
>
> . . .
>
> Let it rest – let it rot – let us throw it aside,
> And smother its vain insignificant pride![14]

When Castlereagh was told in early February that a gang of low people meant to take his head off and assassinate his colleagues, he went to dine at the Lievens', Princess Lieven said, 'looking like a man who had just been hung'. The day after the Cato Street arrests the princess found he had constables quartered in his house and carried loaded pistols in his pockets. When he showed her the weapons at dinner, she nearly fell off her chair in shock; the guest on her other side elbowed her ribs as he cut his meat and so saved her from falling. Castlereagh carried the pistols until he slit his own throat two years later.[15]

People outside the political elites were also pessimistic. Samuel Johnson's ageing friend Mrs Piozzi noted after Hunt's and Watson's great Smithfield meeting in July 1819 that the metropolis was 'distracted with riots' and newspapers were 'quite terrifying'.[16] The poet Shelley repeatedly referred to 'awful times' and a populace 'preparing for a bloody struggle', while Carlile wrote from Dorchester gaol that

> the present is one of the most gloomy moments this country ever beheld ... There is evidently an hostile feeling between the people and the government. The former are oppressed, and the latter the oppressors; and should they not be disposed to conciliate and redress the injuries of the people, a civil war, with all its horrors, must be the consequence of it.[17]

These sundry expressions seem to validate Thompson's sense of a revolutionary situation. But what if they were evidence less of a revolutionary situation than of a moral panic which underestimated the extent to which the state was defended? Thirty years later, Harriet Martineau suggested as much when she wrote that in 1819–20 anxieties had spread 'without any evidence at all':

> how prodigious were the radical forces [then], which were always heard of but never seen; how every shabby and hungry-looking man on the road was pronounced a radical; how country gentlemen, well armed, scoured the fields and lanes, and met on heaths to fight the enemy who never came; and how, even in the midst of towns, young ladies carried heavy planks and ironing boards to barricade windows, in preparation for sieges from thousands of rebels, whose footfall was long listened for in vain, through the darkness of the night.[18]

What is certain is that other variables now need to be added that lay outside Thompson's purview. In 1819 the LCS veteran John Gale Jones welcomed 'Orator' Henry Hunt to London after his stand at Peterloo by referring to the 'triple-headed monster' that kept the British people in their place. It consisted, he said (to loud cheers), of 'a ministerial, a magisterial, and a military despotism', the selfsame complex that had killed unarmed people in Manchester.[19] He saw its power more clearly than Thompson did.

Thompson wrote *The Making of the English Working Class* before the great explosion of research in and after the 1970s into the social-disciplinary history of law, policing, and punishment began at last to explain the relative security of the nineteenth-century social order. (Thompson later helped pioneer the revision.) This work obliges us nowadays to suggest that 'Pitt's barracks', along with the laws, prisons, and gallows that surrounded them, explain very precisely why British plebeians by and large left the business of killing people to their betters, and why no 'fissure' was wide enough for discontent to 'burst through'. As Castlereagh's pistols remind us, aristocracy was protected by something more than the underdogs' love of king and country. Spies, sabres, bullets, and cannon-shot determined outcomes, and courts, prisons, iron bars, and shackles strengthened the arsenal.

Daniel Defoe had noticed long before that London had 'more publick and private prisons, and houses of confinement, than any city in Europe, perhaps as many as in all the capital cities of Europe put together'. By the early nineteenth century strings of prisons bigger than Defoe ever knew covered London. They stretched southwards from Cold Bath Fields prison above Clerkenwell, via the Clerkenwell new prison and the huge Whitecross Street debtors' prison (built in 1813 west of Finsbury), down the axis of the Fleet river (the Giltspur Compter, Newgate, the Fleet, the St Bride's bridewell), and across the Thames to the Borough Compter in Tooley Street, the Marshalsea and the King's Bench off what is now Borough High Street, and the Surrey county prison in Horsemonger Lane. The bridewell at Tothill Fields and the new panopticon at Millbank stood to the west, and the carceral archipelago was completed by a scattering of lock-ups, workhouses, and madhouses. The presence, meaning, and power of these frightful places were inescapable.

LAWS

A couple of weeks after the Cato Street executions William Cobbett wrote:

> Such multitudes of sentences and of executions meet our ears and eyes now-a-days, that they attract little attention. We hear of trials for 'sedition, blasphemy, and treason', of convictions, fines, imprisonments, hangings and quarterings, with feelings much like those with which we hear or read of the killed and wounded in land or sea battles, after a war has been going on for some time.[20]

Politically driven trials, harsh punishment, and public execution under the bloody penal code were central facts in national life in this era, and in regency years became more so, not less. To be sure, with the opening of the Australian penal settlements in 1788, the national execution rate had dropped because increasing numbers of death sentences could be 'pardoned' and commuted to transportation. It had also helped that the French wars initially diminished death sentences and hangings because the half-million neediest and roughest men in Britain were dying on battlefields elsewhere, for the good of their country. The forty-three public hangings outside Newgate prison in 1801–5 marked the lowest execution rate in London since the beginning of the eighteenth century (though it was still the highest in Europe).[21]

That relief didn't last long, though. In the hungry post-war years of 1816–20 ever more need-driven thieving combined with mounting anxieties about demobilisation, immiseration, and disorder to drive prosecution rates upwards. Although 'pardons' remained high, in those few years London saw some 1,058 death sentences and 140 hangings outside Newgate. Forty-three hanged in 1820 alone; and nearly as many died in the year following. London hangings made up 27 per cent of all executions in England and Wales, so, at the time of Cato Street, London was the best place to go in the whole western world if you wanted to see executions. Thereafter, in the 1820s, 672 men and women were executed in England and Wales as a whole. This was more than had been hanged in the whole of either the first or the second quarter of the eighteenth century. Even as humanitarians and people of refinement paraded their new-found 'sensibility' in and after the regency years, most acquiesced in the public scaffold uncritically.[22]

The justice the English courts delivered was rough-hewn. There was no appeal court, and one could only petition for 'mercy' in the hope of replacing death with transportation. Trial by jury was occasionally a blessing if juries stood up for themselves; yet for the most part juries heard evidence casually. As late as 1832 felony trials at the Old Bailey took eight and a half minutes on average, their legal jargon unintelligible to the accused. Poor men and women on trial felt 'knocked down like bullocks, unheard. Full two-thirds of the prisoners, on their return from their trials, cannot tell of any thing which has passed in the court, not even, very frequently, whether they have been tried'.[23] 'I am sold as a bullock that is driven into Smithfield-market,' as Ings the butcher later put it.

Hanging a man was often a political as well as judicial act. In the first twenty years of the new century convictions for 'riot' nominally accounted for twenty-seven hangings, but that number was much swollen by executions for the burglaries and machine-breaking that accompanied most riotous crimes. At key moments, deliberately intimidatory show trials and executions for riot were deployed as acts of policy, never without a dramatic military presence in case of trouble. When Sir Simon le Blanc presided over the trials of sixty-four machine-breakers at York Assizes in 1813, artillerymen with lighted lint-stocks stood by their guns around the court while seventeen men were convicted and ordered for execution next morning. Never before had so many hanged at once in York since ten rebels were executed there in 1746. Since gallows were in short supply, the judge thought they would 'hang more comfortably' if three were hanged on one day and fourteen the next, in batches of seven. Cavalry regiments were on hand and the never-absent dragoons ringed the scaffolds. Henry Hobhouse attended the executions on behalf of the home office. Walking the streets afterwards he noted the defeated and dispirited air of the people. 'The effect was tremendous, for whereas the town had been full of excited mobs of a threatening character, hardly a person was to be seen outside his house on the following day.'[24]

This repressive tally may conclude with the fact that between 1780 and up to (but excluding) the Cato Street executions, thirteen men in

England were hanged and decapitated for the forms of protest, not least Irish, that governments defined as treason. They were de la Motte (1781), Tyrie (1782: the last man to be quartered after hanging and decapitation),[25] O'Coigley (1798), Marcus Despard and six of his co-conspirators (1803), and the midlands stockingers Brandreth, Turner, and Ludlam (1817). Add the five Cato Street hangings and decapitations in May 1820, and later that year the three further decapitations of Wilson, Hardie, and Baird in Glasgow and Stirling for leading the rebellion of distressed Scottish weavers – and the first decades of the new century offered little for the liberal-minded to celebrate, even if it was a blessing that the three Scots were the last Britons to lose their heads literally. Treason prosecutions lapsed between 1820 and the Chartist 1840s; thereafter convicted 'traitors' were transported for life until the executions by noose or firing squad of Irish republicans in 1916 and of Joyce in 1946.

Although the impact of prosecution for sedition was all but drowned in this bloody tide, Pitt's government in the 1790s saw nearly 200 sedition and treason trials at English provincial assizes and quarter sessions; trials in London and Scotland probably matched that number.[26] Many convictions for seditious publication resulted in fines or pillorying, but the list of those imprisoned included great names as well as small, and the list of those intimidated into silence was even longer.

The attack had begun in 1792 with George III's proclamation against seditious writings and publications. It had been followed by the temporary suspension of habeas corpus in 1794 and again in 1798 ('to empower His Majesty to secure and detain [without trial] such persons as His Majesty shall suspect are conspiring against his person and government'); that suspension recurred four times before 1820. In 1795, a stone thrown at the king's coach was used to justify Pitt's Treasonable and Seditious Practices Act and the Seditious Meetings Act. These criminalised so-called 'constructive treason' in publications, and prohibited meetings of fifty or more people. To impede their circulation, stamp duties on newspapers followed; circulating libraries and reading rooms had to be licensed; presses and typefaces had to be registered; and printers had to declare their names and addresses on all publications.

The first notable casualties of this assault were the shoemaker Thomas Hardy and others who had founded the London Corresponding Society in 1792. Fired by Tom Paine's *Rights of Man* and campaigning for annual parliaments and universal manhood suffrage, the LCS at its peak had some three thousand members (five thousand by some accounts), each paying a penny a week. Organised into divisions and competent in propaganda, its tavern meetings spread across London as it 'corresponded' with similar societies in the provinces and France. It pulled in large numbers of professional men, but its novel distinction was its artisan base. Of the small minority whose occupations can be identified, the largest categories were shoemakers, weavers, and tailors.[27] Riddled with spies, its persecution was predictable. In May 1794 a dozen members were arrested and charged with high treason. Three were tried: Hardy, John Thelwall, and John Horne Tooke. The jury ignored the judge's direction and acquitted them because their treasonous intent wasn't proved. Crowds of cheering people drew the acquitted through the streets in unhorsed coaches. But the intimidation was such that the LCS shrunk to 241 paying members. Hardy's wife died while he was in prison, and his business was ruined. Meanwhile the prolific socialist-utopian Thomas Spence, already arrested three times in 1792–3 and imprisoned without trial for seven months in 1794, was sentenced to a year in Shrewsbury gaol in 1798 for seditious publication.

The United Irishmen were more fiercely dealt with. The 1798 Irish rebellion cost thousands of lives, many executed summarily by English troops. James Coigly was hanged, decapitated, and buried beneath the gallows on Penenden Heath in Kent, and Wolfe Tone killed himself before he was hanged. The United Irishmen were proscribed, imprisoned, or exiled. The organisation collapsed after the suppression of Robert Emmet's rebellion in 1803. Meanwhile a second suspension of habeas corpus in 1798 enabled the whole LCS committee to be arrested and imprisoned without charge or trial. Marcus Despard was among those who went inside for three years. Within ten months of his release in 1801 he was rearrested for helping the United Irishmen plot an Irish rising and French invasion. The jury wanted to convict him and his associates only of administering official oaths; it also recommended mercy. But the judge Ellenborough stressed that the group had conspired to destroy the new union with Ireland and aimed to achieve 'the forcible reduction to one common level of all the advantages of property, of all civil and political rights whatsoever'. He sentenced them to be hanged, drawn, and quartered on the roof of the Surrey county prison in Horsemonger Lane across the river. Spared the last infliction, they only had their heads taken off. It was a lesson the Cato Street men failed to remember.

In July 1799 a spy reported that Thomas Evans and a dozen others were trying to form societies of 'United Englishmen' on the model of the United Irishmen in order to promote a revolution ('a more ridiculous project was never entered by the imaginations of men out of Bedlam'). As a result the LCS and the United Englishmen were both outlawed for 'a traitorous conspiracy ... to overturn the laws, constitution and government', a move that effectively extinguished the LCS.[28] Evans and several others spent three years in prison, without trial. His heroic wife Janet gave birth shortly before his arrest; then for a short period she was imprisoned too, despite another pregnancy. Released, she delivered stillborn twins. Evans's undecorated account of his imprisonment is worth full quotation. The experience it describes was never far from the thoughts of every one of our story's protag-onists. This was the threat that even the mildest were obliged to live with:

> I was seized on the authority of a general warrant (an arbitrary mandate of the duke of Portland [home secretary] that was declared illegal in the courts of law) and after laying several days on the floor in Tothil-Fields prison, was conveyed to the Bastile [Cold Bath Fields], and there confined many months in a cell, with the accommodation of a bag of straw, a blanket, and rug; denied books, pen, ink, paper, candle, and much of the time access to fire. Meanwhile my house, in the city of London [Plough Court, Fetter Lane], was taken possession of by a corps of Bow-street officers; who after sending my wife and infant son to the Bastile, detained all persons calling thereat, (whatever their business) and sent them to prison; finally abandoning the house to chance. At the end of sixteen months' confinement in this Bastile, I was banished by authority of an act of parliament (passed for that purpose) to the gaol of Winchester, and there imprisoned in a cell twenty-one weeks, with the accommodation of a bag of straw, &c. as before; denied as before books, pen, ink, paper, fire, candle, &c. or society of any sort. Removed from

thence to London, I was again banished to the gaol of Chelmsford, and confined under the same regulations and instructions, in company with three other persons already in that place similarly circumstanced. In all, two years and eleven months, was I immured on the vague and undefined charge of treasonable practices; and then discharged without trial, remuneration, or redress: my persecutors being unable to exhibit any charge of unlawful conduct for any thing done or said on my part, on any of the numerous persons so maltreated at that time.[29]

Not all was bleak. The legal bombardment of free assembly, speech, and opinion that marked these years fell short of a repression that could credibly be called a 'Terror'.[30] Jury independence had been increased by Fox's Libel Act of 1792, so there were many acquittals; and the rule of law was respected in principle even if less in practice. Criticism was still possible through the medium of satirical imagery (it was difficult to prosecute a 'joke'). Poets supplied another critical chorus, even if Southey and Wordsworth recanted and some of Shelley's works had to be published posthumously. And critical voices abounded in parliament, for liberal-minded whigs were vocal.

George Tierney, the whigs' parliamentary leader in and after 1818, was no firebrand, but he hoped to make the House 'gradually and practically a truer representation of the people' and declared himself 'a friend to parliamentary reform, but not to annual parliaments or to universal suffrage'. His reply to Castlereagh on 30 November 1819 reminds us how capable the culture was of rationality. Even now it provides as good a riposte to high tory reaction as any:

> I see on the part of the government an evident determination to resort to nothing but force: they think of nothing else, they dream of nothing else; they will try no means of conciliation, they will make no attempt to pacify and reconcile: force – force – force, and nothing but force: that is their cry, and it has been the same for years: one measure of coercion has been, and will be, followed up by another, and the result will justify what I assert, that 10,000 [soldiers] will not answer their purpose; one measure of violence must succeed another, and what they gain by force they must retain by the same detestable means.

The people will never rest until they are allowed to live under laws equally administered; until their honest industry will procure them means of maintaining their families, and until they shall again enjoy the blessings of that constitution which their ancestors intended they should partake. If not, discontent will increase to disaffection, and distress will produce discontent, notwithstanding the bold assertions of the noble lord, that the nation is prosperous. ... But if the country gives him [Castlereagh] more troops to put down new meetings, surely it is somewhat hard that he should also ask it for new laws, that are to prevent the possibility of new meetings. If the noble lord thinks that the new laws will be effectual, where is the occasion for the 10,000 men?[31]

But reasoning of this kind was batted away by governments that rode high on the support of provincial electors. The authoritarian mindsets that had been bred deep into the bloodlines of robber barons and landed grandees were expressed in Act after Act curtailing freedom of speech and assembly, and in the Riot Act as well (soldiers could use force to disperse crowds of twelve or more people once a magistrate had ordered the meeting to disperse) – not to mention in the English taste for spying.

Until the twentieth century the British put a touching faith in their governments' rectitude on the matter of spies. The jacobite Francis Atterbury in 1723 inveighed in parliament against the un-English way in which his correspondence had been intercepted: 'In the name of God, what are these decypherers? They are a sort of officers unknown to the English nation. Are they the necessary implements and instruments of ministers of state?' When over a century later the Italian exile Mazzini announced that his letters were being opened, the *Times* declared that the 'proceeding cannot be English, any more than masks, poisons, sword-sticks, secret signs and associations, and other such dark inventions'. Macaulay insisted that his country had 'long ago' determined that spying and letter-opening, like torture, 'were pernicious, debasing and dangerous modes of maintaining its institutions'.

High-minded bluster of this kind had been disingenuous since Elizabethan times. By the late eighteenth century the ubiquity of spies was too well publicised to be doubted. Spies had betrayed the London

Corresponding Society in the 1790s and Despard's conspiracy in 1802. Thistlewood's and Watson's responsibility for the Spa Field riot in December 1816 was shared by the spy and *agent provocateur* John Castle. The Pentrich uprising of 1817 was set up by the spy Oliver, and the Scottish rebels in 1820 were similarly infiltrated.

Both plebeian and liberal opinion drew the line at the notion that a spy might decide a court's judgement when lives were at stake, and tolerance snapped as recognition of the spy system's lethal effects spread. Its full extent was exposed in 1817 in an anonymous pamphlet published by John Fairburn in several numbers at a penny halfpenny each – to reach mass audiences of course. It bore the resounding title, *Spies and Bloodites!!! The Lives and Political History of those Arch-Fiends Oliver, Reynolds, & Co. Treason-Hatchers, Green-Bag-Makers, Blood-Hunters, Spies, Tempters, and Informers-General to His Majesty's Ministers.* In the wake of the Pentrich trials London crowds attacked a butler because he looked like Oliver the 'arch-fiend', and even the *Times* called Oliver 'the wretch'.[32] Lord Liverpool was forced to admit in parliament that governments had 'always employed spies': they were found 'in all the free states of antiquity', and in Britain itself for many years. How else might a modern state monitor its own condition?[33] Henceforth the usefulness of political espionage at home was compromised, however. By 1820 nobody had the least doubt that Edwards belonged to the long line of spies who had infiltrated, manipulated, and reported nearly every subversive plot since Tudor times and earlier.

Paid spies under the regency were usually as low-born as their targets. James Hanley (signing as 'A' in the secret reports) was a Spitalfields tailor; John Shegog ('J. S.' or 'B') an artisan preacher from Lambeth; John Emblin ('J. E.') a clockmaker; John Williamson ('C') a trimming weaver from Spitalfields; John Castle a whitesmith; George Ruthven ('G. R.') a policeman (one of several); Oliver a carpenter and surveyor; Edwards ('W–R', for 'Windsor') a plaster model maker.[34] Most of the twenty or so paid spies known in our era were recruited by John Stafford, Bow Street's chief clerk. These men were brave, clever, and needy enough to risk intimate engagement with dangerous men. They must also have been good actors with the mental recall of practised reporters. Still, as already noted, many were chancers. Castle, who spied on Watson and Thistlewood in 1816–17, was a bawdy-house bully and pimp. When his criminal record was proved in court in 1817 the crown case collapsed; Watson had to be acquitted and Thistlewood and two others released. Edwards was just as crooked. Alderman Wood offered the Commons evidence that he and his brother had trapped a wanted man by bringing him to a spot noted for homosexual encounters 'in order that at a convenient time they might pounce upon him, and receive the money to which his conviction would entitle them'.[35]

When Arthur Thistlewood came to London in 1811 political law was becoming more repressive than it had been even under Pitt. It continued to be so. Modest booksellers and publishers were the most frequent targets. They were also the easiest targets, in good part because the attorney general was allowed to arrest and hold for bail any publisher against whom he chose to file an '*ex officio* information', which meant that he had no need to give his reasons. So the treasury solicitor's papers brim with dossiers on booksellers charged for publishing Paine's *Rights of Man* and similar texts. In seventy such prosecutions between 1808 and 1821, thirty-four resulted in harsh convictions. Radical and liberal editors also caught it for libelling the duke of York, and the radical journalist William Cobbett went inside for two years in 1810–12 for criticising the flogging of militiamen at Ely. In 1812 the brothers Leigh and John Hunt of the liberal *Examiner* were imprisoned for two years for mocking the regent as a mistress-besotted 'Adonis of fifty'. Daniel Isaac Eaton was pilloried at Charing Cross for publishing Paine, and five years later, T. J. Wooler was prosecuted for seditious libel in his radical newspaper the *Black Dwarf*, as was the bookseller William Hone for what was called blasphemous libel, though he was acquitted. For republishing Paine, the freethinker Richard Carlile was imprisoned for six years 1819–25 (and got another two years in 1831–3).

The Spa Fields riots of December 1816 were exploited to justify further controls. In February 1817 Harrowby laid before the Lords a 'Secret Committee Report into the Disturbed State of the Country'. Referring to the riots, it concluded that 'a traitorous conspiracy has been formed in the metropolis for the purpose of overthrowing, by means of a general insurrection, the established government, laws, and constitution of this kingdom, and of effecting a general plunder and division of property'.[36] The so-called Spenceans, it continued, followers of the radical Thomas Spence, aimed at 'the total overthrow of all existing establishments, and ... a division of the landed, and extinction of the funded property of the country'. They sought 'a parochial partnership in land, on the principle[s] that the landholders are not proprietors in chief; that they are but the stewards of the public; that the land is the people's farm; that landed monopoly is contrary to the spirit of Christianity, and destructive of the independence and morality of mankind'. 'These pernicious societies had spread throughout the country,' the report incorrectly insisted, 'in some areas to almost every village'. They employed oaths, intimidation, secret meetings in clubs and taverns, seditious publication, and 'profane and seditious songs and parodies of parts of the liturgy ... They are taught contempt for all decency, all law, all religion and morality, and are thus prepared for the most atrocious scenes of outrage and violence.' So the Spenceans were explicitly named as fit to be 'utterly suppressed and prohibited' in the ensuing Act against Seditious Meetings and Assemblies. The Act had a sunset clause causing it to expire in July 1818, but it was then replaced by one of Sidmouth's Six Acts in the following year. Habeas corpus was again suspended for persons suspected of treason, while sections of the 1795 Treason Act were renewed to make the subversion of soldiers and sailors a capital offence.

In 1817, 107 men were arrested on treasonable charges in England and 37 in Scotland. With the exception of Thistlewood ('gentleman') and James Watson and a Mancunian ('surgeons'), they were all working men. Eleven were Londoners involved in the Spa Fields riots and their aftermath; the rest were from the midlands and Lancashire – artisans, shoemakers, cordwainers, labourers, factory workers, framework-knitters and weavers, spinners, cloth-dressers, colliers, masons, cutlers, coopers, hatters, tailors, printers, and engravers. Of these, 41 were tried for the luddite rising in Derbyshire and Nottinghamshire, and Watson, Thistlewood, Preston, and Hooper were arraigned for the 'treason' of the Spa Fields riots. The rest were discharged after harsh spells in prison.[37]

After Peterloo in August 1819, Sidmouth exploited the panic viciously. In 1820 Henry Hunt was sentenced to two and a half years' imprisonment in Ilchester gaol for 'unlawful and seditious assembling for the purpose of exciting discontent' – that is, for chairing the Peterloo meeting and for condemning the magistrates, militia, and hussars afterwards. In London a campaign of arrests for seditious libel had begun before the massacre and accelerated during the autumn; but it was nothing compared to the attacks delivered by the Six Acts of December 1819. The Acts were as follows: the Training Prevention Act prohibited civilian training in the use of weapons; the Seizure of Arms Act gave magistrates the right to search houses for weapons; the Seditious Meetings Prevention Act revived the restrictions of 1797 and 1817 by giving magistrates the power to ban meetings of more than fifty people that had been called to discuss 'any public grievance or any matter on Church and State'; the Blasphemous and Seditious Libels Act imposed fourteen years' transportation on people twice convicted for seditious libel; the Misdemeanours Act speeded up trial procedures and limited entitlement to bail; and the Newspaper and Stamp Duties Act imposed duties on radical newspapers, periodicals, and pamphlets that had so far dodged duties by pretending to offering opinion rather than news. The fact that Castlereagh introduced the Acts in the Commons was one reason why a few months later the Cato Street men wanted his head off.

A leading lawyer of the age, Lord Redesdale, reminded Sidmouth that 'every meeting for radical reform is not merely an attempt to undermine the existing constitution and government by bringing it into hatred and contempt, but ... [is also] an overt act of treasonable conspiracy against the constitution of government, including the king as its head, [who is] bound by his coronation oath to maintain it'. Governments were happy to be told this. Opening parliament in November 1819, the regent declared that he had the most confident reliance 'upon the loyalty of the great body of the people'. This didn't stop him announcing his government's intention of swelling the already substantial regular army based at home by over ten thousand men, the better to ensure that the great body of the people kept its senses.[38]

SOLDIERS

By later standards civil policing was weak, so military power was indispensable to aristocratic rule. It had long been accepted that at home the army was less a citizens' army than one needed to contain an opinionated populace. In wartime, 12,000 troops had been available to hold down the midlands alone. By 1816, the peacetime army of 150,000 men cost £26,736,017. Their chief purpose was to keep the lower orders in place.[39] Hunt's and Watson's great Smithfield meeting of July 1819 rang with protests at the existence of a standing army, and liberal whigs were critical as well, though to no avail. The whigs were out of power for all of forty-six years between 1784 and 1830. And, if Peterloo proved anything, it was that a tory government and most of its magistrates, clergymen, lords lieutenant, knights, lords, lord mayors, flunkeys, and newspapers were only too ready to maintain hierarchy through violence.

Was the domestic army reliable? Mutiny was vanishingly rare in an army which could flog its transgressors to the point of death, but radicals' appeals to soldiers to join insurrection caused understandable anxieties. In 1780 some twenty thousand soldiers had been deployed in the capital to suppress the Gordon riots, and as a precaution against their Gordonite sympathies most had to be accommodated under canvas in parks and gardens. The danger endured. A month after the Cato Street executions forty years later, Wellington told Lord Liverpool about discontent in one of the Guards battalions. To avoid encouraging the others, he wrote, the battalion was hastily moved from London; but as they marched the men 'made use of the cry of disaffection of the day' (no doubt in support of Queen Caroline), so that 'in one of the most critical moments that ever occurred in this country, we and the public have reason to doubt in *the fidelity of the troops, the only security we have, not only against revolution but for the property and life of every individual in the country who has anything to lose*' (author's italics). The battalion's NCOs were excellent soldiers, he continued, but 'they are taken from the ranks, and [are] of the class of the people, and liable to be influenced by the views and sentiments of the people'. He was alarmed that government and property were protected against insurrection only by 'the fidelity of 3,000 Guards, all of the class of the people, and even of the lowest of that class'.[40]

In these conditions the age-old practice of billeting soldiers in private houses or inns was curtailed. As fear of French invasion and domestic disaffection increased in the 1790s, barracks building became one of later-Georgian and regency England's most profitable enterprises. Learning from the Irish model (Ireland acquired over 270 barracks sites in the eighteenth century), London and the provincial towns were soon sprinkled with almost as many new barracks and prisons as they were with pilastered mansions. In London, barracks were rebuilt and expanded at Finsbury for the Honourable Artillery Company, the Tower of London for the Royal Fusiliers, and Woolwich for the Royal Artillery. New ones were built at Hounslow for the Horse Artillery (1793), Knightsbridge for the Foot Guards, Kensington for the Horse Guards (1795), King Street (now Blandford Street, near Montague Square) for the Life Guards' stables, Portman Street for the Foot Guards, Albany Street (Regent's Park) for cavalry (1820–1), Gray's Inn Lane and Worship Street for the City Light Horse (1812), and St John's Wood for the Royal Horse Artillery (1812).[41]

By global standards the British military didn't murder huge numbers of its own people. The state was relatively merciful at home, if not in Ireland or the empire. A domestic peak was reached during the Gordon riots, when soldiers killed 285 Londoners (some said 700); another 25 were hanged on street corners afterwards. Otherwise 'only' a dozen were killed on St George's Field during a Wilkesite protest in 1768; 18 at Peterloo in 1819, including a child; 24 at Merthyr and 4 at Bristol (with 86 injured) in the 1831 reform riots; and 22 Chartists at Newport, Monmouthshire, in 1839. These were puny numbers compared with the many hundreds shot dead and 1,200 injured at Amritsar in 1919 by Colonel Reginald Dyer and his men, not to mention the 10,000 killed in and after Tiananmen Square, or North American, German, Russian, or Cambodian genocidal horrors. One historian thinks that Peterloo was a rather modest atrocity and that it has loomed large mainly because Britain was 'a country whose history is relatively free of bloody reprisals'.[42] This evades the larger truth that numbers aren't all that count in such cases, and that Peterloo was as cruel and catastrophic in its time and place as other atrocities were in theirs.

But soldiers didn't have to kill in order to bring common people to their senses. Their deterrent displays usually did the trick. When Sir Francis Burdett was arrested in 1810, the spectacular rioting calmed down as soon as it was known that the cannon at the Tower were loaded with grapeshot, that the Tower moat had been flooded, that dragoons occupied Moorfields, that troops and artillery had marched in from Woolwich and Hounslow, and that cavalry were posted in villages round London. In all, fifty thousand soldiers waited on the revolution that for that reason couldn't happen.[43] In any case the occasional riot – or possibility of it – had its uses for the authorities. As Henry Hunt noted, his, Watson's, and Thistlewood's great reform meeting in Smithfield in July 1819 provoked over-the-top military preparations 'under the pretence of quelling some tremendous riot, or some apprehended insurrection ... In the city all was hurry and bustle; and all this was done in order to work upon the fears of the timid and foolish part of the community, to create a prejudice in their minds against the radicals'.[44]

Radicals facing troops were like peasants armed with pitchforks, and were as weirdly innocent as peasants about the mighty powers that faced them. The Spencean Robert Wedderburn crazily told his audience at his Hopkins Street chapel that 'if we cant all get arms theirs them iron railings in front of these big fellows houses ... they will make excellent pikes used by a strong arm'. He thought railings would arm 200,000 men, and that there could be no fear of failure: 'let us lose no time in using them, I am ready'.[45] Only in cooler mood did he realise that soldiers would kill if they were told to: 'I am not such a fool [as] to suppose nor to advise that the poor and half starved part of the population should meet the regular army of the borough-mongers in the field, because they would have no chance.' At another debate a man named Shaw (perhaps John Shaw Strange) thought that if there were a revolution the government would simply call in foreign troops. 'The Holy Alliance entered into by the tyrants of Europe,' he stated, 'had no other object in view, than to send their armies to each other's assistance should their subjects dare to affirm their rights.'

In view of the imbalance of physical power, Byron's friend John Cam Hobhouse raised and answered the following question in 1819:

> What prevents the people from walking down to the House [of Commons], and pulling out the members by the ears, locking up their doors, and flinging the key into the Thames? Is it any majesty which hedges in the members of that assembly? Do we love them? Not at all. ... Do we respect them? Not in the least. *Their true practical protectors, the real efficient anti-Reformers, are to be found at the Horse Guards, and the Knightsbridge barracks.* As long as the House of Commons' majorities are backed by the regimental muster roll, so long may those who have got the tax-power keep it, and hang those who resist.[46]

For this breach of parliamentary privilege the Commons put him inside Newgate for ten weeks; but the liberal whig, Earl Fitzwilliam, had the same thought: 'If we do not set this matter to rights, the military are henceforward the governing power in the British Empire.'[47] Over the ensuing twenty years these views turned into axiomatic truths. By 1839 the military commander of the northern districts, General Napier, wrote this poignant epitaph for the insurrectionary Chartists and the revolution that could never be:

> Fools! We have the physical force, not they. They talk of their hundred thousands of men. Who is to move them when I am dancing round them with cavalry; and pelting them with cannonshot? What would their 100,000 men do with my 100 rockets wriggling their fiery tails among them, roaring, scorching, tearing, smashing all they came near? And when in desperation and despair they broke to fly, how would they bear five regiments of cavalry careering through them? Poor men! How little they know of physical force![48]

Much has now changed, but much has not, except through processes of intensification and elaboration. The imbalance of power between authority and protester is barely noticed today, as are the inequalities that once provoked protest. Thomas Spence's propagandist copper tokens in the 1790s denounced 'LANDLORDS AND STARVATION' and proclaimed 'SPENCES PLAN NO LANDLORDS' and 'PARTNERSHIP IN LAND THE LAND IS OURS' (see Fig. 5.2). But his agrarian socialism did nothing to check today's news that a half of England and far more than a half of Scotland is owned by less than one per cent of their populations. The ratio between the regent's civil list and working-class wages in 1820 is dwarfed by income inequalities today. Surveillance, police entrapment, and the control of public spaces now operate more efficiently than was thinkable two centuries ago. The Cato Street story still speaks to our times.

CHAPTER 5

What They Believed

IDEAS

Great swathes of the urban nation were significantly literate in 1820. Some 60 per cent of English males and 45 per cent of females could sign their marriage registers. In London percentages were higher than this, and among craftsmen higher still.[1] Most people's writing skills were imperfect. When the Cato Street conspirator and bootmaker Thomas Chambers signed his sworn statement, he wrote his 'b' as 'd'.[2] But more than enough reading was achieved for books and newspapers to have a key place in this story. The main sources of textual enlightenment were Tom Paine's endorsement of the French Assembly's *Declaration of the Rights of Man* in his two-volume *Rights of Man* (1791–2), and the writings and propaganda of Thomas Spence. Since these explained deprivation and powerlessness as human and historical rather than divine inflictions, they helped people to make sense of the world and their positions in it, and to blame others and justify protest.

The first volume of Paine's riposte to Burke's *Reflections on the Revolution in France* sold some 50,000 copies. Over the next thirty years, along with his *Age of Reason* (1793–4), it became the most frequent target of prosecution for what the law called seditious and blasphemous libel. Paine's leading idea, from Locke and Rousseau, was that individuals 'entered into a contract with each other to produce a government', and that since this was 'the only mode in which governments have a right to arise, and the only principle on which they have a right to exist', the people's rights were independent of government, so that a government that withheld those rights should be replaced through rebellion. When

94

Burke claimed that royal prerogatives that went back to William of Normandy had earned sacrosanctity, Paine replied 'that there is no English origin of kings and that they [kings] are descendants of the Norman line in right of the Conquest'. It followed that 'if the succession runs in the line of the Conquest, the nation runs in the line of being conquered, and it ought to rescue itself from this reproach'.

Arguments like these could transform people. Well-heeled whig-radicals like Sir Francis Burdett, who learned and suffered for their politics in the 1790s, were 'awakened' when they read Paine, just as Henry Hunt was when he read Cobbett. Poor people were awakened as well. Shoemaker Preston remembered how the 'increase of reading' dispelled his assumption 'that reform meant deform, and that revolution was a compound of blood and madness'. At London Corresponding Society meetings in the 1790s he met people who knew 'the meaning of words' and who dispelled 'the charm of ignorance which had so long lulled my mind into a comparative indifference at the people's wrongs'. 'I now began to read with more attention than I had heretofore exercised: I found there had scarce been a ruler, to whom unlimited power had been yielded, but what had exercised it to the wanton destruction of his species, and in the demolition of every social principle.'[3]

So too Richard Carlile: a freethinking man of unusual independence of mind, he deserves his place in history for his political courage, not to say for his later and then unique affirmation that women 'had an almost constant desire for copulation' and that 'the customs of society alone deter them from it' (Fig. 5.1). Born in Devon as the son of a shoemaker, he had come to London in 1813 as a tinplate worker in his twenties. Finding 'nothing was talked of but revolution', he had been first attracted to politics in 1816 by 'the distress and noise made by public meetings'. He read Paine, Spence, and the Hunt brothers' *Examiner*, and gave up his trade to edit Sherwin's *Political Register* (renaming it the *Republican* after Peterloo). The law soon had its eye on him. He was imprisoned for four months in 1817 for reprinting Hone's blasphemous parodies. In August 1819 he was invited to share Hunt's platform at St Peter's Fields, Manchester. His eyewitness account of the Peterloo

5.1. Anon., *Richard Carlile on His Liberation from Six Years Imprisonment in Dorchester Gaol / Novr 18th 1825* (Carlile, 1825) (© The Trustees of the British Museum)

massacre resulted in further charges of seditious libel. John Keats the poet thought Carlile was immune from reprisals. 'They are afraid to prosecute,' he wrote to his brother in September: 'they are afraid of his defence: it will be published in all the papers all over the empire: they shudder at this: the trials would light a flame they could not extinguish.'[4] He was wrong. Arrested in October, Carlile was held in the King's Bench prison for the blasphemous libel of republishing Paine's *Age of Reason*. During his trial he read out the whole book on the grounds that the jury needed to hear it to assess its blasphemy or otherwise. This secured its republication: the trial report sold 10,000 twopenny copies. In November he was convicted and spent the next six years in near-solitary confinement in Dorchester prison. He continued to publish the *Republican* and other works while his wife and sister ran the Fleet Street bookshop. In these few years eight of the Carliles' shop workers and some 150 people across the country were imprisoned for selling the *Republican*. Jane herself was imprisoned for two years in Dorchester on the information of the evangelical zealots of the Anti-Vice Society.

For a while radical newspapers spread the radical message energetically. They modelled themselves on the twopenny broadsheet version of Cobbett's weekly *Political Register*, which launched in November 1816 and sold 44,000 copies in its first month and 200,000 by the end of

1817. After Cobbett fled to America in May 1817 to escape arrest, T. J. Wooler's satirical *Black Dwarf* (1817–24) took over the *Register*'s lead. Costing four pence, it achieved a national circulation of over 12,000 in 1819 – twice that of the *Times* – and its readers far outnumbered the copies sold. Wooler was tried for seditious libel in May 1817 and was triumphantly acquitted; two years later he was imprisoned for fifteen months for his part in a Birmingham meeting. Another, Thomas Davison, was a prolific printer of Spencean posters and deistical pamphlets, but also editor-publisher of important ultra-radical papers in 1819–20 (the *Medusa; or, Penny Politician*, the *London Alfred*, and the *Deists' Magazine*) until he was imprisoned for two years for seditious libel. It was never easy for radical newspapers to reach large popular markets. From 1815 governments taxed all newspapers at 3d per pound weight on paper, four pence a sheet for stamp duty, and a duty of 3s 6d for an advertisement. One of Sidmouth's Six Acts in late November 1819 required printers and publishers additionally to post a bond of £300 and raised stamp duty to sixpence. This put newspapers beyond the pockets of common readers and most radical papers folded.

Still, in humble radical circles it became axiomatic that 'the right of the people to resist oppression always exists, ... the requisite power to do this always resides in the general will of the people': thus T. J. Wooler in his *Black Dwarf* in 1818. Cobbett could cite the jurist Blackstone to the same effect, while Hunt's speeches referred repeatedly to 'the day of reckoning' or 'the fatal day' when the people would at last overcome their oppressors. Watson and Thistlewood declared at their Finsbury Market meeting on 1 November 1819 that 'the social compact is broken up', that 'the rich are leagued against the poor, and that a legal tyranny supported by a military despotism is prepared to deprive them of every vestige of the freedom guaranteed to them by their forefathers'. By 1820 few who sang tavern songs were unaware that

> Tom Paine, a true Englishman, high in renown,
> Shows that plunder's the system of mitre and crown;
> They thrive by degrading the people's degree,

> But we know that mankind has a right to be free.
> *Ça ira*, ah, ah, the rights of the people for me.[5]

The letters that survive from the largely self-educated people this book is concerned with are laboriously written, sometimes archaic in expression and construction, and badly or not at all punctuated. In their misspellings they deploy street-level and regional pronunciations. 'A dinner *as* been announced,' writes Edwards. Poor people found reading easier than writing, however; and the books, pamphlets, newspapers, and speeches that could be bought or read (or heard read) in taverns and coffee shops could remove scales from the eyes. As in France, where the jacobin revolution was generated in the descent of rationalism 'from the salon to the street, from Voltaire to Marat', so in London countless 'Rousseaus of the gutter'– including shoemaker-poets, writers, and speechifiers like Wedderburn, Preston, and Davenport – flourished in the tavern underworld. The messages they circulated were secular, rationalist, and deistical – the fruits of Enlightenment, in other words, even if mixed with older notions and biblicised language. It was in this culture, with the French example always in mind, that many learned that the social order was other than God-given and that they could change it.

Candid deism or atheism was exceptional in plebeian life. A Mancunian visiting London opined that 'it was the worst thing in the world to mix religion with politicks ... There are not many of us is radicals over religious'.[6] But where deism rooted, it rooted deeply. When the Cold Bath Fields prison chaplain the Rev. David Ruell interviewed the Cato Street men in their cells shortly after their arrests, in February 1820, he was disgusted to find that their reading had destroyed their fear of his god. Thistlewood sourly advised him to read Paine's *Age of Reason*, and when Ruell replied that he had done so 'to ascertain what could be advocated against Xtianity', Thistlewood pretended surprise that Ruell wasn't convinced. Brunt told Ruell that he had read Voltaire, Paine, Volney, and others, while Black Davidson, Wilson, Monument, and Strange stated that they were 'in the habit of reading Paine & other infidel publications'. Tidd declared that he had 'met with no *facts* to prove Christianity true', and John Shaw Strange said that 'Voltaire had given him much clearer views of the Deity & religion than the Bible!' (the chaplain's exclamation mark). Wilson added that he and other shoe-makers 'had been in the habit of reading such books in their leisure time & afterwards discussing their principles & merits during their working hours', thus acknowledging the traditional source of shoemaker literacy and learning.[7]

Cooper, yet another shoemaker though lately a seaman, seems to have been an unenthusiastic conspirator, and in the stable he surrendered to the constables at once, as did Monument and Gilchrist. His autograph signature shows that he could pen a fine copperplate (see Fig. 16.1 (a–b)). We have poignant proof that he valued ideas also. From his transportation ship anchored off Spithead, he wrote to his uncle to ask him to send him his knives, files, and awl blades, his pawned shirts, coat, and waistcoat ('of great value to me'), his silk hat, black handkerchief, and two white ones, and, just as valuable, his volumes of *Natural History* and his second volume of *Speeches of M. de Mirabeau the Elder* to the French National Assembly. A little coffee and sugar would also be a 'rich treat', as would 'all the old newspapers you can send' since 'I am told they are very valuable at Botany Bay'. His letter still lies buried in the home office papers, so he was granted none of these favours.[8]

Texts weren't plebeian London's only educative force. At Westminster elections political argument was played out in the streets. The parliamentary constituency of Westminster was the largest and most democratic in the nation's unreformed electoral system (excepting the City). Virtually all adult male rate-paying householders had the vote – about 12,000 of them, or one in four of Westminster's adult males in 1801. Many of the poorer voters, galvanised by John Wilkes's radicalism in the 1760s, had in effect evolved into an 'informal political nation' committed to voter independence and electoral reform. Because these people could swing elections, the Covent Garden hustings were noisy and turbulent, voter turnouts were high, and even the clamour of the voteless was impossible to ignore.

Then there were the debating clubs and craft societies – a huge range of them. In the few that admitted women, sexual politics were a favoured topic. They tended to ask awkward questions: 'January 30, 1797, at the London Forum, Fleet Street, near Fetter Lane: A Lady's Question concerning Love and Apparitions: Is the assertion of a celebrated author true, – That mutual love between man and wife is like apparitions, talked of by all, but perceived and felt by none?'[9] Otherwise debates were male-dominated. For decades past craft societies had met in tavern club rooms to debate wages and craft controls; and overtly political clubs evolved from them. In the 1790s the artisan-radical London Corresponding Society sprung from a meeting of craftsmen in the Bell Tavern, Exeter Street, and thereafter in taverns in Covent Garden, Soho, and along the Strand and Fleet Street. Some thirty out of the LCS's fifty tavern venues have been identified along and north of the Strand–Fleet Street axis – and only four south of the Thames, four west of Regent Street, three in the City, and one in Whitechapel.[10]

This precedent endured. A spy reported in late 1816 that on Sundays at 8 p.m. the Red Lion in Clement's Lane, the Northumberland Arms in Clerkenwell, and the Roebuck in Union Street laid on public readings of Cobbett's *Political Register*, the Hunts' *Examiner*, and the *Independent Whig*. He added that 'it is a moderate calculation to state that one twentieth part of the public houses in London' also had them read, and collected signatures for parliamentary reform. Fifty to a hundred men would attend these meetings, and 150 were known at the Mulberry Tree. Although they all seemed very poor men, they could usually afford to drink and talk until one in the morning. 'A fund is no doubt appropriated to this purpose', the informant wrote:

> On other evenings there is generally some abstract political question debated – but it is remarkable that the speakers soon forsake the bearings of the original question and deviate into such a path as gives scope for the most violent invectives against ministers Parliament and every part of the government – and suggest the most dangerous modes of obtaining reform – annual elections – universal suffrage & ballot are what they most insist on – and elective annual monarchy is often recommended – there appears nearly throughout the whole class of the regular attendants of these meetings dispositions to become disciples of the wildest and wickedest theories that ever destroy'd the social happiness of civil society. . . . The first moment that opportunity offers the subject of spies is started & violent declarations made as to the manner they would treat a spy if discover'd.[11]

When the Manchester radical Samuel Bamford visited London in 1817, political debate could be rowdy:

> They would generally be found in a large room, an elevated seat being placed for the chairman. On first opening the door, the place seemed dimmed by a suffocating vapour of tobacco, curling from the cups of long pipes . . . in clouds of abominable odour. . . . Every man would have his half-pint of porter before him; many would be speaking at once. [Order would be called, and] a speaker, stranger or citizen, would be announced with much courtesy and compliment, . . . with clapping of hands and knocking of knuckles on the tables till the half-pints danced; . . . then a speech, with compliments to some brother orator or popular statesman; next a resolution in favour of parliamentary reform, and a speech to second it; an amendment on some minor point would follow; a seconding of that; a breach of order by some individual of warm temperament; half a dozen would rise to set him right, a dozen to put them down, and the vociferation and gesticulation would become loud and confounding.[12]

From 1810 through to the 1830s, McCalman observes, this 'apparently innocuous debating club culture' kept a group of ultra-radical leaders intact and provided a springboard of radical action.[13] He lists the British Forum in Poland Street (set up by Gale Jones in 1806), and ambitiously named clubs like the Athenian Lyceum, the Philomathic Institution, the London Institute, a new Robin Hood Society run by Peter Finnerty, the Socratic Club in the Mermaid tavern, and the Polemic Club in the Cock in Grafton Street, Soho. Political continuities were marked. The White Hart in Brook's Market, where the Cato Street men met in the conspiracy's later days, had hosted United Irish meetings in 1798: Irish rebellion was plotted there.[14] All these places were well enough known to the law to be spied on, so meetings were usually thick with paranoia. At the Spotted Dog in 1818,

> some one then said there was a spy in the room. Thistlewood and Watson enquired whereabouts he was, or who he was. The same person answered he was near the door. Then a man near the door got up and said, Gentlemen, I suppose you mean me. The same person answered Yes, by God you are a Bow Street officer, and the sooner you are out the better it

will be for yourself. The man went out instantly. Upon this Roberts, the Manchester man, who had been discharged from prison, took a stick from Thistlewood . . . which he always carries and has a sword in it. Roberts went out after the officer with the stick, and returned in about five minutes and said that he could not catch him, or he would be damned if he would not have given him the contents of it [the stick].[15]

Some of the Cato Street men learned their politics in clubs like the Marylebone Union Reading Society. As William Simmons testified, this met once a week in the schoolmaster William Hazard's house at 54 Queen Street (now Harrowby Street; Cato Street turns off it). There they read 'books and newspapers about reform only, Major Cartwrights Bill of Rights, and Liberties was the groundwork of it, . . . we agreed not to read any works on religion or admit theological discussion we paid two pence a week each'.

> Greening a Blacksmith or Whitesmith living in Paddington was secretary to our society, there also belonged to our society, Bell a Shoemaker living in Paddington Street, Firth of Bryanston Street, cow keeper [*the* cow keeper]. . . . Davidson the man of colour was a member of our society but he did not attend for some time as he was too poor to pay up his Subscriptions.

Being a manservant, Simmons attended under a false name because 'I should lose my place if it was known that I had attended such a society'.[16]

Under the slogan 'knowledge is power', the Marylebone society was among the most militant of the reading clubs set up across London in 1819.[17] Its inclinations were conveyed in the doggerel which Hazard composed and paid to have printed. Prefaced by Isaiah 3:15 ('Ye have eaten up the vineyard; the spoil of the poor is in your houses. What mean ye that ye beat my people to pieces, and grind the faces of the poor?'), it offered Hazard's 'True Picture of Society as Displayed by Certain Rich Characters towards their Poor Neighbours, A Poem':

> Repent, ye tyrants, you have brought
> Distress upon the poor;
> And many men thro you have sought
> Their bread from door to door.

Like cannibals they drain our blood,
Our bread is tax'd, with tea,
And every evil they call good,
Lest mankind should be free. ....

You say the poor was born to work
For you, dukes, lords, and squires;
And you was only born to lurk,
And have your base desires.

In coaches you do proudly ride,
And lord it over them,
That all your comforts, do provide,
Your fellow equal men. – [*etc.*] [18]

THOMAS SPENCE

As others have noted, the conventional narrative of English radicalism gives an apostolic position to Tom Paine. Robert Owen's 'new
view of society' has also loomed large in histories of proto-socialism,
even though his regimented 'villages of cooperation' smacked of
hated factory disciplines and got scant support from the poor. Less
familiar today than Paine's or Owen's names is Thomas Spence's.
Spence's low origins and manners meant that the respectable gave
and still give him little attention; but in the first decades of the
nineteenth century his influence on London's low radicals was all-
pervasive. His many books and pamphlets were less complex and
more repetitive than Paine's. Some have vanished without trace,
and no library today holds his full output. Yet he reached parts
that Paine didn't by imagining an egalitarian utopia achieved
through the abolition of private property and its redistribution by
self-governing parochial communes. He knew the value of political
conviviality as well. On most Tuesday evenings after 1807 or so he
gathered his disciples in his 'free and easy' in the Fleece in Little
Windmill Street. Spencean songs sung there were widely distributed
and were sung in taverns for years to come:

> Thus all the world BELONGS to Man,
> But NOT to kings and lords;
> A country's land's the people's farm,
> And all that it affords;
> For why? divide it how you will,
> 'Tis all the people's still;
> The people's county, parish, town;
> They build, defend, and till.[19]

In its discussions of land reform and class inequality, it was Spencean argument that ruled in the most disaffected regency taverns, and Chartists still cited him in the 1840s.[20] His texts moved readers viscerally. When the shoemaker poet Allen Davenport read them in 1805 he 'immediately became an out and out Spencean' since he saw that by comparison with Spence 'all whig, tory or even radical reformers, were as rush-lights to the meridian sun', and that Spence's ideas in practice would 'make the world a paradise'.[21]

While Paine was relatively well born of Quaker and Anglican parents in Thetford, Norfolk (his maternal grandfather was the town clerk and attorney, and the boy went to the local grammar school until he was twelve), Spence was born in 1750 as one of the nineteen children of impoverished parents in Newcastle upon Tyne. His mother was a stockinger and his father made nets and kept a hardware stall. He had no schooling to speak of, but he and his siblings were taught to read the Bible every day, and in young adulthood he was helped by an extreme Presbyterian of democratic persuasion. In time he became a self-taught schoolteacher. He read More's *Utopia* and Harrington's *Commonwealth of Oceana*, wrote on phonetic spelling reform, and was the first Englishman to explain and endorse the 'Rights of Man' (as early as 1775 in a lecture to the Newcastle Philosophical Society, 'for printing of which the society did the author the honour to expel him').[22] He conceived his redistributist land plan after a dispute over Newcastle's Town Moor in 1774, when freemen burgesses gave up property rights on the moor in exchange for their share of rents, and in effect accepted a right to the proceeds of collective labour on the land.

Having moved to London in 1788, Spence set up a bookstall on the corner of Chancery Lane and Holborn from which he sold radical pamphlets. Although his only known portrait, on the tokens on which he commemorated his imprisonment for treason in 1794, give him an impressive if broken Roman nose and thickly tousled republican hair, he was described as an unprepossessing figure. The radical tailor Francis Place admired his integrity and at one point thought of writing his biography, but found he was

> unpractised in the ways of the world to an extent few could imagine in a man who had been pushed about in it as he had been ... He died as much of a child in some respects as he probably was when he arrived at the usual age of mankind.... Not more [than] five feet high, he seemed feeble when most men still retain their vigour ... [thanks to] a stroke of palsy from which he never entirely recovered. His face was thin and much wrinkled, his mouth was large and uneven, he had a strong northern 'burr' in his throat and a slight impediment in his speech. His garments were generally old and sometimes ragged.[23]

Cobbett thought him 'a plain, unaffected, inoffensive looking creature', though 'beloved by those who knew him'. Hone the bookseller remembered his stall as 'like a baker's close barrow – the pamphlets were exhibited outside, & when he sold one he took it from within, & handed & recommended others with strong expressions of hate to the powers that were, & prophecies of what would happen to the whole race of "land lords"'. In 1792 Hone witnessed Spence's arrest: 'I was passing at the time & heard him in dispute with the officer. He had just got his shutters down in the morning when he was pounced upon. It was early therefore & no one but myself was present at first.'[24]

Spence joined the London Corresponding Society and drew close to Thomas Evans, its then secretary. He was arrested four times in 1792–3 for selling *Rights of Man* and pamphlets of his own, and twice again in 1794, when he spent seven months without trial in Newgate for 'treasonable practices'. On his release friends subscribed funds for him to take a tiny shop, which he named 'The Hive of Liberty', at 8 Little Turnstile (the alleyway off High Holborn still exists), where he traded as a bookseller and coin dealer. Bankrupted three years later, he opened another shop at 9 Oxford Street. He was again imprisoned in 1798, though soon freed, for involvement in Evans's Society of United Englishmen. Then in 1801 he earned himself a cruel year in Shrewsbury gaol for publishing his own *Restorer of Society to its Natural State.* In his verbal defence at the trial he explained his land plan in detail in order to put it on the court record. This ploy enabled him after his release to publish it in his account of *The Important Trial of Thomas Spence* (1803). Further broadsides followed. His pamphlets had resounding titles like *The Constitution of Spensonia, a Country in Fairy-land, Situated between Utopia and Oceana, Brought from thence by Captain Swallow* (1795); *The Meridian Sun of Liberty* (1796); *The Rights of Infants; or, The Imprescriptable Right of Mothers to such a Share of the Elements as is Sufficient to Enable them to Suckle and Bring up their Young* (1797); *The Constitution of a Perfect Commonwealth* (1798), etc. To these he added a collection of Spencean songs in 1807 and a periodical addressed to 'the labouring part of mankind', *One Penny Worth of Pig's Meat: Lessons for the Swinish Multitude* (1793–5).

Aiming at common readers, Spence's messages were simplified, sometimes parodic, but even the simplest demanded consideration. His disciples wrote in the same spirit. In 1816 Thomas Evans's *Christian Policy, The Salvation of the Empire*, price 1/6d, combined jacobin, Spencean, and millenarian ideas with acuity enough to provoke attack by George Canning in the Commons, by the conservative poet Southey, and by Thomas Malthus in the revised edition of his *Essay on Population* in 1817. Canning affected incredulity at Evans's assertion that 'the great and crying evil of the time is the "usurpation of the land, the gift of God, from the people"', and that 'all the land, the waters, the houses, the mines, &c. &c. must return to the people, the whole people; without the restoration of this property, reforms and revolutions are unavailing'. But he conceded that Evans peddled this 'ingenuous creed' with 'intelligence and dexterity' and that it 'circulated with astonishing industry throughout the country'.[25]

Spence followed Paine in advocating universal male suffrage, annual elections, and secret ballots. He followed nobody in supporting female suffrage as well. He made it clear, however, that these reforms alone could never curb the aristocratic usurpers who had secured control of private property through fraud or theft long ago. Land redistribution was a precondition of change. This was utopian thinking, but by pursuing *equality*, that most challenging of all Enlightenment values, and by putting aristocratic theft and corruption in his firing line as the main source of inequality, Spence effected a transformative realisation in British culture. In the new century the common people were able to register the naked facts of inequality with an indignation unknown in the eighteenth. They might lapse into indifference when faced by the impossibility of change, and most thought of themselves as patriots and loyalists. Yet thanks to Spence most had also heard that they deserved the vote, that men, women, and even slaves had rights, and that wealth and land should be taken from a Norman aristocracy and redistributed to honest hardworking Saxons.

The almighty's agency was demoted at these levels. To be sure, the Bible beat Paine or Spence as an educative source, and biblical imagery suffused radical language. Spence's messages were full of biblical references. His vision, he wrote, was founded on divine and immutable justice, and the laws of Moses. These directed that the land must 'be possessed by families, not to be parted with otherwise than by mortgage, nor to be sold, given away, or alienated, but to the year of Jubilee (25th Chap., Leviticus), as no one had other than a life interest therein: Witness – Naboth's Vineyard (21st Chap., 1st Book of Kings)'.[26] Moreover, the ultra-radicals drew support from London's Irish Catholic communities, though the latter were moved by a nationalist anger of their own; and the conspirators Davidson and Wedderburn had once been methodist and unitarian preachers of some kind, and Preston was known as 'the bishop' because he cited the Bible to defend Spenceanism.

Nonetheless, no Spenceans inflicted on others the claim that God was on their side, or thought that the acts of God rather than of man were the source of their troubles. Leaving cant of that kind to their betters, they declared themselves infidels and relished their own blasphemies. In the so-called Spencean 'chapel' which the Jamaican-born Robert Wedderburn ran in Soho, the government spy was shocked to find that on Sundays the male congregation kept their hats on, and even more shocked to hear Wedderburn declare that he'd rather live in hell than in heaven, given 'such a mollock of a God as ours is', and to state after

Peterloo: 'They tell us to be quiet like that *bloody spooney Jesus Christ* who like a *Bloody Fool* tells when we get a slap on one side of the face [to] turn gently round and ask them to smack the other.'[27]

For not all Spencean argument was earnest. Spence announced that he aimed to help not only 'all those who have no helpers' but also 'the discontented of all classes'. Since nobody was too poor to be excluded, his messages and devices had to be simple, direct, and even comical. If, as E. P. Thompson put it, 'the secret press, the anonymous handbill, the charcoaled pavement, the tavern club' were the underground's characteristic methods, Spence deployed them with skill – graffiti, tokens, songs, and satire especially.[28]

London's youth had covered the city with graffiti for generations beyond counting. In the 1760s London was full of chalked 45s to support Wilkes's attack on the government in issue 45 of his *North Briton*, just as Birmingham's walls in the mid-1790s were chalked with slogans calling for 'bread or blood' and gallows emblems. In 1812 the home secretary was alarmed by the number of London chalkings that proclaimed 'SPENCE'S PLAN AND FULL BELLIES'. A year later a spy reported that 'low tradesmen' were chalking slogans announcing 'SPENCE'S SYSTEM', and William Hone noted how curious about Spence's Plan people became after they saw 'the words chalked on the walls, and stamped on shillings'. 'We have all seen, for years past,' Cobbett wrote in 1816, 'written on the walls in and near London, these words, SPENCE'S PLAN.'[29] A Spencean song explained their source:

> As I went forth one Morn
> For some Recreation,
> My thoughts did quickly turn,
> Upon a Reformation,
> But far I had not gone,
> Or could my thoughts recall, sir,
> 'Ere I spied Spence's Plan
> Wrote up against a wall sir.
>
> . . .
>
> Determin'd in my mind,
> For to read his Plan, sir,

I quickly went to find
This enterprising man, sir,
To the Swan I took my flight,
Down in New-Street-Square sir,
Where every Monday night,
Friend Tommy Spence comes there sir.[30]

Spence's ingenuity was further witnessed in the alloy or copper tokens he had cast 1795–6.[31] These emulated the privately minted tokens that tradesmen issued to cope with the nation's copper currency shortage. According to the *Gentleman's Magazine* they were minted in their 'many thousands' to profit from the insatiable demand of token collectors. Not all were political; but those that were mocked the land-grabbing corruption of the high-born in a 'riot of high-impact political imagery' that beat prose for its immediacy. Spence employed a talented medallist, Charles James, to sculpt onto them some 420 different satirical emblems and an array of pithy and varied messages. His shop displayed great heaps of these, and now and then he would toss a few from his window for passers-by to pick up, discuss, and collect. The Rev. W. R. Hay, the Manchester magistrate who shared responsibility for Peterloo, deplored the 'strong impression' they continued to deliver nearly two decades later: 'One could scarcely conceive how industrious and ingenious these jacobins were in the instance of medals to poison the minds of the community.'

What upset Hay and his ilk was that no man, woman, or child who could read letters or decode satire could mistake the tokens' meanings. The irony was rich, and some of it sailed close to the seditious wind; but Spence knew that prosecutors had to go for texts rather than comic images since it was almost impossible to indict a visual joke in pompous legalese without provoking laughter in court.[32] Images were combined back and front at random, but a typical pairing shows 'WE WILL WALK THUS IF THE LAW REQUIRES IT' on one side, with a man in coat-tails crawling on all fours; and on its reverse a king riding a bull (John Bull) with an ass's head and ears, under the protest, 'I AM NOT THINE ASS'. Spence's cat stood for defiant independence; his 'FREE-BORN ENGLISHMAN' became iconic, as we'll see in the next chapter; the hope of 'BRITISH LIBERTY DISPLAYED' is belied in the image of a sailor press-ganging a landsman, while its reverse proclaims, 'WE WERE BORN FREE AND WILL NEVER DIE SLAVES'; and 'THE TREE OF LIBERTY' has men dancing round a pole with Pitt's head impaled on it (Fig. 5.2). Other examples have 'BEFORE THE REVOLUTION' on one side, with a shackled man naked and gnawing a bone in his prison cell, and on the other side, 'AFTER THE REVOLUTION', a well-dressed shepherd taking his ease under a tree in a bucolic landscape. 'ROUSE BRITANNIA!' displayed a Cap of Liberty and on the reverse a donkey bearing four weighted saddlebags of 'RENTS' and 'TAXS' (*sic*). 'THE END OF OPPRESSION' has land documents burning on a bonfire, while the reverse might show a ruined cottage and landscape explained by the fact that 'ONE ONLY MASTER GRASPS THE WHOLE DOMAIN'. Others variously proclaim: 'SPENCES PLAN IS SMALL FARMS & EVERY BLESSING'; 'SMALL FARMS FAT BAIRNS'; 'FAT BAIRNS FULL BELLIES'; 'PLENTY FOR EVER IN SMALL FARMS'; 'PEACE AND LIBERTY FOR EVER'; 'WAR IS STARVATION'; 'LANDLORDS AND STARVATION'; 'SPENCES PLAN NO LANDLORDS'; 'PARTNERSHIP IN LAND THE LAND IS OURS'; 'NO LANDLORDS, YOU ROGUES'; and 'LIBERTY AND NOT SLAVERY'.

5.2. Thomas Spence's copper or alloy tokens (1795–6): 'WE WILL WALK THUS IF THE LAW REQUIRES IT'; 'I AM NOT THINE ASS'; 'MY FREEDOM I AMONG SLAVES ENJOY' (Spence's cat); 'FREE-BORN ENGLISHMAN'; 'BRITISH LIBERTY DISPLAYED'; 'TREE OF LIBERTY'. (© The Trustees of the British Museum)

The historian John Barrell claims that popular radicals were averse to using comic or grotesque visual propaganda in the 1790s lest they belittle their cause in the eyes of their betters, and that Spence's tokens weren't significant propaganda. This is too cautious. Satire would never break an elite, but appreciation of Spence's tokens was assured in the global capital of visual satire, where satire fostered sceptical ways of thought across all classes. Many of the 20,000 satirical print titles published between 1780 and 1820 mercilessly lampooned the regent and his mistresses, royal dukes, government ministers, the pretentious and affected, and the merest magistrate and cleric. Hone's and Cruikshank's overtly radical etchings and woodcuts could be bought for pennies and pinned up in taverns. The power of mockery had been learned from the carnivalesque inversions of fairgrounds, charivari, popular theatre, mock trials, and election meetings.[33] Hone knew this. Tried and acquitted in 1817 for the blasphemous libel of publishing parodies of the Anglican liturgy, he told the court that he would 'laugh his majesty's ministers to scorn':

> he had laughed at them, and, *ha! ha! ha!* he laughed at them now, and he would laugh at them, as long as they were laughing stocks! . . . They were his vindictive persecutors, and his hypocritical persecutors; and laugh at them he would, till they ceased to be the objects of his laughter by ceasing to be ministers. . . . Was a laugh treason? Surely not.[34]

So semi-literate people would understand Spence when he advertised that he would 'treat all the swine with a jest'. Wedderburn too: since the 'ignorant insignificant smock faced stupid fool' of a regent 'turned a deaf ear to our petitions we must redress our own grievances my motto is Assassinate stab in the dark [*sic*]'.[35] Londoners knew how to mock their betters, and unlike most continentals felt fairly safe when they did so.

In September 1814, forty friends and disciples, including Evans, Thistlewood, and Preston, escorted Spence's coffin from Spence's lodgings off Oxford Street to St James's graveyard on the Hampstead Road (now lost under Euston station). The procession was headed by a man carrying a pair of scales draped with white ribbons to denote Spence's sincerity and justness. In each balance an equal pile of earth symbolised the equal distribution of land. Handfuls of tokens were distributed among the crowds that watched the coffin as it passed up the Tottenham Court Road; tokens were thrown onto the coffin as it was lowered into the grave. In accordance with Spence's wishes, a pair of tokens carrying his favourite designs were placed over his eyes and buried with him. One depicted a meridian sun emblazoned with the words 'SPENCE'S PLAN'; the other depicted Spence's favourite animal, the cat. He said that he would have the cat on his coat of arms, because this fine animal 'could be stroked down, but he would not suffer himself to be rubbed against the grain'. 'MY FREEDOM I AMONG SLAVES ENJOY,' the cat says as he glares out at us. On the reverse a pleading dog reminds us that 'MUCH GRATITUDE BRINGS SERVITUDE' (Fig. 5.2).[36]

After Spence's death, Thomas Evans expanded the group into the Society of Spencean Philanthropists, sections of which met in taverns across east and central London on successive nights of the week. Feuds were frequent, and Spenceanism was easily belittled. Place sneered that 'there was nothing which could fairly be called a society . . . the Spenceans were next to nobody and nothing'. Their numbers were indeed underwhelming. McCalman estimates that there were some sixty dedicated activists in London in the post-war years, 200 to 300 committed followers, and 2,000 to 3,000 who attended meetings regularly.[37] Still, in the government's eyes that was enough. We have seen that after the Spa Fields insurrection of December 1816, Sidmouth named Spenceans explicitly as the 'traitorous conspiracy' targeted by the Act against Seditious Meetings and Assemblies. The Act forced them to meet under altered names, which enabled most to get away with it. At the Mulberry Tree in Moorfields, 150 men with enough pennies in pocket to smoke and drink for five hours would crowd 'to suffocation' a club room fit for 100 to hear readings from Cobbett or the *Black Dwarf*, while Wedderburn sold pamphlets to those who could afford them. The landlord monitored everyone entering the room and signalled to the speaker the presence of a stranger, and 'violent declarations [were] made as to the manner they would treat a spy if discovered'.[38] In July 1818 the elder Evans there toasted

'The Public Will. The source and support of all legitimate authority, and of all social institutions.' – *Three times three* [i.e. three cheers] –

'The Natural Rights of Man, neither prescriptible by time, destructible by the sword, nor extinguishable by tyranny.' –

'Agrarian fellowship, the only pure and perfect system of political justice, under which equality and freedom would necessarily and really prevail.' –

'The memory of Thomas Spence, to whose fearless spirit and incorruptible integrity the world may yet stand indebted for its complete emancipation from feudal slavery.' – *Three times three, with great applause.*

Wedderburn compared the gathering to the meeting of Pentecost, when man's salvation was discussed by people of all languages and there was a speaking in tongues. A subscription was opened to publish the society's songs and pamphlets, the younger Evans delivered a panegyric on Spence's character, and more toasts followed, each accompanied by a bumper of the best cordial gin to 'the memory of the suppressed Society of Spencean Philanthropists; may its principles survive the unjust persecution by which their promulgation has been impeded', and to 'The progress of public opinion, the sure and certain means of *demolishing* social and political abuses'.[39] In venues like this plebeian sociability and radical optimism were as yet unfractured.

CHAPTER 6

Fantasy, Myth, and Song

MIXED MESSAGES

'But what say the conspirators themselves?' A week after the Cato Street executions Cobbett answered his own questions by insisting that the written word wasn't their primary propulsion:

> Do they say, or can it be inferred from what they say, that they were urged on by the reading of my book, or of any book, or any paper, what ever? No such thing. They all say [rather] that they were made discontented by the miseries of their country, which they traced to the government; that their minds were inflamed with indignation by the proceedings at Manchester [Peterloo], and especially by the letter of Lord Sidmouth approving of the conduct of the magistrates and the yeomanry, and by the impunity of these persons; that, when they were in this state of mind, they were urged on by Edwards [the spy], who not only advised them to kill the ministers, but who found money to purchase arms and ammunition with, and who gave Thistlewood money besides. – This is what they say; this is their dying declaration; and, what ground is there, then, for ascribing the conspiracy to publications of any sort?[1]

Cobbett was right to see that the instinct to subvert, reform, or abolish the ruling order was primarily driven by hunger, declining or absent wages, high food prices, threatened or lost craft status, the denial of an electoral voice, and resentment of ruling-class callousness. The common people didn't need to read books to register these things. Even the illiterate knew about the French revolution, not least because they had been dragooned or press-ganged into fighting it. For such people, conversation, symbolic rituals, songs, graphic emblems, or Spence's tokens would serve to enlighten just as well.

Historians of political thought can be po-faced about their subject matter. It's their business in life to assume that past people read complex texts with the same attention as they do, and that they valued ideological consistency equally. But in the real world, outside narrow circles, reasoned texts weren't as earnestly ingested as all that. Then, as now, ideological *in*consistency was more common than otherwise. Although men who could barely write might read, they wouldn't read ambitiously. Even the educated would have found books about rights, contract, and despotism heavy-going. Excerpted ideas were more helpful. Even Thistlewood's political education might have depended on a 406-page anthology, *The Manual of Liberty, or Testimonies in Behalf of the Rights of Mankind. Selected from the Best Authorities in Prose and Verse, and Methodically Arranged* (1795). He cited five lines from it when the defence counsel Adolphus asked the doomed conspirators for autographed mementos. The book offered snippets from authors British and foreign, ancient and modern, and poetic, theatrical, and otherwise, on topics like Equality of Mankind, Rights of Man, Rights of Kings, Social Contract, Despotism, Aristocracy, Equity or Justice, Laws and Lawyers, Penal Laws, Laws of Insolvency, Plots Informers and Spies, Oaths, Royalty, Ministers, Parties, Rich and Poor, Origin of Evil, Military Discipline, Features of War, Evils of War, Causes of War, Impress of Seamen, Naval Despotism, and Liberty of the Press. Snippets were easily digested.

The more sloganised and encapsulated ideas were, the better for their circulation. In lodgings, coffee shops, and pubs opinion was shaped less by scriptorial rectitude than by the people one knew, the opinions and public speeches one heard (70,000 or so gathered to hear Henry Hunt and Watson in Smithfield in July 1819), the great public moments one attended, like Hunt's triumphal entry into London after Peterloo, and finally by the contagious excitements of collectivity itself. Even music helped. A loyalist lamented in the 1790s that 'any thing written in voice & especially to an old English tune … made a more fixed impression on the minds of the younger and lower class of people, than any written in prose, which was often forgotten as soon as read'.[2]

What resulted from these diverse exposures was less an ideology than a melange of myths, memories, loyalties, slogans, and resentments – of 'ready-made ideas, commonplaces and intellectual bric-a-brac, the remnants of cultures and mentalities belonging to different times and different places' – whose individual elements would be inconsistent or irrational.[3] That determined disbeliever, the shoemaker Thomas Preston, for instance, had wit enough to read Paine, to be arrested for treason alongside Thistlewood and Watson, and to attempt a memoir. In this, however, he recorded that in his unhappiest time he had consulted a 'cunning woman' in Brentford who told him 'that my enemies would make me a great man, and occasion me to much celebrity; that I should be exposed to great perils; and that I was to make my mind very happy, notwithstanding, for that no prison would long contain me'. He was so impressed by this prediction that he repeated it to all his friends, apologetically.[4]

Thistlewood likewise might be an early member of the Society of Spencean Philanthropists and a friend of Thomas Evans; but there is no evidence that Spence's Plan meant much to him. The son of a comfortable farmer who was a tenant of the county's ruling Vyner family (their patronage got him into loyalist county militias in the 1790s), he lived his first thirty-six years in the conservative and rural county of Lincolnshire. A 'land plan' had no place in that world. When he first appeared in London politics in 1811 it was as a moderately monied quasi-gentleman who joined a committee of respectable reformers led by Sir Francis Burdett. Although he was said to have read Paine in his youth, he never once talked about how to kill a king, and we never once hear the names Spence or Paine on his lips. If anything, he was an old-fashioned jacobin; but although he and his associates sometimes called each other 'citizen', they usually called each other 'Mr' and none mentioned liberty, equality, or fraternity. Nor did Thistlewood invoke France's revolutionary heroes as models; his favourites were Brutus, Cassius, and Cato. His disquisition at Preston's lodging in January 1820, reported by Edwards, brings us as close to his political thinking as we'll get:

> Thistlewood then spoke of the Roman history and said 4 men & a woman destroyed that tyrant Com[modus] and when ever any thing should be done here it would be by a few brave men and not by any arrangement to great extent – he told the story of Commodus death and spoke of his cruelties as also of Galba Calugalas &c and said our George prince of Wales

regent would be as cruel as any of the Romans if he dare indeed added Thistlewood a bigger or crueller villion never lived than our regent is only his cruelties are committed by the bloody minded rascals under him.

Did some part of Thistlewood's authority over his followers stem from his small displays of classical learning? His acquaintance with the history of Roman assassination certainly fed his belief in himself. When Cook protested that they lacked supporters enough to destroy the government, Thistlewood replied that 'he would have done it with a dozen men with nothing but knives', just as the Romans did.[5]

Commonly favoured ideas, whether Paineite, Spencean, or Gibbonian, were aired to signal political seriousness and identity, but most craftsmen would have been more familiar with Paine's or Spence's slogans than with their writings. Even Preston spoke not of Paine but rather of 'a Persian in ancient times ... who overthrew 15 hundred thousand Grecians', adding that 'he would do his duty towards emancipating his fellow countrymen even tho his blood be spilt in the cause'.[6] Perhaps he was too worldly-wise to be doctrinaire. 'We live in an age of fiction,' he wrote in his memoir:

All around us is fiction, – but [except] distress and ruin, – and that unfortunately consists of reality. The king can do no wrong, – that they say is a *necessary* fiction. The ministry are made to be responsible, – that is a *notorious* fiction. The House of Commons is chosen by the people, – this is an *universally understood* fiction. The nation is 'great', because the revenue her governors receive exceed that of all Europe beside, – this is a *consolatory* fiction. The nation is 'glorious', because a numerous body of men clad in red, carry steel at their elbows, – this is both a *burning shame* and a *vexations* and *daring* fiction.[7]

One cost of ideological unfixity was that much radical motivation was driven by fantasy. This wasn't necessarily unfortunate. Fantasy comforts the thwarted mind, but may also channel thought and understanding. T. J. Wooler offered a fine example when his *Black Dwarf* unleashed this wonderful flow after Peterloo, as he imagined himself leading a procession of convicted [Peterloo] yeomanry to the scaffold and a string of reverend and honourable and genteel hypocrites . . . to the [prison] hulks or one of the penitentiaries, and the grandeur and importance of the cavalcade would be considerably improved if a band of the borough-mongers and their tools in power were to close the long line of worthies, each . . . following a cart attended by a posse of . . . Jack Ketches with a cat o'nine tails, administering a wholesome correction to pride and giving a useful lesson to titled insolence. For example's sake, I would have also two or three idle whigs march a breast, handcuffed [and in] shackles which they sit silently by and see riveted upon the people. And if a judge or two could be found . . . I would have . . . them added to the group, adorned with caps and bells to fit them for [their] folly, and secured in straight waistcoats lest in disappointed anger they should be again tempted to bite their keepers.[8]

Here fantasy might seem playful, but it also expressed anger enough to be energising.

The main trouble with fantasy was its evasion of the key questions – how to fulfil the fantasy and get away with it? Just as Spence's advocacy of land redistribution concentrated on fantasised ends rather than on the tricky question of means, so few if any other ultra-radicals had programmes for change that referred to much more than a memory of jacobin violence. Magical thinking could take over. 'For my own part I am ready now,' the Spencean shoemaker Allen Davenport announced: 'I compare the present time to the crisis of the French Revolution, we must arm ourselves as they did and in open day too and though we may loose [sic] a few lives in the onset yet what is the army compared to the mass of the country under the yoke of despotism.'[9] After Peterloo, Wedderburn similarly declared: 'We must all learn to use the gun the dagger the cutlass and the pistols – we shall then be able to defy all the yeomanry of England'. Or as he suggested a month later, since bakers' ovens often ran under the streets and since the bakers were generally radicals or Spenceans, they possessed the means of blowing up London. 'London stands upon nothing, it has no foundations but vaults, stores, ovens, pipes, cesspools so that one shock it would fall like unto the tower of Bable.' With the soldiers bribed onto their side, 'there will not be one left of over groon lords in twenty-four hours'.[10]

Thistlewood and his men also evaded key questions about how to defeat a great army and what to do with the king. At best, in Edwards's account of his words, Thistlewood planned for

> confusion and anarchy until a new government is established, and in respect to plundering we must forbid it on pain of death and wink at it at the same time – We must do as the French did cry out 'peace to the Cottage destruction to the Mansion' but set the poor to go and turn the rich out and take possession of their houses.[11]

The agency he proposed for this enterprise was a 'Committee of Public Safety' of twenty-four veteran radicals. Most of the men listed for the committee would have run miles before they associated themselves with Thistlewood.

Attitudes to monarchy were ambivalent too. In principle radicals knew what kings stood for:

> If a king passes by, *Get ye down! down!–down! Keep ye down!* . . .
> Do you know what a king is? By Patrick I'll tell you;
> He has power in his pocket, to buy you and fell you;
> To make you all soldiers, or keep you at work,
> To hang you, and cure you for ham or salt pork!
> *Get ye down! down!–down! Keep ye down!*[12]

Another song of the 1790s proposed that 'They prosper best who have no king, / To rob them and enthral; / Then let our acclamations ring, / At every tyrant's fall'. Yet another versified that 'Since the reign of kings began, / The Rights of Man are ended'.[13] In the 1810s everyone knew that the regent was a spoiled booby who would say anything if prompted by 'wine and two or three whores' (Wedderburn). After he sent his infamous letter of thanks to the Manchester magistrates after Peterloo, Wedderburn asked, 'What is the prince regent or king to us, we want no king he is no use to us.' 'That great fat booby in Pall Mall', Preston called him.[14]

Yet long-conditioned reflexes would insist on breaking out. They were spurred by the anti-gallic sentiment of wartime and by affection for the afflicted George III: at least a mad king was harmless. Allen Davenport recalled his own loyalism as a young man in the 1790s in these terms:

> Though I was very young, I was a bit of a patriot, and thought, at that time, that everything undertaken by England was right, just and proper ... I shouted 'church and king', as loud and long as any priest or lord in the kingdom ... [it was my] ... bounden duty to put down such a desperate nation of levellers, blasphemers and regicides.[15]

Even Wedderburn usually attacked what Cobbett called 'old corruption' rather than monarchy itself.[16] And one writer suggested that if Thistlewood became an assassin rather than a patriot, it was only thanks to his 'heated imagination and mistaken zeal', implying that at heart he was thoroughly 'English'.[17]

The same might have been said of Dr Watson. During the 1815 peace celebrations, he illuminated his windows and painted his house with loyal insignia along with the best of them. Reporting this, his landlord thought it had been his connection with the Evanses that had 'turned his politics': that is, he was a patriot really. Watson occasionally argued that the regent was misled by bad advisors rather than by his own gross interests. He told a meeting at the White Lion in October 1819 that one of their flags should bear the motto, 'The prince & the people against the borough mongers'; 'this he said would have great weight with the public'.[18]

Even Brunt declared himself a monarchist, although his anger was awesome and he lost his head for it. In his last speech he said it wasn't the king but aristocratic government that he hated. He had intended to 'put those obnoxious characters [the ministers] out of the way – I mean obnoxious to us, not to you, gentlemen, [but] to the man who has nobody to look up to to protect him, and who, when he petitions and cries for bread for his family, can get none'.

> I wish it to go abroad to the world, that I possess a general feeling for those termed the lower orders, who are the stability of my country; that I regard an industrious man, a moral man; and when I see a man, or a set of men, such as my lord Sidmouth or my lord Castlereagh, who have been the cause of millions being murdered, and tens of thousands starved to death, that I have an antipathy against those men; but if I conspired to put them out of the world, is that high treason?

No, this wasn't high treason, he insisted, because he was 'no enemy to my king'. At this point he was doomed whatever he said, so we must accept what followed as honestly felt:

> I have a love to my king and country; but I am an enemy to the borough-mongering faction, that destroys the vitals of my country; but to my king and my country I am a loyal and dutiful subject. I consider the king equally enslaved as the people, by those very men. . . . I never did agree, and Adams has acknowledged at the bar, that when it was proposed to make an attack on London, while the king's funeral was carrying on, I rejected it, and said, nothing short of attacking the cabinet, or some of the ministers, would satisfy me – this I acknowledge I agreed to; but for a verdict to be returned against me, that I conspired to depose his majesty, that I conspired and intended to levy war, is untrue. I never did.[19]

It was consistent with these positions that in the cross-examinations during both the 1817 and the 1820 treason trials reference to Paine or Spence was all but absent. In 1820 such references as there were were made by informers like John Monument or Adams, but only to deny Paine's influence on them. Monument had read Paine's *Age of Reason*, and 'it rather shook my faith; but it did not destroy it, because it was accompanied by the bishop of Llandaff's *Apology for the Bible*'. 'I do not read Paine's works,' Chambers announced as defence witness; 'I only read Cobbett, and have a drawer full of them. I also read the prayer-book and bible.' Adams, the key conspirator-witness, admitted (or lied) that he 'had been a Christian down to the time when I read the infernal work of Thomas Paine, which was given to me by Tidd', and elsewhere he agreed that his mind had been 'perverted' by Carlile's publications and by Paine's 'accursed' *Age of Reason*.[20]

Self-serving statements like these were almost certainly coerced. The fact that Adams's awkward testimony under pressure from the defence counsel ended in a blank refusal to answer hint at this hidden truth of the matter. Richard Carlile believed that Adams was forced to renounce his deism under the treasury solicitor's orders – though the interrogation also conveys the intrinsic fragility of his belief systems:[21]

[Were you] educated as a Christian? – Yes.

You profess that religion, do you, now? – Yes, I do now.

Did you ever cease to profess it? – Yes.

What mode of faith, or disbelief, did you take up while you disbelieved Christianity? What were you then? – was induced . . .

Never mind what you were induced; answer my question first, and you shall tell your inducement afterwards. What were you when you were not a Christian? – A man, certainly, in the same form as I am now. . . .

What faith or persuasion had you when you were not a Christian? – If I must answer that question, . . .

You shall answer the question. – Then I will. I was in faith what they termed a Deist.

Did you believe in God when you were a Deist? – They strove to make me . . .

Did you believe in God when you were a Deist? – Yes.

Then you renounced Christianity to be a Deist, and believed only in God? – Yes, that was the case.

How long may you have embraced Christianity again? – I consider myself to have embraced Christianity again ever since I first received conviction that I was in the wrong.

Give us the day and month. – I cannot.

Was it before the 23rd of February last [date of the Cato Street arrests]? – I was convinced even before I was taken, and my conviction grew stronger after that.

Was it before or after the 23rd of February last you called yourself a Christian again? – After the 23rd.

So much for your religion. How long might you remain in the happy conviction of Deism? How many years? – Of a Deist?

When did you renounce faith in our Saviour? – It first happened since last August [the month of Peterloo, 1819].

Since last August you renounced faith in our Saviour, and since last February you have taken it up again? – Yes.

In your progress downwards, you say you had got down from Christianity to Deism. Did you ever get to the point of Atheism? – Never.

Did you ever profess yourself a Deist? – Never.

Did you ever deny your belief in a God at all, and that the Scriptures were all a fable – I never denied a God, though I was brought by that accursed work of Paine's to deny the Scriptures.

And now you are brought to call the Bible a good book, and Paine's accursed? – [no reply].[22]

MYTH

The belief in a past golden age of happiness and freedom has flourished in all societies, as has the belief that it was an aristocracy that destroyed it. In England the prelapsarian age was understood to be one of Saxon liberty, and its nemesis came with the Norman Yoke that descended in 1066. This primal narrative informed Leveller pamphlets in the civil war, as in Lilburne's insistence that the liberties of common and natural law were the birth right of the 'free-born Englishman'. It was replicated in John Wilkes's and Major John Cartwright's polemics in the 1760s and '70s, and in Paine's and Spence's works as well. When Wilkes fought against curbs on free election and free speech, he appealed to 'every free-born Englishman who ... has been taught to believe in his birthright'. That birth right was the liberty which the Englishman 'hopes and wishes to transmit to his posterity, as he received it from his ancestors, who fought and died for it'.[23]

Common people found the oppressions of the Norman Yoke easier to understand than theories of natural rights. The yoke was visibly inscribed in the mansions, parklands, hunting-grounds, fish ponds, woodlands, game enclosures, and game laws that countless urban immigrants remembered from their younger days. Spence's songs played to this memory:

> THE Golden Age, so fam'd by Men of Yore,
> Shall soon be counted fabulous no more.
> The tyrant Lion like an Ox shall feed,
> And lisping Infants shall tame Tygers lead.
> With deadly Asps shall sportive Sucklings play,
> Nor aught obnoxious blight the blithsome Day.
> Yes – all that Prophets e'er of Bliss foretold,

And all that Poets ever feigned of old,

As yielding joy to Man, shall now be seen

And ever flourish like an Evergreen.

The Mortals join to hail great Nature's plan,

That fully gives to Babes those Rights it gives to Man.

CHORUS. To the Tune of – 'Sally in our Alley':

THEN let us all join heart in hand,

Through country town and city,

Of ev'ry age and ev'ry sex,

Young men and maidens pretty;

To haste this Golden Age's reign,

On ev'ry hill and valley,

Then Paradise shall greet our eyes,

Through ev'ry street and alley.[24]

Similarly, in this song about 'True Antient Liberty', denatured urbanites might well fancy that they could one day return not only to the beginnings of history, but to their own rose-tinted rural childhoods as well:

When wild o'er the woodlands our forefathers stray'd,

As rough as the rocks of our isle,

Fair Liberty wander'd along the deep glade,

And deck'd every face with a smile.

Then they pluck'd the ripe berry bush, and sipp'd the silver tide,

And with nature and liberty their wants were supplied.

The abuse of a throne was to Britons unknown;

They could Tyrants defy![25]

By the regency years radical newspapers, speeches, prints, and songs galvanised the English by referring to the history of aristocratic repression axiomatically. Watson told the Spa Fields meeting in 1816: 'Ever since the Norman conquest, kings and lords have been deluding you.' Wedderburn's audience agreed with him that 'there was no constitution or liberty in England since William the Conqueror'.[26] Shoemaker Brunt declared during the Cato Street trials that he was 'a descendant of the ancient Britons', while Thistlewood announced that 'Albion is still in the chains of slavery'. In their last speeches both Davidson the black cabinet-maker and Ings the butcher cited Magna Carta. Watson's placard advertising a Smithfield meeting in November 1819 urged: 'Think of this ye descendants of the brave and immortal Alfred, who expelled the Tyrant Danes!!!' – and then invoked the 'noble spirit of independence at Runnymede [that] obtained the Magna Charta!!!' Whig-radicals like Sir Francis Burdett wanted country gentlemen to reclaim the 'ancient liberties of Britons' which had been usurped by 'a junto of nobility and placemen'. And tavern songsters sang this in 1820:

> Our ancient rights we ask, and ask no more,
> Our birthrights, which the tyrants now withhold;
> But we will shew them that their day is o'er,
> For British freedom never shall be sold.
>
> *Chorus:*
> In patriot bands we'll join with bravery,
> Break the chains of tyrants' knavery,
> Let our cry be – Down with slavery!
> *Liberty or Death.*[27]

These understandings were underpinned by a satirical emblem of the utmost eloquence. No image better represented radical motivation between 1795 and 1820 than the depiction of the heavily shackled 'free-born Briton' or 'Englishman'. Its origin was probably Josiah Wedgwood's abolitionist medallion of a shackled slave kneeling over the motto, 'Am I not a man and a brother', adopted by the Committee to Abolish the Slave Trade in 1787. But while Wedgwood's shackled slave could talk, the shackled Briton's lips were padlocked. As a comment on the suppression of free speech and assembly, and in its implied equation of this condition to slavery, this device was a brilliant invention of lasting effect.

Its life begins with an anonymous print of *circa* 1795, probably by Isaac Cruikshank, George's father, *The True Born Englishman!!! & Keeper, Now Every Britons Song shall be Give me Death or Liberty etc. etc.* It shows the imprisoned Englishman, in chains and with lips padlocked, gazing hopelessly at a loaf of bread placed just out of his reach, while a gout-stricken Pitt tells the one-legged and one-armed soldiers guards: 'I'll stop the mouths of all the murmuring scoundrell ... Grummbling, grummbling, grummbling the devil grumble them all together ...'[28] (Fig. 6.1). In an anonymous etching of 1795/6 the freeborn becomes a tattered, fettered, and manacled figure over the ironic title, *A Freeborn Englishman. The Admiration of the World; the Envy of Surrounding Nations; &c &c.* (Fig. 6.2). This might have been designed and published by Spence, since the figure reappears on his and Skidmore's tokens in 1796 either as a shackled 'Englishman', hatless and facing right (Spence) or as a shackled 'Briton' wearing a hat and facing left (Skidmore) (see Fig. 5.2 above). (When Spence's shop closed in bankruptcy, his dies were bought by the coin dealer Peter Skidmore, who continued their distribution.) One such token displayed on its reverse a well-dressed French republican sailor wearing a cap of liberty and holding in his hand his own shackles, now broken.[29]

The image's currency was furthered in 1819 in two satires on Sidmouth's Six Acts after Peterloo. Unsigned but attributed to George Cruikshank, both appear over the title *A Free Born Englishman! The*

6.1. Anon. (Isaac Robert Cruikshank?), *The True Born Englishman!!! & Keeper, Now Every Britons Song shall be Give me Death or Liberty etc. etc.* (Roberts; November 1795?) (© Yale Center for British Art)

A FREEBORN ENGLISHMAN,
*the Admiration of the World; the Envy of Surrounding Nations;
&c &c.*

6.2. Anon., *A Freeborn Englishman. The Admiration of the World; the Envy of Surrounding Nations; &c &c.* (1795–6) (© The Trustees of the British Museum)

Admiration of the World!!! And the Envy of Surrounding Nations!!!!! One is a lithograph, the other (here) an etching published by Fores of Piccadilly and dated 15 December 1819 (Fig. 6.3). It sold cheaply for a shilling coloured, a sure sign of popular demand. In it the freeborn Englishman's lips are sealed by a padlock inscribed 'No Grumbling'. With hands tied behind his back and legs loaded with shackles, he is forced to stand on Magna Carta and the Bill of Rights. Birds peck at his scalp, his clothes are tattered, his Cap of Liberty lies on the ground, and the execution axe to his left is labelled 'Law of Libel'. Before a derelict house in the background, a woman and child crouch next to a naked baby and a dead dog. Debtors appeal to a passer-by through the prison grill on the right. One text refers to 'Free Discussion – a farce', the other to the clerical magistrates whom governments use for 'necessary purposes' (Peterloo).

In January 1820 George Cruikshank etched his more elaborate *Poor John Bull – The Free Born Englishman – Deprived of his Seven Senses by the Six New Acts* (Fig. 6.4). Bound by chains and ropes, John Bull has lips padlocked, nose pinched, ears plugged, eyes blinded, and fingers thumb-screwed to

6.3. George Cruikshank, *A Free Born Englishman! The Admiration of the World!!! And the Envy of Surrounding Nations!!!!!* (Fores, 15 December 1819) (© The Trustees of the British Museum)

the table on which Magna Charta and the Bill of Rights are pierced by a blood-dripping dagger of 'Manchester Steel'. Castlereagh, with animal legs and claws, squats on his head and triumphantly tears up Cobbett's 'two penny Trash'.

In a culture that was as relatively starved of images as Britain's was before the advent of steel engraving and photography, this was an un-ignorable visual barrage – though in any era it would be difficult to beat the shackled freeborn as an icon of repression, despair, and anger. The satire's titles became a common idiom. In 1820 Cobbett cited it seven times in his

6.4. George Cruikshank, *Poor John Bull – The Free Born Englishman – Deprived of his Seven Senses by the Six New Acts* (Fairburn, 15 January 1820 (misdated 1819 on the print)) (Universal History Archive/Getty Images)

Political Register, as he wondered ironically of the Cato Street conspirators 'what harm can be done to ... a *constitution which is the envy of surrounding nations and the admiration of the world* ... by a few poor, beggarly silly fellows, who are universally hated and despised?'[30] A year later Hone republished Cruikshank's shackled freeborn as a woodcut in his *A Slap at Slop*, while in the Commons the attorney general referred to these and other 'indecent' caricatures to justify the moral policing conducted by the Society for the Suppression of Vice. In time, misinformed people without a sense of irony or history began to refer to the 'free-born Englishman' as if to a given truth. The prime minister Boris Johnson locked down the nation against the covid pandemic with an apology for 'taking away the ancient, inalienable right of free-born people of the United kingdom to go to the pub'.[31]

SONG

So far as historical memory was concerned, London's long-abused Irish had their own memory to bear. A traveller to Dublin would be struck by the constraints of martial law and 'the ruined mud-cabins – old castles – and innumerable ragged beings soliciting the charity of the traveller – we were surrounded with them at every place at which we stopped'.[32] Escape by migration had a long history, therefore. The Irish made up London's biggest non-English community at the time of the Act of Union in 1801. They probably numbered 37,000 then, or around 4 per cent of the population,[33] and somewhat more after the 1815 peace added discharged Irish sailors and soldiers and influxes of seasonal labour. They crammed themselves into countless courts and alleys outside the old City until the huge immigration after the 1840s famine ghettoised them more closely. There was mistrust, certainly. Radical deists were no fonder of Catholics than Protestants were, and the dislike was reciprocated. The London Irish refused to participate in a Thistlewood rising 'unless the English began it, for they had been deceived so often'. In February 1820 an Irish shoemaker told Brunt that Irishmen 'would not meet with the English before they was redy to carry their [own] object in to execution'.[34] Dwyer's promise to mobilise Irishmen from Gee's Court to join the rebellion was a pretence made under pressure, as we've seen.

All the same, 'Orator' Henry Hunt wooed the Irish, as did Thistlewood and Watson. A printer testified in 1819 that the Irish 'were rude and uncultivated as the mountains they came from', but were 'still men of intellect' even if 'without a shilling in their pockets'.[35] The United Irishmen had collapsed after the suppression of Emmet's rebellion in 1803, but for decades yet Irish nationalist banners were visible at most radical meetings, and Irish songs were heard all over London. Again, songs mattered. 'That something is left us, we all must agree; / Though talking's forbidden – yet singing is free.' When Hunt triumphantly entered London after Peterloo, crowds sang the elegaic 'The Exile of Erin' or 'Erin-go-Bragh':

> Too long have we suffered, and too long lamented,
> > *Bauy youd ma vourneen Erin go bragh.*
> > [*Victory to you my darling Ireland for ever*]
> By courage undaunted it may be prevented.
> > *Bauy youd ma vourneen Erin go bragh.*
> No more by OPPRESSORS let us be affrighted,

But with heart and with band, be firmly united;

For by ERIN GO BRAGH, it's thus we'll be righted.

A song like this was the 'most dreaded of all things. . . . It infects a whole country, and makes them half mad, because they rejoice and forget their cares, and forget their duty, and forget their betters'.[36]

It wasn't only the Irish who found song liberating. As *Spence's Songs* put it in 1807,

> what could hinder small companies from meeting, in a free and easy convivial manner, and singing their rights and instructing each other in songs? Can tyrants hinder people from singing at their work, or in their families? . . . Sing and meet and meet and sing, and your chains will drop off like burnt thread.

Spence's Songs (Thomas Evans composed many of them) was an unsubtle publication but had to be so. It sold to a plebeian market in four unpaginated parts at a penny each, and its balladic metres and homely ditties were set to well-known tunes. They blazoned forth the liberty tale more joyously than any other medium, and (like tokens and visual satires) their messages were difficult to prosecute. Spence's collection followed the precedent of an earlier songbook, Thompson's *Tribute to Liberty: Or, A Collection of Select Songs . . . Sacred to the Rights of Man*, whose 107 pages were published in several editions between 1793 and 1795. Its repeated invocations of 'liberty' gave a small army of Grub Street poets a helpful income at the cost of some tedium, but the book included anglicised translations of the revolutionary Marseillaise (calling it the 'March on, March on') and of the 'Ça ira!' as follows: ''Tis dangerous to eat, / 'Tis dangerous to meet, / 'Tis dangerous to drink, / 'Tis dangerous to think. / *Ça ira, Ça ira, Ça ira'*. These were still being sung in the Crown and Anchor on Fleet Street in 1819. A third collection of lasting influence was *The Wreath of Freedom, or Patriot's Song Book . . . in Favour of Public Liberty*, published in 1820.

Radicals would never sing 'God Save Great George the King' since the version current in the 1790s advised loyalists to 'Let that reformer Payne / Know his vile arts are vaine. . . . / Confound his politics / Frustrate his knavish tricks'. They would, however, sing 'God Save the

Rights of Man!' to the same tune: 'Let us with France agree, / And bid the world be free, / Leading the way. ... / Freedom shall ne'er retire / Freedom shall sway!'[37] They also belted out *Rule, Britannia* as a paean to liberty rather than as an imperialist anthem. Since most radicals were patriotic, Britannia's ruling the waves didn't trouble them. What mattered more was that 'Britons never will be slaves', and that this rule was embedded in the 'charter of the land' when Britain first 'arose from out the azure main': Saxon liberties again.

The most eloquent of all radical songs in this era encapsulated radical thoughts in a full summation of the themes discussed in this chapter. Sung to the catchy tune of 'The Vicar of Bray', it was Francophile, anti-clerical, anti-aristocratic, and anti-judicial, and it looked forward to human perfectability, the return of the golden age, and the sharing of the land. *'Each patriot Briton's song shall be, / O give me death or liberty!'*, its chorus went. Its anonymous verses are often wrongly attributed to Robert Burns, but he only tinkered with the already known song. It first came to light after it was found in the papers of the LCS's shoemaker-founder Thomas Hardy when Hardy was arrested in 1794. Read out during his treason trial as evidence of his evil intent, it had to be published in the official trial accounts afterwards. From this source it was adapted in a cluster of versions in 1794–6 and reprinted in Thompson's *Tribute to Liberty*, from which it passed into common usage:[38]

> Why vainly do we waste our prime
>   Repeating our oppressions?
> Come, rouse to arms, 'tis now the time
>   To punish past transgressions.
> 'Tis said that kings can do no wrong;
>   Their murderous deeds deny it:
> And since from us their power has sprung
>   We have the right to try it.
>
> *Each patriot Briton's song will be,*
> *O give me death or liberty!*
>
> The starving wretch who steals for bread
>   But seldom meets compassion;

And shall a Crown preserve the head
   Of one who robs a nation?
Such partial laws we all despise,
   See Gallia's bright example;
The godlike scene before our eyes,
   We'll every tyrant trample.

Each patriot Briton's song will be,
O give me death or liberty!

Proud Bishops then we will translate
   Among priest-crafted martyrs;
The guillotine on Peers shall wait,
   And Knights we'll hang in garters.
These despots long have trod us down,
   And Judges are their engines;
Such wretched minions of the Crown
   Demand the people's vengeance.
Each patriot Briton's song will be,
O give us death or liberty!

Our Juries are a venal pack,
   See Justice topsy-turvy;
On Freedom's cause they've turn'd a back
   Of Englishmen unworthy.
Now, once for all, the work begun,
   We'll clean the Augean stable;
A moment lost we are undone,
   Come, strike whilst we are able.

Each patriot Briton's song will be,
O give me death or liberty!

The Golden Age will then revive,
   Each man will be a brother;
In harmony we all shall live,
   And share this earth together.

In Virtue's school enlighten'd Youth
Will love his fellow-creature;
And future years will prove the truth,
That Man is good by nature:

Then let us drink with three times three
The reign of Peace and Liberty.

The longevity and provenance of the phrase 'give me liberty or death' (or 'death or liberty') in British radical lore is now smothered by an American takeover. Americans fondly think it was coined by Patrick Henry in his 1775 speech at the Virginia Convention. There are next to no Google references to it other than to Henry's. The trouble is that Henry's biographer first transcribed his speech and improved it from memory eighteen years after Henry's death. The British provenance not only predates the American, it also knocks it sideways (see note at the end of this chapter). Moreover, it had a vigorous life deep into the regency with never a reference to American usage. 'Death or Liberty' (or vice versa) was as British as the weather.

Thus banners proclaimed 'Liberty or Death' at Hunt's, Watson's, and Thistlewood's Smithfield meeting in July 1819, then again at Peterloo, and again at Hunt's triumphal entry into London in September. Hunt himself hailed 'Liberty or Death' as the motto of liberty's heroes: 'the contemptible reptile who would not subscribe to that sentiment, ought to live a slave, and die unlamented'. Wooler's *Black Dwarf* in 1819 described 'Death or Liberty' as 'the generous sentiment that ruled the Grecian and the Roman name', and insisted that it was not only 'the motto of every Briton', but that 'this sentiment, cherished for ages by the wise, the good, and the brave, is now become the emblem of revolt – the call for revolution!' In November one of Watson's and Thistlewood's placards calling a meeting in Smithfield on the 24th shouted 'Join as one family to be free, – Urge on reform, – DEATH, or LIBERTY!!' The doomed insurrectionists of Paisley and Glasgow declared in April 1820, 'Liberty or Death is our motto', their leaders soon to be hanged and decapitated. We'll see that for the defence counsel Adolphus Brunt adapted verses from the song in the memento lines he wrote on his last day on earth. And on the

Newgate scaffold James Ings the butcher bellowed 'O give me death or liberty!' as, blindfolded, he waited for his drop to drop.[39]

A Note on 'Liberty or Death': Its British Provenance

1. An Irish silver token has 'Death or Liberty' and 'No Surrender 1688' inscribed over an Irish harp, re. the Londonderry siege. Irish verses commemorated the same siege with a reference to 'sweet liberty or death' (BM 1952,0904.244). 2. Addison's *Cato, A Tragedy* in 1712 has 'It is not now time to talk of aught / But chains or conquest, liberty or death'. *Cato* was many times republished and performed in London; also performed before George Washington at Valley Forge. 3. Handel's *Judas Maccabeus* (1746) sings, 'Resolve, my sons, on liberty or death'. 4. At Drury Lane in 1774 Jack Bannister sang 'Whilst happy in my native land', with the chorus 'Each free-born Briton's song should be / O give me death or liberty!' (*Covent Garden Magazine*, 3 (1774), 380); the actor Charles Incledon adopted it too. 5. Its tune was used for ballads on liberty subjects: e.g. 'A New Song, called The Triumph of Liberty', 'set to the tune of "Give me Death or Liberty"' (Bodleian Roud no. V1343, Oxford.) All these uses predate Patrick Henry.

6. After Thomas Hardy's verses of 1794 were republished (as above), the phrase entered visual satire in Isaac Cruikshank's *True Born Englishman!!! & Keeper, Now Every Britons Song shall be Give me Death or Liberty etc. etc.* (Fig. 6.1). 7. It was current among the United Irishmen: Napper Tandy proclaimed 'Liberty or Death' after landing in Donegal with 200 men in 1798. 8. Bannister's song was republished in *Edinburgh Musical Miscellany* (2nd edn 1804/8), 44–6. 9. A spoof banknote of 1809 promises twopence to anyone breaching the king's peace by 'coughing, sneezing or the bowel-easing flatus': 'When Justasses take bail for farting, / 'Tis time this land and I were parting. /The British voice by nature free, / Cries "Give me Death or Liberty"' (BM 1868,0808.12614). 10. In Williams's satire, *True Born Britons or a Constitutional Chorus* (1810), Sir Francis Burdett and whig friends sing Bannister's 'very favourite

---

(cont.)

song': 'The noble mind is not at all / By poverty degraded / 'Tis guilt alone can make us fall / And this I am pesuaded [*sic*] / *Each true born Briton's song should be / O give me Death or Liberty'* (BM 1868,0808.7932). 11. One of George Cruikshank's anti-radical prints is *Death or Liberty! Or Britannia & the Virtues of the Constitution in Danger of Violation from the Grt Political Libertine, Radical Reform!* (1 December 1819: BM 1868,0808.8469). 12. Thereafter the phrase was reclaimed by the ultra-radicals of 1819–20, as above.

CHAPTER 7

Rebellion's Habitats

THE SENSE OF PLACE

In 1811 Arthur Thistlewood, his wife Susan, and his illegitimate son
Julian travelled down the Great North Road from deeply rural
Lincolnshire, to arrive at the Spread Eagle in Gracechurch Street three
days later. Their resettlement in the capital would have been a liberation
for a resentment-riddled man from a remote county. One could not
express dangerous ideas in Lincolnshire, let alone meet like-minded
people. The county was dominated by great landowners whose rule was
unchallenged. The Anderson Pelhams held one county seat from 1774 to
1823. The Vyner family, part of this oligarchy, ruled the Thistlewood
roosts directly: Arthur's father was one of their tenant farmers. The city of
Lincoln boasted a population of a mere 8,600 in 1811, and only five other
Lincolnshire towns had over 5,000. Now a metropolis of over a million
people awaited them – twice the size of Paris. How did they cope? Where
and how did they live? And how did metropolitan living direct their
views? If Thistlewood couldn't have embarked on his madcap career
outside the great city, the same went for Thistlewood's humbler supporters. Nearly all were born in the provinces. One came from Scotland
and a couple from Ireland, and only two or three were London-born.
Coming to London didn't necessarily improve their lot, but it did
broaden their sense of the world's possibilities – including the world's
worst possibilities. Had they stayed in their birthplaces they wouldn't
have been executed or sent to Australia.

The Thistlewoods first moved into lodgings at number 64 Edgware
Road, on the very edge of western London.[1] This was an oddly distant
location to choose, offset by the fact that their lodging in a fine new

regency house did justice to their standing, and the semi-rural outlook might have been comforting. Faden's map of 1819 shows number 64 as a large newly built terrace house with a small front garden and a larger rear one, facing unbuilt gardens and fields across the road to the west (see Map 1). Cato Street stood immediately behind the house two blocks to the east, but this was an uncanny coincidence that had no meaning then. It was almost as coincidental that number 64 stood just north of Géricault's lodging during the artist's first visit to London in 1820, when he arrived to show his work and also to draw Thistlewood's execution. Géricault lodged at number 39 with a master bootmaker and his family in a smaller terrace house. A delicate drawing he did of his landlady and her children displays that family's equal gentility.[2]

Provincials were two-a-penny in London. One in six of the eighteenth-century English are thought to have lived in the capital at some stage in their lives. Ceaseless immigration, along with rising fertility and declining child mortality, had doubled London's population in the eighteenth century; and the total of a million or so in 1801 was increased by a further half-million in the twenty years following. Into London they came daily in hope of employment and better futures – on foot or horseback, in cart or boat, over short distances or long. Young females outnumbered males thanks to the pull of domestic service, and the inflow peaked in years of bad harvest or after harvests were over. In the metropolis the clash of accents and dialects, often unintelligible to others, was deafening. For many, a reference to 'my country' still as like as not signified 'my county' or 'parish'.

The Thistlewoods could look after themselves in this enlarging world, but humbler people's first encounters with London could be bewildering. When the young shoemaker John Brown walked from Cambridge to London in search of work, he was terrified by the traffic, streets, and shops. John Cashman, the discharged Irish sailor hanged for his part in the Spa Fields riots, testified that when he was swept up by the riotous crowd he had no idea where he was, other than that he was standing near 'a large church and castle', by which he meant St Paul's cathedral.[3]

It was an unkind city they came to. Deprivation was written into the crowded soot-blackened, smoke-filled, and rat-infested tenements in which most had to live. Francis Place recalled that his boyhood home off Drury Lane was 'filled with rats mice and bugs' and had 'always a reservoir of putrid matter in the lower part of the house'.[4] Later, the deaths from cholera in London's darker tenements matched the plague deaths in their cruelty and horror. In such places, too, where some people changed lodgings every few weeks, newcomers could find communal understandings and mutuality less dependable than they had been in the village. Courtyards and alleys generated as many feuds as acts of kindness. Employers, when found, were as like as not mean, cruel, or fickle, and women without a position were exploited or prostituted. Newcomers learned quickly about landlords' and employers' penny-squeezing exactions.

Police and moral missionaries seldom if ever entered poor territories until the sanitary panics of the 1840s prodded their self-interest. Until then comfortable people assessed poverty by counting beggar sailors and soldiers on street corners – men who had been discharged from service 'like dogs', as Henry Hunt put it, 'broken down in body and in spirit' and feeling that they had fought 'for despotism instead of liberty'.[5] Constables were thin on the ground, but prisons, workhouses, spies, and military barracks adequately encased its people, as we've seen, and on eight days a year men and women were choked to death outside Newgate before crowds of polite people as well as low. When poor people looked beyond their small territories they saw how marginal they were to the world's greater doings and pleasures. Not far from the alleys of Fetter Lane where the shoemaker Thomas Preston lodged and plotted, the great lawyers and their clerks passed up and down Chancery Lane and the Strand in black suits and foot-manned coaches, heading for the Old Bailey to pass sentences of death or transportation after the five-minute trials of poor people.

Still, London offered gains for some, perhaps most newcomers. Most of our protagonists had a skill to sell, and on first arrival wouldn't be as vulnerable as, say, single young women or unskilled lads were. The luckier incomers would be greeted by relatives or friends from home, and in years of high wartime demand the more enterprising would find masters, trade clubs, and networks to sustain them. Some taverns became specialised havens for provincials: the Saracen's Head in Snow Hill for

Yorkshiremen, or the Scotch Arms for Scots in Round Court behind St Martin-in-the-Fields.

As most made their way into the central 'town' between Covent Garden and Fetter Lane, or into the warrens above Holborn, or into Seven Dials or Spitalfields, few would have romanticised the rural world they had left behind. London was frightening, but in courtyard and tenement the big world might be comfortingly narrowed and the metropolis's immensity made bearable. London, too, was a city of spectacle and laughter in which wit, irony, and humour insisted on declaring itself. You would see more laughter in its streets than tears, for the fullness of life was vivifying. The 'town' was a place of available sex, drink, and energetic discussion; radical, artistic, and unseemly views flourished there. This would be the first place newcomers lived in in which they might mock and malign the great with impunity.

Neighbourhoods mattered to common people, and intimate business was conducted there. The local patch was where they assessed each other for trust- or credit-worthiness, and marked out this and not that pub as good for carousing or safe for politicking. Here both sexes could mix more freely than in their villages, and acquire spouses for themselves and employment for children, and flit to affordable lodgings round a corner or two when landlords demanded their rent inconveniently. London also offered both the taverns and beer shops in which opinions were debated, and the public spaces in which women as well as men could meet and express them. Radical networks lived near each other for communication and safety, since in a spy-haunted world the more one knew about one's neighbours the better. Although only tiny minorities were purposeful revolutionaries, under provocation and among like-situated neighbours the possibility of radically changing the world was at least thinkable, especially as poor people learned to read, write, and argue, in an era in which France had shown the way.

For these reasons and more, topographies are more than the incidental settings that most historical writers take for granted, and we should take them seriously. 'We live in places, relate to others in them, die in them. Nothing we do is unplaced. How could it be otherwise? How could we fail to recognize this primal fact?'[6] The territories Thistlewood moved through and which our conspirators occupied were the base-lines from which ideas and ambitions sprang and in which they were tested and shared. Live elsewhere, and attitudes changed. John Thelwall, the London Corresponding Society veteran who was tried for treason and acquitted in 1794, later spent ten days hobnobbing with Coleridge and the Wordsworths in Nether Stowey in Somerset. The Quantock hills, he said, were 'a place to make a man forget that there is any necessity for treason'.[7]

The Cato Street conspiracy was hatched not in Cato Street but two and a half miles to the east of that humble mews, in a square half-mile of an older London outside the City, much of it built before the Great Fire of 1666 and untouched by it. Activist by-lines extended out of this quadrilateral, but the key territory was bounded by the Strand and Fleet Street in the south, Stanhope Street in the west (where Thistlewood lived after 1817), Holborn, Gray's Inn Lane, and Brook's Market in the north, and in the east by Fetter Lane as it returned from Holborn back south to Fleet Street (Map 2). In Fetter Lane's courtyards Thomas and Janet Evans lodged, and later Thomas Preston and Dr Watson. In Wych Street between Drury Lane and the Strand stood the White Lion tavern, the favoured meeting place of the ultras in 1819–20. In the White Hart in Brook's Market the conspirators laid their plans and stored their weapons in early 1820. Tidd and Adams lodged minutes away from this tavern in a dire alley called Hole-in-the-Wall Passage, while Brunt lodged in Fox Court, a block or so to the west.

Outside the quadrilateral lay Wedderburn's 'chapel' in Soho, public meeting spaces in Spa Fields, Smithfield, and Finsbury Market, and safe public houses whose landlords could be trusted: the Cock in Grafton Street, Soho,[8] the Spotted Dog in Clement's Lane, the Black Dog in Gray's Inn Lane, the Rose in Great Wild Street, the Mulberry Tree in Long Alley in Moorfields, and the Scotch Arms behind St Martin's-in-the-Fields. As one of Edwards's spy reports reads, 'In the evening there was a meeting at the Rose – about 20 present. From there we went to the Scotch Arms, where the party increased to about 30.... The committee to meet at the Rose at 7 tomorrow (Tuesday), and to go from there to the

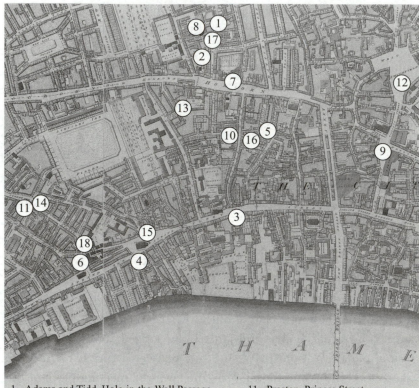

1. Adams and Tidd, Hole-in-the-Wall Passage
2. Brunt, 4 Fox Court, Grays Inn Lane
3. Carlile (1819–), 55 Fleet Street
4. Crown and Anchor, Strand and Arundel Street
5. Thomas and Janet Evans (1796–8),
   14 Plough Court
6. Thomas and Janet Evans, Newcastle Street
7. Furnival's Inn
8. Monument and Cooper, Garden Court
9. Newgate Prison and Old Bailey
10. Preston, Greystoke Court,
    Fetter Lane
11. Preston, Princes Street
12. Smithfield market
13. Thistlewood (1816),
    Southampton Buildings
14. Thistlewood (1817–20) 41
    Stanhope Street,
15. Watson (1817–20),
    Three Kings Court, Clements Lane
16. Watson (1816), 1 Dean Street,
    Fetter Lane
17. White Lamb, Brooks Market
18. White Lion, Wych Street

Map 2. The Strand, Fetter Lane, Holborn, Drury Lane (from Horwood's *PLAN of the Cities of LONDON and WESTMINSTER, etc.* 1799) (MOTCO Image Database)

White Hart White Harts Yard Brooks Market, where there is to be a general meeting.'[9]

Men walked to meetings from two or three miles away. Cook lived in Hackney, Palin in the Borough south of the Thames. Several lived in

Marylebone, not far from the Thistlewoods' first lodgings, and their local knowledge explains the choice of the Cato Street stable as assembly point for the final assault. Davidson lived with wife and children in a rickety tenement at 12 Elliot's Row at the back of Lord's (old) cricket ground on the New (now Marylebone) Road. It was a 'hovel', the Bow Street magistrate Birnie wrote after his officers had searched it.[10] A substantial black community of freed or escaped slaves and naval veterans had lived in the neighbourhood for decades. The shoemaker-turned-tailor-turned-milkman Wilson lived a couple of doors from Davidson, John Shaw Strange lived near Lisson Green, and Robert George lived with his wife, a mantua maker, in Chapel Street north of Southampton Row. The Cato Street stable was five minutes' walk from each of these. Davidson's radical reading club met next to Cato Street in Queen Street; and Frith, the cowman who lived in the stable before he sublet it to the conspirators was a member of the club as well.

In November 1816 the Thistlewoods, more affluent than these, moved from Edgware Road (or subsequent lodgings, unknown) into the operative quadrilateral, in the genteel mid-seventeenth-century Southampton Buildings behind the south-eastern corner of Chancery Lane and Holborn. It was full of solicitors and law stationers and literary men. Charles and Mary Lamb lodged there in 1800 and 1809–11; Coleridge stayed with them in 1811; and Hazlitt lived there that year as well, and again in 1820–1 when he became helplessly besotted by his landlord's fickle daughter. The Thistlewoods lodged in 'two pair of back rooms' (two rooms up two pairs of stairs?) for two or three weeks; after the Spa Fields riots of 2 December they disappeared without notice and went into hiding.[11] They might have moved here expressly to impress Henry Hunt, since this was where Thistlewood and Watson first met Hunt and persuaded him to speak at the Spa Fields meetings in 1816–17. Hunt was struck by the fact that a female servant showed him into 'a very neat and well-furnished dining-room', where he found Thistlewood wearing 'a handsome dressing-gown and morocco slippers'.[12]

A year later, after Thistlewood's arrest and failed arraignment for treason, with funds fast diminishing, the family moved to two rooms on the second floor of 41 Stanhope Street (between Drury Lane and Clare Market, the latter now obliterated by the Aldwych development). Built in the mid-seventeenth century, it had been 'a pretty broad, well built and inhabited street', and was still reasonably respectable.[13] Thistlewood couldn't hold meetings there because 'there is an officer that lives so opposite to me that if that officer should perceive men coming backwards and forwards to my place it will be a means of giving some suspicion [that] there is something in it'.[14] But Stanhope Street was minutes' walk away from his associates' lodgings and the White Lion meeting room in Wych Street. Despite its spread, London was built on a human scale suited to pedestrians. Even today it takes no more than six minutes to walk from Fleet Street up Fetter Lane to Brook's Market, despite the traffic.

THE KNOTTY PROBLEM OF ALLEYS

The Great Fire that raged across the City in September 1666 determined London's habitats for the next two centuries. In four terrifying days it destroyed some 80 per cent of properties within the square mile of the City walls, and a third of the City properties outside them – altogether some 13,200 houses, 87 churches, and most public buildings. A half of the walled City burned down within two days. On the third day wind drove the flames westwards to engulf St Paul's cathedral, the City's western gates at Newgate and Ludgate, and across the Fleet Ditch. They then swallowed the City's extra-mural extensions northwards across Shoe Lane up to Holborn, and down Fleet Street and across the Temple, stopping only at Fetter Lane, its western terminus. The ruins stretched for nearly two miles from Tower Hill in the east to Fetter Lane, and from the Thames in the south to Pie Corner below Smithfield in the north and the Fleet bridge at the beginning of Holborn. Only the north-eastern corner of the walled City escaped obliteration (Fig. 7.1).[15]

The speed of reconstruction was astonishing. The first stone of Wren's new St Paul's was laid in 1675, and his fifty-one rebuilt parish churches were completed soon after. Houses went up more quickly. The Building Act insisted that they be rebuilt in brick and roofed in tiles. No upper storeys were to project over the street, and sizes were standardised in the 'Rules and directions to be observed in the rebuilding of the City of London'. The smallest 'sort', with two storeys and a garret, were to be

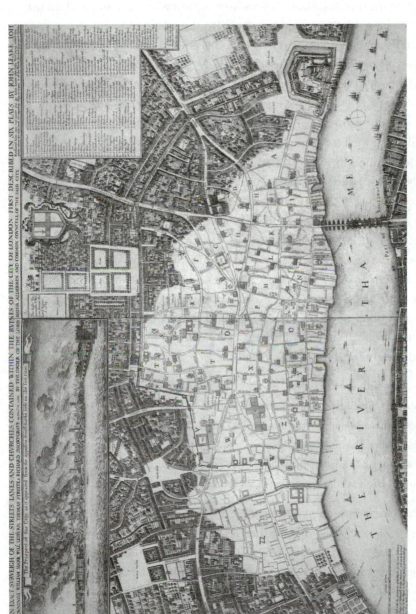

7.1. Wenceslaus Hollar, *Map showing the Extent of the Damage caused by the Great Fire of London, 1666* (1666) (Universal History Archive/Universal Images Group via Getty Images)

built on by-streets and lanes; the second sort, of three storeys and a garret, were for streets and lanes 'of note'; the third sort, with four storeys and a garret, were for 'high and principal streets'; and the fourth sort were to be mansions for people 'of extraordinary quality'. By 1672 nearly all was rebuilt in these styles. Many houses were meant to last no longer than the ground lease of fifty or sixty years. By the early nineteenth century hundreds were in decay and had become tenements and lodgings.[16]

The old street patterns changed little. Vested interests, absent owners, and the rush to recovery checked the geometrical replanning of the City that Wren, Evelyn, and others advocated. Some streets and yards were widened, but most of the ancient maze of 'bye-lanes, rooks and alleys, huddled up one on the neck of another' survived or was replicated, often still determined by ancient field patterns. Half a century later the architect Nicholas Hawksmoor lamented the survival of 'a chaos of winding crooked passages (scarce practicable) lakes of mud and rils of stinking mire running through them'. A half century on, Henry Fielding was writing of London as 'a vast wood or forest, in which a thief may harbour with as great security as wild beasts do in the deserts of Africa or Arabia'. By 1820 improvements were beginning to make the intricacies of court-yards and alleys look antique and undesirable, but leaseholders continued to open passages to areas behind houses which they subdivided and built round. In 1821 Thomas de Quincey's opium-befuddled rambles through London would bring him

> upon such knotty problems of alleys, such enigmatical entries, and such sphynx's riddles of streets without thoroughfares, as must, I conceive, baffle the audacity of porters, and confound the intellects of hackney-coachmen. I could almost have believed, at times, that I must be the first discoverer of some of these *terrae incognitae*, and doubted, whether they had yet been laid down in the modern charts of London.[17]

The Great Fire displaced some 65,000 Londoners. Thousands took refuge in Moorfields outside the northern City wall, and beyond that 'severall miles in circle', as Evelyn the diarist put it: 'some under tents, others under miserab[l]e hutts and hovells, without a rag, or any necessary utinsils, bed or board . . . [in] extreamest misery & poverty'. As winter deepened many refugees crammed themselves into the courtyards and alleys outside the walled City that the fire hadn't touched – in Aldgate, Bishopsgate, and the artisan alleys of Smithfield and Clerkenwell. A few crowded south into the unburned riverside alleys across the Thames.

Most moved into and trebled the densities of the crooked dwellings and courtyards above Holborn – in Field Lane, Saffron Hill, and Turnmill Street – and in Drury Lane and off the Strand. Strype's *Survey* in 1720 described these quarters as 'ordinary and nastily kept'. The rackety timber-framed dwellings up Saffron Hill and Field Lane and along Chick Lane to Smithfield – 'none of the best', Strype wrote – became the habitats of the destitute and dispossessed, their adjacency to the sewage and animal carcases in the Fleet Ditch making them stink more than London generally stank. Although these streets accommodated more skilled labour and tradesmen than *Oliver Twist* later suggested, they remained disease-ridden and neglected for two hundred years yet.

Two-thirds of London's seventeenth-century spread was untouched by the fire. In the central 'town' great swathes of medieval and Tudor houses survived into the nineteenth century – with timber frames and lathe-and-plaster in-fill, or with whitewashed or tarred plank cladding, gabled roofs, and overhanging storeys. By 1800 the grimmest shacks and shanties of the pre-fire city were gone, but the ancient houses north of Temple Bar up Clement's Lane, Ship Yard, Shire Lane, and Little Shire Lane survived for decades more. From the fire's terminus at Fetter Lane they also stretched westwards along the Strand to Charing Cross, north up St Martin's Lane, Drury Lane, and Chancery Lane, along Holborn and up Gray's Inn Lane, and south from Charing Cross to Thieving Lane and Tothill Street behind Westminster Abbey.[18] Many were of such extraordinary construction and character – gnarled, carved, tottering, and unstable, their walls sometimes propped against their neighbours' walls with poles and planks – that they seemed living things. In our imaginations we must coat all of them in soot, for London was a blackened city in which the air itself was soot-laden and winter fogs were impenetrable. These battered environs were where most of this book's protagonists lodged, some in bearable comfort alongside tradesmen and shopkeepers, others alongside people living in bleak resignation or in thwarted hope of improvements to come.

By the 1840s urban reformers were to find it impossible *not* to regard the oldest and poorest places as 'receptacles of filth in every corner, the bane of old London, and a sort of nestling-place for the plague and fevers', or as 'a huge overcrowded den, where blasphemy, rags, gin hollow-eyed poverty, and stinted industry, were all fearfully huddled together' – etc., etc.[19] Yet that was how parts of London had always been. The parish of St Clement Danes was in fact fairly prosperous by London standards thanks to the richer streets leading down to the Thames. But now and then the chimneys of ancient edifices 'fell down', as the kindly phrase went, and fires were commonplace. In 1772 over thirty lathe-and-plaster houses burned down at the end of Wych Street; a new Newcastle Street was laid out between the Strand and Stanhope Street to fill the gap this opened.[20]

While merchants rebuilt their bases in the old City, late seventeenth-century aristocrats and gentry and their dependants had begun a steady migration westwards into new and fashionable streets carved into these pre-fire territories around Covent Garden's Piazza, Lincoln's Inn Fields, and Leicester Fields, and between the Thames and the Strand. Artistic and brothel-keeping, brothel-using, and gambling people followed them. By the 1720s affluent new streets and squares were also being laid out north and south of Oxford Street and westwards to Grosvenor Square, where the Cato Street men planned to slaughter the cabinet. In due course Covent Garden's polite classes moved west to fill them. Those who dallied were finally propelled by the Gordon riots of 1780. New terraces and squares multiplied off Pall Mall and Piccadilly, and by 1820 estates were being planned to fill the fields of Paddington east of the Edgware Road and north of the New (later Marylebone) Road.[21]

As the finer people moved westward, thousands of immigrants doubled or trebled up in the increasingly neglected and subdivided houses of the central town, as well as in the substantial stock of antique wooden houses and gabled tenements which the fire hadn't touched. In some courtyards and alleys population densities were lethal. Pauper burials in the courts around Covent Garden and between Clare Market and St Clement Danes had made them 'one of the great killing grounds of Europe': death rates were higher there than they were in the northern cotton towns.[22] 'Corridors of misery' ran northwards into St Giles's, Holborn and Smithfield, and the expanding East End as well. Covent Garden, St Giles's, Holborn, and Smithfield became sleazy, and antique locations like Field Lane and Chick Lane came to be regarded as 'dangerous'. Dickens made Fagin, the wicked receiver of stolen goods, live there.

FETTER LANE AND CHANCERY LANE

Fetter Lane marked the boundary at which the Great Fire ceased its westwards rampage. Its southern half on both sides had been destroyed, so the lost houses were replaced with brick-built terraced houses of the second or third sorts, many with ground-floor shops built in. The northern stretch of the street escaped entirely and retained its crooked half-timbered constructions. The whole had been heterodox territory for nearly two centuries (Map 2). The anabaptist Praise-God Barebone had been a Fetter Lane leather seller, and the conventicler Richard Baxter had preached in the Moravian chapel in 1672. From the same pulpit Wesley and Whitefield had done their bit against the devil in 1739. Their preaching elicited cries of such exceeding joy as the congregation fell and rolled on the floor, and the preachers were so surprised by the sight, that the Fetter Lane community has a claim to have launched the Wesleyan revival. A baptist congregation ruled Greystoke Place and Elim Court next to it.[23] If the street's radical credentials were muted by Thomas Hobbes's lodging there when he endorsed sovereign power in his *Leviathan* in 1651, Tom Paine made up for it by lodging in Harding Street off Fetter Lane as he was finishing his *Rights of Man* in 1791, and later in 10 Dean Street.[24]

One centre of operation for Thistlewood and his men were the two impoverished rooms in number 9 Greystoke Place, off Fetter Lane, where Preston lived with his daughters after his wife had absconded. Their back room was lit by a dirty skylight on the landing, and the daughters, 'pinched with hunger and cold', as he wrote, had wretched beds on the floor 'with scarcely any covering, and hardly a chair in the room'.[25] The alleyway's disordered antiquity is apparent in a watercolour painted sixty

7.2. John Emslie, *Greystoke Place, Fetter Lane* (*c.* 1880) (© London Metropolitan Archives)

years later (Fig. 7.2). It was disreputable enough for a gate at its furthest end to be locked every night to safeguard the lawyers of Cursitor Street and Chancery Lane. When Henry Hunt called on Preston on his way to his first meeting with Thistlewood in November 1816, he found 'no one there but two or three dirtily dressed, miserable, poor children, who told me that I should find their father at some house in Southampton-buildings, Chancery-lane. Thither I repaired, meditating as I went along on the wretched emblem of the distresses of the times, which I had just witnessed in the family of Mr. Thomas Preston.'[26] Preston's den continued to be a meeting place for several years. 'I went to Preston's, where I met Thistlewood who desired me to come to his lodgings ... to make some pistol-balls with him, wch I did' – thus Edwards the spy in December 1819.

Greystoke Place stood opposite the openings to Dean Street and Plough Court. These had their own radical histories. Thomas and Janet Evans had lodged in 14 Plough Court in 1796–8 while making a living by watercolouring prints for the printshops. He was the LCS's last secretary, and its committee met in their house. Dr James Watson the apothecary also gravitated towards this patch. In November 1816 he and his son flitted from the single room they shared in Hyde Street in Bloomsbury (now erased by New Oxford Street) and moved into a room at 1 Dean Street. Dean Street had post-fire houses of the 'second sort', and it looked stylish; but although the houses were three floors and a garret high, they had only a single room on each floor.[27] In this cramped space father and son shared a bed while the Spa Fields insurrection was being plotted.

Not long after, Watson moved to Three Kings Court, at the foot of Clements Lane off Fleet Street. Preston and his daughters likewise moved to 'one room and a small bedroom adjoining' in Princes Street just north of Wych Street, its disadvantage being that from the other rooms on the same floor one could hear everything they said.[28] These movements meant that by 1818–20 London's insurrectionary leaders lived a street or two away from each other, as well as from the Rose tavern in Great Wild Street and the White Lion in Wych Street nearby. The Thistlewoods in Stanhope Street and Preston in Princes Street could have waved to each other from their windows if a couple of houses hadn't stood in the way.

What sense of the world's fairness or otherwise would our men have assimilated from Fetter Lane? Nothing untoward, it has to be said. The region had its equalising features and didn't teach the lessons one might learn in the slums of Seven Dials. Strype in 1720 had found Fetter Lane and the surrounding streets – Holborn, Chancery Lane, Shoe Lane, Fleet Street – 'well inhabited'. A century later there prevailed the usual cheek-by-jowl intermingling of middle-class houses and plebeian taverns, shops, and workshops. The Fetter Lane trades listed in *Johnstone's London Commercial Guide and Street Directory* (1818) included respectable solicitors and agents, oil and colour men, printers, stationers, goldsmiths, gold-beaters, tobacconists, tallow chandlers, grocers, and tea-dealers, as well as one each of a musical instrument maker, furrier, cabinet-maker, pewter-maker, marble-paper maker, glass-warehouseman, cutler, tinplate-maker, and wine and brandy merchant.

The neighbourhood's social tone was raised (also deadened) by the legal precincts within it. Lincoln's Inn, Gray's Inn, and the Temple were on Fetter Lane's peripheries, the old Chancery Inns – Clifford's, Barnard's, and Staple – were inside them, while Sergeant's Inn was across the way in Fleet Street and Furnival's Inn was across the way in Holborn. (Since medieval times the nine Chancery Inns had been schools that prepared young lawyers for the Inns of Court, but by the late eighteenth century they had mainly become social clubs for attorneys and solicitors and apartments for bachelors, clerks, and tradesmen.) Chancery Lane, the Rolls Buildings, and interstices like Cursitor's Alley and Duck Court, 'well built', Strype wrote, were full of lawyers, though not necessarily great ones. Dickens's Mr Tulkinghorn lived in a once fine house that was divided into chambers in whose 'shrunken fragments of its greatness, lawyers lie like maggots in nuts'.

The presence of the Law in these streets stunted the artistic energies that enlivened nearby Covent Garden, but liberal-minded literary men did consort here. In the Southampton Coffee House Hazlitt spent evenings with William Hone and George Cruikshank – Cruikshank dipping his finger in beer to sketch suggestions for this or that satire on the table. Coleridge, Scott, Southey, Lamb, and Leigh Hunt frequented the Clifford's Inn chambers of the reformer George Dyer. Coleridge and Southey recanted their earlier radical enthusiasms, but others kept their critical reflexes in good order. Hazlitt was only a marginal commentator on the Cato Street drama, but he must have had the conspirators' entrapment in mind when he declared in 1821 that he 'could endure the brutality (as it is termed) of mobs better than the inhumanity of courts. The violence of the one rages like a fire; the insidious policy of the other strikes like a pestilence, and is more fatal and inevitable. The slow poison of despotism is worse than the convulsive struggles of anarchy.' Men like these had a fully developed awareness that British justice couldn't really count among the crown's brighter jewels in this era. They took its dimness as read.[29]

For despite its mild respectability, Fetter Lane did have at least this lesson to teach them. Plebeian byways and alleys, 'meanly inhabited' or 'of mean repute' (Strype), wove tortuous paths between every main street, so there was roughness in the district. And it generated historic criminal sensations. Sarah Malcolm, the murderess painted in her condemned cell by Hogarth, was hanged in Fleet Street opposite Fetter Lane's entrance in 1733, while in Flewer de Lis Court (as the map-maker Horwood spelt it), which paralleled Fetter Lane's southern end, Eliza Brownrigg flogged her servant girl to death in 1767 and was then hanged at Tyburn and dissected. Flower de Lyz Alley (another map spelling) accommodated a mysterious Mousetrap House, a lockup which has left no record other than Strype's description of it as a 'receptacle for leud persons'.[30] Fetter Lane featured in over 500 prosecutions at the Old Bailey between 1700 and 1820 – for burglaries and larcenies mainly.

The biggest criminal sensation locally exposed the dubious quality of Old Bailey trials not long before Cato Street. In July 1815 a twenty-year-old servant girl named Eliza Fenning was hanged for attempting to murder her Fetter Lane law-stationer employer and his family by lacing their dumplings with arsenic. The court ignored the fact that she had eaten the dumplings too, and sentenced her on narrow circumstantial evidence. The travesty of a trial, along with her protestations of innocence and the helpful fact that her body was 'of the most perfect symmetry', together with the evil reputa-tion of her judge, Sir John Sylvester (a reprobate who was reputed to demand sexual favours from women who begged him for mercy or justice), unleashed an unsuccessful but noisy campaign for mercy which marked a significant stage in the movement against the death penalty. William Hone revealed himself as that era's most powerful radical publicist when he published his *Elaborate Investigation into the Mysterious Case of Elizabeth Fenning*. It delivered a forensic broadside against the law's casual injustices, warning readers 'to put little confidence in the reasonings of fallible magis-trates, who have grown old in the ministration of death'. The law was only too easily 'converted into an engine of oppression, and an instrument of vengeance' and should be perpetually scrutinised lest it be left 'in the hands of the crafty and vindictive'. Fenning's fate was determined, Hone added, by the fact that her employers' respectability ('by which is understood their opulence') was 'pitted against the humble poverty of their servant maid'. A good part of London agreed. After her death and spectacularly well attended funeral, a thousand or so protesting people caused a near riot outside the Turners' house. For days afterwards it had to be guarded by Bow

Street officers.[31] Even though he only briefly lived round the corner from the crime (its victims lived at 68 Chancery Lane), Thistlewood as well as Preston would have heard every detail of the case.

WYCH STREET

In September 1819 relations between the more moderate radicals and the ultras fractured over how best to celebrate Hunt's return to London after his heroism on the Peterloo platform (see Chapter 11). The fracture was also inscribed topographically. The moderates met in the grand edifice of the Crown and Anchor behind the Strand in Arundel Street. Rebuilt in 1790 with a dignified entrance on the Strand (Fig. 7.3) and an ambitious banqueting hall behind that could hold two and a half thousand people, it

7.3. Anon. (J. Findlay?), *The Strand Entrance to the Crown and Anchor 1851* (Guildhall Library & Art Gallery/Heritage Images/Getty Images)

became the informal headquarters of Westminster's whig-radicals. Anniversaries of the fall of the Bastille were celebrated there, as was Charles James Fox's birthday in 1798. It was too grand for common conspiring; but from it you could walk across the Strand to the antique White Lion tavern in a narrow side alley on the northern side of Wych Street. This, by contrast, was a galleried pre-fire town house with creaking timbers and uneven floors, and until the magistrates withdrew its licence in October 1819 it was the low radicals' headquarters and Watson's and Thistlewood's venue of first resort. The building remained disreputable long after their deaths. In the late 1840s a female corpse was found on the pavement below three of its ancient windows overlooking the New Inn. The Inn's governors declared that the house was tenanted 'by a very doubtful class of people', and bricked up the windows.[32]

Watercolour drawings made by John Crowther just before the building's demolition in 1881 tell us what the White Lion looked like.[33] They reveal a galleried building, once a modestly fine one, which one approached down a passage squeezed between the walls of the New Inn and a neighbouring shop in Wych Street (Fig. 7.4). On the ground floor there was a parlour of

7.4. John Crowther, *View of White Lion Court, Wych Street* (1880) (© London Metropolitan Archives)

some kind; but you entered the house proper up a wide staircase with barley-twist balusters that led onto an open gallery overlooking the entry passage (Fig. 7.5). Above this the second and third floors were weather-proofed by slates and topped by an attic. The end of the gallery gave access to a large and once fine room, panelled to the ceiling and flanked by columns with carved entablatures, with landscapes and musical instruments painted in *grisaille* over the fireplace. On the second floor was another large room, and above that another, its floor suspended from the roof by massive oak pillars.[34]

By July 1819 Thistlewood's committee met here almost daily, and were often joined in the upper room by supporters notified by word of mouth: 'no stranger admitted'.[35] Wilkinson described the scene in his *Authentic History* (probably citing a visitor from the Crown and Anchor):

> [The parlour] was the room in which the most private transactions were carried on; Mr. Thistlewood or Dr. Watson always came out into the passage to speak to any person who called there on business. In a very large room up stairs ... upwards of a hundred ill-looking persons have assembled of an evening; ... it had ranges of forms all round and across the room, and had hardly ever more than two or three candles to illuminate it. Here their processions, etc., were arranged; their flags, etc., kept; whilst the more private business was carried on below in the parlour.[36]

By the time of their demolition to make way for the modern Aldwych in 1901–2, Wych Street and the adjacent Holywell Street survived as London's only near-complete streets of pre-fire houses. Figure 7.6 shows Wych Street's southern side as photographed in 1867. Both streets offered a comfortable territory for would-be insurrectionists. They were notorious for street robberies, prostitution, and dirty books, and Wych Street leavened its sleaziness with a population of Burdett-voting tradesmen. The 1818 election poll-book lists a couple each of plumbers, victuallers, box-makers, law-stationers, and bakers, along with a sheriff's officer, painter, coal merchant, musical

7.5 John Crowther, *Staircase in the White Lion, Wych Street* (1880) (Guildhall Library & Art Gallery/Heritage Images/Getty Images)

instrument maker, carpenter, bootmaker, eating-house keeper, broker, watchmaker, plasterer, hardware merchant, coffee house keeper, coal dealer, wire worker, and fishmonger. Radical views were common among them. From 49 Wych Street the radical deist Robert Shorter edited or published *The Theological Comet; or, Free-Thinking Englishman.* Further up the street a ballad seller named Price subverted Edmund Burke's famous indictment of the French revolution ('learning will be ... trodden down under the hoofs of a swinish multitude') by declaring himself 'Printer and Publisher to the Swinish Multitude, (late of His Majesty's Gaol of Newgate, for a libel on the duke of York) at his Pig-Sty, 19, Wych Street, Strand' – here picking up on Thomas Spence's equally parodic title for his weekly *One Penny Worth of Pig's Meat: Lessons for the Swinish Multitude* (1793–5). Price was imprisoned in 1810 for publishing a scurrilous ballad on the duke of York's affair with the courtesan Mary Anne Clark.[37]

7.6. A. J. Bool, *Wych Street* (1867) (© The Trustees of the British Museum)

Similarly inclined and more active in this story was a wire worker named William West, at number 54. His 'manufactory' advertised 'invisible pleasure-ground fences' for the nobility and gentry 'to prevent hares and rabbits from exotics [plants], should the situation require it'. Despite his presumed clientele, he was one of radical London's indispensable facilitators. He organised the support committee for Watson, Thistlewood, and Preston during and after their treason arraignment in 1817, accommodated Henry Hunt after the Smithfield meeting in July 1819, travelled with James Harmer to the Lancaster Assizes in September to advise Hunt after Peterloo, and sheltered Susan Thistlewood during and after the 1820 trials. In one shop window West displayed his iron pallisades, and in the other a stock of 'radical breakfast powder' – Hunt's invention, an unappetising rye-based substitute for coffee that advertised the great orator's abstinence from excisable goods. Thistlewood wrote to his son that he could always rely on West.[38]

Wych Street was flanked on either side by two Inns of Chancery: to the north the tidily gardened and flourishingly respectable New Inn, full of solicitors, and to the south the decaying Lyon's Inn, which provided shabby-genteel lodgings to 'all kinds of men about town – good and bad, clever and rascally, gamblers and swindlers', including at least one famous murder victim in 1823:

> They cut his throat from ear to ear,
> His head they battered in.
> His name was Mr William Weare,
> He lived in Lyons Inn.

Lowering the tone further were the Olympic Theatre at the western end of Wych Street, on the Drury Lane-Newcastle Street junction, and the Adelphi not far away in the Strand. Serving boisterous plebeian audiences, these minor theatres' burlettas, farces, and melodramas could determine their audiences' self-fashioning.[39] Thistlewood's and Davidson's melodramatic tropes and postures were probably learned here. Not the least of the Olympic's consequences was a 'downright neighbourhood' for drinking and whoring, as the poet Thomas Hood put it. Opposite Lyon's Inn door in Holywell Street was 'a small passage into the Strand, called Pissing Alley, perhaps in contempt'.[40] The alley was well used, because common life went on noisily nearby and encouraged urinary incontinence. At the street's eastern end two women took up Saturday night pitches to 'chaunt' the lewd ballad 'Sandman Joe', concluding it 'amidst roars of laughter' by bucking their pelvises and shamming orgasm:

> He star'd awhile, then turn'd his quid
> Why, blast you, Sall, I loves you!
> And for to prove what I have said,
> This night I'll soundly fuck you.
> Why then says Sall, my hearts at rest
> If what you say you'll stand to;
> His brawny hands, her bubbies prest
> And roaring cried, white sand O,
> Why here's your lilly lilly lilly lilly white sand O.[41]

FOX COURT

After the White Lion lost its licence, the White Hart in Brook's Market north off Holborn became the conspirators' main venue. Many decades later sewers had cleansed the area, and the pub was thought charming. Built in seventeenth-century clapboard and sporting a cow's portrait on its signboard, it had 'a quiet countrified air'.[42] But there was nothing charming about it in 1820: the meat market outside was squalid. The conspirators rented a 'hut' in its yard for a half-crown a week. Access was through an adjoining hut with an old couple in it who could hear conversations through the wall. Still, the White Hart had hosted United Irish meetings in 1798, and the current landlord, Hobbs, could be relied on to let the conspirators know if officers arrived to ask awkward questions. When officers did just that in mid-December, Hobbs apologetically asked the group to adjourn to the Black Dog in Gray's Inn Lane.[43] In early January 1820 they returned to the hut until constables again called. So on 24 January, the group moved to a 'two pair of stairs [second floor] back room' in 4 Fox Court, behind Thomas Brunt's two front rooms on the second floor of a tenement. He and his wife, son, and apprentice made shoes in one room and slept and ate in a smaller one.

Hired for three shillings a week in the name of Ings the butcher, the meeting room had no furniture. 'They used to borrow Brunt's chairs to sit on', and a table sometimes to make weapons on. On the day of the Cato Street assembling Mrs Brunt had to reclaim the table for her teatime. The place was used for meetings, bomb-making, and storing weapons, while Ings continued to lodge penuriously a mile and a half away in Spitalfields, reassuring the Fox Court landlady that 'he might bring in his goods in a week or better, but he never did'. The room had one advantage:

Is there a door that people may go up without going through your shop? – Yes, there is a private door in a passage leading to the staircase. There is also a back door which lodgers come in at and go up stairs without coming to the shop.[44]

Fox Court was a couple of minutes' walk west of the White Hart. Immediately to its north the bootmakers Richard Tidd and Robert Adams lodged next door to each other in Hole-in-the-Wall Passage, a virtual tunnel that connected Dorrington Street and Baldwin's Gardens. Tidd shared one or two rooms here with his wife, his daughter, and her two 'orphan' children (their father had died or disappeared). Adams's and Tidd's windows 'nearly join each other', Tidd told the court. Seriously poor, the men counted among Thistlewood's leading henchmen. John Monument and Charles Cooper, two more shoemaker conspirators, were neighbours in the misnamed Garden Court off Baldwin's Gardens.[45] Through chance proximities of this sort, radical networks were constructed.

The Hole-in-the-Wall dated from the seventeenth century. It was too humble to be described by Strype or to be drawn into Rocque's great London map of 1747, but it was included in the Horwood-Faden maps of 1799–1819 as a wavering scratch of an alley, narrow and crooked, barely wide enough for a fat pedestrian or two thin pedestrians side by side. The map shows it flanked by three minuscule dwellings on the western side and five on the eastern side, crammed against the backside of the George tavern-yard off Leather Lane. An Old Bailey trial in 1789 described one dwelling as 'a one pair of stairs' – i.e., it had a ground and a first floor. In another trial in 1794 a watchman described a thief running 'up a pair of stairs, called the Hole in the Wall Passage, I ran up these pair of stairs, and catched him at top in the Passage, it is a pair of stairs belonging to a house, it has no under floor nor street door at all, I asked him what he did there? he said, it was his lodging.'[46] In other words, the tiny dwellings had external staircases and entries along open galleries in a pre-Fire mode.

Neither the maps nor the 1841 census dignified alleys like this with house numbers; but in that census year the enumerator counted forty-five people in eleven one- or two-room lodgings there. Twelve were children and six or so lived with families who were lodgers themselves. Only two were born in Ireland; the rest were London-born. The largest male occupation was shoemaking, and most of the occupied women called themselves charwomen or needlewomen. Naming an occupation for the census man didn't mean that you had one. Ten adults gave no occupation at all.

The environs of Fox Court and Brook's Market once had 'some relish of ancient greatness' about them (as Dickens wrote of Bleeding Heart Yard nearby). The terraced houses of Brook, Greville, Dorrington, and Charles Streets and Hatton Garden had been laid out in the late seventeenth century over the Elizabethan courtier Fulke Greville's house and gardens; in 1720 Strype found them full of 'good new brick buildings' and 'well inhabited'. Brook's Market in the centre had been 'a good large and convenient place, with shambles, a market house, and stalls, &c. for that use' – not yet the rat-infested market it became. Turn left from Brook Street into Holborn and you passed the new neoclassical facade of Furnival's Inn. It was rebuilt in 1818–20 after the antique Chancery Inn was sold when Lincoln's Inn refused to renew its lease. Demolished in 1879, it was replaced by the great pink brick pile of the Prudential Assurance Company, its facade still preserved.

At a critical period in his younger life Dickens lodged precisely in these environs. In his mid-teens he worked and lived as a solicitor's clerk in Gray's Inn before moving to Furnival's Inn in his mid-twenties (in 1834–7). There he married and wrote *Sketches by Boz*, *The Pickwick Papers*, and the first two chapters of *Oliver Twist*, and agreed to write what became *Barnaby Rudge*. Yet his writings only twice mentioned the Cato Street conspirators and their Brook Street haunts, and that incidentally.[47] Not once did he look westwards from Furnival's Inn and so to Fox Court. His gaze was directed only southwards to the Gordon rioters' burning of Langdale's Holborn distillery opposite Furnival's Inn (*Barnaby Rudge*), and eastwards to Field Lane, Saffron Hill, and Newgate (*Oliver Twist*). This was odd because in his early novels he was drawn to insurrectionary moments, but his neglect of the conspiracy was typical of subsequent generations' amnesia about it.

Brook Street's social tone was declining even in the 1760s. When young Thomas Chatterton lodged there in the attic of a bawdy-house, his landlady allowed him to have sex with her, and put up his rent after he had had it. In 1770 Chatterton swallowed the arsenic that killed him and turned him into a romantic hero. By Dickens' time, if he is to be believed, 'of colour, brightness, gaiety, there is no trace [in Brook Street]; and even if the sunshine, on some favoured summer sunset, does stream down upon the eastern side of the street, it soon fades away, as if unwilling to make the dullness and dinginess of the locality seem greater upon its departure'. Dickens's rhetorical flourishes on the subject of slums are unreliable, but the decline was obvious, and it extended to Fox Court.

Developed in the late seventeenth century to provide a passage between Brook Street and Gray's Inn Lane, Strype had found it 'well inhabited' and 'large and open, with very good brick buildings'. In 1697/8 the countess of Macclesfield secretly gave birth there to the illegitimate Richard Savage, later to be Samuel Johnson's low-living poet friend. Calling herself Madam Smith, she wore a mask during her delivery to protect her anonymity, but the aggrieved earl heard about it and divorced her anyway. By the regency, it was no place for aristocrats. Dickens later described it as a 'miserable alley' and Brook Street as 'dingy, quiet, sordid' and 'dirty', the neighbourhood's tone lowered by 'the low-brewed costermongers of Brook's Market, the unkempt roughs of Fox Court, the wild Irishmen of Greville Street, and the mocking [Italian] organ-boys of Leather Lane'.

The overcrowding and filth in the saddest of the courts east of Gray's Inn Lane would worsen after the influx of Irish refugees from the famine in the 1840s. The tenements were chronically damp because they were undrained and because they used sea-sand for the cement: '[I]t always becomes damp; it "gives", as it is called,' said the Health of Towns Committee in 1840. The committee targeted Spread Eagle Court (by then renamed Tyndall's Buildings) for its three-storey, eight-rooms-per-house and two-families-per-bed habitations, for its typhoid and its cellar cesspools, and for its predominantly Irish tenants who shared rooms with their pigs.

By the 1850s Fox Court was also an alleged hotbed of disease and vice: Henry Mayhew described it as full of low lodging houses, one of which was a 'thieves' kitchen', alarmingly illustrated. However, its buildings were older and more solidly built, so it might have been more habitable. The 1841 census has its 235 inhabitants living in eighteen staircases, each accommodating up to some twenty people on three floors; but among its inevitable run of shoemakers, bricklayers, and laundrywomen it included a smattering of skilled printers and clerks, and hardly any Irish.[48] Neither the Health of Towns Committee nor Chadwick's sanitary report two years later thought Fox Court worth mentioning. As for today, nobody now remembers that this was where the Cato Street conspiracy was planned. 'Fox Court' is now a block of brick, glass, and steel, and nobody lives there.

PART THREE

THISTLEWOOD: HIS STORY

CHAPTER 8

A Terrorist in the Making: 1774–1816

WHAT MANNER OF MAN?

In an age when most felons were brought to the scaffold weeping, urinating, or defecating in terror, four of the Cato Street men had spirit enough on the scaffold to show their contempt for the aristocracy that was set to kill them. The exception was William Davidson, the Jamaican-born mixed-race methodist carpenter. In his last speech to the court he was in despair and panic. He had been innocently enticed into the Cato Street stable, he lied in desperation; he knew nothing of the plot and had no intention of hurting anyone. On the scaffold he prayed, wept, and acknowledged his infamy. Yet he had shown a bolder face earlier. 'Scots, wha' hae' wi' Wallace bled,' he sang exultantly as he ran from the police on the night of the Cato Street arrests: having lived in Scotland, he knew his Robert Burns. The policeman who caught him restrained him from singing the rest:

> Lay the proud usurpers low!
> Tyrants fall in every foe!
> Liberty's in every blow! –
> Let us do or dee!¹

It was Arthur Thistlewood's defiance that was most remarkable. On his last day in court, Friday, 28 April 1820, he was called to speak in his own defence immediately before his death sentence was delivered. He hated public speaking at the best of times, so he now began to read from several closely written sheets of paper 'with such tremour and in so feeble a tone, that it was difficult for some moments to collect distinctly what he said'.

At several points he lapsed into portentous tropes, perhaps with an eye to posterity:

> A few hours hence, and I will be no more, but the nightly breeze, which will whistle over the silent grave that shall protect me from its keenness, will bear to your restless pillow the memory of one who lived but for his country, and died when liberty and justice had been driven from its confines by a set of villains, whose thirst for blood is only to be equalled by their activity in plunder. For life, as it respects myself, I care not; but while yet I may, I would rescue my memory from the calumny which I doubt not will be industriously heaped upon it, when it will no longer be in my power to protect it.

But his confidence returned as his speech proceeded.[2] In 1817 he and Watson had spoken at their treason hearings 'like men of firmness and with the air of public orators – a sort of *forumizing* tone and manner'.[3] Now he recovered quickly enough to speak like that again. Although his phrases were mannered, they rank among history's braver pleas for justice in the country at large and from the court that was denying it. As he spoke he looked straight at the heavily wigged judge beetling his brows down on him. That took some doing. On Monday morning that personage would have him choked to death and his head removed.

Thistlewood first denounced the ministers and military force deployed against the people, and then the court's failure to call the spy who had instigated parts of the plot. The agents of oppression, he announced, were the government – 'privileged traitors to their country, who lord it over the lives and property of the sovereign people with barefaced impunity'. He recalled Peterloo and the government cover-up afterwards:

> My every feeling … was [for] the welfare of my starving countrymen. I keenly felt for their miseries: but when their miseries are laughed at, and when, because they dared to express those miseries, they were cut down by hundreds, barbarously massacred, and trampled to death; when infants were sabred in their mother's arms, and the breast, from which they drew the tide of life, was severed from the parent's body, my feelings became too intense, too excessive for endurance, and I resolved on vengeance; I

resolved that the lives of the instigators should be the requiem to the souls of the murdered innocents. ... High treason was committed against the people at Manchester, but justice was closed against the mutilated, the maimed, and the friends of those who were upon that occasion indiscriminately massacred.

Next he declared the tyrannicidal principle that was an article of faith among London's ultra-radicals, and that had been so since the seventeenth century: 'With respect of the immorality of our project, I will just observe that the assassination of a tyrant has always been deemed a meritorious action. Brutus and Cassius were lauded to the very skies for slaying Caesar.' At this point chief justice Abbott, outraged, tried to check his statement, but Thistlewood ignored him and continued:

> Indeed, when any man, or any set of men, place themselves above the laws of their country, there is no other means of bringing them to justice than through the arms [weapons] of a private individual. If the laws are not strong enough to prevent them from murdering the community, it becomes the duty of every member of that community to rid his country of its oppressors. ... Insurrection then became a public duty, and the blood of the victims should have been the watch-word to vengeance on their murderers. ...
>
> Albion is still in the chains of slavery: I quit it without regret; I shall soon be consigned to the grave, and my body will be immured beneath the soil whereon I first drew breath. My only sorrow is that that soil should be a theatre for slaves, for cowards, and for despots. My motives, I doubt not, will hereafter be justly appreciated; I will therefore now conclude by stating, that I shall consider myself as murdered, if I am to be executed on the verdict obtained against me, by the refusal of the court to hear my evidence.

At the end of his address Thistlewood 'leaned against the side of the bar, and seemed more like an indifferent spectator of, than a prominent character in, the awful scene which ensued.' As the chief justice prepared to deliver his judgement, Thistlewood took a pinch from his snuffbox and looked round the court 'as if he were entering a theatre'.[4]

What manner of man could this be? Thistlewood had his problems, but he fits no easy stereotype. He was certainly not the madman 'totally void of courage' whom Carlile described.[5] All the same, he was a graceless, truculent, and unforgiving figure, and as alienated, resentful, and fantasy-laden as any modern jihadist. While Thomas Preston made jokes and William Davidson sang songs, he seems never to have laughed, and he quarrelled with what few friends he had. Everyone commented on his truculence – a permanent sulk, it seems, without lightness. There might have been something of the bipolar about him. On the other hand, he was a group actor; and we're told that it's the lone-wolf terrorist who is most likely to be psychopathic.[6] He was neither poor nor less justly dealt with in childhood than anyone might be; but dependent as he was on a father who expected him to work and prosper as his brother did, he would have felt pressed to prove some competence in life when a fair amount of evidence showed that he had none. His intense hatreds might have been primally directed at a disapproving father and successful brother, and he bristled with that sense of exclusion and thwarted entitlement that move many marginalised people to violence. Despite his moderately good schooling and family money behind him, he failed at farming and land surveying, and stuck with none of his obligations. To top it all, he became an addicted gambler who squandered a good deal of his family's money as well as his own – a man who in life as well as at the card-table would chase his losses in a fixed hope of offsetting them. Just as he shut his mind to the likely arrival of bailiffs, so he shut it to the presence of spies.

It's easy to imagine the youthful Thistlewood as a lost soul and a wastrel, not unlike Thackeray's feckless adventurer Barry Lyndon but without the charm. He was well enough read to recommend Gibbon's *Decline and Fall of the Roman Empire* to his son and to cite the Roman heroes Brutus, Cassius, or Cato when need be; but he was no man of ideas. He was unnerved when called on to speak in public and hardly ever made speeches; and we hear no solid statement of his purposes until this last statement in court. He anticipated an English revolution on jacobin lines, but never once spoke of Spence's redistribution of land and property, even though he belonged to Evans's Spencean Philanthropists. Nor do we hear him opining what to do with his revolution should he achieve one. He had charisma, however. How else to explain the puzzle, as Adolphus put it, that 'seven or eight men, two of them soldiers, should have met to act on so ridiculous a proposal' as Thistlewood's? It must have been the charisma of the withdrawn but driven man who intimidated others by his moody silences. For all that, he was either insanely reckless or the bravest man in England.

We have an exceptionally good sense of Thistlewood's appearance in both 1817 and 1820, and of his associates' appearances as well. Historically this is unusual. Thornhill and Hogarth had been able to paint Jack Sheppard and the murderess Sarah Malcolm in their condemned cells; Richard Newton produced a group portrait of radicals imprisoned on the state side of Newgate in 1793; and the artist Henry Richter portrayed the LCS leaders Hardy, Thelwall, and his own brother John as they awaited their treason trials in the Tower in 1794. Otherwise nearly all non-aristocratic prisoners passed through English courts and prisons without leaving a visual trace other than a stylised woodcut if they were lucky.

Thistlewood and friends were twice drawn and engraved conscientiously and without caricature. The first portraits – of Watson, Thistlewood, Preston, and Hooper – were drawn by George Scharf as they awaited trial for treason in the Tower in 1817. The second and more remarkable batch was made by Abraham Wivell in March and April 1820. It depicted Thistlewood and six of his men after the Cato Street arrests. It is Thistlewood who signifies here, so we return to the other men's portraits later.

Scharf came to London from Germany in early 1816 in order to launch his career as a portrait miniaturist or as a lithographer of London life. There was no better way of publicising himself than by aiming at the latest sensation, so he painted the Spa Fields prisoners in watercolour and body-colour on vellum.[7] Though gaunt, his Thistlewood looks respectable, self-contained, and stylishly dressed in a high cravat, buff waistcoat, and blue coat with the extravagant lapels of the day. His trademark side-whiskers are carefully shaped, and his short hair is brushed forward in the radical manner. He stares out at us unflinchingly (Fig. 8.1).

8.1. George Scharf, *Arthur Thistlewood* (1817) (© The Trustees of the British Museum)
8.2. Richard Dighton, *Arthur Thistlewood at the Old Bailey, Monday, 17 April 1820* (photograph: the author)

More dynamic portraits of the prisoners were taken during the 1820 trials. Richard Dighton's fine depiction of *Arthur Thistlewood at the Old Bailey Monday April 17 1820* catches the man's stolidity in the dock (Fig. 8.2). But it's Abraham Wivell's work that impresses most. Commissioned by the publisher Thomas Kelly, Wivell owed his access to his acquaintance with a keeper of Cold Bath Fields prison. His portraits made his reputation, and he progressed to being a society portraitist of distinction.[8] His flattering profile of Thistlewood shows a handsome and gentlemanly figure. It was sold as an independent print and then as a frontispiece in the first printing of Wilkinson's *Authentic History* (Fig. 8.3) His second Thistlewood portrait is the most riveting of the whole collection. Published in the *Authentic History*'s second printing, it was taken nearly full-face in the Old Bailey Sessions House on the day Thistlewood heard his death sentence. In this haunting and haunted image, his face is powerful, heavy, and brooding, and his sunken eyes make him look older than his forty-five years. Here the greatest would-be terrorist of his century faces his end. He has two days left to live (Fig. 8.4).

8.3. Abraham Wivell, *Arthur Thistlewood* (Wivell, 15 April 1820) (© The Trustees of the British Museum)
8.4. Abraham Wivell, *Arthur Thistlewood: Engraved by Mr Cooper, from a drawing taken by Mr Wivell, taken in the Sessions House, on the day sentence of death was passed* (in second printing of Wilkinson's *Authentic History*, May, 1820) (Hulton Archive/Getty Images)

In 1817 Thistlewood was said to be 'a stout, active, cheerful-looking man, with something of a fearless and determined cast of features. His deportment at that time was free and unembarrassed.'[9] The advert for his arrest described him as walking 'very upright' with 'the appearance of a military man', five feet eleven inches tall, with a sallow complexion, long face, dark hair (a little grey), small whiskers, dark hazel eyes and arched eyebrows, a wide mouth with a good set of teeth, a scar under his right jaw, and usually dressed in 'a French gray-coloured coat, buff waistcoat, gray coloured Wellington pantaloons, with Hessian boots under them, and at times a dark brown great coat'. A year later, when tried for challenging Sidmouth to a duel, 'his hair was cut short behind, and combed over his face, as he wore it during the state trials; his whiskers were unusually large, and his face extremely pale; altogether a most forbidding countenance'.[10] Then decline set in, together with what sounds like a mania. Just before his 1820 arrest he was

> seen constantly in the streets, dressed in a shabby manner; his countenance squalid and emaciated, and his whole dress and the expression of his

features, denoting a man who was reduced to a state of extreme indigence. He was generally observed walking or running through the streets with eager impetuosity, and his shoes and an old surtout coat, which he generally wore, bearing all the marks of the poverty and distressed circumstances of the wearer.

Captured on 24 February, he wore a threadbare coat and the corduroy breeches and worsted stockings that he had slept in, and he had not a farthing in his pocket. Awaiting interrogation in Whitehall, his mood changed. 'There was nothing of agitation in his manner. He sat with his eyes chiefly fixed on the ground, except when he occasionally raised them to survey members of the privy council, as they passed through the hall on their way to the council-room.'[11] Lord Hardwicke saw him 'sitting over the fire without his hat; it was easy to distinguish him from the rest, by the character of ferocity which marked his countenance, which had a singularly bad expression' – as well it might.

The admiralty secretary described him as 'looking mean, squalid and miserable' but admitted that 'if he was dressed, and above all at the head of 10,000 men, he would be called a good-looking man'. And when Lord Harrowby gave the poet Thomas Moore a detailed account of the conspiracy and his share in detecting it, 'all seemed to consider Thistlewood as a very extraordinary man'.[12] When the journalist Cyrus Redding saw him in Paris in 1815, his countenance showed such 'indomitable determination' that Redding said he would never forget it.

YOUTH

Condemned prisoners' life stories had once been gleaned from the 'accounts' compiled by the clerical 'ordinary' (i.e. chaplain) of Newgate, but these ceased publication in the 1770s. In any case, the ordinary in 1820, the Rev. Horace Cotton, was the last man likely to be favoured with the conspirators' intimacies. Even the penitent Davidson mistrusted him; the other four rejected his moral bullying outright. They mistrusted the Rev. Ruell, the Cold Bath Fields prison chaplain, as well.[13] The men are more likely to have spoken to their visitors. Men and artists of standing from Hogarth to Wivell had always found access to notorious prisoners easy to come by. The state prisoner Thomas Lloyd in 1794 got one or two visitors on most days, and dined with them too.[14] Still, many details in Thistlewood's and others' early lives culled from these or other sources are unverifiable, and some were fabricated. When discussing notorious men like Thistlewood and Black Davidson, neither contemporaries nor historians have allowed truth to stand in the way of a good story. The men didn't allow it, either.

On the eve of Thistlewood's execution, on 28 April, the freethinker Richard Carlile in his journal the *Republican* was among the first to relay hearsay tales about his life. Carlile gave neither dates nor sources, and admitted that until December 1816 he had no knowledge of how Thistlewood spent his time further than that

> he spent a considerable property at the gambling table, and reduced himself to indigence. His name was scarcely known in London until the proclamation of 1817, which appeared from the secretary of state's office, offering a reward of, I believe, £1000 for his apprehension on a charge of high treason. This was the first time I ever saw his name or heard it mentioned.

This didn't stop Carlile's affirming:

> In the early part of the French revolution, he held a lieutenancy in the militia, from thence he exchanged into some regular regiment, and went out to the West Indies. He left the army, from what cause is not generally known, and visited the United States: from this moment may be dated the origin of those principles which have brought him to his present hapless state. From the United States he embarked for France, and remained in Paris during the whole career of the Robespierrian party, and has unfortunately shewn himself, ever since, to be deeply impregnated with the principles of that party, and all the worst passions that disgraced the French revolution, and finally tended to destroy its benefits. From Paris he returned to London, and being quite a stranger to the political characters of that day, his return from France formed the ground of an introduction to many of them, who were in the habit of assembling at the shop and house of Daniel Isaac Eaton, a bookseller in Newgate-street.[15]

The *Times* circulated most of these same details after the execution, declaring that they were 'sent to us as authentic'. They were further embellished in the 'Biography of some of the Conspirators', which the *Observer* published a week later. 'Furnished from various sources', they were again unspecified. Variants on Carlile's account were widely repeated – and still are. Some said that Thistlewood went to France to serve in the French grenadiers, fought for the French at the battles of Zurich in 1798–9, and served in the West Indies. Others followed Carlile by having him go to America, and others again had him involved in Despard's plot to assassinate the king in 1802. Much of this was recycled in the brief *Lives of … the Leaders of the Cato Street Conspiracy … Collected from the Most Authentic Sources*. This explained that it was compiled from newspapers and from the conspirators' 'immediate friends', but the publisher Kelleher was a tory loyalist in whom immediate friends were unlikely to have confided.[16] Nonetheless his account was recycled in Wilkinson's *Authentic History*, and again in the *New Newgate Calendar* which Wilkinson also edited.

Such are the shaky foundations that have determined every scholarly as well as popular account of Thistlewood from that day to this. No known evidence supports any of these stories.[17] Never averse to giving self-lauding accounts of his own valour, Thistlewood later and falsely told one of his intended recruits that he had been involved 'in five or six different revolutions', implying that he could easily run one of his own if he had to. This was a shameless fabrication.[18]

The firmest evidence about Thistlewood's early life – though lethally biased – comes from an anonymous correspondent who signed himself 'X.Y'. In November 1819, well before Cato Street, he sent a letter post-marked 'Lincoln' to Francis Freeling, the secretary of the General Post Office in London. In March 1817, Sidmouth had issued a warrant to intercept and forward letters addressed to 'Mr Thistlewood' or to 'Mr or Miss Wilkinson' (Susan). Freeling needed little encouragement. He had been opening radicals' letters and passing on titbits to the home office since the early 1790s. In any case, X.Y's covering letter told Freeling to use his information as he saw fit. X.Y was a partisan informant moved by unknown grievances. But he claimed to have known Thistlewood since childhood, and his view of the man was confidently expressed.[19]

Thistlewood's father, X.Y writes, was 'a very respectable well informed man', a stock-breeder and a commissioner for several enclosures, who lived in the scattered Lincolnshire farming community of Tupholme, outside Bardney, a few miles west of Horncastle. This worthy had an 'unfortunate connection' with a widowed servant-cum-shopkeeper in nearby Horsington, which resulted in the birth of this 'worthless fellow', this 'pest to society' – little Arthur. Enclosed with the covering letter, X.Y sent a longer letter to Thistlewood himself. It gets to the point without ceremony. 'You are such a despicable character,' it heartily announces, 'that I have never heard a person speak well of you in your own neighbourhood and when you was last down in the country you was scouted as a disafected [sic] designing disgraceful scoundrel, every honest man avoided as he would a mad dog.' The writer charges villains like Thistlewood with responsibility for all the troubles that had beset France and England, and reminds him that he might have been a respectable farmer like his brother had he not kept such bad company – and read 'Pain's' books.

> You never liked work, and was always idle and poaching about the house ... did you not rob your mother of two hundred pounds to start you in search of liberty? After some years did you not return [home] and like a fawning sychophant [sic], disavow your real principles and get a lieutenancy in the supplementary militia under the earl of Buckinghamshire?

Next comes the charge that while in the militia Thistlewood deceived a rich young woman into marriage and squandered £8,000 of her fortune. From this cruel treatment, X.Y writes, she died broken-hearted two years later. 'Did you not leave Lincoln in a great deal of debt and disgrace? Was you not blanketed and horsewhipped for not discharging your gambling engagements?' Thistlewood returned to take refuge with his mother in Tupholme until he pursued further 'plunder' by 'breaking the peace' of a respectable Horncastle family. This he did by marrying 'their poor giddy daughter, your present wife, who you have contaminated and made equal to yourself in all kinds of deceit and wickedness – have you not made her an atheist and disaffected to government?' After that (in London), Thistlewood joined 'a pretty set of villains' and set about deceiving 'poor idle weak deluded people who like yourself are bent on plunder. ... You are aiming, like Hone and Carlile, to make a fortune by your popular villainy.' X.Y then reminds Thistlewood that when he was in France the police were so suspicious of him that they inspected his and his wife's papers two or three times a week. So much for French liberty, he snorts. 'Dare such liberties be taken with the press there [France] as in England? No. In England we have more libertys [*sic*] than we have sense to value. ... It is the garden spot of the world and the envy of all other nations.' After which wholesome affirmation the letter ends with a rant against the expense of the Poor Laws.

Thistlewood's baptismal certificate proves the 'unfortunate' birth X.Y referred to. Dated 4 December 1774, it identifies the child as 'Arthur, a baseborn son of Ann Burnet'. Ann was the daughter of a small shopkeeper in neighbouring Horsington and was now a servant of John Thistlewood, Arthur's comfortable tenant farmer father. John worked the land of the Vyner family, one of whose mansions was in Tupholme. To confirm these details Sidmouth made exhaustive enquiries among Lincolnshire worthies, including Sir Joseph Banks, the naturalist, who owned a substantial estate at Revesby Abbey not far from Tupholme, and Earl Brownlow, a major slave-owner, of Belton House, near Grantham.[20] Thistlewood's parentage, illegitimacy, and surname were of interest to the home office lest he be acquitted under a plea of misnomer, so we know a lot about them. The enquiries showed that John and Ann's relationship was born of no casual seduction. John had two other children by her, and after his first wife's death he married her and the children were legitimised.

The Thistlewood clan were well known in the county, and Arthur's modest affluence in adulthood owed everything to his family connections. His sister married a local vicar (and soon died in childbirth), while his brother John became a prosperous tenant farmer who was described as 'Esq.' when he married in 1819. He and Arthur shared some brotherly trust, we'll see, though on John's part it was misplaced.

Arthur's uncle was the Jamaican slave-owner Thomas Thistlewood (1721–86), also born in Tupholme. This man is now infamous for the brutality to and sexual exploitation of his slaves, which he himself recorded in eighty-four notebook diaries – a man without inwardness, it seems, for he wrote in 'dry, flat, serviceable, and completely unreflective prose' that contains little by way of explanation or opinion, most of it being 'occurrence'. It was one of the Vyners who first gave this ogre his leg-up by providing him with a letter of introduction to William Beckford, twice lord mayor of London and the largest slave-owner of his time (despite the banner across his house, which celebrated John Wilkes's release in 1770 with the three-foot high word, 'Liberty'). Since uncle Thomas lived in Jamaica from 1750 until his death, Arthur never encountered him, though in youth he shared both his easy way with women and his unimaginative stolidity. Since they were not later listed as recipients of emancipation compensation there is no evidence that slave-made wealth helped the Lincolnshire Thistlewoods, though it's unlikely that there were no investments, now obscured.[21]

X.Y prepares us for the evidence that Thistlewood's early life was louche, spendthrift, and provincial. The father was said to have sent the boy to the Horncastle free grammar school and had him trained as a land surveyor before trying his hand on the family farm. In 1795 'Arthur Thistlewood of Tupholme, grazier' appears as a surety for a marriage bond in Lincoln's diocesan records.

The *Militia List* next confirms that from July 1798 he was an ensign in the West Yorkshire militia. He resigned the commission in February 1799, but from July to September 1803 he served as a lieutenant in the Lincolnshire militia. Family interest secured him both positions, but why he so abruptly resigned from them is unknown. One possibility is implied in the story of his horsewhipping for unpaid debts in Lincoln. Another may lie in X.Y's claims that Thistlewood had read Tom Paine when young and that he when he joined the militias he betrayed his 'real principles'. (In March 1798 seditious handbills circulated in London encouraging radicals to enlist in the militia and cavalry the better to subvert them.)[22] Thistlewood did learn how to use a sword. In the Cato Street stable he killed constable Smithers with a perfectly aimed thrust to the heart. But militias were reserve forces; they seldom left English shores or saw military action. Although a reward for his arrest in 1817 described him as lately a lieutenant in the 'army', later reward adverts in 1820 said nothing about army service. The well-informed X.Y would have mentioned army service and other biographical embellishments had they been true.

Certainties return somewhat in 1804, his thirtieth year. As X.Y confirms, Thistlewood had standing enough to marry a woman of some wealth. She was Jane Worsley, daughter of one Joseph Worsley of Manchester. The marriage was reported in the *Gentleman's Magazine*. According to the *Times*, she brought him a fortune of at least £10,000. With her he moved to live in some style in Bawtry, south Yorkshire. The ruling story is that she died in childbirth fifteen months later. Alas, her wealth reverted to her family, and Thistlewood was allowed only a small annuity. The plaque he erected to her memory in St Nicholas's church in Bawtry withheld affection. 'Near this place Lie the remains of Jane Thistlewood Wife of Mr Arthur Thistlewood of Bawtry who Died April 29th 1805. Aged 30 Years.'

Thistlewood returned to Lincoln (the *Times* reported), and there bought a 'mansion' and lived respectably for two or three years. He joined the Lincoln freemasons in 1805. Then 'an unfortunate gaming transaction at cards during the Lincoln races ... involved him in difficulties which he found it impossible to meet, and he fled, to avoid the importunities of his more fortunate associates. This seems to have been the decided breaking up of his character, and he has been since known only as the professed gambler or the factious demagogue.'[23]

Not only a gambler, but a seducer also. Taking refuge with his mother, Thistlewood got himself a bastard son by a woman named Ann Thornelly, the servant of an affluent Horncastle butcher's wife named Wilkinson. Julian was born on 3 October 1806.[24] Meanwhile Thistlewood had been consorting with the butcher's 22-year-old daughter Susan. He niftily ended his relationship with Ann by paying one John Hunt, a local man, to marry her in February 1809 ('Amelia Thornley', she called herself in the register). Thistlewood married Susan in 1808, detached Julian from his mother, and took on the child as one of his family. This second marriage was a lucky break. He and Susan had no children, but Susan brought him £2,000 (the *Times* reported), accepted little Julian, shared her husband's views, and stuck by him to the end. Amelia's grief at being forcibly parted from her son may explain why the Hunts later followed the Thistlewoods to London. There, as we shall see, John became a Spencean and briefly gave the Thistlewoods refuge from the police after the Spa Fields fiasco.

After the marriage, Arthur's father and brother were said to have set him up as a farmer. If so, that venture failed too, perhaps because rents and taxes were high and selling prices low. At last, in the winter of 1810/11 the Thistlewoods came to London. His wastrel habits didn't improve. He lived off his annuity and his family's and wife's money, and X.Y was right about his gambling. In early 1813 his brother John asked him to collect £900 that was due to him from a land sale. With this in his pocket, Thistlewood dined and got drunk with a party of West End rakes, and late at night 'found himself by accident in a house in St. James's Street, eminent for the resort of persons addicted to deep play.' In a single game of hazard with the black-leg gamester Hill Darley he lost £841 of his brother's money. Moving on to another gaming house in Pall Mall, he lost over £400 of his own. He tried to bring an action against Darley but the case failed and his brother had to recover the money for himself later.[25] Press reports of this affair described Thistlewood as 'of no business himself, but a man of small fortune'; a government spy thought him 'quite the gentleman in manners and appearance'. The title page of the 1817 trial report identified him as 'Gent'. Everyone called him 'Mr', even after the executions.

He had wit and wealth enough twice to go to Paris, first after Napoleon's exile to Elba in 1814 and then after Waterloo. It was a fashionable thing to do. After the Treaty of Paris was signed, 13,832 Britons passed through Calais, and in the following year over three-quarters of foreign visitors in Paris were English. Their carriages, grooms, horses, dogs, fashions, and shops were seen everywhere. 'London now is out of town / Who in England tarries? / Who can bear to linger there? / When all the world's in Paris?'[26]

On his first visit, Thistlewood took with him sixteen-year-old Thomas John Evans, his Spencean friend's son, to introduce him to some of the English and Irish radicals in exile there. Thistlewood also associated with a one-time secretary of the London Corresponding Society, John Ashley, and with the exiled United Irish agent William McCabe, whose secret return to England a year later Thistlewood helped to fund.[27] An unverifiable story that may belong to his second visit had Thistlewood imprisoned in Calais with another Englishman because they lacked passports. His companion insulted a French officer, and when the officer retaliated Thistlewood knocked him down with his fist. The two Englishmen were imprisoned for 'several weeks'.[28]

The gaming tables in the Palais Royale would have cheered him – at first. In the breakfast room of the Hotel de l'Europe he was spotted by the writer Cyrus Redding. Redding described him as

> a square built man dressed in a green coat, sullen of expression, of pallid complexion, and a low compressed brow indicating great firmness of purpose ... On seeing us come in, he rose up and went away, without the smallest recognition on either side. At breakfast we asked who he was, and were told he was a Lincolnshire gentleman, named Thistlewood, a man of property, reduced. He was in an awkward predicament.

Thistlewood had gambled away £200, which he had acquired through a dishonoured bill discounted for him by one 'Astly', and was now looking for someone to renew the bill. It was 'a bad case', Redding was told.[29]

THISTLEWOOD THE RADICAL

It had taken Thistlewood several years to achieve these Parisian connections, though after his arrival in London he had moved quickly. He inserted himself into London's radical circles as early as March 1811 by becoming the secretary of a subscription committee for a United Irish journalist, Peter Finnerty, who had been imprisoned in Dublin in 1797 for charging Castlereagh and the Irish administration with 'massacre and rape, military murders, desolation and terror'. When he repeated the accusation he was imprisoned again for eighteen months.[30] His support committee met at the Crown and Anchor. It invited supporters to leave money for Finnerty's relief at 167 Fleet Street, the shoemaking shop of Thomas Hardy, the LCS founder.[31] Thistlewood at this point must have had relatively respectable political and perhaps social ambitions. The Finnerty committee included the veteran Major John Cartwright, who had advocated universal male suffrage as early as 1776, and Alderman Matthew Wood, later champion of the Cato Street widows. It was chaired by Sir Francis Burdett, the radical-whig MP for Westminster who had been recently imprisoned in the Tower for breaching parliamentary privilege.

Though wealthily married into the Coutts banking family, Burdett had radical form. His popular following had blossomed in 1799 when he befriended Despard and his black Jamaican wife Catherine while campaigning to improve the nightmare conditions of Cold Bath Fields prison, where Despard languished without trial for the three years 1798–1801. In 1802, Burdett won the seat for Middlesex in one of London's most tumultuous elections since the 1760s. At the hustings a band played the revolutionary 'Ça ira!' and the crowd cried 'No Bastille!', in reference to Cold Bath Fields' reputation. In 1807 another turbulent election gave him the key constituency of Westminster, and in 1809 he was the first MP to move for parliamentary reform since 1797. He supported the Cobbettite radicals in denouncing flogging in the army and the duke of York's corrupt relationship with the courtesan Mary Anne Clarke. He then published a letter in Cobbett's *Register* protesting at the Commons' imprisonment of the popular radical, Gale Jones, for criticising the Commons' inquiry into the Walcheren naval disaster. This provoked the Commons on 5 April 1810 into voting for his arrest for breach of privilege. Appealing to Magna Carta, Burdett refused to accept the warrant's legality and denied the serjeant-at-arms entry to his Piccadilly mansion. News of the stand-off drew in huge crowds to support him, and his eventual arrest provoked the most violent riots London had seen since 1780.[32]

Gentlemanly radicals like Burdett stood to what we would now call the left of the parliamentary Foxite whigs, and initially Thistlewood tried to be on good terms with them, though Carlile later observed that 'he was never sufficiently countenanced by any of them, so as to form an intimacy with them'. Sure enough, when he sought Burdett's patronage to get him onto the committee of the West London Lancastrian Association, he was thwarted by the radical tailor Francis Place, once of the LCS and now a man with fingers in several reformist pies. Thanks to wartime demand, Place's breeches-making shop was making an annual profit of £2,270, which Thistlewood so resented that he accused him of being a government informer – the first of his many quarrels in ensuing years, though Place gave as good as he got.[33] He was to spread the rumour that Thistlewood compensated for his gambling losses by bringing false accusations against miscreants in order to collect 'blood money'.[34]

Class differences simmered beneath these relationships. Thistlewood thought of affluent shopkeepers as 'a set of aristocrats' altogether, and stated that he would 'glory to see the day that all the shops were shut up, and were plundered', because 'there was no person who was worth ten pound, who was worth anything for the country'.[35] He wasn't alone in this. Henry Hunt also condemned the 'petty shop-keepers, and little tradesmen, who, under the denomination of tax-paying housekeepers, … set themselves up as a sort of privileged class, above the operative manufacturer, the artizan, the mechanic, and the labourer'.[36]

Thistlewood quarrelled with men of higher status too. The tenant farmer's son, with his Lincolnshire accent, belonged to a humbler social breed than the likes of Burdett, who had salon manners and wealth to match them, and was only 'a democrat in words, and an aristocrat in feeling', as Cobbett put it later. Even Hunt was a Wiltshire gentleman farmer and a substantial independent freeholder. Influenced by Cobbett, Hunt was on his way to becoming the most flamboyant and self-lauding narcissist in that era's radical politics, but Thistlewood was to quarrel with him as well. Soon Thistlewood was dismissing all the genteel classes as 'mean and contemptible'.

The key problem, probably, was that most of the LCS veterans had learned the wisdom of political caution even as Thistlewood's views became more extreme. The suppression of free speech and assembly, the brutal executions of Despard and friends in 1803, and their own experiences of prison squashed the old radicals' faith in the prospects for revolution. Meanwhile and conversely, Thistlewood's advanced political views were first exposed in February 1813, when he offered to finance a wild plan proposed by an unrepentant LCS veteran named Maurice Margarot, who had lately returned penniless from fourteen years' transportation for sedition and who now lived off Thomas Hardy's charity.

According to a home office informant named Arthur Kidder, Margarot remained a true believer in Bonaparte long after most London jacobins had lost faith in him after the retreat from Moscow. Margarot planned to hire a smuggler's boat in Jersey or Guernsey and to cross 'the pond' (Kidder's phrase) to France while the dark winter nights provided cover. There he would invite Bonaparte to invade England and would promise that armed radicals would greet the hero as he landed. In return Bonaparte would restore the old Saxon laws, confiscate and sell the aristocratic estates, abolish and destroy 'those damned nobles and clergy', and give everybody 'a bit of land' – altogether a nice reprise of the Spencean programme. Margarot calculated that if land were evenly distributed across England's population, each male would gain four or five acres. Oddly, much the same is true today.[37]

Soon one fantasist was proposing to mislead the other. Thistlewood assured Margarot that he could fund Margarot's plan because he had been awarded a £10,000 annuity in a chancery suit and that he could discount a £160 bill to do so. A few days later Thistlewood had to tell Margarot that he couldn't find anyone to discount his bill after all, and talk of the annuity evaporated. Kidder reported that Thistlewood's once considerable property was now 'so embarrassed with contingencies & other circumstances, that he has not yet been able to realize from any of the money lenders from whom they are negotiating'. All he now possessed was 'the wreck of his former estates'. What he also had was the wreck of his reputation. Soon even Hardy was dismissing Thistlewood as 'a mixture of a rogue and a fool'. Kidder commented that 'from his past life, his present pursuits, principles & low connections &c, he [Thistlewood] seems to be a second edition of Colonel Despard'. This was a foresightful observation.

In the days of the LCS radical reformers had called others 'citizen' this and 'citizen' that, but now fraternal intimacies were easily fractured. Truculent and taciturn by nature, Thistlewood felt increasingly comfortable with rough-and-ready shoemakers and Irishmen who had lived hard lives and knew failure in their callings, as he did. The big world continued to call him 'Mister', but among his close associates he discarded gentlemanly pretensions: *'Did you ever hear them call Thistlewood by any name? –* Yes; they used to call him sometimes T. and sometimes Arthur.'[38] In these conditions Thistlewood gradually moved towards the outer fringe of metropolitan radicalism. He began an association with Thomas Spence himself, whose utopian-socialist arguments all but ruled debate in London's noisier tavern clubs, and with Spence's disciple, Thomas Evans. He attended Spences's funeral, joined Evans's Spencean Philanthropists, and grew close to James Watson and Thomas Preston, who were also members. The way was opening to insurrection.

CHAPTER 9

The Spa Fields Insurrection: 1816–17

PLOTS

In the first years of peace after 1815 Arthur Thistlewood came to associate with men who were rougher diamonds than Evans or Spence – or at least with men who were easily made to look that way. Robert Cruikshank's unsubtle engraving of a scowling, crop-haired, and ill-clad Dr James Watson shows a veritable thug whom one would best avoid on dark nights (Fig. 9.1). An anonymous portrayal of the shoemaker Thomas Preston with unkempt hair, untrimmed whiskers, hunched shoulders, and staring profile suggests yokel-like stupidity (Fig. 9.2). Each image illustrated published reports of Watson's trial and Preston's arraignment for treason in June 1817.

Yet in person the men presented themselves better than these carica-tures conveyed. 'Watson was genteelly dressed in black and wore powder [on his hair]. Under his arm he carried a large bundle of papers. Preston and Hooper were also dressed in black.'[1] Turn to the colour drawings in Scharf's little gallery, and we meet Watson alert and not without dignity. Preston may look shabby, but his face would be unremarkable if you passed it in the street. And the shoemaker John Hooper's curly and undisciplined hair suggests humble standing, but not maliciously. None of the portraits suggests anger, hunger, or madness. Each wears respect-able clothes and looks as unexceptional as any of us might (Figs. 9.3 (a–c)). Yet all four had just lived through the major crisis and disappoint-ment of their lives.

Who were these men of the Spa Fields fiasco? Thomas Preston first. He was born in 1774 in a court off Wood Street in the City of London. He called himself a cockney and spoke like one, replacing Vs with Ws,

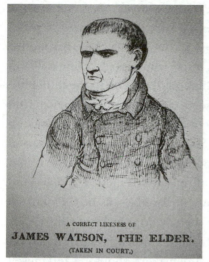

9.1. Robert Cruikshank, *A Correct Likeness of James Watson, the Elder (Taken in Court)* (Fairburn 1817) (from Fairburn, 1817) (photograph: the author)
9.2. Anon., *Thomas Preston* (from Lewis, *Trials at Large*, 1817) (photograph: the author)

9.3 (a–c). George Scharf, *James Watson, Thomas Preston,* and *John Hooper* (1817) (© The Trustees of the British Museum)

dropping Hs, flattening As, and inserting glottal stops – as a parodist made clear: 'Vy that's the way the bisniss to perform, / And vork a vide and raddercal Reform, / Vich, as I proves, must vone day end the strife; / You'll read it for a shilling in "My Life".'[2] The reference was to the 37-page unfinished autobiography which he published after release from the treason trials in 1817. Its jaunty title caught something of Preston's teasing garrulity: *The Life and Opinions of Thomas Preston,*

Patriot and Shoemaker; Containing Much that is Curious, Much that is Useful, More that is True, and A Great Deal More, Perhaps, than is Expected.

The book tells how his father died in his infancy, how his mother remarried and 'distributed' him to a nurse whose neglect one day crippled him permanently, and how he then 'waded through the difficulties of neglected childhood'. When another accident ended his brief apprenticeship to a silversmith, he was apprenticed to the craft of shoemaking, 'of which I have been since the victim and the slave'. His master was cruel, so Preston absconded and spent a good part of his teens on the tramp, offering his labour to local masters throughout England and Ireland. After helping to organise a shoemakers' strike in Cork (he claimed), he returned to London around 1794. He then made good by reading widely, joining the London Corresponding Society, and marrying an ingenious wife with whom he was soon running shoemakers' shops in Clerkenwell, Swallow Street, and Holborn, which put out work to some forty people. Then disaster struck. In 1807 his wife ran off with a paramour to America ('where I am since told she died', he added evenly). This left him to bring up their four daughters, the youngest aged four. In 1811 he became an intimate of Thomas Spence, and on Spence's death three years later joined Thomas Evans's Spencean Philanthropists, as Watson and Thistlewood did independently. But the girls were 'a clog to all future proceedings', he lamented. He took to drink and his shops collapsed. He was reduced to taking in piecework as he and the girls crowded into the two dingy rooms in Greystoke Place off Fetter Lane (see Fig. 7.2) that became one of London's insurrectionary headquarters.

James Watson is a more mystifying character. Born in Lincolnshire in 1766, he was the oldest of our constellation. He claimed to have been trained as a surgeon, and everyone called him 'Doctor', but there is next to no record of his surgical practice. He lived as an apothecary, rather, dispensing medicines both real and otherwise in the most marginal and insecure of the professions: 'An apothecary on a white horse / Rode by on his vocation; / And the Devil thought of his old friend / Death in Revelations' (Coleridge). In its higher reaches it was a calling of some status, however. Those who could afford it would be trained by a member of the Company of Surgeons, and might join this company in due course. The veteran radical Gale Jones was one such.

When the Manchester reformer Samuel Bamford met Watson and Preston soon after the 1817 trial, he thought of them (not Thistlewood) as the most influential reform leaders in London. Watson, he found, had 'somewhat of a polish in his gait and manner, and a degree of respectability and neatness in his dress. He was educated for a genteel profession, that of a surgeon; had practised it, and had in consequence [once] moved in a sphere more high than his present one.' He failed, Bamford thought, because 'he had probably a better heart than head.' Watson himself explained his failures by the impact of the war on middling-class incomes: his clients lacked the means to 'repay the ordinary attendance which a man in his situation was at all times bound to give'.[3] So Watson shared in the apothecary's more common fate, his career unsuccessful and peripatetic. Given 'the pressure of the times and the poverty of neighbourhoods', he was chronically in debt.

Watson's ten children – later rumour expanded them to sixteen – were born across London, Yorkshire, Norfolk, and Staffordshire. After his Staffordshire business failed, he and his vast family came to London around 1808. The capital defeated them. One of his daughters died in 1810 'for want of nourishment'. As she lay dying 'the bed that was under her was seized for rent', a disaster which Watson understandably thought 'too much when the affluent were wallowing in riches'.[4] In May 1816 his wife left him, taking four of their youngest children with her to find refuge with her nephew in Lynn. The couple allegedly broke up because 'he beat the younger children cruelly', but it was likely that, like other big families, they split up simply to survive.[5] We hear a little about two or three of the children, nothing about the rest. Watson's eldest daughter Charlotte, aged sixteen and 'very amiable', was in service in Lamb's Conduit Street until her employer dismissed her after the Spa Fields insurrection. In January 1820, while Watson was in Whitecross Street debtors' prison, an eleven-year-old son collected his father's coded message to the troops (the one cut into strips: see Fig. 1.5).[6]

Watson's oldest son James ('young Watson' because of their identical names) stayed with his father too, though he sometimes worked as a surgeon in the Greenland fisheries. He shared his father's taste in black coats and waistcoats, drab breeches, and long gaiters. Born around 1797, he was said to have trained with an apothecary in Bath, where 'his wild and unmanageable temper induced a belief that his mind was rather disordered'.[7] He brought his temper to London. In a public house in Long Acre in November 1816 he challenged a nobleman's servant who had betrayed his calling by the coat of arms on his buttons. 'How had it come about that this lord [the servant's employer] had so much property?' he demanded: 'the servant had an equal right with the lord, and ... the time was fast approaching when he would have as much money and land as his master.' Argument ensued; and when young Watson announced that English soldiers 'would not fight for such a government as this: they had been abroad, and had seen how merit was rewarded in France', the conversation ended in a rowdy quarrel.[8]

Meanwhile one might call old Watson's life uncentred. He moved lodgings and shop from Newcastle Street on the Strand to Catherine Street, then 'in difficulty' to Somers Town, then back to Newcastle Street, then to a single room shared with young James in Hyde Street, Bloomsbury.[9] A week before the December Spa Fields meeting, he flitted from Hyde Street by night 'as he owed so much rent' and went to Dean Street off Fetter Lane, where father and son shared a bed. After young James scarpered to America, he moved to Three Kings Court off the north side of Fleet Street, where he stayed until at least 1819, and lastly to Surrey Street off the Strand.

It's impossible now to unravel the fullness of Watson's inner world. His failures in life suggest the influences less of mischance and a big family than of a quixotic relationship to reality. There was something childlike in his taste for secret codes and recipes for letter- and fire-bombs. And his political conversion was impetuous and sudden. It was probably during one of his sojourns in Newcastle Street that he formed his connection with Thomas and Janet Evans, who lived there too, and joined the Spenceans as a result. He was visibly radical only between 1816 and 1820, and even then his politics were occasionally moderated, as we've seen. Still, there is no doubting the Spencean and jacobin tenor of his speeches at Spa Fields, or his hatred of inequality. Unlike Thistlewood, he never shrank from public speaking, so from 1816 to early 1820 he and not Thistlewood was regarded as London's ultra-radical leader.

THE SPA FIELDS INSURRECTION

At a Spencean meeting in the Cock in Grafton Street in Soho in October 1816, a whitesmith (metal-worker) named John Castle was approached by Thomas Preston. Castle described what ensued to Stafford, the Bow Street spymaster:

> Got acquainted [with] the old Watson by going to the Spencean societies which are open to any one Preston is a member, the same night I was made [a member] Preston called me out and we had a drop of gin together at the bar of the Cock, he asked me to meet him and the others at the Mulberry Tree the next night which I did, and met old Evans, young Evans, Watson, Preston and Thislewood [*sic*], and in returning home, we got into conversation, Watson said how easy it was to upset the government, if it was only handled as it ought to be, it might be done without any blood being spilt.[10]

Castle of course shouldn't have been trusted – but how else to pull in recruits except by taking chances? It was later proved in court that Castle had been a bigamist and a bawdy-house keeper, and that he had saved himself from a conviction for coining by informing on his accomplices, one of whom was hanged and the other transported. He had then allegedly connived with the down-at-heel George Edwards to persuade French prisoners to abscond in order to collect the rewards for detecting them. He was currently living on blood money – and the blood he had in view now was Watson's, Preston's, and Thistlewood's. Stafford had provided him with clothes 'as the incipient price of his testimony'.[11]

Castle played his hand well, and Watson was easily led on. For some months the ultra leaders had been discussing a new policy, the first important radical initiative for some years. This was to hold great outdoor meetings, the first since 1795, in the hope of catalysing insurrection.[12] Their enthusiasm for the idea and their hunger for supporters laid them open to Castle's blandishments. On 26 October, Watson visited Castle's lodging, and 'a sort of intimacy' commenced between them. Watson told him that he and his friends planned 'to collect as many of the labouring poor who might be out of employment as they could; to take advantage of the distresses under which they suffered', and to bring about a revolution to achieve the 'equal division of the land of the country'. According to Castle's report as relayed by the attorney general, Watson added his view that money was no object (thanks to Thistlewood's funding), and that nothing but a revolution would alleviate the poor people's sufferings. With Castle making all the right noises in response, he was soon invited to meetings in Preston's lodging in Greystoke Place and in taverns like the Cock, the Nag's Head, and the Mulberry Tree, where Thistlewood paid the reckonings.

An action committee was formed. Evans and the ex-soldier John Harrison distanced themselves from it, however, because young Watson's taste for violence was excessive and dangerous. So Castle and an unemployed shoemaker named John Hooper replaced them.[13] 'The Committee met every morning to settle what to do, and in the evening to report what had been done, they met at No. 9 Greystoke Place, we generally went two and two, Thislewood [sic] and I generally went together, sometimes I went with young Watson.'

Another informant stated that Preston and others canvassed sailors at the George in Shadwell. They took chances here too. 'Preston's appearance was dirty and shabby, the 3 others decent and respectable'. One was a medical man (old Watson), one had lately been to France (Thistlewood), the third was 'a young man who seemed of very clever abilities' (young Watson):

> Their conversation was very wild & seditious lamenting the state of the poor, and stating that they could raise many thousand men in arms to join them & shewing a printed bill respecting a meeting at the Bear in Bear Lane Southwark to petition the prince to put down machines in factories, and other printed bills which they would not trust out of their hands, and stating that they should be in the neighbourhood again in about 3 weeks when something would be done.

Elsewhere, Castle reported,

> Thislewood gave the poor sailors money, and treated the soldiers, he has treated them when on guard at the theatres, at a public house in Long Lane, where the soldiers use, and at a house in Vinegar Yard, Drury Lane, they used to sound the soldiers and ask if any thing happened would they

fire on the mob. And they [the soldiers] generally said No, they would not that they wanted a big loaf as well as other people.[14]

Treating soldiers to beer was always easy. Soldiers never refused a gift, a footguard from the Knightsbridge barracks told Castle. That didn't mean they listened to the spiel. Castle found this man more attentive to the beer and their game of bowls than to the 'chat'.[15] Those who benefited from Thistlewood's treats told him what he wanted to hear. In Paddington they canvassed the labourers who had been laid off after cutting the Regent's Canal. Thistlewood plied them with beer and urged them to come to the Spa Fields meeting with any weapons they could – 'a spike-nail in the end of a stick or any thing that would run into a fellow's guts'.[16] One told him that the men 'wished for a good row, and would sooner be killed than starved to death', another that 'he could collect five or six hundred any morning, so many were without work'.[17] Castle reassured the committee that, as a whitesmith, he could mobilise 500 smiths in the Borough south of the Thames.[18]

By November Thistlewood, Preston, and party had persuaded themselves that they could muster 2,000 men over the next days – men who would 'act and not debate and talk'. People said that the Scots had risen and that soldiers had refused to act against them; that the Irish in St Giles were ripe for rebellion; and that people were crying, 'Wait, wait; the day is not far distant when some men will carry their heads under their arms!', and 'Our oppressors must go!' If they could only find a rallying point, Thistlewood said, they could raise the whole of London's population in a few hours and effect 'a complete revolution'.[19]

And that is how on 13 November 1816 Thistlewood's committee invited Henry Hunt to that first meeting with him in Thistlewood's lodgings in Southampton Buildings. Ignoring Cobbett's advice not to tangle with Thistlewood, and impressed by Thistlewood's gentlemanly lodgings, furnishings, and Moroccan slippers, Hunt agreed to address a series of public meetings on Spa Fields between November 1816 and February 1817 to petition the regent for the relief of distress. A petition movement was accelerating in the midlands and north and Hunt wanted to be part of it. Thistlewood and Watson wanted Hunt to also lead a march to Carlton House to force the regent to endorse Spencean proposals, which they laid out over several closely written pages. Hunt drew the line at this and insisted that the meeting concentrate only on peaceful reform and the relief of distress.[20] Thistlewood and Watson gave way, though they privately meant to turn one of the meetings into an insurrection.

Hunt was by now the unavoidable choice as figurehead and speaker. Since the 1790s his record as a parliamentary reformer was unbroken, and he had good looks and charisma. When the Lancashire weaver-poet Samuel Bamford met him at the first Spa Fields meeting, he found him 'gentlemanly in his manner and attire, six feet and better in height, and extremely well formed' – though the good looks collapsed somewhat when he was excited in speaking:

> [his eyes] seemed to distend and protrude; and if he worked himself furious ... they became blood streaked, and almost started from their sockets. Then it was that the expression of his lip was to be observed – the kind smile was exchanged for the curl of scorn, or the curse of indignation. His voice was bellowing; his face swollen and flushed; his gripped hand beat as if it were to pulverise; and his whole manner gave token of a painful energy, struggling for utterance. ... He was always beating against a tempest of his own or of others' creating.[21]

It was Hunt's stentorian voice and eloquence that mattered – the cadenced and theatrical sentences, the forceful repetition of simple messages and anecdotes, the powers of ridicule, the candid narcissism, and the professed readiness to die in the cause of reform. He later made his white hat the emblem of reform, and acquired the habit of displaying the scars he got at Peterloo rather 'like Mark Anthony exhibiting the mantle of Caesar', as a newspaper put it.[22] It was around now that Robert Southey the poet coined the sobriquet 'Orator' Hunt.

As for the committee's choice of Spa Fields as venue, Thistlewood had perused the map of London and decided that it was 'the best place and nearest the City to hold [the meetings] so that we could get at the old Lady [the Bank of England] and the old Gentleman [the Tower] before the soldiers could get near us ... we could from there get directly into town and block up everything'. In a typical flight of fantasy he added that 'some men were to get on the tops of houses and if the soldiers would not join us they were to be destroyed, as a stone, brick or tile or a bottle thrown from a house top would knock a man or horse down'. After the insurrection the group would appoint a Committee of Public Safety on the jacobin model. It would include an implausible mixture of moderate and veteran candidates, most of whom knew better than to touch insurrection with a bargepole: 'Sir F. Burdett, the Lord Mayor, Lord Cochrane, Gale Jones, Hunt, Thompson, Fowkes, Roger O'Connor. Major Cartwright, old and young Evans, the editor of *The Statesman* and *The Whig* and many more names were mentioned which I cannot call to mind at present to the amount of twenty-four in number were to be appointed.'[23]

If you walked up Gray's Inn Lane from Fox Court in 1816, or up the Islington Road from Clerkenwell, you would have had access to Spa Fields, the largest open space to the north of built-up London. It offered a gently rising landscape of reservoirs, spas, and wells, and you went here in the eighteenth and early nineteenth centuries to bathe if you could afford to, or to watch prizefights, bull-baitings, female fisticuffs, cudgel-playing, grinning competitions, donkey races, ox-roasting, or attend the Whitsuntide Gooseberry Fair.[24] Bagnigge Wells tea garden, once famous for its clientele of highwaymen and ladies of easy virtue, was on Spa Fields' western flank and a stone's throw from the top of Gray's Inn Lane beyond it. At the bottom of the hill, at what used to be called Codpiece Row but was now bowdlerised into Coppice Row, the Spa Fields pie-house marked the beginning of the streets to the south. From it you could see at the top of the hill to the east the Merlin's Cave tavern from whose upper window Orator Hunt spoke at the meetings. The vista was shadowed by the daunting walls of Cold Bath Fields prison a few hundred yards to the south-west, and was about to be destroyed by the building of Merlin Street and Wilmington Square a couple of years later.[25]

Hunt's arrival at the first of the meetings, on 15 November, was cheered by 'much the largest concourse of people [he] had ever seen together in [his] life'. Most accounts put the number at 10,000. Thistlewood and friends forgot to provide the hustings they had promised, so Hunt addressed the crowd from an upper window of the Merlin's

Cave tavern. He lectured for an hour on the iniquities of the civil list and the blood-sucking of sinecurists – 'the fathers, the brothers, the mothers, the sisters, the cousins and bastards of the borough-mongers' (*Laughter*) – who lifted huge sums out of the taxes 'without doing any thing for it'; and he pleaded for parliamentary reform. A petition to the regent was proposed, seconded, and allegedly signed by 24,479 people. When Burdett refused to present it at Carlton House, Hunt treated him as a renegade, as did the ultras. Hunt tried to deliver it instead, but was three times turned away with the information that the regent replied only to petitions from the City and the universities of Oxford and Cambridge. The prince sent £4,000 to the Spitalfields soup kitchen instead. After the meeting a part of the crowd (a 'mob of boys', said the *Times*) broke away to loot bakers' and fishmongers' shops in the Strand, Cranbourne Street, and St Giles's and butchers' stalls in Newport Market, but the disturbance wasn't serious.[26]

The Watsonites, as newspapers called them, planned the second meeting carefully. A couple of hundred girls in virginal white were to carry flags and cockades at the front of a column of men in order 'to work powerfully upon the humanity of the troops', which was a nice way of putting it, and the meeting was advertised for 2 December in printed posters whose draft was later found among Watson's papers:[27]

England

Expects every Man to do his Duty

The Meeting at Spa Fields

takes place at 12 o'clock

on Monday December 2nd 1816

To receive the answer of the Prince Regent to the Petition determined

upon at the last Meeting held at the same place and for other important

Considerations

The present state of Great Britain

Four Millions in Distress!!!

Four Millions Embarrassed!!!

One Million and a Half fear distress!!!

Half a Million live in splendid luxury!!!

Our Brothers in Ireland are in a worse state

The climax of misery is complete, it can go no further

Death would now be a relief to millions. Arrogance
Ffolly and Crime have brought affairs to this dread crisis –
Firmness and Integrity can only save the Country!!!

In the event the girls in white couldn't be mustered; but the crowd was swollen by the old custom, still observed in many London trades, of taking 'Saint Monday' off work (a full week's work in any case was hard to come by). It was also an execution day at Newgate, when 'master-coach-builders, frame-makers, tailors, shoe-makers, and others' would observe to their customers that 'that will be a hanging-day and my men will not be at work'.[28] Outside Newgate at eight that morning four men were hanged, two for stealing handkerchiefs, one for robbery, another for sodomy. Once that was over, several hundred hyped-up people walked to Spa Fields via Smithfield, and another crowd came from Finsbury up St John's Street. This last included a wagon full of sailors from Wapping, where Thistlewood's recruiting and perhaps the placard's citation of Nelson had had an effect. The activists had been provided with tricoloured flags and banners that proclaimed: 'Nature, Truth and Justice!', 'Feed the hungry!', 'Protect the oppressed! Punish crimes!' A white flag advised that 'The brave soldiers are our brothers; treat them kindly'. Susan Thistlewood made what her husband called 'the real' tricolour, its bands of green, red, and white symbolising the revolutionary unity of Ireland, England, and Scotland. Over 20,000 people gathered; some thought the number well over twice that. William Hone found Spa Fields 'covered with people, and stalls for the sale of fruit, gingerbread, &c.': it looked like a fairground.

Hunt was late, so large numbers of people were drawn down from Merlin's Cave to the waving flags on the sailors' wagon at Coppice Row Gate. Hone thought that four or five thousand congregated there. They were described by reporters as 'poor distressed sailors, and other starvelings, the famishing victims of times out of joint, whom want of protection and relief let loose from society without attachment or fealty'. Francis Place dismissed them as 'a contemptible set of fools and miscreants, whom twenty constables could have dispersed'. They can't all have been such derelicts, but they were low enough to drive many of the middling sort back to Merlin's Cave in disgust, while the two Watsons and Hooper, sporting the tricoloured cockades in their hats that Susan had made, jumped into the wagon and were hailed with loud cheers.[29]

The speeches that followed were taken down in shorthand by one Vincent Dowling for the *Observer* newspaper. Dowling had made his mark as a reporter in 1812 with an eyewitness account of the prime minister Spencer Perceval's assassination. He might already have signed up as a paid government informant; if not, he soon became one. Immediately after the speeches Dowling took his notes to the home office, and was to read them out at Watson's trial seven months later. Hunt later called him 'Mr. Spectacle Dowling', a man who had 'written so many falsehoods ... that he actually believed at last that what he had written was true'. His Spa Fields report, Hunt added, was suspect for its 'astonishing degree of minuteness, although other reporters who were present declared that not one-tenth of what was said could be heard'. Still, it is the fullest of all reports of the meeting, and it wasn't contradicted elsewhere.[30]

According to Dowling, Watson senior addressed the crowd as 'friends and countrymen', and then expanded on the iniquities of a nation in which half a million people enjoyed luxury while 8 million were in dire distress or in fear of it. 'Are we to go on from ... year to year, crying to the Father of his People, as he is called, in vain for redress? [*No, No!*] The present, then, is the time to do something. ... We have been placed in a state of bondage for years, and this because ... the calls of the multitude have been neglected [*Cheers*]':

> There is not a day in which we pass through the streets of this great metropolis, that we do not see people starving to death. Are [the 'great'] ignorant of this? [*No!*] ... They know well that the people are starving in every part of the kingdom; and yet will admit of no measure to relieve them. [*Groans.*] Will they now hear our cries? [*No, No!*] ... Have we not been in a state of bondage longer than the Israelites? They were in bondage but four hundred years, but we have been longer. Ever since the Norman Conquest, kings have been admitted by you to do as they liked: they have in many instances converted you to their own wicked purposes; but this must not last any longer! [*Cries of 'No, No!' and loud shouts.*]

Watson was followed by his twenty-year-old son. The hostile press described him as drunk; he was certainly exuberant. He too rehearsed the inequalities of the age, the ways in which the regent profited from them, and the Spencean utopia that awaited:

> We have been told very truly, that trade and commerce have been annihilated; but still the earth was by nature designed for the support of mankind. The earth is at all times sufficient to place man above distress, and in a comfortable situation. If he has but a spade and a hoe, to turn up his mother earth, he has the means of averting starvation.

He went on to lament Ireland's plight and to remind the crowd of its own mythic memories – of Wat Tyler's peasants' revolt and martyrdom in Smithfield in 1381, no less.[31] The next day's precis by the *Times* conveniently summarised the ultra-radical credo:

> I am sorry to tell you that our supplication to the prince has failed. … And is this man the father of the people? – [*No.*] Has he listened to your petition? – [*No*]. The day is come. [*It is – It is, from the mob.*] We must do more than words. We have been oppressed for 800 years since the Norman Conquest. If they would give ye a hod, a shovel, a spade, and a hoe, your mother earth would supply you. [*Aye, aye, she would. Loud applause.*] Countrymen, if you will have your wrongs redressed, follow me. [*That we will. Shouts.*] Wat Tyler would have succeeded, had he not been basely murdered by a Lord Mayor, William of Walworth. Has the Parliament done their duty? – [*No.*] Has the regent done his duty? – [*No, no.*] A man [the regent] who receives one million a year public money gives only £5,000 [*sic*] to the poor. They have neglected the starving people, robbed them of every thing, and given them a penny. Is this to be endured? Four millions are in distress; our brothers in Ireland are in a worse state, the climax of misery is complete, it can go no further.

Young Watson rounded this off with three rhetorical questions that echoed Camille Desmoulin's questions to the Parisians at the Café de Foy before they stormed the Bastille:

> If they will not give us what we want, then, shall we not take it? [*Yes!*]
> Are you willing to take it? [*Yes!*]
> If I jump down among you, will you follow me? [*loud acclamations, Yes! Yes!*][32]

Whereupon the two Watsons and Hooper led several hundred people down Coppice Lane towards the City while the greater body of the crowd stayed behind to listen to Hunt. The Orator arrived at last (whether he was delayed by accident or design was much debated; he claimed later that Castle had tried to divert him to the Tower) and delivered one of his rousing speeches in favour of reform. It kept within the bounds of the law; and his audience behaved themselves too – unlike those who followed the Watsons and Hooper.

THE RIOTS

What ensued in the City, the *Observer* noted, were the worst riots London had seen since the Gordon riots of 1780. One difference between 1780 and 1816 was that now there were no deaths other than a later execution. Another difference was that in the febrile post-war conditions and chilly economic climate of 1816, serious disturbance was predictable, so the authorities were prepared. Across past months the Spenceans had been watched by more than a dozen spies and informers, and Castle warned that disturbance was imminent.

A few weak points were left uncovered. The commander of the Portland Place artillery depot admitted that 250 stand of small arms and four fieldpieces with ammunition were guarded at night by no more than three watchmen.[33] But preparations were otherwise impressive. Bill-stickers covered the town with posters warning against riot, and 'several thousand' special constables were sworn in. They included over half the householders in Candlewick Ward, and members of Lloyd's and the Stock Exchange joined as well, as such personages have in nature always been inclined to do. On Sunday evening the Bow Street staff remained on duty, and magistrates were posted at Cold Bath Fields prison and the Clerkenwell house of correction to receive charges against prisoners who might be brought in. Constables from all the police offices and county parishes were stationed at Cold Bath Fields under the command of Bow Street's chief clerk, John Stafford, who was required to send hourly reports to Sidmouth in the home office. Magistrates monitored the crowd's mood and behaviour from the house next to the Merlin's Cave tavern, and every five minutes received and relayed reports from strategically placed observers. Soldiers were posted at Newgate, the Bank, and other public offices; cavalry and infantry were stationed inside King's Bench prison and a company of Guards lurked in the Poultry Compter, a debtors' prison. At the Tower, gates were closed, drawbridges raised, and cannon overlooking Tower Hill were loaded. Its walls were manned by Coldstream Guards and the Artillery, and the humble ordnance workers were required to parade with firelocks on the Tower's glacis. Life Guards arrived at the west end of Cheapside, and behind them waited the 9th Dragoons.[34]

Thanks to its spies, sabres, guns, and bullets, Liverpool's government was a long way from a revolutionary situation. Nonetheless fearsome disorder erupted, and most shops in the City and town barricaded their doors and put up their shutters. Manuscript posters urged: 'Britons to Arms! Break open all Gun & Sword shops Pawnbrokers or other likely places to find Arms. Run all Cunstables thro' who toutch a Man of us. – No rise of Bread &c! No Castlereagh off with his Head! … The whole Cuntry waits the Signall from London to fly to Arms.'[35] No constables were run through, but on their way into the City the crowd looted a gun shop at Skinner Street on the Snow Hill corner near Newgate, and stole guns and ammunition valued at £1,349 15s 6d. In the mêlée young Watson accidentally shot and wounded a shop customer named Platt when Platt tried to seize him. It must have been accidental because Watson apologised profusely and, himself a surgeon, set about comforting Platt until he felt it wiser to escape through a window.

Down Cheapside they all went, next to lay siege to the Royal Exchange. Hone reported that fifty or sixty were armed. Shots were fired over and under the Exchange gates before police repelled the attackers, and several were arrested. They included Hooper, armed with two pistols and his pockets full of incriminating papers, and a sailor called John Cashman, who carried a loaded musket. Outside the Bank young Watson, sword in hand, shouted 'Follow me, brave men!' Not more than a hundred did so, and most were 'boys and old men, many of them sailors'. Undaunted, young Watson led the crowd on to the Tower. 'A great many were firing in the air; there were about two hundred men and boys.'[36]

In the Minories they had liberty to loot more gun shops for over an hour. By late afternoon gangs were still marauding down Threadneedle

Street and into Bishopsgate and Whitechapel. Until now the authorities' communication lines were in poor order despite the earlier preparation, but at last the Life Guards checked the crowd in Aldgate. Rioters fired at the troops and a horse was wounded. Chased into the Whitechapel cattle pens, the looters escaped after discarding muskets, piles of which were found next day in a Houndsditch dung heap. Of the casualties treated at the London Hospital, one had a bullet hole in his hat, but others were the casualties of their own faulty weapons. A man with his thumb blown off explained that he had gone out that morning 'for the express purpose of shooting some person; ... he was in a state of starvation and did not care for his life'. He ran away before his treatment was finished. Another had his thumb and forefinger blown off, and another was wounded in the wrist.[37]

Meanwhile another part of the crowd had left Spa Fields to rampage by way of St Giles and Catherine Street down into the Strand, and looting spread from Soho to Holborn. Although dragoons and footguards with fixed bayonets put a stop to this, the streets were disordered for hours yet, and peace was secured only after nightfall. Most looters' ambitions were simple. They did smash some of the windows of Somerset House and pelt its facade with dung, but then they moved on to loot the second-hand clothes shops in Holywell Street and the food stores of the Dog tavern opposite. Butchers' stalls and a Tottenham Court Road eating-house were pillaged for food. An eleven-year-old Irish lad named Patrick Sullivan was later indicted for stealing two quartern loaves from a bread shop in Seven Dials. The shop servant testified:

> There was three men with bludgeons in their hands, the shop was full of people, taking the bread. I was alone in the shop. It was shut up before I went out. I left the door upon the latch; they asked for bread. As they were going out I saw the prisoner with some loaves; I laid hold of [Sullivan], and he dropped them. He had two loaves under his arm.

Later in the Bow Street court his mother went on her knees to beg the magistrate to send him to a boy's charity. No such luck. He was tried and convicted in the Old Bailey instead, though his punishment was respited. Two years later he was convicted of pickpocketing a handkerchief in Oxford Street: off he was sent to New South Wales for twenty-one years.[38]

Thistlewood, old Watson, and Preston kept clear of the looting. Instead they headed straight to the Tower to call out the soldiers. Preston clambered onto a wall and shouted that soldiers were the people's protectors and that any who joined them would get a hundred guineas and a promotion of rank. 'The men gazed at him – laughed; no one fired a shot – and soon after he fell down, or was pulled off by his companions.'[39] Thistlewood, no public speaker, had taken no part in the Watsons' oratorical performances, so he passed unremarked and unnamed in newspaper accounts; six days later the *Observer* still referred to him as 'a Mr Thisselton'.

At six o'clock that evening Castle the spy found Thistlewood and the Watsons packing their clothes in Watson's room in Dean Street. Castle's perfidy was still unsuspected. Thistlewood told him that they were departing for a house in the country and under an alias would leave messages at the Red Hart in Shoe Lane. He added that the day left him 'perfectly well satisfied that the people were not ripe enough to act' – which put it mildly.[40] Some planning had been evident in the flags and the raids aimed at separate targets. But the leaders' disappointment acknowledged the distance between the riots and old Watson's fantastic plan, found on his person after his capture, for the revolution that didn't happen:

> Smiths [blacksmiths], Westminster-road, to form three divisions, and collect as great a number as possible together, and meet the London division at the London-road, and proceed to the Old Man, Paddington, to proceed to St Giles's. – Barricado each street to Holborn-Bars, and the approaches to T. B. [Temple Bar]. – Barricado Chancery-lane and Carey-st. St Giles's division to barricado as far as St. Andrew's Holborn, to include Chancery-lane; 3d, Gray's Inn-lane; 4th, St. John-street and Old-street; 5th, Whitechapel; 6th, Tower; 7th, Bank; 8th, Picket-street.[41]

Next day it was reported that an unnamed leader of the riots rode on horseback to a tavern in Bouverie Street off Fleet Street, doffing his hat and bowing to the applause of the crowd that followed him. This was Hunt returning to Cooper's Hotel. Back at Merlin's Cave, after mocking the regent for his meanness, he had delivered his now familiar reform speeches, but he dissociated himself from violence and had nothing to do with the riots.[42] This didn't stop newspapers tainting him by association or visual satirists from betraying him. George Cruikshank, living in Salisbury Court three streets away from Cooper's Hotel, that night persuaded Hunt to pose for him while holding a scrolled 'Petition of Rights'. But Cruikshank was always happy to woo loyalists with his other hand, so in March his satire on Hunt's third Spa Fields meeting, *The Spa Fields orator HUNT-ing for Popularity to Do-Good!!* (Fig. 9.4), showed his audience at Merlin's Cave as lumpen grotesques and Hunt at the window as a posturing poltroon.

Hunt now had new fame to deal with, and new strategies to ponder. Narcissist as he was, he noted that the next day's newspapers 'were crammed full of the most wonderful accounts of this most wonderful plot and insurrection; attributing the whole of it to ME. ... If ten thousand of the inhabitants had been massacred, there could not have been greater consternation produced throughout the whole country; which consternation was sedulously kept up by the most abominable falsehoods.'[43] The fame of 'Spa Fields Hunt' henceforth eclipsed that of moderate tax-focused radicals like Burdett, Cobbett, and Major Cartwright. At the three Spa Fields meetings between November and February, spurred on by Watson and Thistlewood, Hunt had redefined the nature of popular politics by agitating for universal male franchise, annual parliaments, and secret ballot, in a strategy that was for the first time independent of privileged men within the political nation, and that was aimed instead to engage the small employer 'who wore a good coat' as well as 'the artisan, with a dirty waistcoat upon his waist'. As Thistlewood was sorry to see, however, Hunt repudiated violence as a tactic of first resort. With northern radicals galvanised, the way was opened to the great mobilisation that culminated in Peterloo.[44]

Five men were arrested and tried for the thefts from Beckwith's gun shop. In a hasty and ill-conducted trial Hooper and three others were acquitted. This left the sailor John Cashman as scapegoat. A 28-year-old Irishman of stunted stature and thin visage, his role in the looting was affirmed by a shop apprentice; he had also been seen waving a flag on Watson's wagon. In court no defence attorney or witness spoke for him,

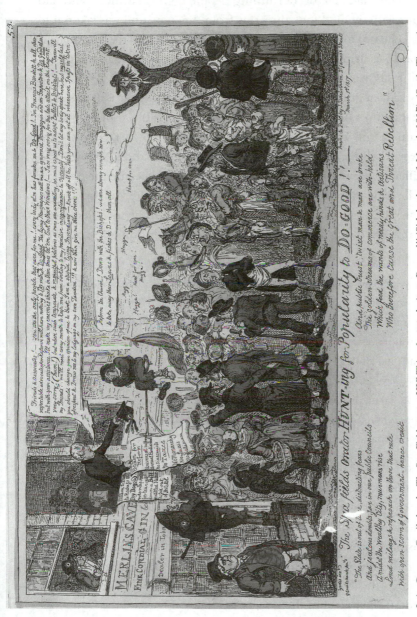

9.4. George Cruikshank, *The Spa Fields orator HUNT-ing for popularity to Do-good!!* (Sidebotham, 1 March 1817) (Sepia Times/ Universal Images Group via Getty Images)

and his own defence statement totalled ninety-seven words.[45] All he said was that he had gone that morning to the London Hospital to see an ill shipmate, had taken a letter to the admiralty, had returned to Rosemary Lane in Whitechapel where he sometimes lodged, had returned again to the admiralty, had met lots of running people on his way there, and had run along with them. 'I took the arms from the men, and was taken into custody. The two men, when they were examined before the lord-mayor, said, that I was drunk; and so I was. The man who took the musket from me, said I was drunk.' And that was it.

Only radical newspapers added that the shop had been full of sailors in similar clothes and that misidentification was possible, especially since the promise of fifty pounds reward encouraged false testimony. Moreover, Cashman had been nine times wounded and his father had been killed at sea; and his mother had to go begging because the pound a month he tried to send her never reached her. When he was swept up in the crowd, Cashman had been walking to the admiralty to collect prize money that was owing to him – and it wasn't only the admiralty that owed him:

> Four years' pay, at the rate of one pound per month, was due to him from the owner of a transport, in which he served; ... seven months' pay, at the rate of three pounds ten shillings per month, was due him from a ship in which he afterwards served; from another ship, five months' pay, at five pounds ten shillings per month; ... he was entitled to prize money from the *Sea-horse* [a Navy frigate], but lost all his papers in a schooner, in which he was taken in an action off the coast of America, and carried to Philadelphia; on which occasion he was wounded, and under the surgeon's hands for a long time.[46]

It didn't increase Cashman's chances of mercy that the authorities had further alarms to deal with. In January 1817, on his way to open parliament, the regent was mobbed in his carriage, and a stone or bullet broke its window. In February Sidmouth introduced his Habeas Corpus Suspension Bill by deploring the existence of 'a traitorous conspiracy' working for the government's overthrow, and the 'malignant spirit' which since the French revolution 'had brought such disgrace upon the domestic character of the people'. Castlereagh asked the Commons 'whether on the eve of an insurrection ... they wished the executive to sit with arms folded and make no effort to arrest it till it exploded against the state'. On 4 March habeas corpus was suspended for a year.[47] On 17 March a Treason Act renewed the Act of 1795 against 'the compassing, imagining, inventing, devising or intending death or destruction ... of the heirs and successors of George III'. And on 31 March assent was given to the Act preventing Seditious Meetings and Assemblies of more than fifty people called to deliberate 'upon any grievance, in church or state'. Meant to expire in July 1818, this was renewed by the Seditious Meetings Act of 1819.

It clinched Cashman's fate that two days before his hanging some 5,000 unemployed weavers assembled in Manchester with the intention of walking to London to petition the regent for relief. Each carried a rolled blanket to sleep in: hence 'the Blanketeers'. 'We will let them see it is not riot and disturbance we want, it is bread we want and we will apply to our noble prince as a child would to its father for bread,' an optimistic leader declared. Another invoked one of the myths that so moved poor English radicals: 'In the reign of Richard II about 40,000 men went to London to demand their rights of the king; & he granted them their rights & they went home again. But they only came a little way from London, they did not go from Manchester.'[48] The Blanketeers' assembly was broken up by dragoons and constables and twenty-seven were arrested. The cavalry chased others towards Stockport to terrify them, though they killed nobody this time.

In this climate Cashman's appeal for mercy hadn't a chance. On 12 March Newgate's unwieldy new drop was trundled out from the prison door to the corner of Skinner Street and Snow Hill where Beckwith's gun shop stood (it is now erased by the Holborn Viaduct). Overseen by soldiers, Cashman bowed, cavorted, made jokes to the crowd as best he could, and frightened the gun shop owner by saying he would return to haunt him. He told the priest that he wanted no mercy from a protestant God, and protested his innocence to the end. The crowd hissed the hangman and sheriffs as he dropped to his choking and kicking death.

FLIGHT AND CAPTURE

It is unlikely that Thistlewood and the Watsons father and son thought twice about the collateral damage inflicted on the wretched Cashman. They had their own plights to worry about. On the night of 2 December the three disguised themselves and escaped on foot into the dark countryside up the Holloway Road, heading (Thistlewood said) for Northampton. Alas, they were stopped near the Highgate village church by a Bow Street horse patrol which happened to be looking for a gang of footpads. Questions were asked, shots were exchanged, and Thistlewood and young Watson ran off into the night, firing pistols as they did so. Old Watson was caught and taken to a nearby tavern. Left in the care of its patrons while the patrol chased and lost the others, he stabbed a man with his cane-sword and had to be handcuffed. He was found to be carrying draft plans for the Spa Fields meeting and the list of radicals who might run a future Committee of Public Safety. He was taken to Bow Street to await Sidmouth's directions.[49]

Thistlewood and young Watson wandered the fields that night, before finding their way undetected back to London. There they hid among a network of LCS veterans and Spenceans. We know what ensued because one of the network's members, an ex-LCS man and Spencean tailor named Robert Moggridge, was at last caught with Thistlewood in late April and was interrogated over the next several days by Nathaniel Conant, the Bow Street magistrate. In sworn statements that covered sixteen closely written pages, Moggridge spilled all the beans the home office could have hoped for, and gave the details of an extraordinary story.[50] His exposure of the manoeuvres that kept Thistlewood and young Watson hidden in early 1817 illuminates the relative cohesion and loyalty of the Spencean underground, at least up to that date, though the Evanses' part in it was about to be forcefully ended.

The two fugitives had spent their first four or five nights in the lodging of a Lincolnshire couple, John and Amelia Hunt, in East (now Chiltern) Street, Marylebone; Susan and Julian Thistlewood seem to have joined them there shortly after. The Hunts had come to London after the Thistlewoods settled there, perhaps to be near Julian, for the sad truth was that Amelia was Julian's mother by Thistlewood, and her boy was now in the Thistlewoods' care. The fact that John had also joined the Spenceans might suggest a warm relationship were it not that Thistlewood had paid Hunt to rid him of Amelia by marrying her, as we have seen elsewhere (page 180).

It wasn't a happy ménage, therefore. Hunt relieved some of the pressure by persuading one William Carr, a victualler who was Moggridge's old LCS friend, to hide young Watson in the garret of his Tottenham Court Road shop. Young Watson wasn't a model fugitive. He took risks by venturing out for air in Mrs Carr's clothes. The Thistlewoods added to the danger by visiting him. Thomas Evans wanted to separate them lest the young man be provoked into further rash action. He promised to pay a pound for the young man's board and lodging, but was powerless to help otherwise. On 9 February 1817, on the same morning as old Watson and Preston, he and his son were arrested and imprisoned until January 1818.[51]

In their absence, Moggridge proposed a refuge for young Watson remote from Thistlewood's influence, in the house of William Holl. Aged forty-five and no longer politically active, Holl had also been a LCS man and was now a noted engraver. He lived with his wife and sons in Bayham Street, Camden Town, out of the way both of police surveillance and of Thistlewood. The young man wasn't easy to live with, and after three months Mrs Holl, now pregnant, wanted him gone.

Young Watson was next protected by Charles Pendrill, a Newgate Street tailor who had been arrested as a member of Evans's United Englishmen in 1798 and who had narrowly escaped being hanged with Despard. Pendrill came up with the obvious solution. He persuaded young Watson to flee to America. So at four o'clock one dark morning young Watson, Pendrill, and Moggridge walked for three hours out of London along unlit and muddy lanes to the village of Plaistow on the Essex border. From there another veteran named Stephen Casey, now a licensed madhouse keeper and deaf with it (so Dickensian!), led them across the Plaistow marshes to the wharf from which they were ferried across the Thames to Dartford. From Dartford they walked another ten miles to Gravesend, and there young Watson boarded the *Venus* to await the crossing to New York.

While his thirty-eight-pounds passage money was being raised, Moggridge made young Watson a pepper-and-salt coat, a striped waistcoat, and woollen cord breeches by way of a disguise. He was still recognisable: his drooping eye couldn't be helped, and the caustic he applied to the mole on his cheek had no effect. An informer spotted him and told the home office that he was on the *Venus* and about to depart ('shall call on Monday for the reward').[52] Still, off to New York he sailed, just in time. He troubled Britain no further. In 1823 the *Observer* reported that he was sentenced to death for burglary in Nashville, Tennessee, but that he was pardoned and given twenty lashes; after that he 'wandered about' in the hope of resuming life as a physician until a bilious fever killed him in Mount Vernon, Kentucky. But who knows? In 1835 someone else claimed to have met him in New York and found him a 'well-ordered man of good conduct' who was practising as a doctor.[53]

Meanwhile, with a £500 reward on his head, Thistlewood, with his wife Susan and son Julian, flitted between John Hunt's lodging and a private lodging near Marylebone church, and then back to Hunt's again because Susan didn't like the landlord. Susan had asked her father in Horncastle to send her £200 on the pretence that it was needed for Julian, so at least the Thistlewoods were adequately provided for. A fortnight after young Watson's departure, she met Moggridge and Pendrill at Carr's to arrange a meeting with Thistlewood in Marylebone. Moggridge and Pendrill told the Thistlewoods that Watson had escaped to America and advised them to follow his example. The boat *Porteus* would take them to New York for twenty guineas. Under her maiden name of Wilkinson, Susan and Julian joined the *Porteus* at Tower Wharf on 23 April, intending to pick up Thistlewood downriver at Gravesend.

So it was that Moggridge and Pendrill took Thistlewood along the same wearisome road to Casey's in Plaistow. Thistlewood left a poor impression there. Brandishing a dagger, he 'used such violent language that Casey came to town the next morning to tell Pendrell that Thistlewood should not stay there ... [he] was only fit for a straight waistcoat'. Nonetheless, three days later, Casey disguised Thistlewood in a sailor's jacket, trousers, and a red neckerchief, and took him to Tilbury, from which the fugitive crossed to Gravesend. Before joining his family on board, he was told to report to the Aliens Office vessel moored nearby. There he was at once surrounded by Bow Street officers, arrested, shackled, and taken by boat to Whitehall to face several hours' grilling by the privy council.[54] No evidence was forthcoming that he had been directly involved in the riots and looting, but Castle's reports had exposed his role in their planning. They put him in the state prisoners' cells in the Tower alongside old Watson, Preston, and Hooper.

Thistlewood initially suspected that he had been betrayed by John Hunt. But Moggridge was the obvious culprit. He had been visited by the spy Oliver five days before Thistlewood's arrest. On the day before Thistlewood's embarkation he had been arrested, interrogated by Conant, and after disclosing Thistlewood's whereabouts locked up in Tothill Fields prison until June. The madhouse keeper Casey was arrested and released on the same date, and Carr and Holl were arrested on 3 May and held for six weeks.

Moggridge agreed to become a paid government spy and duly infiltrated the White Lion committee that organised Hunt's triumphal entry into London. He had nothing to do with Cato Street because by then he was in Whitecross Street debtors' prison, like Watson. But on the day after the Cato Street arrests he wrote to Carr, who was then in a similar plight in the Marshalsea – all these men chronically haunted by debt. Here Moggridge explained the motive behind his betrayal. Signing himself 'Citizzen Moggridge' and addressing 'Citizzen Carr' ('has [as] wee have been politically engaged together'), he complained about the Thistlewoods' ingratitude for his efforts on their behalf in 1816. 'Neither the wants of my family nor their being forced from the home they have occupied for ten years, has made any impression on their flinty hearts.' This, he added, confirmed Henry Hunt's adage: 'save a man from the gallows [and] he will turn round and cut your throat'.[55]

THE 1817 TREASON TRIAL

Watson, Thistlewood, Preston, and Hooper were charged with high treason on 29 April and arraigned on 17 May 1817; Watson's trial, meant to be the first of four, opened at the court of King's Bench in Westminster on 9 June. As many as 229 government witnesses were summoned. One distinguished lawyer, Sir Samuel Romilly, knew that ministerial showmanship was behind this overkill: the prisoners were committed to the Tower and arraigned for treason merely to 'give an extraordinary degree of importance to every appearance of disaffection or turmoil'. The strategy backfired in this case. Had the men been committed to Newgate, tried at the Old Bailey, and indicted merely for aggravated riot, Romilly thought they would have been convicted.[56]

The defence counsel Wetherell argued that the prisoners made implausible revolutionaries: 'two broken-down apothecaries [the two Watsons], a broken-down gentleman, and two cobblers: these five solitary individuals were to oppose the whole world'. But in court the prisoners looked better than that, as Scharf's prison portraits have shown. Watson's trial lasted a week and was one of the year's many sensations. The liberal whig leaders from both houses of parliament attended – Holland, Grey, Lauderdale, Tierney, Lambton, Stanhope, Burdett, along with the tory Robert Peel.[57]

Unhappily for the government, the first day of the proceedings coincided with the breaking of a spy scandal. Three hundred desperate stockingers and miners in Nottinghamshire and Derbyshire had assembled in the deluded belief that they might form part of a national insurrection. 'Oliver the Spy' (W. J. Richards) had persuaded their leader, Jeremiah Brandreth, that there was to be an armed rising in London. On the appointed day, 9 June, Brandreth led his men to Nottingham, only to be surrounded by troops and arrested after a skirmish at the village of Pentrich. On 14 June, Edward Baines of the *Leeds Mercury* revealed that Oliver had provoked the uprising as part of a wider government strategy – of instigating plots and letting them run to prosecutable conclusions in order to squash them and justify repression. Sir Francis Burdett read out one of Baines's articles in the Commons on 16 June and it caused a sensation. According to one of Oliver's associates, when he and Oliver presented Sidmouth with their bill of expenses 'his Lordship abused Oliver for a great fool, for being detected'.[58]

None of this helped the Pentrich men. In October a jury of county landowners found them guilty, and chief justice Ellenborough sentenced Brandreth, Ludlam, and Turner to hanging and decapitation for treason. Fourteen others were transported to Australia, and more were gaoled. The executions took place outside Derby gaol on 7 November,

9.5. Anon. (W. Pegg?), *Decapitation of Jeremiah Brandreth* (1817) (Hulton Archive/Getty Images)

their brutality proclaimed in an uncompromising etching of Brandreth's fate (Fig. 9.5). The *Examiner* described the occasion:

> Troops of horse, with keen and glittering swords, hemmed in the multitudes collected to witness this abominable exhibition. When the stroke of the axe was heard, there was a burst of horror from the crowd. The instant the head was exhibited, there was a tremendous shriek set up, and the multitude ran violently in all directions, as if under the impulse of sudden frenzy. Those who resumed their stations, groaned and hooted.

The duke of Devonshire was the rioters' landlord. Himself comfortably housed in his vast palace at Chatsworth, that noble man had the rioters' cottages demolished and their families evicted, thus cutting Pentrich's population by a third.

The Pentrich trials and executions disgusted liberal England. Hazlitt sprang into print with a scathing piece 'On the Spy System', while in Shelley's polemic, 'We pity the plumage but forget the dying bird' (originally Tom Paine's phrase), the poet contrasted the nation's extravagant mourning for the regent's newly dead daughter princess Charlotte with the indifference shown to the Pentrich executions. Many in the polite world were too cautious to protest publicly, and Shelley's protest was published posthumously; even so, his words reveal what it was possible then to know and to take for granted:

> Thus much is known, that so soon as the whole nation lifted up its voice for parliamentary reform, spies were sent forth. These were selected from the most worthless and infamous of mankind, and dispersed among the multitude of famished and illiterate labourers. It was their business if they found no discontent to create it. It was their business to find victims, no matter whether right or wrong. It was their business to produce upon the public an impression, that if any attempt to attain national freedom, or to diminish the burthens of debt and taxation under which we groan, were successful, the starving multitude would rush in, and confound all orders and distinctions, and institutions and laws, in common ruin. The inference with which they were required to arm the ministers was, that despotic power ought to be eternal.

It was 'a national calamity that we endure men to rule over us' who themselves engineered a plot of this kind, which would succeed only 'through such a frightful pouring forth of human blood and agony. Liberty is dead!'[59]

The *Leeds Mercury*'s exposure of Oliver was probably why the government abandoned Watson's and Thistlewood's treason trials in 1817. Oliver's exposure switched attention to the key prosecution witness against Watson, John Castle, who had enrolled as a Bow Street spy in February. Henry Hunt destroyed Castle's credibility in court by revealing his criminal record as pimp, brothel keeper, and extortionist, and by claiming that he had tried to entrap Hunt himself after the first Spa Fields meeting in November. When the defence counsel Wetherell proposed that Castle had 'invented, organised and framed the whole of the projects which he represents were moulded into a system of conspiracy', the judge Ellenborough objected that he was 'at a loss to know whether it be necessary thus to divulge the sources of the information of government'. On 16 June, Watson's jury defied the judge and returned a verdict of not guilty. Watson was released, the attorney general dropped the other trials, and Thistlewood, Preston, and Hooper were freed next day.[60]

Street-level communication was speedy in those days, and popular celebration was infectious. News of the verdict spread quickly. You could hear the word *acquitted* 'a hundred times in every five minutes', the diarist Crabb Robinson recorded. In St Martin's Lane, he met a crowd in what he thought was an ugly mood, but when one drunken fellow shouted out 'England's glory for ever!' he realised they were cheering the jury.[61]

Watson now enjoyed his finest hour. After he had dined with the defence attorney James Harmer in Hatton Garden, a cheering crowd removed the horses from their harness and pushed and pulled his hackney coach down Holborn and Fetter Lane to William West's, the radical wire worker of Wych Street. '*Lights, Lights!*' the crowd demanded; so West surrounded his first-floor window with lighted candles, and Watson displayed himself at it, bowing with his hand on his heart as the crowd cheered. Next day a group of cheering supporters unharnessed Thistlewood's horses and drew his coach as he left Westminster, while Preston and Harmer left by boat, alighted at the Strand steps, and walked through cheering crowds to join Watson in Wych Street. From West's window, Preston addressed the crowd fulsomely. Thistlewood was briefer: 'I am scarcely able to address you, my feelings have been so much over-powered by being so suddenly set at liberty, after the anxiety I have experienced through so long a trial. I have ever tried to do my duty; my life shall be devoted to your cause.'

In a calculated act of appropriation on the ultras' part, a dinner was held for them four days later in the grand room of the Crown and Anchor. Preston coloured his speech after dinner by announcing that he would offer a free piece of bread to anyone who turned up at his new lodging in Clement's Inn Passage: 'he had put the names of his noble and independent jury over his fire-place, and would teach his children for ever to lisp them – (*Great applause.*)' Again Thistlewood's response was cooler. Public speaking embarrassed him, he confessed, and he would say little. A half-dozen sentences followed, to exhort the audience to support the Evanses father and son, still imprisoned.[62] In view of their mounting disagreements this was generous to the Evanses, but it was a singularly laconic speech for so rhetorically loquacious an era.

Poor Hooper was rather side-lined in all this. Having faced two trials for his life within several weeks, he died in St Thomas's Hospital seven months later of what the doctors understandably called 'exhaustion'. (Hunt later wrote that he died from a cold caught in prison.) His body was exposed for a week to sympathetic spectators before it was buried at his own request in St Dunstan's churchyard, Stepney, near the grave of the hanged sailor Cashman. The mourning procession of forty men in black cloaks was led by Watson, Thistlewood, and Preston and followed by what the *Morning Post* called 'a numerous mob'. Bow Street officers oversaw the proceedings.[63]

The jury's triumph in the Spa Fields trial anticipated an even greater triumph in December when the jury three times acquitted William Hone of the charge of publishing blasphemous parodies. In court Hone inveighed against the government's reliance on *ex officio* information, packed juries, and a shackled press. He rebuked Mr justice Abbott and lord chief justice Ellenborough for their many prejudicial interjections, and the audience in court laughed and cheered him. Hone's mockery and acquittals made him the hero of liberal and radical London.

Ellenborough had long enjoyed persecuting radicals. He had prosecuted Lord George Gordon in 1787 and Thomas Hardy in 1794, and had sent Despard and colleagues to their gruesome traitors' deaths in 1803. He had also presided over the trials of the journalists Leigh and John Hunt and the midland luddites. After Hone's acquittals, Ellenborough affected not to care that the jury had ignored his instructions. As he rode into the jeering crowd he 'laughed at the hooting and tumultuous mob who surrounded his carriage, remarking that their saliva was more dangerous than their bite'. At one point he stopped his coach and sent his coachman to buy kippers.[64] But his health declined after his humiliation, and a year later he passed away to whatever afterlife the almighty had prepared for him.

CHAPTER 10

Thistlewood Unhinged: 1818–19

THISTLEWOOD AT BAY

After their narrow escape in the Spa Fields prosecutions, Watson and Preston had sense enough not to talk openly of violence. Not so Thistlewood. The collapse of the prosecutions seems to have filled him with a sense of his own invulnerability and worsened his manic disposition. As a 'half-pardoned rebel' (Mrs Piozzi's phrase), he knew he would be under surveillance, but he broadcast his insurrectionary ambitions with suicidal candour. Henceforth his behaviour suggests the bipolarity that was mentioned earlier.

His later Cato Street indictment was to note his febrile condition in prose that was itself overexcited. Thistlewood 'was in [a] constant state of restlessness devising plans and endeavouring to enlist partizans for overthrowing the government and wild as such a plan may seem to be to others, the practicability of it or at least of creating the utmost confusion in the state appears to have got the full possession of his mind'.[1] Richard Carlile levelled the same charge in his *Republican* two days before Thistlewood's execution. He believed, bluntly, that Thistlewood was insane. The Spa Fields trial, he wrote, had raised the man 'into an importance which otherwise he could never have attained'. When he was then deserted by his friends and betters, he embarked on projects that were 'desperate, random and futile', and 'changed his company almost every month':

His mind was never without a plot or project of some sort, which he never hesitated to unfold to the greatest stranger if he would only listen to him; every one who saw and heard the wild notions he had conceived, immediately shunned him, and thus Thistlewood has ransacked all London to find some one willing to be hung with him. . . . If ever the plea of insanity should be allowed to excuse the act of any individual, that plea might be fairly and justly put in for Thistlewood. . . . Could anything but insanity induce a man, with such projects in his mind as Thistlewood has been proved to hold, to go almost to every alehouse to announce it, and to every prison in the metropolis to tell the prisoners of his intention, and that they must prepare themselves for a release? . . . Whoever has known Thistlewood for the last three years, must have been assured, that he was a candidate for the gallows.[2]

And so it was within months of their release that Thistlewood led Watson and Preston into a series of sorry misadventures, each tolerated by a home secretary who looked forward to a sensational but also easier prosecution in the fullness of time. In September 1817 the trio tried to provoke rebellion among the pleasure-seeking crowd at St Bartholmew's Fair in Smithfield. A great deal of placard-posting and weapon-sharpening forewarned the government as usual, so Horse Guards were deployed around the Mansion House, the Bank, and the prisons, and the fair-goers' taste for martyrdom evaporated. Preston 'was so disappointed, that if he had had a pistol by him, he thinks he should have blown his brains out'. In his twopenny satire on the *Bartholomew Fair Insurrection*, William Hone pretended that the attempt had been a hoax on Sidmouth, but the government knew better. A few days later the ultras began talking about an attack on the privy council 'in the manner of Despard', but the government knew about this too. In October an attack on the Tower and Bank of England was abandoned when too few men mustered to deliver it.[3]

By the new year of 1818 Thistlewood's moods were brittle. Hunt's evidence on Watson's behalf during the latter's treason trial had strengthened Watson's rapport with the orator and endorsement of his anti-insurrectionary tactics. Although Hunt was distancing himself from the moderate Burdettites, Thistlewood thought that he and Watson were going soft. At a meeting in the Spotted Dog in Clements Lane on 1 February he charged Watson with 'not being the man he professed to be'. Why had Watson written cravenly to thank Sidmouth for the visiting privileges the home secretary had allowed him in the Tower? Watson replied that so many country friends visited him while he awaited trial there that he had to write to Sidmouth for permission two or three times a day; so it was his duty to thank Sidmouth, and that hardly 'made him the worse man in the political view'. 'After this high words passed between them, and Thistlewood challenged Watson out on Monday either with sword or pistol which[ever] he liked. The company interfered and made them reconciled and agree to be friends and not conceal anything from each other. They shook hands.'[4]

Thistlewood's relations with the Evans family were also tense. Their separation was to mark the next and biggest fracture in Thistlewood's friendships. According to Francis Place, Evans had been a difficult man 'with very contemptible reasoning powers, a sort of absurd fanatic, continually operated upon by impulses'. Place added elsewhere that he was 'a fanatic of a peculiar description, ignorant, conceited and remarkably obstinate'.[5] But the simpler truth was that the Evans family had had enough of Thistlewood's violent conduct and language, as well as of being put into prisons.[6] Evans wasn't averse to violence in principle, but he mistrusted Thistlewood's indifference to the restoration of land to the common people. Until that was achieved, attempts at insurrection would be no more than 'effusions of madness, which rise like a mob, and subside, or are put down like a mob, and the oppression continues or returns with redoubled force'. Moreover, Evans had been detained without trial for the three years 1798–1801, and Janet had been briefly detained with him while pregnant and nursing her infant son. She bore stillborn twins soon after. When freed, their business and health were ruined and their political energies tamed. Funded by Janet's brother, the engineering employer Alexander Galloway (an ex-LCS man and Despard supporter now turned Burdettite), the couple had opened a shop in Newcastle Street to sell patent steel braces and springs for carriages. The family now avoided talk of jacobin violence and advocated Spence's agrarian socialism simply. Their change of heart didn't stop Evans and his son Thomas John, now nineteen, being arrested 'out of their beds' on the same morning as Watson and Preston (9 February 1817), on a general warrant issued by Sidmouth for complicity in the Spa Fields insurrection. They were detained in Cold Bath

Fields for a month until the repeal of habeas corpus enabled Sidmouth to put them into solitary confinement in the Surrey county gaol at Horsemonger Lane to await their trial for treason.[7]

There as state prisoners they enjoyed privileges that had been denied Evans in 1798–1801. Their rooms measured twenty-five by eighteen feet and eleven feet high, fire and coals were supplied by the county, and there were two large windows they could 'open as they please'. Thomas's upstairs room had 'a fine view of the Surrey hills, Shooters Hill &c, and with the assistance of a telescope which he has with him he can command a very extensive prospect'. Their comforts were offset, young Evans soon complained, by the 'wanton inhumanity' with which the keeper prevented his mother from visiting him freely. He could talk to her only through iron gratings and could hardly see her. 'I am not able to conceive how it is possible for your Lordship [Sidmouth] to deny this demand, without a direct infringement of the fundamental securities of English liberty, and a voluntary departure from all rectitude of character.'[8]

Father and son stayed in prison until January 1818, long after the Watsonites were acquitted and discharged after Watson's treason trial. In their absence the Newcastle Street business collapsed, and Janet had to open a coffee shop and newsroom from which she issued Spencean pamphlets. After their release the family's spirits recovered a little. Father and son sat on the Crown and Anchor committee that tried to plan a dinner for Hunt after Peterloo (in the event Watson and Thistlewood beat them at it), and they also supported the Cato Street wives after their husbands' deaths or transportation. Otherwise they washed their hands of ultras. It hardly helped friendship with Thistlewood that Thomas was a rate-paying Westminster voter and so one of the shopkeepers whose pusillanimity Thistlewood hated. Worse, he was one of the very few popular radicals to appear in the electoral poll-book for the 1818 Westminster election. He voted for Burdett and snubbed the candidacy of Henry Hunt, who was badly defeated.

The two old friends did sup together before the Spa Fields meeting, but Evans discouraged talk of violence and advised the Watsonites not to get carried away next day.[9] In April 1818, young Evans told a meeting in the coffee shop that he and his parents detested riotous assemblies; all they wanted was the redistribution of land. 'Evans had lost his soul since he lost his liberty,' Preston commented a few days later. The tory writer John Gifford's view was crueller: 'a hero in words, but a coward in action'.[10] In 1820 the family moved to Manchester and disappear from this story. Young Evans was later briefly the proprietor and editor of the radical *Manchester Observer*.

What Thistlewood did next speaks for a loosening of all reason. In late 1817 he had printed at his own expense a twopenny pamphlet entitled *An Interesting Correspondence between Thistlewood and Sidmouth concerning the Property Detained, in Consequence of an Arrest, on a Charge of High Treason.* It reproduced four letters he sent to Sidmouth between July and September 1817 from the family's new address at 41 Stanhope Street. The first letter demanded the reimbursement of the £180 passage money he had wasted when his escape to America was blocked in April. He also wanted to be paid the value of the clothes that had been spoiled while he was in the Tower, and to have the family possessions returned that had been confiscated when he was arrested. He listed:

> A new black coat, a pair of blue pantaloons, a black silk waistcot, three shirts, two pair of black silk stockings, a hat; those articles belonged to myself; my little boy, a new coat, waistcoat, and trousers, his bed, a box of colours, a glass inkstand, two writing books, a large quantity of goose quills, some music books; Mrs Thistlewood was more fortunate, she only lost a large silk umbrella.

The pamphlet also published Sidmouth's secretary's curt dismissal of his plea together with three of Thistlewood's replies. These last can only be called immoderate. Denouncing 'that unfeeling brutality, and that unhesitating dishonesty which so pre-eminently distinguishes the British Cabinet', he invited Sidmouth to 'cast off your hypocritical saintlyness, and appear in no other character but your own, that of the willing tool of the vilest of mankind.' He, Thistlewood, remained 'the avowed enemy of every species of villainy, whether disguised in the hypocritical cant of a supercilious aristocrat, or exhibited in the more vulgar depravity of a commissioned executioner'. These ripostes were ignored, so on

3 February 1818 he sent a letter by twopenny post to challenge Sidmouth to a duel: 'I leave the choice of sword or pistol to your Lordship, and [the] place. As for time, I shall admit of no delay, and an immediate answer is expected.' This was sent two days after he had challenged Watson to a duel as well.

Liverpool's cabinet responded by prosecuting Thistlewood for what it chose to call a breach of the peace. Sidmouth demurred at first because he would be required to swear that the challenge had put him in bodily fear; but he gave way next day and swore the peace against Thistlewood in the King's Bench. An impossible bail was set, and Thistlewood was put in the Marshalsea prison to wait three months for his trial and sentence.

The press reported that he now fell 'wretchedly ill'. When he was brought to court on 14 May he was so unstable that a surgeon had to attend him, and Watson was allowed to sit next to him as his advisor. During the proceedings, he laughed at the prosecution and then shouted in anger. Found guilty, he had to wait another fortnight for his sentence. He was imprisoned for a year in the Sussex county gaol in Horsham, distant from London friends. His sentence included an obligation to provide £600 as sureties of good behaviour for three years after his release, a half paid by himself and a half by two others.

From Horsham Thistlewood wrote to the home office to complain about prison conditions and to plead against his sentences on grounds of health and poverty. Horsham gaol had been rebuilt in the late 1770s as a 'reformed prison'. It had twelve cells for male felons on each of its two upper floors, six for women, and thirteen for debtors, and in its grounds there was an infirmary and a pleasantly named Hard Labour Shed. His cell measured seven by nine feet, he wrote, and in it he had to share a single bed with two other men. The sureties amounted to a sentence for life because he was in no position to pay them. For what the treasury solicitor admitted was only a misdemeanour, these were vindictive inflictions. The ministers would have felt that they were disposing of a madman.[11]

His mental condition wouldn't have been improved had he seen Robert Cruikshank's slander on the ultras in his *Modern Reformers in Council, – or – Patriots Regaling*, published on 3 July 1818 (Fig. 10.1). The print shows Henry Hunt, who a fortnight earlier had been hopelessly

10.1. Isaac Robert Cruikshank, *Modern Reformers in Council, – or – Patriots Regaling – vide the Resolutions of the Spa Fields & Spencean Societies* (Humphrey, 3 July 1818) (Sepia Times/ Universal Images Group via Getty Images)

beaten at the Westminster election, addressing his grotesquely lampooned supporters – Gale Jones, Preston, the Evanses, and Wooler among them, all sporting revolutionary *bonnets rouges* and rosettes. The wall behind them is adorned by portraits of 'Tom Payne' and Napoleon, and images of a judge dangling from a gas-light gibbet and of the Bank of England on fire. Front right sits the pipe-smoking James Watson, barelegged and ragged. Tied to his back are an 'Old Stocking full of Gunpowder Spa Fields' and an enema-pipe 'for the Regent'; at his feet a bottle contains 'Poison of Contention'. On his left sits cobbler Preston, while on the extreme left Thistlewood sits drinking 'venom' from a skull goblet and holding a blunderbuss inscribed with his name.

Thistlewood's fragility is betrayed in a letter he wrote to Julian on 11 June, his only domestic letter that survives.[12] (It never reached the boy, and is now in the home office papers.) In it he rebukes his son for unspecified misdeeds, and instructs him to be a good and studious boy and to read Gibbon's *Decline and Fall*. Julian's stepmother Susan he terms 'Mrs Thistlewood'. The letter castigates the 'infernal monsters' the

Evanses and the Lincolnshire 'scoundrel' John Hunt whom Thistlewood had paid to marry Julian's mother (and who had sheltered him and young Watson after Spa Fields).[13] The letter is littered with street-level pronunciations and phrases, and punctuation and spelling are disordered.

Horsham Gaol
11th June 1818

My dear Julian,

A copy of a letter which you intend sending to that scoundrel John Hunt Mrs Thistlewood has just shown me. Send it by all means you have hit him hard but he wants hiting [sic] harder. Ask him if he has the impudence to call again whether if you should go with him if he can teach you to steal so as not to be found out. For he was such a clumsy hand when at Horncastle he did it in such a Bungling manner that if he had not got of [off] pretty quick he would [...?] most likely have been hanged or transported. Tell him what ever you learn you are determined if possible to be taught by a man that understands his business, also give him to understand it will be well for his health to keep away from you for you are determined to expose him in the street both as a spy and a thief. Rest assured Julian I for give all that is passed that [...?] excellent disposition which Nature as [sic] given you and which was so near being destroyed by them infernal monsters the Hunts and the Evanses. I am glad from my heart that you have got your eyes open never shut them again from your real friends. My imprisonment is only for a year if they give me the whole extent of it and that will soon be over, and you and your mother shall come and spend a week or two at Horsham in the course of the summer. I hope you will always speak french to Mr Faggs. You must when you go to the Kings Bench [prison] again get the address of mr Askam Junr.[14] He lives I think in Sergeants Inn Chancery Lane you must corespond [sic] with him in short hand once or twice in the week, you must also go to Mr Lawsons and learn to play the flute. I would have you also begin and read through Gibbons Roman History, take care and keep up on the best terms with William West [of Wych Street] quarrel with nobody except the Hunts and Evans your mother tells me you are a good boy I surely hope you will keep so and I remain your affectionate father

Arthur Thistlewood.

On his release from Horsham a year later, in May 1819, Thistlewood seemed a broken man. Two years earlier he had been described as active and cheerful-looking. Now he was to be seen walking or running through the streets 'with eager impetuosity', shabbily dressed, furtive, and emaciated. Sidmouth recognised that he was moved by 'a strong desire of revenge superadded to his previous feeling of hatred to the government'.

While Thistlewood was in gaol, Watson continued to be regarded as London's ultra-radical leader. He strengthened links with provincial and Irish radicals, moved closer to Hunt during the June 1818 Westminster election, and endorsed Hunt's non-violent platform campaign of 1819 as the best way of attracting people to the radical cause. But he began to advocate this in class terms, hitherto uncited by the ultras and certainly not by Hunt. Mechanics and labourers, Watson argued, were 'a class of people from whom all the good that man enjoyed was derived'; they were 'the sole support of the superstructure', the foundation from which 'all the other classes rise pyramidically to the Throne'.[15]

THE SMITHFIELD MEETING

After he left Horsham, Thistlewood rejoined Susan and young Julian in Stanhope Street. He still had money enough to fund the making of iron pike-heads and hand grenades, and on his tavern recruiting forays to buy cheese and beer for any number of potential insurrectionists.[16] Some of the expenditure was raised in sixpenny donations from trade-club and Spencean meetings, with several pounds now and then donated by richer people. Among the least expected of these was Jeremy Bentham the philosopher, who paid to send a visiting radical, Walker, home to Manchester. Bentham had helped previously, it seems, though his vast correspondence contains no reference to Thistlewood, Watson, or street politics generally; as a friend of Burdett he had no affinity with the ultras.[17]

Eventually Thistlewood's money ran out. In October 1819 he sent another fiery letter to Sidmouth asserting that he had been illegally arrested and wanted his £180 back with three years' interest – 'compound interest of course'. Sidmouth ignored it.[18] By February 1820 he was selling family possessions to buy weapons. The two pounds he got from

Colnaghi's printshop for his set of twenty-three prints depicting Napoleon's battles he spent on 'combustibles'. He called on Jane Carlile to ask her for two or three pounds, but with her husband in gaol she was too poor to oblige.[19]

Despite his hardships, Thistlewood retained credit enough to be a prominent member of the 'Committee of 200' that gathered round Watson in the White Lion. Its most significant initiative was to invite Henry Hunt to address a great reform meeting in Smithfield on 21 July 1819.[20] It was a prelude to Peterloo three weeks later. Hunt committed himself to a non-violent platform, and at this point Thistlewood and Watson had no choice but to follow his lead.

To the north of Newgate, Smithfield was the ancient site of livestock sales as well as of executions and burnings (Map 2). It occupied a space twice as big as it does now, after the meat market was built in 1868. Despite the cattle pens in the way, the *Examiner* estimated that some 70,000 people gathered there on this occasion, one of the largest assemblies London had seen. Moderates like Major Cartwright, Sir Charles Wolseley, the Evanses, and Galloway did the Watsonites a favour by absenting themselves. It was Watson, therefore, who escorted Hunt to the meeting, the Orator riding behind him on his high horse, in the wake of a procession bearing leafy wands. And it was Thistlewood, Watson, Preston, and the Stockport reformer, Rev. Joseph Harrison, who stood on the platform by Hunt's side as he addressed the meeting, with not a moderate in sight. The platform was decorated with a white flag inscribed 'Peace and Good Will', a red flag inscribed 'Universal Suffrage', and another striped red, white, and green inscribed 'ENGLAND', 'SCOTLAND', 'IRELAND', signifying the three nations' revolutionary unity. Everyone cheered when Hunt announced that this was to be the new Union flag. Then another flag of 'blood red hue' was unfurled to display the words 'LIBERTY OR DEATH', which Hunt hailed as the motto of liberty's heroes (*Loud and long cheering*). A print of the assembly was published the day after by George Thompson's printshop in 43 Long Lane (Fig. 10.2). Despite its broadside-woodcut style, it does justice to the scale and excitement of the event. Hunt sits at 'A' with a paper on 'Universal Suffrage' on his lap; Thistlewood, side-whiskered, stands behind him at 'D', while Watson proposes a vote of censure on

10.2. *Smithfield Meeting 21 July 1819* (Thompson, Long Lane, 23 July 1819) (Guildhall Library & Art Gallery/Heritage Images/Getty Images)

Sidmouth to the fore at 'C'. On the left of the print, top-hatted and truncheon-bearing constables approach the platform with practised efficiency to arrest Rev. Joseph Harrison (B), as they did in reality.

To the authorities, the meeting was scarily reminiscent of December 1816 in Spa Fields. Anxieties were increased by the advertisements posted about town. The *Times* transcribed one to show how wicked the radicals were, despite their protestations otherwise:[21]

> No riot, no bloodshed, by choice; but blood-thirsty despots must grant our
> rights. If that overgrown pauper [the regent], if the puppet of C—
> [Castlereagh], of L— [Liverpool], and S— [Sidmouth], whose villainous
> impudence at his [the regent's] late prorogation of the Houses of
> Corruption, could mock the miseries of the non-represented by jargoning
> about our happy constitution! – if he can be put down without breach of
> peace, let peace be preserved. . . . Peace is our wish; but let us never forget that
> resistance to oppression is the constitutional privilege of every Briton. . . .
> Shall a million of stout non-franchised hearts, reduced to the abject
> condition of slaves, lick the feet of such a comparative handful of rascals,

who trample upon us. ... If the unspeakable grievances of non-representation cannot be redressed without vengeance, 'tis better to break our chains upon the heads of our common tyrants, than longer to endure our servitude.

Reading this and similar posters led the lord mayor Atkins to anticipate the 'firing [of] this great city and murdering all its peaceable inhabitants'. Or so he said. He made sure that soldiers lurked behind the gates of St Bartholomew's Hospital, and that 6,000 special constables were sworn in the day before.

In the event the only danger point came when the Bow Street men marched in to arrest Joseph Harrison. Hunt later commented that the arrest was meant to provoke a tumult so that the military might 'have a pretence for bloodshed' and be 'let loose upon the people, with some apparent show of necessity'.[22] Certainly the arrest might have provoked a riot had Hunt not controlled the meeting so skilfully. 'Order, Order', one of the platform banners shouted. In his speech Hunt insisted that Londoners should follow the example of the northerners whose peaceable meetings denied the government the chance of 'special commissions, dungeons and hangings'. Any violence 'would damn the cause altogether', he said: 'By great public meetings being peaceably but firmly conducted, the public feeling of the whole country may be so concentrated as to cause the consummation of our wishes.' So Hunt's familiar attacks on sinecures, taxation, and parliament's criminal complacency and corruption ruled the day.[23] Working the crowd with his usual skill, he added that anonymous letters had threatened to kill him, but that if need be, like Wat Tyler in 1381, he would glory in 'dying at your head'. Watson and Joseph Harrison followed the cue. Wat Tyler's supporters had assembled 'in those very fields', Watson said, which proved that 'a spirit of morality was inherent in every British heart'. Harrison before his arrest declared that he stood 'in the same place where many martyrs have suffered death and where Wat Tyler was assassinated'. John Gast, the Rotherhithe shipwright allied to Hunt, concluded the meeting by moving a long series of resolutions, beginning with the motion 'that every person born in Great Britain and Ireland is, by inherent right – FREE'.[24]

Apart from a disturbance or two on the margins of the gathering and a couple of beaten-up constables, the crowd remained peaceful.[25] When it broke up at four o'clock Hunt again cautioned the people against violence and led them to the Wych Street house of William West the wire worker. From its casement window he bowed to the people and basked in their cheers.[26] In less than a month he would be the hero of Peterloo.

CHAPTER 11

Peterloo in London: 1819–20

MANCHESTER, 16 AUGUST 1819

There's no passing over the horror of Peterloo in this book. Even today, familiarity with the *idea* of Peterloo doesn't prepare one for its bloody detail: the deaths, the wounds, the mindless gung-ho of sabre-wielding tories on horseback. Its miserable story should never *not* be repeated. In importance one historian thinks it 'up there with Magna Carta'. Many of the middle classes had been icily indifferent to popular demands for the vote, so as a Mancunian put it at the time, what now occurred was like 'the breaking up of a great frost'.[1] For a while it transformed political understanding in all Britain:

> The mask for a century worn,
>> Has fallen from her [Tyranny's] visage at last;
> Of all its sham attributes shorn,
>> Her reign of delusion is past.[2]

Peterloo makes Thistlewood's and his supporters' driven fury and thirst for vengeance over the winter of 1819/20 not at all mad, but intelligible. We've already heard Thistlewood: 'High treason was committed against the people at Manchester ... The prince, by the advice of his ministers, thanked the murderers, still reeking in the gore of their hapless victims! ... Insurrection then became a public duty, and the blood of the victims should have been the watch-word to vengeance on their murderers.' We've heard Brunt, too, insisting that the conspirators had never called monarchy into question, and that it was the ministers who deserved assassination. In liberty's name he wanted them dead:

the circular [letter to the magistrates] issued by Lord Sidmouth was nothing but a thing sent out to instigate the cavalry to murder those men at Manchester; and if a man murders my brother I have a right to murder him. What does the scripture say 'An eye for an eye, and a tooth for a tooth'[?] ... Try me for murder – hang me – draw me – quarter me – but let me have justice, that is all I have to say.[3]

The butcher James Ings said the same:

There is another thing, my Lord. A meeting was called at Manchester, under the protection of the great charter of England, which our forefathers bled and fought for, and made King John sign in the open air. Those men were met under the protection of that law, to oblige parliament to give them their rights. My lord, previous to the meeting, the Manchester yeomanry cavalry carried their swords to the cutlers to be ground; for my own part I see no harm in grinding swords, but they cut down unarmed men, women and children; that was a disgrace to the name and character of Englishmen. .... I hope my children will live to see the day that there will be justice administered in the country; that they all will be freemen, and live like men; I had rather die like a man, than live like a slave. I am sorry I have not got abilities to address you, but I have not, and therefore I must withdraw.[4]

This from the man who had planned to enter Lord Harrowby's dining room with the words, 'Well, my lords, I have got as good men here as the Manchester yeomanry. Enter, citizens, and do your duty': and off the heads would come.[5]

The crowd flocking to Manchester's St Peter's Field on Monday, 16 August 1819 to hear Orator Hunt address them on parliamentary reform was, by modern calculation, at least 35,000 strong.[6] At the time, the *Times* reported 80,000 people, while the *Manchester Observer* worked from densities per square yard to conclude that 153,000 were present. Henry Hunt and Richard Carlile, both on the platform, respectively calculated 180,000–200,000 and 300,000 people. William Jolliffe, a young lieutenant of the Hussars who rode in the fatal charge, remembered that the space was 'so filled with people that their hats seemed to touch'. They had assembled peaceably and unarmed, Jolliffe wrote, apart from a stone in the occasional pocket. As they walked with their banners and bands of music from neighbouring towns as well as Manchester, unemployed weavers and their families mostly, everyone was 'full of good humour, laughing and shouting and making fun'. The poorest wore their best clothes; the slightly less poor dressed like Jemima Bamford – 'plainly as a countrywoman, in my second best attire'.[7] The day was fine and hot.

The magistrates who had to deal with this influx were pumped-up social disciplinarians, high tory and Anglican landowners, commercial men and clergy – 'the worst ... most bigoted, violent and active' magistrates in England, Lord Brougham wrote after the event.[8] The home office papers of the preceding decade crawl with their anxieties about the jacobins, trouble-makers, and strangers that infested their localities. They dealt with them forcefully. An assembly of 20,000 Manchester handloom weavers in 1808 calling for a fixed wage prompted the magistrates to read the Riot Act and call out the dragoons. A weaver was killed and several injured.[9] And when in 1812 desperate handloom weavers set fire to a mechanised weaving mill at Westhoughton, the high sheriff William Hulton of Hulton Hall outside Bolton ensured that four were hanged, among them a twelve-year-old boy, and nine transported. Hulton was a landed gentleman and coal-owner of ancient family who was infamous for squeezing his workforce. He was one of the magistrates attending Peterloo, and it was he who ordered Orator Hunt's arrest and the hussars' charge that achieved it.

Well before the meeting, the home office undersecretary Henry Hobhouse had privately informed the northern military commander of Sidmouth's belief 'that your country [county] will not be tranquillized until blood shall have been shed either by the law or the sword. Lord Sidmouth will not fail to be prepared for either alternative, and is confident that he will be adequately supported by the magistracy of Lancashire.' In July Sidmouth gave the magistrates what Robert Poole calls another 'get out of gaol card'. This was the infamous circular that promised a parliamentary indemnity should they be confronted by 'an extreme case'. It also advised the magistrates to 'keep this delicate subject as much as possible to yourself'.[10] So it was, amid stories of men marching and arming on the moors, of women making *bonnets rouges,* of advertisements for a monster meeting, and of Hunt's planned arrival, that the magistrates prepared for the worst by swearing in three or four hundred volunteer special constables and calling for the help of the soldiers.

An intimidating force was assembled: six troops of light cavalrymen of the 15th Hussars; seven companies of the 77th and 88th Foot; 400 men of the Cheshire yeomanry cavalry; and a troop of the Royal Horse Artillery. The military were commanded by one Lieutenant Colonel Guy L'Estrange. He was deputed to do so because Major General Sir John Byng, commander of the northern district, stayed in York to watch the races. The 15th Hussars were hardened professionals who had fought with Wellington in Spain and at Hougoumont Farm at Waterloo. They knew how to fight English civilians too. In 1810 they had stopped the Burdettite riots in London, in 1812 they had put down luddites in Yorkshire and Nottinghamshire, and had controlled Nottingham crowds celebrating the prime minister Spencer Perceval's assassination, and in 1817 they had captured the Pentrich rebels and policed the crowd when Brandreth and his fellows were executed for treason in Derby. These ungentle souls had been quartered in the Hulme cavalry barracks in Manchester since May.[11]

Meanwhile the Horse Artillery took up their posts with two 'long six-pounder' cannon. Six-pounders! These machines had been standard equipment on both sides at Waterloo and remained the army's staple artillery piece for decades yet. Long six-pounders were drawn on four-wheeled carriages, which made them manoeuvrable for street use. Each could shoot a solid iron ball weighing six pounds (2.7 kg) up to one kilometre at four degrees elevation. If it ploughed through human beings as it then bounced along, it would kill or maim dozens. For short-range decimation the cannon could discharge tin cans filled with small iron balls, the first 'shrapnel'.[12] Nobody meeting in Manchester was unaware of the guns' reputation and effects.

This unlovely edifice was crowned by some 120 of the Manchester and Salford yeomanry cavalry. These were the incompetent villains in what unfolded, a mixed bag of tradesmen and cotton masters swaggering in uniforms on horseback and waving sabres that they had freshly sharpened that morning. The cutler assured them that they were sharp enough to shave reformers.[13] The posse had been formed in 1817 after the aborted march to London of 5,000 blanket-carrying weavers (the 'Blanketeers') to petition the regent for relief. Eleven of them were cotton manufacturers and merchants, and twenty-one had no declared occupation. These included ten 'Esquires' and a 'Gent'.[14] The rank and file included shopkeepers, publicans, watchmakers, insurance agents, tobacconists, farriers, butchers, attorneys, horse-breakers, brewers, and an unexpected dancing master. They had to provide their own horses, so they were comfortable men whose membership brought martial colour into their lives, not to say profitable hobnobbing with the gents in command. The gents in command were a landowner Thomas Trafford and the cotton manufacturer Hugh Hornby Birley. The last named led the fatal charge.

Such were the men whom the panicking magistrates ordered to help arrest Henry Hunt and other speakers after the constables failed to do so. No reliable evidence was brought that they read the Riot Act first. Into the people the yeomanry charged with 'zeal and ardour', as one witness observed, 'seeming individually to vie with each other which should be first'.[15] As they did so, the Hussars blocked the eastern side of St Peter's Field, the Cheshire yeomanry blocked the southern side, and the 88th infantry regiment with fixed bayonets (and the cannon behind them) blocked the main escape route into Peter Street. Everyone panicked. So did the horses, confused by the screaming crush of trapped people. The Hussars and the Cheshire yeomanry were ordered in to help. As Jolliffe again recalled, the Hussars 'swept this mingled mass of human beings before it; people, yeomen, and constables, in their confused attempts to escape, ran one over the other; so that by the time we [the Hussars] had arrived at the end of the field the fugitives were literally piled up to a considerable elevation above the level of the ground'. The regular troops at first escaped execration because their officers were twice heard ordering their men and the yeomanry to desist: 'For shame, gentlemen; what are you about? The people cannot get away.' Yet according to Jolliffe the professionals slashed and cut as zealously as the amateurs. They caused nine out of ten of the sabre wounds, he thought – and the special constables' vigorous way with truncheons injured many more.[16]

A cheerful letter to the home office from the Hussars' Major Dyneley caught the spirit of things at the close of day: 'The first action of the Battle of Manchester is over, and has I am happy to say ended in the complete discomfiture of the enemy.' He was gratified to see 'the field of battle covered with hats, sticks, shoes, laurel branches, drum heads &c &c in short the field was as complete as I had ever seen one after an action'. And, he added, 'I was very much amused to see the way in which the Volunteer Cavalry knocked the people about during the whole time we remained upon the ground; the instant they saw 10 or a dozen mobbites together, they rode at them, & *leathered* them properly.'[17]

Henry Hunt was leathered as well. Two yeomen cavalrymen and a half-pay major general named Clay attacked him as the constables conducted him to the magistrates: 'I received three cuts from them,' he wrote later, 'a slight one on the back of my hand, and two others in my head, which cuts penetrated through my hat. As I entered into Buxton's house, ... a ruffian came behind me and levelled a blow at my head with a heavy bludgeon, which would have felled me to the earth, had I not been supported by the constables.'[18]

After the disaster, the lists of killed and wounded lengthened. By January 1820 it was possible to name eleven killed and over 400 injured. But there had been so much intimidation and under-reporting that only now can modern research give eighteen killed (since seven died of wounds later) and some 670 injured. The report of the London relief committee lists how they died: 'sabred'; 'sabred and trampled on'; 'sabred and stabbed'; 'rode over by the cavalry'; 'sabred'; 'inwardly crushed'; 'thrown into a cellar and killed on the spot'; 'shot'; 'trampled on by the cavalry'; 'rode over by cavalry'. The dead included four women and a two-year-old boy, 'trampled on'.[19]

One dead victim, John Lees, was a veteran of Waterloo, though aged only twenty-two. Because he was the illegitimate son of a cotton manufac-turer, he was the sole victim to be given an inquest. A witness testified that he saw him receive 'a cut on the back of his right arm from a sabre; he was parrying off the blows of one of the military, and another came and cut him; he had his right arm up over his head protecting it with a walking-stick'. He died of injuries three weeks later. 'I have seen many dead people,' said another, 'but I never saw such a corpse as this, in all my life.' His body was discoloured and 'his inside was putrified'; it continued to bleed as it was put into the coffin. The London radicals' attorney James Harmer was sent to Manchester to assess the inquest's conduct. Despite the difficulties put in his way, he managed to keep the proceedings going for a month before they were corruptly dismissed in order to avoid a verdict of unlawful killing. It was left to Hone in London to expose the scandal by publishing *The Whole Proceedings before the Coroner's Inquest at Oldham, . . . on the Body of John Lees, who Died of Sabre Wounds at Manchester, August 16, 1819.*

Most casualties were struck down by horses' hooves and crushed or trampled; at least a half were slashed by sabres or battered by special constables' truncheons. Every strike and slash was delivered with a curse and 'horrible imprecations'. At least seven men and a woman were bayoneted by the regular infantry as they tried to escape into Peter Street. By far the majority of casualties were weavers: 145 are named in the metropolitan relief schedule (which supplies occupations as the Manchester relief book does not). There were also ten labourers, two plasterers, a dozen spinners, four shoemakers, and eight tailors. None was armed. The manuscript Manchester relief book lists ninety-one injured women, as well as the four dead ones. Mary Heys of Oxford Road was one who was killed. The metropolitan committee reported her as 'knocked down and trampled on by a cavalry horse, her foot stripped of the flesh and great toe nails; was pregnant at the time, and so much bruised, she continued to have fits almost daily till the 17th December when she died. Was prematurely delivered of a seven month's child, which caused her death. Her husband is nearly blind.'

Women were nearly twice as likely as men to be sabred or trunch-eoned. A dozen stood in white dresses on the speakers' platform, an unnatural display of female assertiveness which military men found beyond bearing. Some 150 female reformers came from a club in Oldham, and another group from Royton. 'Respectable' women taunted them for their unseemliness, and the constables and yeomanry attacked them with particular malice. Mary Fildes was on the platform as president of the Female Radical Reformers of Manchester, conspicuous for her white dress and the banner she held, inscribed 'Annual Elections,

Universal Suffrage, Vote by Ballot'. This was 'a most singular and interesting situation for a woman at such a meeting,' Carlile wrote; 'Joan of
Arc could not have been more interesting ... On the first appearance of
the cavalry I was standing by Mary Fildes, but I found her above everything like fear.'[20] She 'was much beat by constables and leaped off the
hustings when Mr Hunt was taken [and] was obliged to absent herself
a fortnight to avoid imprisonment.' Jemima Bamford, Samuel's wife,
described her own escape:

> The people shouted, and then the soldiers shouted, waving
> their swords. Then they rode amongst the people, and there was a great
> outcry, and a moment after, a man passed without hat, and wiping the
> blood off his head with his hand, and it ran down his arm in a great stream.
> The meeting was all in a tumult; there were dreadful cries; the soldiers kept
> riding amongst the people, and striking with their swords. I became
> faint, and turning from the door, I went unobserved down steps into
> a cellared passage; and hoping to escape from the horrid noise, and to
> be concealed, I crept into a vault, and sat down, faint and terrified, on
> some fire-wood.[21]

Wounds were horrific. Thomas Hayward of Pendleton was 'inwardly
injured by the crowd ... so dreadfully crushed, the blood issued from his
mouth and nose: three weeks in the Infirmary and eight weeks off work,
disabled'. Treatments were rudimentary. Those sent to the Manchester
infirmary might be 'huffed and insulted' and turned away if they admitted to being radicals. James Lees (not John) had

> 2 desperate cuts on the head one 5 inches long by one of the 15th
> [Hussars] – He was taken to the infirmary and after being dressed one of
> the junior surgeons ordered him to a bed ... Dr Ransome asked him if he
> had enough of Manchester meetings and on his reply in the negative he
> was told there was no room for him.

William Barnes of Salford, a weaver with a 'sabre-cut on left eye-brow and
right side of his head, legs trampled on', was arrested but discharged on
the recommendation of his master 'who said he had been very ill used'.
Appended to this: the magistrate 'Mr Ethelstone said, notwithstanding,
that he thought him a very dangerous fellow.'[22]

We should recall these people's poverty, their risks of 'mortification' (sepsis), and the disaster delivered on fragile family economies when injury forced them out of work. Hunger would kill if sabres failed. Agents sent by the London relief committee found some of the people 'now almost generally clothed in rags', their hovels and cellars nearly stripped of furniture and themselves subsisting solely on potatoes. 'Here and there a little fat or dripping [was] mixed up with the potatoes ... but in no one instance among the weavers did your deputation see a morsel of animal food; and ... in most families where there were children, the taste of meat was unknown from one year to another.' This was no wonder, they added, when six shillings per week was the average wage of an able-bodied and industrious weaver. Many couldn't obtain even that amount. One source gives the advanced ages of some of the injured: 'a man aged 61, four 60, two 64, one 67, one 65, two men 50, a man 70, a woman 55, one 63, three men 63, a man 76, one 69, a woman 71, a man 62 (disabled for life), a woman 70, one 66, one 79, a man 74, one 75, a woman 64, and so on.'[23] In bald notes and hasty formatting, but in a neat script that somehow deepens their sadness, 179 pages of the Manchester account book give the names, addresses, and injuries of 347 people, along with the relief provided.[24] The *Times* reported a few days later that 'Manchester now wears the appearance of a ... town conquered in war'.

What people saw and reported was unforgettable. Henry Hunt remembered one man 'with his shoulder-blade cut in two', and

> another with the fleshy part of the arm just below the shoulder, with a wound 7 inches long, & cut so deep as to injure the bone materially, several splinters having been extracted. One poor woman has her left breast taken clean off, leaving her ribs bare; one man his nose off; one with his ear cut off close to his head, which he actually picked up and carried home in his pocket.

Everyone also remembered the yeomanry's trumpeter Edward Meagher. He 'could hardly sit on his horse, he was so drunk; he sat like a monkey'. 'Damn you, disperse,' he shouted at William Cheetham, a Bolton weaver.[25] Cheetham begged for room to pass, so Meagher 'moved his horse a little, and as Cheetham went betwixt him and the wall, he cut him and said, I will cut off your damned head'. Cheetham had to be treated for severe sabre cuts on the back of his neck, and missed two weeks' work, for which he was compensated with '40 shillings final'.

The man Hunt saw with the split shoulder blade turned out to be a journeyman hatter named Thomas Redford; he had carried a banner on or near the platform. Three years later well-wishers funded his private prosecution of Captain Hugh Hornby Birley and three of his troop for causing the injury. Of the hundred witnesses heard in the trial, one was another of Birley's casualties, John Leigh of Cheetham. On his prancing steed, Birley had recognised Leigh as one of his own workers. He 'made a stroke and cut him on the left lip a very respectable man'. Leigh managed to name Birley as the perpetrator before the presiding judge Holroyd silenced him for his insolence. Holroyd reminded the court of the disturbed state of the town before the meeting, and said that the magistrates had merely reacted against a provocative if not strictly unlawful assembly. Prosecution was futile, since 'no action, unless brought within six months, can lie against any persons who act in obedience to a warrant of the magistrates'. The special jury, six of whom were 'esquires', took six minutes to decide that such assault as there had been 'had been properly committed in the dispersal of an unlawful assembly'.[26]

Birley deserves special commemoration. A Pittite tory and one of Manchester's largest cotton spinners, he ran a huge iron-framed, six-storey mill, built in 1814. It employed 549 people two years later, and that number trebled as decades passed. He squeezed wages like all his kind, but with a malice of his own. His men stoned his mill windows during the 1818 spinners' strike; within three years spinners' average wage had dropped from 24 to 18 shillings. Starving, they had to return to work ten weeks later, wages unchanged. Birley escaped Peterloo scot free. For decades ahead, the only penalties he paid for his brutality were the mocking 'rough music' and 'groaning' performed outside his Mosley Street house on every Peterloo anniversary. He died in 1845 lauded for charitable works because he had helped endow a church or two. He was a progenitor of a well-padded dynasty of which eighteen members now cohabit in *Who's Who*, their family name paraded there despite its taint.

Manchester's tory cabal wasn't to be easily defeated. One of the magistrates, the Rev. Charles Wickstead Ethelston, insisted that he had read the Riot Act on St Peter's Field (inaudibly, if so), and he it was who had signed the warrant for the speakers' arrests. The attorney James Harmer advised the London relief committee that Ethelstone's actions and the other magistrates' support constituted 'murder, as to those who were slain, and a capital offence as to those who were sabred', but he admitted that there was no chance of winning a legal case in the face of tory obstructionism, and the whig lawyers Denman, Brougham, and Tindall agreed. That assessment was confirmed a few days after Peterloo when Sidmouth forwarded the regent's thanks to the magistrates 'for their prompt, decisive, and efficient measures for preservation of the public peace'. In January 1820 one of the magistrates, the Rev. W. R. Hay, was granted the clerical living of Rochdale worth £2,000 a year for 'his services in putting down the demand for reform'.[27] It was the platform speakers and their friends who were punished. Sidmouth's first instinct was to try them for treason, but evidence was lacking. Nine were tried at the York Assizes in March 1820 for unlawful assembly and the exciting of discontent. After a fortnight's trial five were found guilty, Henry Hunt among them. He was imprisoned in Ilchester gaol for two and a half years.[28]

PETERLOO IN LONDON

In mail coaches that might reach speeds of eight miles an hour in good weather, it usually took two days for Manchester news to reach the London papers. News about Peterloo arrived more speedily. Richard Carlile had been on Hunt's platform in St Peter's Field as an intended speaker. Having escaped the arrests and caught the early mail coach to London, he had London's walls placarded with the headlines 'Horrid Massacres at Manchester' by Wednesday morning. On 18 August, his *Weekly Political Register* described the massacre graphically: 'The yeomanry cavalry made their charge with a most infuriate frenzy; they cut down men, women and children, indiscriminately, and appeared to have commenced a premeditated attack with the most insatiable thirst for blood and destruction.' Bow Street officers closed the newspaper and confiscated his stock. Carlile changed the paper's name to the *Republican* and in it a week later demanded that

> the massacre of the unoffending inhabitants of Manchester, on the 16th of August, by the yeomanry cavalry and police at the instigation of the magistrates, should be the daily theme of the press until the murderers are brought to justice ... Every man in Manchester who avows his opinions on the necessity of reform, should never go unarmed – retaliation has become a duty, and revenge an act of justice.

The *Times* was early with the news too. Late on Tuesday night, a courier provided it with a brief report of a disaster on St Peter's Field the day before. The press was kept open until early in the morning in the hope of further news, but the reporter who had been on the platform had been arrested along with Hunt, so it was only on Thursday that the paper broke the news in full. Although it lamented the people's ignorance and the 'brawler' Hunt's influence, it deplored the 'dreadful fact that nearly a hundred of the king's unarmed subjects have been sabred by a body of cavalry ... in the presence of those magistrates whose sworn duty it is to protect and preserve the life of the meanest Englishman'. In the same edition it published the liberal Manchester merchant John Edward Taylor's eyewitness account, sent in haste to prevent the magistrates' account from becoming the received version in London. Taylor also published in Manchester his serial narrative of *The Peter-loo Massacre*. Selling in fourteen parts at twopence each, it covered the events of the day in detail and the corrupt inquest on the Peterloo victim John Lees as well; and it listed the known killed, wounded, and maimed. In London it sold from radical printshops and presses like Dolby's on the Strand and Thomas Davison's in Duke Street, West Smithfield.

It was more difficult for the law to prosecute satirical images than words, so prints, medals, plaques, jugs, and even handkerchiefs delivered the truths of Peterloo to the popular market. On this occasion the market-savvy Cruikshank was confident that his purchasers were politically primed and ready to buy, so he pulled no punches. The first of his Peterloo prints, *Massacre at St. Peter's or Britons Strike Home!!!*, claimed the impossible publication date of 16 August, but he doubtless reached for his burin as soon as the news reached London, since he armed his fat

11.1. George (and Isaac Robert?) Cruikshank, *Massacre at St. Peter's, or 'Britons Strike home'!!!* (Tegg, 16 August 1819) (©Library of Congress)

yeomanry cavalry with axes rather than sabres (Fig. 11.1). In his turbulent composition people fall beneath the horses and one cavalryman kicks a mother with infant who kneels beseechingly as he raises his axe to smite her. Another shouts from behind him 'Down with 'em! Chop 'em down! my brave boys! give them no quarter, they wan't to take our Beef & Pudding from us! – & remember the more you Kill the less poor rates you'll have to pay so go it Lads show your Courage & your Loyalty!' In September, Fores's printshop published Cruikshank's modified version of this under the title *Manchester Heroes*.

The most accomplished image was by an anonymous but highly competent artist, probably Cruikshank, and was published by Carlile on 1 October, just before his own arrest (Fig. 11.2). He dedicated it *To Henry Hunt, Esqr. ... and to the Female Reformers of Manchester and the adjacent Towns who were exposed to and suffered from the Wanton and Furious Attack made on them by that British Armed Force the Manchester and Cheshire Yeomanry Cavalry.* On the platform a woman in white holds a banner inscribed 'Manchester Female Reformers'. Other banners proclaim 'Liberty or Death', 'Universal Suffrage', and 'Universal Civil and

11.2. [Richard Carlile,] *To Henry Hunt, Esqr. as Chairman of the meeting assembled on St. Peter's Field, Manchester on the 16th. of August, 1819 and to the Female Reformers of Manchester and the adjacent Towns who were exposed to and suffered from the Wanton and Furious Attack made on them by that British Armed Force the Manchester and Cheshire Yeomanry Cavalry this plate is dedicated by their fellow labourer Richard Carlile; Published, Oct 1st, 1819, by Rd. Carlile, 55, Fleet Street, London* (Rischgitz/Getty Images)

Religious Liberty'. Their poles are topped by Caps of Liberty. The magistrates direct proceedings from a window on the left, while in the foreground a banner-man is pursued by one of the yeomanry with a raised sabre; the rest of the design is filled by cutting and slashing. In December, too, Cruikshank recycled the Spencean image of the freeborn Englishman in chains with padlocked lips (see Fig. 6.3), and in the same month Hone published his shilling pamphlet, *The Political House that Jack Built*, a parodic nursery-rhyme doggerel that catalogued the ills and the villains of the age, accompanied by thirteen Cruikshank woodcuts. It went through seventy reprintings and was said to have sold 100,000 copies over the following couple of years, many of them read out loud and thumbed through dozens of times.

A meeting of the Crown and Anchor moderates on the Saturday following the massacre passed resolutions deploring the magistrates' and yeomanry cavalry's conduct. The veteran Gale Jones proposed that they should form a committee to press for an inquiry. This would also relieve the sufferers 'in person and purse', support Hunt and others who had been arrested, and fund James Harmer to go to Manchester to collect evidence.[29] On 2 September the Metropolitan and Central Committee for the Relief of the Manchester Sufferers was formed to liaise with the relief committee set up by the liberal caucus in Manchester.

The radical whig John Cam Hobhouse was said to have written its *Report ... with an Appendix containing the Names of the Sufferers, and the Nature and Extent of their Wounds.* Published by Hone, it was authenticated by three attorneys, notably Harmer and Charles Pearson, later the City solicitor. It tells us that £3,408 was raised in subscriptions, but that while the subscribers were individually generous they were few in number. In the event, only £1,206 went to the victims (of which £250 came from the Manchester committee); the rest went on administration and lawyer's fees. Complaints about this were many, not least from Hunt, who was still smarting from his defeat in the 1818 Westminster election, which he felt was the responsibility of some on the Burdettite committee.[30] But the committee later explained that it had cost £1,077 to send the attorneys to Manchester to collect evidence against the magistrates and yeomanry and to attend John Lees's inquest. Coaches, inns, hire of rooms, stationery, and subsistence cost another £355.

The biggest expenditure funded the despatch of two committee members and a paid secretary to authenticate nearly 500 cases for relief. Covering the ten miles around Manchester and taking forty-two days, they found that people were reluctant to declare their woes for fear of persecution and insult. In any case it was

> difficult for humble persons to call the laws to their assistance in the hours of need, when they are to be employed to punish powerful men ... The forms and legal obstructions with which they have had to contend have interrupted and delayed justice, and have thereby proved our laws to be more admirable in theory than useful in practice.

Still, in its final report the committee's nightmare catalogue of injuries and hardships was worth paying for. Like the labours of its Mancunian equivalent, its work endures.[31]

The aftermath of Peterloo saw deepening disagreement between the Watsonites and the respectable Burdettite radicals. It marked an important turning point in this tale. Each group was physically separated as well. While the respectables continued to meet in the elegant Crown and Anchor, the ultras hived off to the creaking rooms of the White Lion off Wych Street a couple of hundred yards away.

The Watsonites' first move was to call a public meeting in Smithfield on 25 August 1819 to capitalise on anger about Peterloo. Even the pacific Thomas Evans plastered his shopfront with a summons 'To Arms – and avenge the Blood of the Manchester murdered', adding that now 'there must be either a Revolution or a military Despotism'.[32] Faint hope of revolution, however. By earlier standards the Smithfield crowd was impressive, between 8,000 and 20,000 people; but that was far fewer than the 70,000 or so who had mustered in July to hear Hunt. It didn't help that the veteran Sir Charles Worsley refused to take the chair because he was otherwise engaged, while the *Black Dwarf* editor Wooler and his patron Major Cartwright refused to attend at all. Nor was it helpful that Bow Street police were stationed in a Smithfield inn-yard, that 500 special constables and another 500 men provided by the East India Company were quartered in St Bartholomew's church, that Foot Guards were lurking in the same Company's arms store in Bishopsgate, and that the Guards were ordered to remain in London for the next several days instead of going to Brighton as was intended. Despite all, Dr Watson told the meeting all about Peterloo, and then they passed thirty or so resolutions asserting the people's rights to annual parliament, universal male suffrage, and vote by ballot. Thistlewood seconded a resolution that reformers who absented themselves from public meetings were only pretended friends of reform.

The meeting dispersed peacefully, as it had to. Its most pronounced consequence was the intimidation and prosecution of the obscure men who had advertised it. This process was reported dismissively; yet there were countless attacks on such people, mostly unrecorded. They ranged from men who had printed the meeting's posters, like Samuel Waddington, the dwarfish vicar's son and mocking sprite of the Hopkins Street Spencean chapel, down to the humblest of bill-stickers charged with defacing the walls with 'bills of an inflammatory nature'. Waddington was arrested for 'unlawfully publishing a certain printed seditious hand-bill' that appealed to the regent 'to stay the hands of merciless and blood-thirsty tyrants, and to save the country from massacre and murder, thereby intending to excite, stir up, and provoke tumult, riot, sedition and disaffection'. He explained that he worked alone as a printer-cum-shoemaker in a 'one pair of stairs [first floor] back room' in 12 New Bolton Street, Long Acre, and that he was one of the committee named in the handbill. He also rented a shop in Holborn opposite Gray's Inn Lane 'for the sale of pamphlets and pike heads', and in it he hung three nooses which were respectively labelled LS, LC, and LL – Lords Sidmouth, Castlereagh, and Liverpool. But he refused to say who had employed or paid him and chose to be committed to trial instead. He was acquitted.[33]

The radical publishers Carlile, Dolby, and Wooler were likewise arrested and forced to apply for bail. One Thomas Farrell of Chandos Street was discharged, but only after he had been terrified by the lord mayor seated in full fig on his platform in the Mansion House courtroom. Farrell admitted that he had posted bills in Fleet Market and the Borough, etc., but would not have done so 'if he had been aware that he was acting improperly'. Another target was 'a wretched looking man, most shabbily dressed', who had designed placards and openly carried a pike in the street. This was Edward Blandford, an impoverished hairdresser-printer-poet who was a member of Wedderburn's chapel and one of Watson's White Lion committee that planned the Smithfield meeting. The police officer reported that at the doorway of Blandford's lodging in Hackney 'his wife leaned as if she were fainting'; upstairs he found 'three or four naked children lying on the floor, and one naked child lying on the bed'. He 'searched room and found papers', along with a powder-horn, pistol, and bullets. Blandford was sent to Giltspur Street compter (gaol) for distributing 'seditious and inflammatory bills'.[34]

After this it was in a demoralised state that 'Watson, Preston, Thistlewood, Waddington, Moggeridge, and Co.' (thus listed: that

Moggeridge was now a spy was unsuspected) planned their recovery by proposing for Hunt a triumphal entry into London, along with a dinner for Hunt that would be cheaper than the one the Crown and Anchor party proposed, because they wanted poor men to attend it.

The moderates protested that they had already planned a dinner and that the White Lioners were trying to usurp their role. They sent a deputation across the Strand to invite the White Lioners to further discussion. Their delegation, including Galloway and Evans, reported back to the Crown and Anchor that the White Lioners were 'men of intelligent minds, but evidently and unfortunately depressed by poverty' – which was condescending of them, since that fact was obvious. The meeting that ensued was marred by a squabble about the choice of a chairman, and then by Galloway's and young Thomas Evans's angry insistence that a dinner would win the support of all radicals, while a triumphant procession so soon after Peterloo might not only provoke their enemies into reprisals, but also be *vulgar!* A 'raree-show [peep-show] of a procession with drums, kettles, fifes, flags' and a few 'gilded and tawdry decorations' and much 'noisy effervescence' would achieve nothing.

Too late, however! The Watsonites had advertised the procession and its route a week ago. Watson read out the printed placard to prove it. One of the respectables charged Watson with lying and called him out of the room. Watson replied that they would settle the matter in private. Galloway and his circle withdrew in high dudgeon. Watson, Thistlewood, Waddington, and Preston were left to instruct the remaining audience about Hunt's patriotism: Preston declared that no thinking or reading man could be insensible of his '*wirtues*'. At one o'clock in the morning they started arguing over who should pay for the room. Waddington swore 'he'd be damned if they should pay, for "they were in*wited*"'. This is the *Times* reporting, in amusement. At which point its exhausted reporter took himself off to bed.[35]

Watson and Thistlewood were gratified by their success. On the Thursday after Peterloo they had walked together to the home office to ask about Hunt's safety, only to be dismissed as 'impudent'.[36] Now the celebration of Hunt's arrival in London would prove their importance and organisational skills beyond doubt.

HUNT'S TRIUMPHAL ENTRY

On Monday, 13 September, nearly a month after the Manchester massacre, Hunt made his apotheotic entry into London. Gale Jones said that he entered 'like an Alexander'. Hunt had already enjoyed similar celebrations in Lancashire. Granted bail at the Lancaster Assizes, where the charge of treason at Peterloo was replaced by one of sedition, he was cheered in every village and town as he made his way from Lancaster via Preston and Bolton back to Manchester; some half a million people turned out to see him. People strewed flowers before him and unyoked his horses and drew his carriage themselves. At one point he was told of the sad death of his favourite horse, Bob. 'Alas, poor Bob,' he said, and the tears he allowed publicly to roll down his cheek were widely and approvingly reported. At the next village he compared Bob's nobility with the murderers on St Peter's Field. 'This faithful beast,' said he, 'would not tread on the toe of the poorest subject of his Majesty's dominions; whilst brutes in human shape are to be found base enough to plunge the sword into the breast of the innocent and unprotected.' The *Times* circulated this touching tale two days before he arrived in London.[37]

The day's proceedings began at half past nine that morning when an elegant landaulet arrived outside Watson's lodging in Three King's Court at the foot of Clement's Lane. Watson entered it, leaving no doubt about his importance as the day's chief instigator. He wore a hat with a red cockade and black crape in mourning for Peterloo. Thistlewood, Preston, Waddington, and other White Lioners sat in hackney carriages that followed. Two further carriages bore Hunt's friends, male and female. People and horses wore red favours and ribbons, and the motto 'Hunt for Ever' decorated the men's white hats. Off they all clattered northwards to the Angel inn at the foot of Islington High Street. There they had bread and cheese, arranged the procession, and trooped north to meet Hunt at the Holloway turnpike.

Hunt mistrusted Watson's committee. He could hardly forget how they had exploited him to his own discredit by trying to turn his December 1816 Spa Fields meeting into an insurrection. And everyone talked about Thistlewood's loss of control in provoking Sidmouth into gaoling him for a year. Hunt was himself now on bail and anxious that no disorder should erupt. In any case, he still believed in the moral power of peaceful mass meetings, which was more than the White Lioners did. So, exhausted by his long journey south, he sent Watson a message from Barnet, where he had spent the night, that he wanted to take as direct a route to the Crown and Anchor as possible (via Goswell Street and St Paul's). But Watson had already had posters printed and horn-boys employed to advertise a route, five miles in length, from Islington down the newly built City Road to Finsbury Square, and then via Sun Street, Bishopsgate, Cheapside, Ludgate Hill, and Fleet Street to dinner at the Crown and Anchor in the Strand.[38] Hunt had to give way.

As usual, Hunt was unpunctual. Having said he would reach Islington at one o'clock, he arrived at three, in a chaise and pair accompanied by two comely women. When he and Watson met at the turnpike they saluted each other frigidly. From the Holloway Road southwards the crowd was such that it took Hunt another hour to reach the Angel, a further three and a half hours to reach the Crown and Anchor, and a further hour before he sat down to dinner. What unfolded was the largest and most expressive of all mass responses both to Peterloo and to a people's hero. The *Times* reporter thought it one of the most imposing spectacles he had ever seen.

This was the first time in memory that the rituals and symbols of a triumphant procession were appropriated by the common people for their own and their hero's gratification. The nearest equivalent had been Burdett's triumphal procession after his victory in the 1807 Westminster election. On that occasion a draped 'Roman' carriage pulled by white horses had conveyed him from his Piccadilly mansion through Covent Garden to the Crown and Anchor. Burdett sat on a fluted Corinthian pillar, and a statue of Britannia was at the fore. The carriage was preceded and followed by buglers, beadles, and electors bearing Roman banners. But although the streets and windows along Burdett's route were just as crowded as Hunt's was now, his procession travelled no great distance, and relative to Hunt's it was thinly reported. In any case, Burdett's flags and banners mildly recommended 'Purity of Election'; Hunt's replicated the flags of Peterloo. Invoking Magna Carta and the Bill of Rights, they called for religious and civil and Irish liberty, for free speech and a free press, for trial by jury and universal suffrage, and for 'Liberty or Death'. To have persuaded such crowds to turn out and cheer these contra-loyalist invocations made Hunt's triumph a Watsonite propaganda coup without equal. It was also a carnival, an embodiment of common happiness. Every newspaper agreed that it was unequalled in memory – and this in a city that remembered the celebrations of Hardy's, Tooke's, and Thelwall's acquittals in 1794, the splendour of Nelson's funeral in 1806, and the Peace celebrations of 1814–15.[39]

Hunt at first looked pale and jaded, but despite the heat he stood upright in his carriage with head uncovered and bowed to the people as he passed. Shouting crowds accompanied him down Islington High Street, throwing up so much dust on that hot sunny day that breathing was difficult and distances obscured. At the Angel he exchanged his chaise for the landaulet. Some tried to unyoke its six beribboned horses and pull it themselves, but Hunt persuaded them not to. 'Wherever the slightest disposition appeared to disorder, a general cry of "Order!" was thundered out, until it passed through the crowd, and quietness succeeded, as if the creation of some talismanic influence.'

Here is the procession's structure from the first to the last of its twenty-six orders as the press reported it:

> Some hundreds of footmen bearing large branches of oak, poplar, and various other trees.
> A footman, bearing the emblem of union – a bundle of sticks stuck on a pitchfork, supported by groups of men on horseback and on foot.
> A horseman with a scroll inscribed on it, Magna Charta and Bill of Rights [this line added in Black Dwarf]
> The Committees bearing white wands, and all wearing knots of red riband and laurel leaves in their hats.

A green silk flag, with gold letters and Irish harp; inscription, 'Universal, civil, and religious liberty'; borne and supported by six Irishmen, and numerous other footmen.

A band of music.

Horsemen.

A white flag surmounted and bordered with crêpe; inscription in black, 'To the immortal memory of the Reformers massacred at Manchester, Aug 16, 1819.'

Groups of horsemen and footmen.

A large tricoloured flag, red, white, and green, with the words 'England, Scotland, and Ireland' in gold letters.

Groups of men, bearing white wands and red favours.

The old red flag, with the inscription 'Universal Suffrage'.

Two barouches, in which were some friends of Mr. Hunt.

Two carriages, in which were some gentlemen connected with the press.

A sky-blue flag; inscription 'The palladium of liberty, a free press'.

Groups of footmen.

A carriage containing Messrs. Watson, Thistlewood, and Preston, and other friends of Mr. Hunt.

A scarlet silk flag; inscription in gold letters, 'Hunt, the heroic Champion of Liberty'.

Groups of men on horseback and on foot.

A Band of Music.

Mr. HUNT

Standing in a landaulet, drawn by six handsome bays, decorated with scarlet ribands.

Behind the carriage stood a man, bearing a large red flag, which waved over Mr. Hunt's head; inscription, 'Liberty or Death'.

Groups of Horsemen and Footmen.

A white Silk flag; inscription, 'Trial by Jury'.

Most of the flags had small pieces of black crape fastened at the ends out of respect for the memory of the unfortunate persons who fell at Manchester.

To this description we should add the colour and noise of clattering horses, mules, and carriages, the dust clouds rising from the unpaved

roads on that hot day, 'the waving of hats and handkerchiefs, the clap-
ping of hands, the shouts of applause mingled with the sounds of musical
instruments, and the voices of some thousands who accompanied them
in the national air of "Rule, Britannia".' In other words, people were
singing as well, and the two bands played patriotic and Irish tunes all the
way. Nobody counted the footmen and horsemen in the procession, but
there might have been hundreds. Pedestrians followed behind 'as far as
the eye could reach', and 'all appeared one solid mass of human beings
from the pavement to the tops of the houses'. The *Times* said that to
people waiting ahead of the procession its approach 'seemed like that of
a moving grove. The mixture of green boughs gave no faint idea of the
approach of Birnham-wood to Dunsinane'.

The same paper estimated that by mid-afternoon the crowds on the
streets numbered not less than 300,000, and thousands more waved from
rooftops and windows. If so, up to one in five of London's population
turned out to watch – 'half London', another newspaper thought.

> The houses and walls [were] literally roofed and covered with human
> beings, and teeming with them at every door or window. ... The
> thousands and tens of thousands ... moved slowly and regularly along, in
> one solid mass. ... Solid masses of people covered the roads;
> handkerchiefs and red ribbons floated from the windows; cheers and
> acclamations were heard at every side of the immense cavalcade. ...
> Thousands entreated to know – 'Have we a chance of seeing him?' –
> 'Oh, the brave fellow' – 'Success to Hunt' – 'They would not have sabred
> the people at Manchester, if they [had] expected this.'

London's narrow streets and spilling crowds slowed the procession, and
there were accidents in the crush. But there was exhilaration as well: the
streets were unchallengeably in the people's control. A terrier dog was
cheered as he trotted along sporting red rosettes on each side of his head.
He wore a placard proclaiming 'Universal Suffrage' round his body, and
a paper collar inscribed 'No Dog Tax' round his neck. Every reporter was
impressed that the people remained orderly and good-humoured and
that the soldiers who waited out of sight weren't needed. 'There never
was an assembly of persons,' the *Examiner* declared, 'even to the one-
fortieth part of the number, conducted in so peaceable a manner.' Nor, it

added, had there before been 'any [gathering] where the proportion of the middling and ... the upper classes was so great. ... Persons of both sexes, of every rank and condition, in the houses and in the streets, joined in the applause.' Every newspaper noticed the waving and cheers of women. Hunt's semi-scandalous devotion to his common-law wife Mrs Vince was well known, but he looked fetchingly handsome, heroic, and manly even so. John Keats was there as well. 'It would take me a whole day and a quire of paper to give you any thing like detail,' he wrote to his brother and sister-in-law: 'The whole distance from the Angel Islington to the Crown and Anchor was lined with multitudes'. Six days later, Keats wrote 'To Autumn', a poem which achieves 'an apotheosis of contemporary Spencean articles of faith about English natural abundance and fertility'.[40]

In the course of his progress, Hunt contrived his usual theatrical moments. Outside the *Black Dwarf*'s office in Sun Street he halted his carriage, bowed to the women at every window, and drew attention to a Manchester lad now seated in his carriage. The youngster had a sabre scar across his head, so cries of 'mixed compassion and indignation' filled the air. At the Mansion House Hunt bowed ironically to the lord mayor, who could be spied peeping from his window.

Visual enactments and song catered to a populace familiar with and hungry for spectacular but familiar effects, so the images, symbols, and allegories deployed in mass celebrations of this kind were fully displayed. In its beribboned horses and banners, its antique symbols imported from remote countrysides (that 'bundle of sticks stuck on a pitchfork' was an emblem of union – a 'simple *fasces*', the *Morning Chronicle* explained) – in its waving laurel branches and its sticks pared down to white 'wands', its red tokens and ribbons and cockades sported in white 'Hunt' hats or pinned on horses and on female bosoms, and in its two raucous bands and rank upon rank of footmen and horsemen – in displays like these, immigrants from the north and midlands saw reflections of their own trade, guild, and May Day pageants, while Londoners would have relished the replay of celebrations whose forms and symbols had evolved over centuries.

THE QUARREL

Arriving at last at the Crown and Anchor, Hunt told the crowd that they had celebrated not his triumph but the triumph of reform, and that that great cause had been further advanced by the cowardly Manchester magistrates and yeomanry than it could possibly be by the people. Then, after attacking the press for its biases and congratulating himself for achieving 'the pinnacle of popularity' as a result of Peterloo, he described some of Peterloo's nightmare moments and his own harassment and injury, before repeating his promise not to touch taxed beer, wine, spirits, or tea until he had brought the Manchester murderers to justice (*Cheers*). He was ready to die for the cause of reform (*Continued and thunderous applause*), but he urged people not to disturb the peace as they dispersed (*Cries of 'No, No'*). Inside, the dinner announced for six o'clock began two and a half hours later. After Hunt had said grace, near on 400 men (no women mentioned) attacked the meal for which they had each paid 7s 6d. Nobody reported how it tasted.

After dinner, there was the usual tussle over the appointment of a chairman. When Hunt took the chair Watson was offended. He had nominated Gale Jones as chairman, and never imagined that 'the hero of the piece would ever wish to become the master of ceremonies'; but this time Watson had to give way. Hunt urged the audience not 'be led by the nose by the sophistical declamation of interested individuals' (*Applause*). For a while the toasts and soul-stirring music hid the discomfort caused by this put-down. When Hunt proposed his provocative toast to 'The only source of all legitimate power – the people', fiddles and 'clarionets' played Handel's 'See, the Conquering Hero Comes!' The Bow Street magistrate Birnie was spotted taking notes in the gallery. The audience laughed when Hunt and other speakers called him out. Then they played the revolutionary 'Ça ira!' after the toast to 'Universal Suffrage, Annual Parliaments and Vote by Ballot, the undoubted right of every Briton'; and the Marseillaise made its statement too, after 'May arms be taken from those who abuse them, and given to those who have the courage to use them'. The musicians abstained from asking God to save the king. Instead they played Thomas Arne's 'Rule, Britannia' with its advice that Britons would never be enslaved. Another of their tunes, the haunting

Scottish love-lament 'The Land of the Leal', was played after the toast to the Peterloo victims. It had the same music as Robert Burns' rowdily insurrectionary 'Scots, wha' hae' wi' Wallace bled', which William Davidson was to sing in Cato Street as he tried to run away.

Gale Jones's toast to Hunt for championing the people 'against a ministerial, magisterial and military despotism' was greeted with loud cheering for several minutes. Hunt's orotund reply bubbled with his own grievances against Burdett and the whigs, who had humiliated him at the 1818 Westminster election, against the as yet unnamed radicals who had accused him of being a government spy, and against his treatment by the *Times*. (Actually that newspaper reported Hunt's London triumph and dinner fully and fairly; only in its leader column did it condemn 'these trifling, squabbling pennyless boobies'.) He also described at length episodes in the Manchester massacre and his own arrest and heroic resistance. The audience cried '*Shame!*' in sympathy.

Then the divisions surfaced. The most divisive part of Hunt's speech the newspapers failed to report, perhaps because it challenged their view of the man as a rabble-rouser. Yet it showed conclusively that Peterloo had brought home to him the moral power of the peaceful mass meeting and that he was now aligning with moderation. This escaped neither the audience nor the note-taking magistrate Birnie in the gallery. Birnie transcribed the key passage for the home office:

> He should [Hunt said] cheerfully lay down his life at any time to procure happiness and comfort for the poor man and his family (*Loud applause*). How often had he been accused of a design to excite the poor to insurrection against the rich. But he would solemnly declare – and he called upon any man who could to contradict him – that *he never had in any one instance been so incautious as to point out to the poor that they were entitled to the property of the rich.* He had always preached up to them that their sole claims to property rested upon their honest industry, and that all they were fairly entitled to was a sufficient reward for their labours.[41]

Hunt made a point of rephrasing this in a narrative, *The Triumphal Entry of Henry Hunt*, that was published shortly after: 'He had never said that there should be an equal division of property, and that there should be no poor people. No, the whole front of his offending, was an earnest wish that the man, poor and industrious, who laboured from one end of the week to the other, should have something more than the necessaries of life.'

In the concluding speech Gale Jones, hovering between both sides in the quarrel, rebuked Hunt and the moderates for cold-shouldering Watson, Thistlewood, and Preston simply because they had been contaminated by being tried for treason in 1817. The critics forgot, he said, that 'but for the treason of our ancestors in 1668, the tyranny of the Stuarts would have been perpetuated; and even the rights that remained to Englishmen would not now have been enjoyed (*Continued cheers* [from some])'. In any case, the jury's acquittal proved that far from being traitors Watson and friends had honestly exerted themselves at Spa Fields, and he expected that 'an English assembly of reformers would not allow a prejudice to operate where an obligation was due (*Cries of Bravo Jones!* [from some])'.

The evening broke up with toasts to 'Liberty, the first lesson we learn, and [to] resistance to oppression the first we teach'. Then came toasts to the attorneys Harmer and Pearson, and to 'the memory of the elder Brutus, whose exertions led to the abolition of tyranny in Rome'.[42] Hunt departed 'with great urbanity of manners', though not in a manner Watson appreciated, since he left it to Watson to foot the bill for the dinner. This parting insult saved Watson's life. Since the debt was still unpaid five months later, Watson languished safely in Whitecross Street debtors' prison as his friends gathered at their life-changing rendezvous in Cato Street.

As the celebrations drew to a close, Carlile saw Thistlewood for the first time. He was sitting by himself in a sulk, 'a well-dressed man' with 'a more respectable appearance than any other person in the room'. But 'he was a silent observer, as on no occasion did he interfere or open his mouth, or appear interested by any thing that was said and done'.[43] Thistlewood was angry, but knew that a new chapter in his story was opening.

Within days of the dinner, each faction was smearing the other in letters to the newspapers, and this to the newspapers' amusement, for what ensued really was unseemly. First Palin, Harrison, Chambers, Hall, and two others, each a member of the Committee of Five Hundred that had planned Hunt's entry, demanded that

Hunt should explain his ill-treatment of Watson. Then Thistlewood declared that Hunt's behaviour was a 'premeditated insult'. He knew, he wrote, that Carlile, Waddington, Mrs Vince (Hunt's mistress), and others had met Hunt at Barnet before his entry to London to persuade him to join the Westminster moderates. 'Lord help their conjuring souls!': he and the doctor didn't deserve such treatment 'after our unwearied exertions in the cause to raise your fame.'

Worse followed. When Hunt learned of Thistlewood's intention to visit northern radicals to persuade them to join the nation-wide protest he had in mind for 1 October, he accused Thistlewood of being in government pay. Thistlewood replied that he had once believed that Hunt would advance the great cause of liberty but now regarded him as a 'damned coward', 'a man that was no friend to the people', and 'a spy for government'. He added that Cobbett, 'with all his writings, was of no good to the country' either, since he 'was a spy equally the same as Mr. Hunt himself'. Then he announced that Hunt had embezzled £4 14s 6d of the committee's Peterloo funds and a £5 payment which Hunt forgot to declare. Watson joined this slanging match by denouncing 'the paltry scoundrels, the lying villains, who, by open declarations, would place him [Thistlewood] at the mercy of the tyrants of the people. Oh the wretches! Is this patriotism? Is this unity and unanimity? … Who are the fiends? Who the monsters? Who the tricksters? Who is now the Machiavellian, to divide and destroy?'[44]

So ended the ultras' three-year dalliance with Henry Hunt. As Preston put it, Hunt had deserted the 'trusty fellows' who had raised him to his present popularity and had surrendered to a 'set of puppies'. Isolated, the ultras were now free to pursue their own way, and Thistlewood found his own voice as their leader. A well-informed writer later suggested that Hunt's charge so shook Thistlewood that it explained his resolution henceforth to perform 'some bold and daring act to wipe away the imputation'.[45] If so, he had willing associates. In October 1819

the triumvirate Watson Thistlewood and Preston were indulging in their usual luxury of a pipe when it was observed by Preston 'that a dozen of determined men might do the business at once. Let each man take his bird, said he, let us begin by the prince, Lords Castlereagh and Sidmouth' – upon which he took out his loaded pistol and swore he was ready were eleven good fellows to join him.

Now that the government had let the first blood at Peterloo, only violence could fit the case. The aim, Preston declared, must be 'nothing short of a revolution'.[46]

FINSBURY MARKET

The breach with Hunt reinvigorated Thistlewood. With much anger to vent, he got busy. He attended a score of larger meetings in the White Lion and raised money from well-wishers. He was seen drilling a posse of men on Primrose Hill with Preston, Harrison, Chambers, Davidson, and Hall. In October he persuaded Gale Jones and Gast the Rotherhithe shipwrights' leader to attend a meeting at the White Lion. And he toured the midlands and north with T. J. Wooler of the *Black Dwarf* to plan country-wide protests to coincide with a meeting he proposed for 1 November in Finsbury Market in the City.

The polite newspapers reported all these proceedings in states of high anxiety and indignation. Watchful magistrates described a state of insurrection in the north, and letters of advice to Sidmouth flowed in from the nation's country houses. In a garrulous twelve-page letter from Garboldisham Hall in Norfolk, Sir John Jervis White Jervis (*sic*) warned Sidmouth that civil war was imminent, and expressed incredulity that the scoundrel Hunt had been allowed a 'revolutionary' triumph through London in defiance of all law and decency, an event which even females deplorably cheered. The only right reply was lethal force, he insisted. He provided a detailed plan for its deployment.[47]

In the event Hunt's rejection of Thistlewood's plan for concerted meetings persuaded many northern radical groups to withdraw from Thistlewood; but Thistlewood and Watson still had high hopes for London. Union societies were being formed in Marylebone, Battlebridge, and Fleet Market, and by the 'mostly Yorkshiremen' who met in the Saracen's Head in Snow Hill. Their White Lion meetings were drawing audiences of up to seventy. Expectations ran high in these gatherings. A smith displayed paper patterns for pike-heads which he would have ready for sale on the Sunday before the Finsbury meeting. The union society from Drury Lane announced that they would attend Finsbury in a body, with a green flag declaring 'He that hath not a sword / Let him sell his garment and buy one'.[48] The committee itself sent a band of musicians and a banner inscribed 'Let us die like men and not live like slaves' round Shoreditch, Bethnal Green, Spitalfields, and Whitechapel, and horn-blowers posted placards. Thistlewood's signed poster advertising the Finsbury meeting reminded London of the 'noble spirit of independence at Runnymede which obtained Magna Carta'.[49]

Sidmouth was sufficiently alarmed to despatch several lords lieutenant home to take command of their counties. And when Finsbury landlords complained to the Worship Street police magistrates about the damage the mob would do to their properties, Thistlewood published another letter to remind them that 'since the great plague in London, all fields and open plots of ground within the bills of mortality are free to the people to assemble in'.[50]

The Finsbury Market meeting of 1 November was held on a Monday as usual. In principle this was a good day for it since at eight in the morning a wife-murderer was hanged at Newgate twenty-five minutes' walk away. But the meeting turned into a rain-sodden fiasco. Only twenty men and boys turned up at the White Lion to join the intended flag-waving and band-playing procession from Wych Street to Finsbury. Bearing the symbolic bundle of sticks and the banners that had featured in Hunt's triumphal entry, they trudged through the rain via Drury Lane and Holborn, in which last they 'paddled up to their knees in mud', and took back-alley shortcuts to Finsbury rather than face the main thoroughfares as planned. Eighty or more idlers and a volunteer piper joined them as they went, but the newspapers delighted in their wretched appearance. Thistlewood, Watson, and Preston waited till noon for the rest of the procession to arrive, before giving up and travelling to the market by coach. Preston was said to be drunk by then.[51]

The *Chronicle*'s account put the people attending the Finsbury meeting at a thousand or so, and thought that most of them were vagabonds, sweeps, and dustmen 'without shoes, or wearing such apologies for shoes that their toes were exposed to the wet ground'; 'from their shivering aspect, [they] might be considered as anything but warm in the cause'. The *Black Dwarf* put the attendance at five times that number. It explained that numbers were lessened both because Hunt disapproved of the meeting and because the market was 'half-knee-deep' in mud. This forced most people to stand so far from the platform that they could hear nothing of the speeches.[52]

Another deterrent was so familiar that few mentioned it. In the morning the City sheriff and his deputy had ordered five cartloads of brickbats, stones, and broken bottles to be removed from the market lest they be used as weapons. By midday the area was surrounded by all London's available policemen and by armed detachments of the City Light Horse, the Horse Guards, and the City Artillery. Life Guards lurked in the City Light Horse stables in Worship Street round the corner. Not surprisingly, this force had not the least hint of public disorder to deal with throughout the whole of the miserable day, mud-fights notwithstanding. There were plenty of these. The rougher sorts passed the time by pelting each other with dung, mud, and cabbage stalks, as anyone would.

Just before one o'clock Watson took the chair, and he and Preston spoke at length, and Wedderburn had to be called to order when he told people to come armed to the next meeting. Thistlewood stayed silent. A radical coffee house keeper took an hour to explain the petition to ask the regent to alleviate distress, and this was followed by twenty-seven voted-on resolutions. The *Morning Chronicle* mentioned the most inflammatory of them: that it was an inherent principle of justice that power belongs to the people; that an armed people, who have courage to use their arms, cannot be a nation of slaves; and that attempts to disarm the people violated the laws of nature. As the speeches ended, 'ruffians' pulled the waggon into the swamp to immobilise it, and pelted Watson, Thistlewood, and friends 'like wretches who are pilloried for unutterable crimes'. Others – 'pickpockets', said the newspapers – drew the orators in an unhorsed hackney coach back to Wych Street, during which procedure 'several persons were robbed and beaten in a most dreadful manner'.

The newspapers' derision was predictable. The lampooning of radical reformers had been incessant since the 1790s. Like a malign Greek chorus, mockery accompanied every stage in this story. Visual satirists

11.3. George Cruikshank, *The Radical's Arms* (Humphrey, November 1819) (© Library of Congress, Washington, DC)

amplified it. Caricaturists like George Cruikshank swung both ways as expedience, subject matter, or printshops and markets dictated. By 1819–20, for every one of his indictments of the attacks on free speech and assembly, he produced two that depicted the ultra-radicals as depraved and derelict thugs. Shortly after the Finsbury debacle he etched his poisonous *The Radical's Arms* for Humphrey's upmarket printshop in St James's Street (Fig. 11.3). A disreputable man and woman flank a guillotine decorated by nooses, execution axes, and a cap of liberty. 'No god, no religion, no king, no constitution', the floating banners proclaim above it. In the guillotine's frame the world is in flames and turned upside down (with 'N' at the south). The pistol-packing male cheerily holds up a blood-dripping knife and a glass of gin, while the blowsy woman waves her own bottle of 'Blue Ruien' (*sic*). They trample on Magna Carta, the Bill of Rights, and a mitre, coronet, and Bible, and blood spills from the guillotine into an overturned crown.

The Finsbury disaster lost Thistlewood and Watson the credit they had won by organising Hunt's triumph. A widely advertised meeting in Smithfield on 24 November to hear the results of the Finsbury petition attracted barely a thousand people. Most attended out of 'curiosity', the newspapers were pleased to report. The force supervising their behaviour included two regiments of the London militia and 750 special constables, ward officers, and firemen.[53] In December the *Morning Post* described a further Smithfield meeting as led by 'twenty or thirty dirty looking fellows' who unfurled flags 'with the usual texts of sedition' ('Let us die like men and not be sold like slaves', and another a black flag emblazoned with a skull and crossbones, carried by 'Black' Davidson). Most of these fellows 'proceeded with their flags to a gin-shop opposite Newgate, where the greater part regaled themselves with the articles sold by the landlord, until they were desired by the officers to move on'. It didn't further the cause that after Wilson carried his flag back home he somehow lost forty rounds of ball cartridge from his pocket.[54]

These humiliations ended the ultras' hopes of mass support. They also marked a turning point. The great days of public meeting seemed over, and only violence offered a way forward. As Edwards reported it, after the Smithfield failure Watson, Thistlewood, Preston, Palin, Bradburn, Cook, Edwards, and two others adjourned to lick their wounds in the Black Dog in Gray's Inn Lane and then in Preston's lodging in Princes Street. Deciding that they could count on fifty-one armed supporters, but needed two hundred at least, they divided their known number into groups of four, every fourth man to be a 'captain', in order to drum up recruits and 'do something that would rouse both London and the country'. At this stage the alleged treason went no further than that 'something'.[55]

CHAPTER 12

Edwards the Spy: 1819–20

THE ARTS OF SPYING

It wasn't only his year in Horsham gaol that changed Thistlewood's fortunes. It mattered more that the spy George Edwards was awaiting his release. 'Thistlewood is the boy for us,' he told his friends; 'he's the one to do our work: he will very soon be out of Horsham-gaol.'[1] It was Edwards rather than Thistlewood who orchestrated the last stages of the story. He was the conspiracy's fount, origin, and undoing – 'the contriver, the instigator, the entrapper', as Thistlewood realised too late. 'A rogue by nature ... a diminutive animal, with downcast looks and stealthy face, [he] seemed capable of any evil' – thus Charles Knight the radical, drawing on hindsight.[2]

Edwards's early life was grim. Born in London around 1786, his mother was a lottery-shopkeeper whom the father wooed in a gin shop and then deserted. He reached five feet three inches fully grown. He had a talent for drawing, so he was apprenticed to a statuary-maker in Smithfield and for a while wandered round London selling plaster models – without shoes or stockings, according to Alderman Wood later. He took up thieving in boyhood and, as Wood added, extortion from homosexuals in his teens.[3] There followed a miserable marriage from which he absconded for several months. He allegedly collaborated in a scam with John Castle, helping French prisoners of war to escape and then betraying their whereabouts in exchange for a reward. Around 1814 he opened a shop on Eton High Street. From it he sold schoolboys statuettes of Dr Keate, the flogging Eton headmaster, which the boys used for target practice.

Edwards's brother was already a Spencean, though according to Carlile he was also an officer of the Hatton Garden police office, and so probably an informant. Edwards became a Spencean himself, establishing his credibility by commemorating Spence in plaster busts. Wood believed that he was active at the 1816 Smithfield meeting. His shop failed, and in the grim winter of 1817/18 he returned penniless to London to lodge in a single room behind Picket Street in the Strand. He was 'without a bed to lie upon, or a chair to sit in', Thistlewood said in court: 'straw was his resting place; his only covering a blanket; but, owing to his bad character and his swindling conduct, he was driven from thence by his landlord'.[4]

In January 1818 Edwards began sending reports on Spencean meetings to Stafford, the chief clerk and spymaster at Bow Street.[5] How and when he learned to write is unknown. His reports were unpunctuated and used the cockney 'ham' for 'am', but they were usually to the point and written in a practised hand. He had a sharp ear for dialogue and phrasing and transcribed the key parts of conversations more or less verbatim. As like as not he was questioned when he delivered his strips, so fabrication was unlikely.[6] Now Edwards prospered. Wood told the Commons that 'all at once ... he got supplied with cash, and was enabled to purchase several other weapons of defence, and arms'. When they met again, Thistlewood found Edwards 'dressed like a lord, in all the folly of the reigning fashion'. Edwards claimed that he had inherited the title and property of a German baron and that Castlereagh and Sidmouth were financing him while he awaited the legacy. 'From this period,' Thistlewood said, 'I date his career as a government spy.'[7]

Edwards next enmeshed himself in Carlile's life. When Carlile set up his radical bookshop in 55 Fleet Street in January 1819, he found Edwards ensconced as a plaster model maker in number 55½, a tiny shop carved out of 55. Edwards's first step was to pester Carlile to give him a lodging in 55, 'but the shrewd suspicions of Mrs. Carlile, re-acting upon his villainous countenance, put it aside', so Edwards and family took up a lodging directly opposite at 166 Fleet Street. In late February or early March he modelled and coloured for Carlile a full-length figure of Tom Paine.[8] Carlile later wrote that he 'had little ground to suspect his spyship' and 'never for a moment suspected [him] to be any thing further than an idle, dissolute character'.[9]

In truth, Edwards was casting about for dupes whom he could induce to attempt subversions which he could then expose and profit from. Carlile was an obvious target. His bookshop, Carlile wrote later, was the haunt 'of almost every forward man in London, by their coming to my shop for pamphlets'.[10] The Cato Street butcher James Ings frequented the shop in September 1819 to buy pamphlets to resell in his ailing Whitechapel coffee shop. Edwards befriended him and drew him into his net.

Arrested in October 1819, Carlile was held in the King's Bench prison for republishing Paine's *Age of Reason*. Edwards visited him there with William Davidson. When Davidson offered to spring Carlile from gaol with the help of 'sixty or seventy [men] of the same mind as the writer, . . . even at the hazard and sacrifice of their lives', Carlile rejected the offer as lunatic and convinced himself that Davidson was a spy. After the executions he apologised to Davidson's widow: 'Little did I think that villain Edwards was the spy, agent, and instigator of the government, and Mr. Davidson his victim. I now regret my error, and hope that you will pardon it as an error of the head, without any bad motive', reassuring her that 'the heroic manner in which your husband and his companions met their fate, will in a few years, perhaps in a few months, stamp their names as patriots, and men who had nothing but their country's weal at heart'. He sent her two pounds by way of compensation, all he could afford.

'When he failed to get me hanged,' Carlile wrote, Edwards 'caused the death of Thistlewood and others'. By now Edwards had ingratiated himself with Watson. Within days of Thistlewood's release from Horsham in May 1819, Watson introduced Edwards to Thistlewood at Preston's lodging. Soon, in Brunt's words, Edwards was pinned to Thistlewood's coat-tail. Henceforth everything Thistlewood did and said was known in Bow Street and the home office. Fully informed, Stafford, Birnie, and Sidmouth were to play Thistlewood and friends like fish on their lines, before reeling them in.

Why Thistlewood trusted Edwards is a mystery. He and his colleagues never ceased worrying about spies in the camp. They tried to hide supporters' identities behind number codes and to vet attendance at meetings, and they planned to hunt down spy lists in Stafford's and

Sidmouth's offices when their great day came.[11] They suspected that Hunt and Cobbett were spies. According to Carlile, Thistlewood was often warned that Bow Street agents were among his group; he boasted that he was continually watched by the police: 'this has been his pride and pleasure'.[12] Yet Edwards was never once suspected – even by Carlile, who disliked him but was his immediate neighbour for a year. Did Edwards simply play his game brilliantly? He had the persistence, loquacity, and persuasive skills that had been polished in the course of his earlier criminal extortions, and now he seems to have won favour by fine acting, by regular and vocal attendance at meetings, and by matching Blunt and Ings in blood-thirstiness. He was also an energetic recruiter – too energetic sometimes, since his zeal could invite suspicion. The veteran Spencean George Pickard, for example, met Edwards at the great Smithfield meeting and again at the White Lion in Wych Street. 'What a pity it is, Pickard, that we can't destroy these bloody vermin,' Edwards said to him, meaning the ministers. He then broached a plan to enter the Commons with hidden explosives:

> Anybody can get into the House of Commons with an order, nor does it require that they should go clean. Suppose we have an iron case made in the shape of a book (for any person is allowed to carry in a book), and have some old gun-barrels, which may be got cheap, cut into pieces about three or four inches long; let them be plugged up at each end with lead, and the centre filled with powder, and a touch-hole made; half a dozen of cases may be made full of them for a similar number of men to take into the House. One man might have a bottle of phosphorus, and a lighted match might be taken with a piece of rope without giving any alarm to the persons present, and applied to the fuze, which would communicate with the contents of the cases; they should be thrown when the House was full from the gallery; the opportunity should be taken when some important business was going forward. What bloody destruction it would make.

Pickard replied that he 'must know him better before I would have anything to do with him'. 'Oh, you are a damn'd fool,' Edwards exclaimed, 'you know nothing.' Edwards pestered Pickard again in the Scotch Arms in Round Court. He 'talked about destroying the ministers, and invited me to go to a meeting, and Adams gave me a grenade and Edwards gave me a small-pike'. Pickard avoided Edwards thereafter.[13]

Another whose suspicion was aroused was the bootmaker Thomas Chambers. He had carried flags at meetings in Smithfield and at Hunt's triumphal entry to London. He swore that he had met Edwards 'by accident' at the White Lion in Wych Street. When Edwards called on him and talked politics 'in a strange and violent manner', he got worried:

> On Christmas Eve he again called on me with several person amongst them were two Irishmen who were drunk and whom I had never seen before. Edwards on this occasion had with him an old cavalry sword which he kept under his coat and also a sword stick in his hand. He said to the Irishmen 'Wouldn't you wish to have Castlereagh's head to carry about on a pole for the good he has done your country'. One of the Irishmen said: 'He (meaning Lord Castlereagh) is a big rogue '– At which Edwards drew out the dirk from his stick, and said 'Here is what will cut off his bloody head'. Edwards called on me again about a week after, much against my wish, and held forth in violent language about the government, and said that 'After the tyrants were cut off, [moderate radicals like] Hunt and Cobbett must go to pot [too]'.

Two days before Cato Street the spy arrived at Chambers's lodging with a very tall man with a cast in his eye – Adams:

> Edwards had a large bag with him which he requested me to allow him to leave in my room. I asked him what it contained. He replied: 'Oh, only a few pistols and such like'. I instantly bid him take them away, that I should not have such things in my place. He urged me very much to permit the bag to remain, but I again told him I would on no account have anything to do with such things and immediately made him take the bag away assisted by the person who came with him. . . . I answered I would not be at such a Despard business. He then clapped his hand on the wall of the house and said: 'This is all lathe and plaster, you shan't be safe, we'll blow you out of your bed'.[14]

WAITING

Across the frozen weeks between the Finsbury Market meeting on 1 November 1819 and the Cato Street arrests on 23 February, Edwards sent some hundred reports to John Stafford at Bow Street and latterly to Henry Hobhouse in the home office. Signed 'W—r' for 'Windsor', they were scribbled in ink on narrow hand-cut slips of paper (the better to conceal them, presumably). They record near-daily and sometimes twice-daily meetings in the White Lion, the White Hart, the Scotch Arms and other taverns, and in Preston's or Watson's lodgings. From late January they met in the newly hired back room behind Brunt's lodging in Fox Court. Between 11 and 24 January, Edwards suspended his reports because, he said, 'nothing particular took place', though that had been true across most of December and January as well. Even as matters heated up in February, Edwards could still report: 'conversation much as yester-day'. For months Stafford, Birnie, Hobhouse, and Sidmouth must have twitched with impatience as they read these tediously repetitive missives and waited for a prosecutable action to jump on.

Most though not all meetings were attended by Brunt, Tidd, Davidson, Ings, Harrison, Robert George, Cook, Bradburn, Hartley, Palin, Potter, and Adams. Thistlewood and Edwards attended them all. A trivial debt, the recurrent curse of all these people, put Adams in the Whitecross Street debtors' prison from 13 to 30 January 1820; for another debt he was returned to it after the trials. Debt also saved Watson. Not paying the bill for Hunt's dinner put him into gaol in early December and excluded him from the active conspiracy. When Thistlewood reassured him that 'he should soon fetch him out', 'Watson replyed you will of corse do that but make sure of your aim first and be sure to make a stand and die to a man rather than be taken'.[15]

Instead of fetching him out or dying to a man, Thistlewood and Edwards met Watson in his prison-yard – Edwards to consult him on the wording of a proclamation, Thistlewood to pick up his recipe for 'combustibles'. Watson's eleven-year-old son, hitherto unheard of, brought from prison his father's coded message to the soldiers (see Figs 1.4 and 1.5). From Whitecross Street, Watson also sent Thistlewood condolences on his death sentence, sure that he would 'rise superior to the fear which agitates little minds'. He asked to see him for a few minutes before his last moments: Sidmouth refused.[16] That is the last we hear of Watson's activity until over a year later he headed the funeral procession of two labourers who had been killed by rogue soldiers during a fracas in Knightsbridge. In the 1830s he went to New York (perhaps to join young Watson, if he was still living). He died there a pauper in 1838.[17]

We are at Edwards's mercy in assessing the conspirators' states of mind in these cold waiting months. He had to abbreviate their inter-changes and elide nuance and qualification as he did so, and he wrote very little about personal relationships or how discussions were regu-lated. This would obscure their subtler judgements, if they had any. But his reports do answer the questions that the defence counsel Adolphus raised in court in April. As disappointment followed disappointment, how against all reason could the conspirators sustain their commitment? How could they persuade themselves that their ramshackle plots were viable?

Basic answers are provided by anger, ignorance, and deprivation, and by their need to prove London's valour to the rest of the country. But Edwards's notes also illuminate the unifying bond between men who had time on their hands and no profitable paid work to occupy them – a needy sociability, in other words: the importance of mutual exhortation and bravado, the difficulty of reneging on one's own fantasies and boasts, the obsessional fixation on assassination – and their total lack of focus as their discussion ranged loosely and at random from topic to topic. What comes over is a disordered medley of fantasies. Living day after day with dreams of action, and repeating grindingly familiar arguments or scen-arios to pass the time, it was next to impossible to bring themselves down to earth again. The last thing they had was an agenda. 'Turn the rich out and put the poor in their houses,' someone said, and then felt no need to say anything further.

One effect of these processes was a breezy optimism melded with a numbing of thought about their own and others' deaths. They came to anticipate the cruellest of killings with equanimity. At one meeting they argued what to do with any of their men who might be wounded in the coming 'row':

[Thistlewood] said you must not mind about murder. They must have a hackney coach handy and convey the wounded in them order the coachman to drive us to a place where we must murder him as also the poor hall porter that shows us the room where the ministers are if we have a man wounded that cant live cut his head off and carry it away with us then every one must take care of some party for himself.[18]

When Cook worried about the insufficiency of their numbers, Thistlewood lectured him on the history of Roman assassination; this taught that it was the determination of a handful, not numbers, that counted. When Cook worried whether the cabinet at dinner would be armed, Thistlewood reassured him that ministers carried arms only out of doors, and 'besides, we should take them by surprise'.[19] Now and then Thistlewood advised caution. 'Sufficient was said that evening to hang them all,' he warned at one point; they must collect 200 armed men before they could move. But then he added that once they had them, 'they would not wait one hour more'. He kept promising action 'within days', reassuring his men that 'he would bring it to an end soon if they would follow him' and that 'he did not wish them to go where he would not he would place himself in all the danger and share the same fate as them'.[20]

In a typical report in early January, Edwards described a peripatetic meeting between Thistlewood, Preston, Ings, and Bradburn, with Brunt and Hall joining later in the day – peripatetic because it moved from Preston's to Thistlewood's lodgings with breaks and errands in between. One notes Susan Thistlewood's presence in the group and her readiness to challenge her husband; but more striking is the wishful thinking and disordered discussion:

Monday morning Met Mr [Mrs?] Thistlewood at Prestons . . . B[runt] went to Peels coffeehouse to look at the Morning Post on his return said there was nothing that would do [i.e. no cabinet meeting]. . . . he said there was to be [a] rout [party] at one of the ambassadors and no doubt they [the ministers] would be there but it would be better to catch the devils all together [than] by themselves We met afterward at Mr Thist[d] and was joind by Hall he said he had seen all his men except Rose who had moved Thistlewood said he thought that Rose, Hartley, Payne & George had grabbled about 600 guineas from an old gent a little way out of town & that Hartley's house had been searched [There is no record of this robbery.] He said Hartley would spoil the cause for nothing should be done that was felonious but after the ministers were destroyed he T— would take them to Childs or Coutts Bank Besides he said none of them would give a shilling of it to him towards carrying into effect the overturning of government The method of attack was spoken of which was much as before Brunt said he longed to have a cut at them all This[d] said above all he wished to kill Wellington What said Mrs T[histlewood] would not you rather kill Sidmouth he said he should like to have a thrust at them all Brunt said Tidd wished to kill Canning and that his Blue [ex Horse Guard Adams] would play Hell among them with a sword Thistlewood said if any of them should be taken those that are at liberty must immediately assassinate several of Carlile's jurors and label them as a warning to the jury that may have to try those that are taken.[21]

December was the conspirators' bleakest month. The country itched for 'something big' to happen, but Finsbury Market had taught them that Londoners could sink into torpor as well as mud. The number of armed supporters they counted on never exceeded fifty, and most were impatient for action. Ings 'bought a knife and a steel in the true style of a butcher' and 'enjoys the idea of carrying off several of the heads in a bag that hangs in the room at the White Hart'. Robert George (in Edwards's words) announced that

> nothing but fighting would do for him there has been all talking and no fighting for long enough it was now time they left of [*sic*] talking and began fighting he had begun by telling [the] magistrates that he would pay no king's taxes and had drove away the tax gentlemen and been obliged to leve his house he was now a wanderer & therefore was determined to fight.

Cook made

> a leather bag to bring away one of the heads and says he will carry it on a pike as soon as the people assemble. He has received three letters from Leeds the last (he says) states their determination to form into little parties to murder all those in that part of the cuntry who has been obnoxious to them – in addition to the arms stated before he has in his possession 2 horse pistols.[22]

What hurt was the public shaming. In December a visiting Manchester ultra boasted that in the north 170,000 armed men could be assembled within an hour, and that over a million were ready to march from Scotland and the north and arrive in London within ten days. By comparison, he added sourly, their London counterparts lacked 'talents, money, influence and respectability', and couldn't be depended on for anything. On Christmas Day Thistlewood told the committee that that day's *Courier* reported an insurrection in Glasgow and Paisley. Three days later a letter from Ireland told Bradburn that Ireland was also rising. If true, Thistlewood said, 'they ought to muster all hands and begin directly'. All they actually did was meet tamely at Preston's next morning. When Davidson suggested that it would be 'a great slur on the Londoners if they let the country begin by themselves', Thistlewood bleakly replied that the country seemed not to need them.[23]

In the event, it was in Scotland and Yorkshire that 'something' was done in response to London's defeat, though as usual they were outgunned. In April 1820 insurrection swept through the Scottish midlands as desperate weavers proposed a provisional government and a national strike. Betrayed by spies, they were contained by hussars and militia in a 'radical war' that resulted in the usual killings. In August and September leaders Wilson, Hardie, and Baird were hanged and decapitated for treason. In Yorkshire, twenty-two men were sentenced to death for treason though mercifully sent to Australia on the prison ships, after an abortive rising on Grange Moor. With Thistlewood and friends heading for the gallows, London could do nothing to help.[24]

Meanwhile, Edwards reported several Sunday gatherings of fifty or sixty men, some from the unions and one group from 'over the water' (Thames). Admissions were poorly controlled, so the meetings were insecure and fractious. In the Scotch Arms on 22 December the newcomer Ings – at his first meeting – drew a loaded pistol and declared that he would shoot Sidmouth, Castlereagh, Liverpool, and Canning, and that he itched to 'bring away one of [the ministers'] heads stuck upon a pole to rouse the people with'. In protest at the stupidity of saying this in public, Hartley, Palin, Tunbridge, and Cook surrendered their 'captaincies'. A couple of days later Ings proposed killing the ministers one at a time as they left the Commons; Thistlewood said that would make them look like thieves and fail to rouse the people. A proposal that each committee member hide his name behind a number was dropped because everyone forgot the numbers. The group agreed 'not to meet in large parties any more' and to suspend its collective leadership. Management of the cause was given to Thistlewood, though the others continued to chair meetings. Ings was admitted to their number.[25]

Money was a constant worry. Thistlewood had splashed out family cash to fund the Spa Fields rising in 1816, but he was heading for destitution now, and had to sell family prints and books. Yet when an unnamed gentleman subscribed £10 to buy pistols, £4 was held back to buy rum and bread and cheese for the day of the attack. On 27 December Edwards and Bradburn extracted a twopenny subscription from an acquaintance to help pay for a room to store weapons. Impoverishment didn't stop the twosome treating themselves to a mix of beer and a quarter-pint of gin 'made hot'. On New Year's Day Brunt and Edwards toured town to find a room to store arms ('at any rent, as it was expected none would be paid'), and afterwards knocked back hot gin and beer as they dined off a beef steak at the Cross Keys in Brownlow Street.[26]

Such positive news as there was was eagerly reported, but there was little of it. During an interchange with a soldier at the Rose, Thistlewood asked 'how many of his comrades he could get to ingage in something'. The reply was cautious 'Can't answer for many.'

> *Question*: Suppose we should some night begin and kick up a row would your regiment pike us in the gutts?
>
> *Answer*: Our regiment seems to wish there was something done and [I] don't think they would fight against the people.

One day Brunt treated a soldier to beer and said it was a rascally shame that a soldier should work for 15 pence a day while the officers who did nothing earned £15 a day: he hoped the soldiers would unite with the people. At this suggestion the soldier became 'rather shy and left'. On another occasion Thistlewood 'had no doubt that the soldier we was in company with the night before ... would join in any thing if he was furnished with disguise'. This didn't bode well either.[27]

On 13 December Thistlewood summoned Edwards to his Stanhope Street lodging to help him make pistol balls. Here he proposed a new policy. (Edwards promptly reported it to the home office.) Since their numbers were too few to attack the Commons, how about murdering the whole cabinet at their next dinner? This was due to be held at Lord Westmorland's house in Grosvenor Square (a few doors from Harrowby's). When Thistlewood went to spy on Westmorland's he found the house ringed by policemen, so that had to be dropped.[28]

On 24 January Thistlewood told his committee at the White Hart (Brunt, Ings, Tidd, Hartley, Edwards, and Harrison present) that a cabinet dinner had been advertised for Harrowby's house on 1 February. This time they embarked on frenetic preparation. The first thing they did was rent the new and safe meeting place in the back room on Brunt's floor in Fox Court. Palin drafted an address to the people and the soldiers, and Edwards took it to Whitecross Street prison for Watson to polish it. Thomas Davison the printer prevaricated about printing the posters, and Thistlewood declared that he was a coward and needed skewering. Over the next couple of days bullets, pistols, and pikes were collected, Davidson and Harrison made hand grenades, supporters across town were visited, cajoled, and alerted, and Harrowby's was watched to be sure it wasn't guarded. Then on Sunday evening, 30 January, Thistlewood arrived with an anticlimactic announcement. 'The damned old king' had died the previous evening. Dinner at Harrowby's was cancelled.[29]

There was no returning to the earlier torpor, however. At a meeting in the Fox Court room on 4 February, Thistlewood, Ings, Brunt, Bradburn, Adams (just out of debtors' prison), and Edwards argued about their new plan to kill individual ministers on the 16th, the day of the king's funeral, when all the soldiers and most of the police would be in Windsor attending it. (Ministers too, surely?) They would appropriate the three artillery pieces in the Finsbury artillery ground. Harris, the letter-foundryman near Finsbury Square who was busy making pikes and polishing swords for them, told Thistlewood that the guns were six-pounders like those deployed at Peterloo. 'They can be got easily,' said Harris, though they would have to make cartridges to fit them. When the soldiers returned to London after marching from Windsor they would be tired. They should be disarmed at once and then given free run of the silversmith shops 'to satisfy themselves'.[30]

Adams wanted to use the guns to set free the felons in Newgate; 'they would make a good mob' of natural plunderers. Thistlewood agreed that they had 'several man-of-wars-men and they all understand the use of field pieces'. Harrison most fancied killing 'that villian Wellington'. He made a large grenade for the purpose by packing three quarters of a pound of gunpowder into an iron coffee roaster. He would 'give it out that Wellington was the greatest coward in the room and that he beged for mercy on his knees ... such a report will be degrading to his friends and relations'. Ings just wanted to get on with killing Castlereagh and Sidmouth:

> It was all nonsense for a man to be afraid of his life he had made up his mind to die (swearing and marching about the room like a mad man) ... he would never cease untill he had killed some of the bloody villins ... we can go in small parties to their houses at seven in the morning as soon as the servants open the door and murder them in their bed.

Thistlewood preferred to find where they dined after the king's burial and to kill them there. He would then use the guns to attack the Bank, 'his old favourite object', he said. That 'would destroy all confidence in bank notes and prevent their passing ... besides we should find a quantity of silver and gold and that would bring thousands to join our standard'. They talked of capturing the military telegraph to Woolwich and, if Adams is to be believed, of capturing Brighton to prevent the regent escaping.

> Thistlewood gave me [Edwards] 15 shillings to purchase cumbustibles to fire houses. Ings bought a half gallon of spirits of turpentine 3 lbs of tallow 8 ounces of brimstone & 2 lb of pitch. Harris gave Ths[d] a quantity of old rope to be pulled to pieces to make old junk to be formed in to balls and dipped in the above ingredients. Harris apprised Thistlewood that he has got above 20 pike blades & 10 swords he gave me one of the pike blades for a pattern for fitting them to the shafts. Ings said he had been watching Lord Castlereagh that afternoon and that he should know him again and he would be damned if he don't kill him and one or two more before long – Thistlewood said he must not, as it will be better to kill all the

ministers at the same time. A great deal of the old rope was picked to pieces by Thistlewood Harrison Ings and Brunt.

The next three weeks were spent reiterating murderous hatreds and intentions in this mode, making pikes and grenades, spying on ministers, and hunting recruits. Ings and Wilson itched for immediate slaughter, and on Saturday, 19 February Brunt agreed with them that if no dinner took place before Wednesday they should 'put as many of the rascals out of the world as we can get at'. 'Let us divide into small divisions and cast lots who shall kill the man allotted to the party and the rest secure his retreat and [if] he don't kill whomsoever is allotted to him the other shall kill him for being a coward. . . . Carried unanimously.' If they killed only Castlereagh and Sidmouth, the country would still rise behind them.

Thistlewood's larger ambition won through, however. On Sunday, 20 February in the Fox Court meeting room he addressed a crammed assembly of twenty or so, including Brunt, Hall, Ings, Potter, Palin, Strange, Adams, Wilson, Davidson, Harrison, and Cook, with Tidd in the chair. 'Gentlemen,' Thistlewood began – then corrected himself: 'no I shall drop that old way of addressing you and shall use the word Citizens'. As he talked, Davidson chipped in: 'don't call it murdering use the word bottling of them'. 'Well then,' Thistlewood agreed, 'we will bottle them this I consider to be the first and grand object.' Even if only forty men turned up to 'destroy them villains', that number would do the job as well as five hundred.

So plans were relaid. While women and boys (Susan Thistlewood and Julian included) kept watch on houses, barracks, and police offices, Dwyer's fifty imaginary Irishmen and a party from the Marylebone union would capture the artillery pieces in Gray's Inn Lane. The Finsbury party, '80 at least', would meet at Cook's house behind the Antelope pub in Hollywell Lane, in Shoreditch, and would move to kill the sentry and appropriate the guns in the artillery ground at Bunhill Row. A hundred-weight of cast-iron railings awaited them at Harris's type manufactory in Chiswell Street nearby. With sledgehammers brought for the purpose, Thistlewood said, they should break them up for the cannons' ammunition. Then 'we shall be able to beat all the horse soldiers that they can send against us'. They would then take the Bank and make the Mansion House their 'seat of government' while starting fires across London – for 'nothing will call the people together like fires'. Bills must be posted 'to inform the people that the Tyrents are no more [and] that the Provisional Government is sitting at the Mansion House and that they call upon the people to assist them. – Carried unanimously.' Soldiers worried them chronically, but not as much as they should have. The day before assembling at Cato Street, Cook said he knew the soldiers were waiting for 'something to be done'; he drew comfort from the fact that they had sworn to serve George III but not as yet to serve George IV. Harrison added that 'the horse soldiers couldn't make a move without his knowing, and that he was sure they could not get sadled and out of the barracks in less than an hour, and that all the men are out of the barracks from eight to ten every evening and that the King Street barracks can be set on fire very easily'.[31]

By that weekend Sidmouth, Hobhouse, Birnie, and Stafford would have had enough of these endless reports. Most of their deliberations were verbal and so leave no record; but Edwards's daily notes must have made it obvious that Thistlewood and men were pumped up for action. And so it was at last that the trap was laid.

On Tuesday Edwards 'discovered' in the *New Times* the planted announcement of the cabinet dinner arranged for the following evening in Harrowby's house, Grosvenor Square, and reported it to the meeting in Fox Court. Hall was sent to Fleet Street to buy a copy, and on his return Thistlewood 'read the advertisement very loud which immediately inspired the whole room with hilarity. Brunt exclaimed now I believe there is a God I never belift it before he has called all the ministers together for us to murder them.'

That same Tuesday afternoon Edwards used a secret messenger to deliver a for once carefully written letter to Hobhouse in which he specified every detail of the conspirators' intentions next day. 'We meet again this evening at Brunts [i.e. Fox Court],' he wrote, 'and as many alterations may then take place, I promise to wait on you this evening before I go to rest.' He added that at Hobhouse's home (provided Hobhouse saw 'nothing improper in it') he would like to meet the officers who would lead the attack on the conspirators, and to answer any questions he had overlooked. He suggested that rooms should be taken as near as possible to Brook Street, Queen Street, Cato Street, and Holywell Lane in Shoreditch, and that they should be all taken in one name 'to prevent mistake on my part'. 'A trusty person with a messenger should sit at each place and if the room can be obtained in houses were [*sic*] the street doors are open all day it will facilitate our correspondence. Yours faithfully, G. Edwards.'[32]

With this letter Edwards's thick dossier of reports comes to an end.

TREACHERIES REPAID

What happened to the spies, turncoat witnesses, and informers whose reports and testimony laid the Cato Street men low? After the trials and executions they were subjected to such execration, plebeian and other-wise, that they had good cause to worry about their futures. One who escaped public anger was Abel Hall. In May he 'felt clear with them all' – so clear that a month later he contrived to join the widows in indicting Edwards, and was able, undetected, to become a spy himself. A few others got away with it too. Hall reported that Firth bought two new cows to keep himself out of politics, George gave up politics on his master's orders, and Simmons took a job in the country.[33] Others were less lucky. The Irish bricklayer Thomas Dwyer told Sidmouth that he was

> under the greattest conptent by the lower class of people. . . . My lord I am threatened every hour by people of every discription my child can not go into the street and [an] that [lest] he should chanch to be known but he is insulted in the worst of manner I hope my lord that your lordship will removed me from these deficutyes which exposes me and my family to the scoffs and frowns of an inhuman publik.

He would happily emigrate as a 'working mecanik' if Sidmouth would help him, since he was 'friteful of being assinated every moment by some of their friends or some of these disafected people that serounds this metropoliss'.[34]

Adams suffered most. In May he asked Stafford at Bow Street for support in the 'daingeras sitturation i now stand in for what i have dun'. His eyesight was failing, and his imprisonment in Tothill Fields and in debtors' prison left him too ill to work. And after what i have dun it is more than a hundred to one if any master should employ me for if the master whould be willing as sone as the men . . . knew it [they] whould directly strike against the master for employing me then the men whould convey it to the hole trade not for a man to go on for the shop so long as i was on for it.

A few weeks later he lamented: 'My life his in worse dainger than if I had run the risk of my trial for then I should have had some protection. . . . I have a life worse than a dog, for my life his [is] fretand [threatened] in many directions as sone as any of the party see me.' To Sidmouth he lamented 'the disgrace theas [these] knowing falsiths [falsehoods] to me will bring upon my children, not myne only but upon thear children as well, what must the riseing genaration think, not only the riseing but the present.' He asked for some shirts and neckerchiefs, adding in November that he also needed medicines and 'a sute of close a hat one flannel wescoat and drawers and par of short legans', as well as money for his poor wife.[35] There's no knowing if he got them.

Of course Edwards was the most hated. Thanks to Thistlewood's accusation in his final statement in court, the news spread rapidly that he had set up the conspiracy and then betrayed it. 'The ministers were the instigators of this business' and Edwards was their agent, Carlile stated in the *Republican* on 28 April. Voices in the scaffold crowd on May Day called for Edwards's death. Soon after the executions the shoemaker John Brown saw him 'soused with stinking water from shoemaker's shop tubs, as he sneaked through narrow courts and alleys; he was a most repulsive and cadaverous looking wretch'.[36]

Edwards's biggest threat came from the reformer and City MP, Alderman Matthew Wood. He laid evidence of Edwards's role before Sidmouth on 26 April, but Sidmouth dismissed it. He gathered further evidence from Thistlewood as the latter was having his shackles struck off in the Newgate press-room. He then raised the matter in the Commons on 2 May and brought it to full debate a week later. He proposed a secret committee 'to examine evidence touching the criminal conduct and proceedings of George Edwards and his associates for the last two years, and especially his connexion with the parties forming the plot lately discovered in Cato Street'. His speech was thick with testimonies to

Edwards's and the ministers' guilt, and he argued that Edwards's sudden elevation from poverty to wealth confirmed them. The opposition agreed. The MP for Southwark, Sir Robert Wilson, 'was not prepared to say that spies were not necessary under certain circumstances, but ... an organised spy system was most abominable':

> Under any circumstances, those who engaged spies, were placed under an awful responsibility. They should take care that their agents should not become incendiaries – that they should not have the means of providing arms and ammunition in order to seduce those who from distress or a feeling of unredressed wrongs were likely to become easy dupes to their machinations. ... In such a case, the distresses of the people would enable such miscreants to bring, not tens, but thousands to the scaffold. ...
>
> The unhappy persons in the [Cato Street] case to which he alluded were accused on the secret evidence of a spy of the police. The accused demanded that the accuser might be brought forward, but that demand was rejected; they were found guilty, and executed under circumstances of peculiar barbarity – with a barbarity which never disgraced the French revolution, even in the very height of its rage. But, barbarous as it was, the execution of those persons did not excite so much indignation as the unjust transaction, disgraced as it had been by the interference of spies.

'The basest materials of which the human race was composed' was how the future judge Thomas Denman defined Edwards in the debate. He had it from the conspirators' defence counsel that 'they had not the smallest doubt that Edwards had been an active instigator from the beginning of the plot; but that fact they could not state in the defence, because Edwards had not been examined on the trial'.

Led by George Canning, tory speakers dismissed Wood as 'meddling, busy and mischievous' and his motion as 'folly'. Even the whig Henry Brougham told the Commons that he didn't blame government for employing spies: 'As long as society can furnish such desperate characters as Thistlewood and Ings, government is not only justified, but bound, to employ such men as Edwards.'[37] The clincher came from the attorney general Robert Gifford. He stated outright that Edwards 'had never been employed by the government as a spy, and it was not in that character that he furnished that information which had enabled ministers to defeat one of the most horrible plots that had ever been formed'. He sought to justify his lie through an elaborate review of Thistlewood's deviousness and of other conspirators' responsibility for informing on him. He was the readier to lie since he had blood on his hands already. He had appeared against the Derbyshire rioters in 1817 while fully aware of the spy Oliver's role in the case; and he had replied for the crown in Watson's treason prosecution while fully aware of the spy Castle's culpability. He knew the truth of the Cato Street case as well, which is why Edwards's testimony was dispensed with in court. Since Castle's exposure in the Watson trial had laid the prosecution low, the government had no choice but to lie if the Cato Street prosecution was to retain any credit. Still, even today it would shock some if not all of us to hear an attorney general lying to parliament as bare-facedly as this man did.[38]

Wood's efforts came too late. Nobody outside the home office and Bow Street knew this, but on 4 May Edwards wrote to undersecretary Hobhouse that he had arrived on the Channel island of Guernsey and was short of money. In late May he heard it rumoured that he was in Guernsey and thought he'd be safer in London after all. 'It really seems I shall find it difficult to obtain a resting place for every one seems to rail against me (instead of which I anticipated praise from all).' But 22 May was the day on which the Middlesex Grand Jury found a true bill on the indictment for treason against him brought by Susan and Julian Thistlewood, Mary Brunt, Robert George, and Abel Hall. They were aided by Alderman Wood, ex-sheriff Philips, and a current sheriff, Parkins. Harmer the solicitor was authorised to offer a hundred guineas reward for his arrest. So a week later, still in Guernsey, Edwards asked Hobhouse how he was to be 'protected from the insult of a vile and indiscreet rabble . . . every turn I take I am obliged to hear the invective utterances against me it really allarms me'. Two days later Edwards lamented that 'after what has been said against me it would be impossible for me to [pursue my career as an artist] even in the most remote part of the world'. When his family joined him in June he asked for £31 to pay for their comforts, and in July asked for more to rent a house and furniture. Signing himself 'G. Parker', he thanked Stafford for the £20 sent to him but asked for another £70 because Guernsey rents were inflated by wealthy English visitors.[39]

In August, Edwards and family were sent to the Cape of Good Hope. This was the obvious place to go. In 1819, £50,000 had been voted to assist strategic settlement on the eastern Cape frontier, a policy that would alleviate distress at home at the same time. Brunt, Preston, and Hartley each thought of applying for a passage, and possibly did apply; but of 90,000 applicants only some 4,000 were accepted. Castle, who betrayed Watson and Thistlewood in 1816/17, might have been one of them. William Oliver, who helped send the luddites to their deaths, certainly was. Under the name William Jones, he was granted land and employed as deputy inspector of the colony's buildings. He was buried in Green Point Cemetery in 1827. Edwards was buried in the same cemetery in 1843. He had turned himself into 'George Parker', plaster modeller.[40]

Before he left Guernsey, Edwards told Stafford that in his spying he had been moved by 'an internal conviction of innocence'. Charles Lamb was one of thousands who thought otherwise:

> ... And all about the detestable pit
> Strange headless ghosts, and quarter'd forms, did flit,
> Rivers of blood, from living traitors spilt,
> By treachery stung from poverty to guilt.
> I ask'd the fiend, for whom these rites were meant?
> 'These graves,' quoth he, 'when life's brief oil is spent,
> When the dark night comes, and they're sinking bedwards,
> – I mean for Castles, Oliver, and Edwards.'[41]

PART FOUR

ORDINARY BRITONS

CHAPTER 13

Conspirators and Others

OTHERS

Except at carnivalesque moments like Hunt's entry into London, most common and middling folk in the regency years kept their distance from subversives – whether out of principle, contentment, inertia, or fear. The Cruikshank brothers' anti-radical caricatures aimed at this audience and higher. Letters poured into the home office not only to castigate but also to congratulate Sidmouth on his victory over the wicked. And more tavern landlords pinned 'No Jacobins' to their doors than ever welcomed radicals to their club rooms. 'Nine tenths of the publicans are your enemies,' Henry Hunt warned his supporters; 'they are tools in the hands of the magistrates' to secure their licences.[1] For all manner of reasons, the anger that animates this story was not universally shared.

Even so, as suggested earlier, in the big real world many contrary-seeming facts may be true at once. The people who thought *well* of radicals in regency London were also beyond counting. When, for instance, Daniel Isaac Eaton was sent by Ellenborough to the Charing Cross pillory in 1812 for publishing Tom Paine, people didn't pelt him with dead cats as they were meant to; instead they applauded him and urged him to stand so that the pillory would shield his head from the sun. Government didn't forget this lesson. When two years later the naval hero and critic of naval abuses Lord Cochrane was sentenced to the pillory, the government dared not execute the sentence. In 1816 the pillory was abolished except for wilful and corrupt perjury and subordination.[2] The ultras' faith in this vast reservoir of support was not delusional. By 1819, plebeian support of this kind was probably predominant in London. Individuals' enthusiasm for the likes of Thistlewood was qualified in all sorts of ways, but nobody doubted that it was wide-ranging and expressed a culture that was deeply at odds with its rulers.

When the home office informant Vincent Dowling made nocturnal visits to a series of taverns between Fleet Street and Whitechapel, he met 'much of the tone of "the mobocracy"', 'a strong revolutionary taint', and political topics discussed 'everywhere'. In the Red Lion off Lombard Street, a 'nest of democrats' met to read Cobbett aloud once a week. Most Whitechapel butchers had 'the right [loyalist] feeling', but others with the wrong feeling told him that the Spa Fields rising had been badly managed and that insurrection must be better organised next time.[3] Again, an unnamed correspondent in November 1819 wrote a series of 'notes' in a practised hand which were so confidently expressed, and so well informed about the Thistlewood camp, that their author might have been an official like Stafford. 'Trash publications pollute every corner in the island,' he stated. You found them 'in the pothouses, the streets and workshops of London, and the manufacturing districts and most isolated corners of Hampshire and Devonshire. The country people on the highway and in the fields are stopped by wandering demagogues and hawkers who live by preaching and selling blasphemy and sedition.' Yet again, a City cabinet-maker told the correspondent that only two of his sixty men were 'moderate'. The other fifty-eight were 'rendered furious by the reading of these publications – they bind them up in volumes, and read them to their wives and children – they observed to the foreman, "these publications are food and drink to us"'. The correspondent noted that although 'the old London Corresponding Society men' were jealous of the ultras, they still met them and contributed money. The ultras' committee comprised about 700 individuals, he added, and 'they could muster about 1,500 determined men who would do whatever Thistlewood might desire them'.[4]

We meet this great array of dissidents in one form or another in just about every spy report in 1818–20, and the catalogue that emerges from them is remarkable. First came the men who were known to Bow Street but who escaped arrest in 1820. Some spoke violently in Wedderburn's Spencean chapel in Soho or in the White Lion – men like James Hartley, ex-soldier and unemployed servant; George Pickard, who later testified against Edwards; Samuel Waddington the diminutive shoemaker and printer; Allen Davenport the shoemaker; Blandford the poor hair-dresser; or Thomas Davison the journeyman printer who supplied many of Thistlewood's and Watson's posters.[5] Other names float in and out of the reports, impossible to identify now. For decades yet, ageing radicals boasted of their Cato Street credentials; and in select circles in New South Wales it was a mark of distinction, even in the 1850s, to be known as one of the five Cato Street transportees.

Beyond such men we should include the printers who cast lead shot for pistols and blunderbusses, or who took chances by printing radical and deistical pamphlets and posters; the bill-posters who stuck them up across London; the bookshop, coffee house, and street vendors who sold radical papers; the newspapermen who risked prison and whose readers (and listeners) outnumbered those of the *Times*; the cabinet-makers who read Cobbett or Wooler to illiterate wives and children; the tavern landlords who hosted meetings and kept sharp eyes on strangers; the blacksmiths who beat out iron pike-heads at cost price; the cutlers who sharpened cutlasses and pike-heads; the tavern people who contributed their sixpences to help buy weapons or to aid bereft wives and children; the shoemakers', coachmakers', tailors', and typefounders' societies that contributed for the same; the men who paid sixpence to attend debates at Wedderburn's chapel; the families of radical veterans and old LCS men like Pendrill or Holl the engraver who sheltered the fugitives Thistlewood and young Watson in 1816; the malcontents who sent anonymous letters before and after the executions to damn ministers' eyes and threaten them with assassination; and the neighbours who put the fear of God into the conspirators who had informed or turned into crown witnesses.

Then one should add the cheering celebrants who unhorsed Hunt's or Thistlewood's carriages and pulled them to their destinations; the rowdy thousands who went to hear Hunt and Watson at Spa Fields and at Smithfield; the constellation that flocked to Islington to welcome Hunt into London after Peterloo; the lawyers like James Harmer who worked in court for the poor to expose rough justice and malign judges. Add the crowds at executions that hissed the hangman and sheriffs and shouted support for those about to die – not always as 'barbaric' as critics liked to think; the sardonic gallows jokes and street ballads that lauded the scaffold's victims; the caricaturists and versifiers, so wounding to the regent and government that the fat booby had to bribe them into silence the moment he became king; the women's and children's cheers or lamentations for imprisoned or fugitive husbands; the people who chalked graffiti on walls, as they had for centuries.

Finally add the men of literary, cultural, or political standing who made panicky ministers believe that even gentlemen might favour revolution. Whiggish radicals like Burdett and poets like Shelley, Byron, and Keats were vocal critics of government. Jeremy Bentham contributed funds to radical groups, and Byron's friend John Cam Hobhouse was put in Newgate for breaching parliamentary privilege. The informant Abel Hall reported that Thistlewood visited Hobhouse in prison and persuaded him to lead the conspirators' provisional government should their revolution succeed. According to Mrs Arbuthnot, the duke of Wellington had no doubt of the truth of this story, unlikely though it sounds.[6]

Finally there were the prudent people who hardly ever stuck their necks above parapets but who couldn't resist doing so under provocation. Typical were two printers, George Thompson and John Evans (unrelated to the Spencean Evans), who had collaborated in printmaking since the 1790s and who traded next door to each other in Long Lane in West Smithfield. Since the 1790s their output of bucolic scenes and simple descriptive prints of state occasions had been innocuous and apolitical. Suddenly in 1819–20 Thompson allowed himself a trio of stylised prints whose sympathies were betrayed in their subject matter: Hunt's and Watson's Smithfield meeting in July 1819 (see Fig. 10.2), another of Peterloo three months later, and his horrific classic on the Cato Street executions (see Fig. 17.1). John Evans likewise had issued countless sentimental and loyalist ballads over the past quarter-century until he too broke loose by publishing a ballad in 1819 which commented on politics *seditiously*, as if his reticence had also snapped. Entitled 'The White Hat', it celebrated Henry Hunt as the future king 'Harry the Ninth':

> We'll have not pension, place, nor court,
> No king nor regent to support;

No priests to feed, no taxes to pay:
And we'll go to the devil our own way.

…

Now march, my boys, in your Radical rags;
Handle your sticks, and flourish your flags;
Till we lay the Throne and the Altar flat,
With a whisk of Harry the Ninth's White Hat.

And Hey for Radical Reform,
To raise in England a glorious storm;
And level each proud aristocrat,
With a whisk of Harry the Ninth's White Hat.[7]

THE RANK AND FILE

The information we *do* have about prosecutable or prosecuted individuals concerns only the most exposed of this vast and resentful populace. As an impoverished artisanate, none of them securely employed, and some seriously hungry, the radicals among them had long been the targets of upper-class contempt. Since the 1790s home office spies would always gratify their paymasters by reporting that the men who met and plotted in low taverns were ignorant ruffians and desperados. Print satirists did the same. James Gillray set his *London Corresponding Society, alarm'd* (1798) in 'Tom Treason['s] Hell-Fire Celler, Chick Lane', and showed assembled there a bevy of blubber-lipped Corresponding Society delegates named 'Forging Sam, Barber Joe, Dick Butcher, Dissenting Nick, Sheepshead Will, and Cut Down Lary', none of them a figure of manly fortitude. That tradition endured into the loyalist prints of George Cruikshank and others throughout the regency.

The truth was, however, that the Cato Street men were very different from the 'parcel of mechanics from the lowest orders of society' referred to in the trials. They weren't *sans-culotte* or *lumpen* proletarian either. Thistlewood was a middle-aged quasi-gentleman, while Dr Watson had some medical knowledge to his credit. Beneath these two we meet a sample of 'ordinary' Britons who had craft skills, craft pride, workable literacy, and despite their poverty a certain moral weight to them. The street kids and young tearaways who had made themselves felt as the 'mob' in the Spa Fields lootings aren't visible in this company.

Nearly all our known actors were male craftsmen in their thirties or forties who were married with children, and nearly all were literate, or could at least read when they couldn't write. None had a previous conviction against him that is traceable today, even if Tidd's early life was allegedly spotted with illegalities and frauds, and Harrison was implicated in planning the Spa Fields insurrection.[8] Tidd and Davidson were repeatedly noticed in spy reports from July 1819 onwards, and Harrison was noticed in 1816; yet each was in person no more sinister than any other craftsman out of full employment. The shoemakers involved in the Cato Street conspiracy were so numerous that the plot was virtually a shoemakers' plot – and shoemakers have never been intrinsically wicked, sinister, or stupid.

Most of the conspirators rose from these common origins, but commentators felt free to project every form of monstrosity onto them. On the night of the arrests the *Morning Chronicle* described butcher Ings (the youngest of the group, at twenty-six) as a 'short and squat ruffian … of the most determined aspect'. It added that his hands were 'covered with blood' but failed to explain that it was his own blood that covered them, since a constable had beaten him up an hour earlier. 'As he stood at the bar, manacled to one of his wretched confederates, his small fiery eyes glared round upon the spectators with an expression truly horrible'. In that situation whose eyes wouldn't? When the prison chaplain David Ruell interviewed Ings in prison, he found him 'a most desperate & turbulent character & a political enthusiast of the first order'.[9] Harrison was described after his transportation to New South Wales as 'a gaunt muscular man, upwards of six feet in height, with large black eyes starting from his head, and thick jet-black hair hanging in profusion over a pale and rather forbidding visage … the very impersonation of a conspirator, fit to have been enrolled under Catiline'. This judgement was undermined by the fact that he was 'of feeble intellect'.[10]

People saw in these men what they needed to see. For a more credible reality we should return to Abraham Wivell's etchings (Figs 13.1–13.6). He included seven of the arrested men in his gallery. Like his prints of Thistlewood discussed above, he sold each as a single-sheet etching at

13.1. Abraham Wivell, *James Ings, Butcher* (Wivell, 15 April 1820)
(© The Trustees of the British Museum)
13.2. Abraham Wivell, *James Ings and Thomas Brunt* (Kelly, 2 May 1820)
(© The Trustees of the British Museum)

13.3. Abraham Wivell, *Charles Cooper: A Seaman* (Wivell, 15 April 1820)
(© The Trustees of the British Museum)
13.4. Abraham Wivell, *John Monument: Shoe Maker* (Sherwood, Neely and Jones, 1820)
(© The Trustees of the British Museum)

13.5. Abraham Wivell, *William Davidson* (Sherwood, Neely, and Jones, 1820)
(photograph: the author)
13.6. Abraham Wivell, *Richard Tidd* (Kelly, 2 May 1820)
(© The Trustees of the British Museum)

one shilling and sixpence before having it reproduced in Wilkinson's *Authentic History*. No other criminal portraits from any pre-photographic era compare with their quality. Each does justice to its subject's humanity, and none caricatures its subject as a monster or a bumpkin.

Ings is allowed to dress stylishly and look less of a thug than reports suggested: he is shown as a trim, neat man, troubled in expression. Brunt looks mild too – rather as he was described (by Kelleher): a man of piercing and intelligent eyes, with long dark hair combed to one side. Long-faced Charles Cooper, with trimmed seaman's beard and a dashing quiff to his hair, has decided character and presence. The young shoe-maker John Monument looks as vulnerable and startled as in fact he turned out to be. Wivell gave Jamaican-born Davidson two portraits. Both show him well dressed and confirm Kelleher's description of him in *Lives of the Leaders of the Conspiracy* as 'broad-sholdered, sinewy, and athletic; large mouth, black curly hair, fierce aspect, and, upon the whole, rather well made than otherwise'. His depiction here shows braided hair across his forehead, as if to affirm his mixed-race identity. Dreadlocks were then a rare sight in London; I know no other image like it.

Wivell's wonderful portrait of the shoemaker Richard Tidd is the most moving of the set. It shows him ageing, heavy, and tired. Of all the condemned conspirators, Tidd is the one we can say least about. Inarticulate and semi-literate, he gave no account of himself when he was called on for his last words in court, but simply apologised for being 'an indifferent orator'. His first appearance in newspaper reports was as one of the committee that organised the Smithfield reform meeting of July 1819.[11] Wise after the event and using sources unknown, the early biographers wrote of a vagabond youth and thieving inclinations, and said he was involved in the Despard conspiracy of 1802–3. This may be a garbled version of the fact that in the 1802 Middlesex election he had posed falsely as a freeholder in order to vote for Burdett. Another story had him adopting sundry disguises during the war in order to join several regiments across the country, then to abscond from each one with the bounty money; and once he robbed a recruiting sergeant before escaping through a window. He would address a serjeant thus: 'Measter, oon a body be a sowjer when do em gee ame the brass?' ('Master, when one becomes a soldier when do you give him the [bounty] money?')[12] But no evidence is referenced for any of this. He was latterly described as 'a respectable, good-natured, elderly man who sometimes wore spectacles and was bald and rather stout'. Everyone thought him sober and industrious, and character witnesses endorsed that. As the conspiracy came to its head, he proved to be the most nervous of all his colleagues. In late December Brunt had reported that Tidd 'would have no more to do with it', though he stuck with it nonetheless.[13] In his lodging in Hole-in-the-Wall Passage in the week before the Cato Street assembling, 'he had been in a drunken state, and his family had been at a loss to account for the extraordinary change in his conduct. On [the critical] Wednesday night three men came to Tidd while [he was] in such a state of drunkenness as scarcely to be able to keep his legs, and forced him away, notwithstanding the earnest entreaties and remonstrance of his wife and family.'[14] Drunkenness didn't stop him putting a bullet through a sergeant's cap during the fight in the stable.

The smartish clothes which the men wore for their portraits were intended to signal their craft status and distinction from the common labourer. They might have been borrowed or shared since they concealed the real conditions of their lives. Their work clothing was different, though it too would have signalled craft standing. The day before the arrests an informant noticed a group of 'remarkable good looking men' in Lincoln's Inn Fields discussing foreign affairs and saying they were damned 'if they will have soldiers fight for Spain or against the liberties of this country', and expressing delight at the duc de Berrie's assassination in France. They were 'well dressed for tradesmen some had aprons roled round their loines which I took for respectable tinmen or shoemakers, I having the same dress, I joined in amongst them to hear their conversation'.[15]

They lived in poverty, however. Bow Street officers referred to each of Tidd's, Adams's, and Davidson's lodgings as 'hovels', and Edwards referred to Davidson's as a 'hut'; and when constables searched Davidson's after the arrests they met a man distraining the family's few possessions in lieu of rent.[16] Henry Hunt found the lodging in which Preston lived with his daughters 'miserable' and Preston's daughters 'dirtily dressed, miserable and poor'. Watson's daughter died young, and after his wife left him he had to share a bed with his son. Few men in these conditions could afford the accoutrements of revolution. When Brunt told Monument to buy a five-shilling pistol to bring to the stable, Monument replied that he 'was too poor to do anything of the kind'.[17] In the stable Tidd wore a pistol belt improvised from leather off-cuts 'such as they use for ladies' shoes'; Bradburn's belt was made of string. James Gilchrist, we've seen, was starving. Adams was in Whitecross Street debtors' prison for a small debt of £1 3s 8d, and after the trials he was sent there again.[18]

Thanks to his advantages Thistlewood seems to have been healthy, except for the mental states reported in 1818. He was advertised as having 'the appearance of a military man' and good teeth. Teeth were a reliable indication of condition. Even in high society, natural teeth could be blackened, broken, or absent, which is why you don't see them in the portraits of the time. Watson's twenty-year-old son had a very wide mouth that showed 'very black teeth' when he laughed: the pain would have been chronic. He also had smallpox scars on his face, a hairy mole near his left eye, and an eyelid that drooped, and his clothing was 'shabby genteel'.[19] At one point he was said to have been treated for insanity.

A very high proportion of the radicals mentioned in this book, together with their wives and children, shared the common afflictions of the poor – not to mention the horrors they or their husbands endured in courts, in prison cells, and afterwards. Brunt's face was marked by smallpox and an oddly twisted chin. John Palin was 'of meagre aspect, shabbily dressed', while Monument was so diminutive in size that he looked 'ludicrous' by the side of Adams the soldier-shoemaker. Adams was over six feet tall and 'athletic', but his left eye squinted badly. Preston was lame in one leg and walked with a stick because a nurse had dropped him when his mother farmed him out as a child. The schoolmaster William Hazard was also lame. In Australia, Harrison was thought to be of 'limited intellect'. The shoemaker John Hooper, obscure in everything other than his treason arraignment with Thistlewood, Watson, and Preston after the Spa Fields riots, was too lame to ride a horse (the court heard in 1817), though he 'could walk fast enough' to keep up with the rioters. He died of 'exhaustion' shortly after the trial. The dwarfish Spencean Samuel Waddington was only four feet two inches high, though that didn't stop him having eight children. The shoemaker Allen Davenport was 'thin, pale and poor', and cursed by ill health and poor eyesight.

The veteran radicals of the 1790s had afflictions of the same sort too. Thomas Spence, born into deep poverty in Newcastle as one of nineteen children, was barely five feet tall; a stroke or attack of palsy left him with a limp and a speech impediment. John Gale Jones was 'afflicted with a paralytic affliction, which causes ... an almost constant convulsive twitching of his head, shoulders, & arms'; John Thelwall was 'a very mean looking man, of a sickly sallow complexion'; and Joseph Gerrald was 'of a slender make and puny constitution'. Every one of Thomas Hardy's six children died in infancy; his wife died in childbirth after their house was attacked by a church and king mob, and the child was stillborn. Thomas Evans, in gaol without trial for nearly three years in 1798–1801 and again in 1817, suffered from 'prison dropsy' (malnutritional oedema) for the rest of his life.[20] Afflictions of these kinds would have darkened their views of the world.

SHOEMAKERS AND LITERACY

The number of shoemakers in Thistlewood's circle was remarkable. In addition to a dozen or more shadowy figures recruited from shoemaker's societies throughout London, the chief of them were Adams, Brunt, Cook, Cooper, Davenport, Gilchrist, Monument, Preston, Strange, Tidd, Waddington, Wilson (and Hooper in 1816–17). Only one tailor, Wilson, was directly involved in the conspiracy, but he had been a shoemaker before becoming a tailor and then a milkman.

All were down on their uppers, to use the shoemakers' idiom. Nearly all were immigrants into London, though it would be pushing it to call them 'rootless' since trade taverns and clubs, subcontracting networks, and burial and benefit clubs quickly knitted skilled newcomers into wider communities. When young John Brown (uninvolved in our story) looked for work in London, he was introduced to a 'countryman' of his – i.e. both came from Cambridge – who advised him to put himself under a first-rate workman for instruction. His patron took him to a house in Green Arbour Court which was occupied by eight or nine lodging shoemakers; he reserved a stool next to the most skilled of these by paying five pounds. When Brown gave evidence against policemen who had brought false charges of assault against two Irishmen, the Irish rewarded him by appointing him cobbler to an Irish boot club. Each of its hundred members paid weekly subscriptions and drew lots to decide the order in which he would make boots for the other members, to an agreed price list. Brown enjoyed their good humour and conviviality.[21]

Shoemaker networks accounted for many of the patterns in Cato Street recruiting. Brunt was a kingpin. By January 1820 the spy reports contain more details of 'Brunt's men' than of any other conspirator's. One 'is a clicker in a boot-makers shop in Fleet Street … another of his men is … a boot maker [who] declared in the public room in the Sun in Windmill Street that nothing would do but the murdering of all the ministers just before the meeting of parliament'.[22] John Shaw Strange entered the plot because he knew Brunt, and in Fox Court Brunt lived a minute's walk away from Tidd and Adams, who in turn lived next door to each other in Hole-in-the-Wall Passage, while Monument and Cooper lived a couple of blocks away in Garden Court. Thomas Chambers, a shoemaker who had kept his distance from the conspiracy and who gave evidence for the prosecution, had known Davidson since the time of 'Mr Hunt's procession, when he had himself carried a banner inscribed Manchester Massacre'; and Tidd he had known since the meetings in Smithfield (where he had carried banners too) because Tidd was 'in the trade, we are brother shoemakers'.[23]

Literacy and book knowledge were common among shoemakers. Just as Thomas Preston published the beginning of a memoir before life's excitements overtook him, so Brunt knocked out satirical doggerel in the Tower:

> The home Department's Secretaire,
> His orders they would make you stare;
> An hour a day allowed to walk,
> But mind you neither wink nor talk!
> For these are gifts of human reason,
> And you are adepts in high treason:
> No bigger rogues on earth there be on,
> For so says Edwards the espione!

Rough stuff, it seems, until at the bottom you find him adding a couplet from Pope's *Essay on Man*: 'In modes of faith let graceless zealots fight, / He can't be wrong whose life is in the right' – and another from John Gay's *My Own Epitaph*: 'Life's but a jest, and all things show it, / I thought so once, but now I know it!'[24]

Literacy at these levels is to be expected of radical craftsmen. One reason Spence had written in favour of the phonetic alphabet was to improve speech and spelling in order to remove 'one of the worst curses of poverty'. His first book on the subject was published as early as 1775; he continued to propagate his phonetic alphabet for the rest of his life. The LCS veteran John Thelwall taught elocution in the last three decades of his life for the same reason, while Cobbett compiled his *Grammar of the English Language* (1818) for 'soldiers, sailors, apprentices, and plough-boys', drawing his examples of faulty grammar from Castlereagh, Wellington, and George III. Autodidactic effort and dame and charity schools completed the process.

Literacy was particularly to be expected of shoemakers. Nearly fifty shoemaker-poets were published in print in Britain between the late seventeenth and the late nineteenth centuries. No other craft matched that record; nor could any other match shoemakers' reputation for political independence and acuity.[25] Tailors had similar reasons to resent the plight of their craft, and they were not without their radicals. But poets they never produced.

A Victorian account of the *Lives of Illustrious Shoemakers* explained their peculiar talent by noting that the shoemaker 'as a rule, sits alone; that his occupation stimulates his mind without wholly occupying and absorbing its powers; it leaves him free to break off, if he will, at intervals, and glance at the book or make notes on the paper which lies beside him'. And because the craft was not strenuous, parents tended to apprentice small, weak, or lame boys to it – it helping that the cost of apprenticing a boy to a shoemaker was lower than it was to many other trades. Physical disability doubtless fed a need to affirm oneself through learning and independent views. The 'radical shoemaker' became an archetype in this era. In the south and east of England in 1830 the rural labourers' riots against the introduction of threshing machines were at their fiercest around towns with many shoemakers.

Countless shoemakers in eighteenth-century towns if not villages were either workshop masters or men working alongside fellow apprentices and journeymen. This could be an educative experience. In his master's shop in London, the young shoemaker-poet Robert Bloomfield read newspapers aloud to the others at work, and claimed that nine-tenths of his *Farmer's Boy* (1798) 'was put together as I sat at work; no one in the house has any knowledge of what I have employed my thoughts about when I did not talk'. John Brown, fresh in London in 1811 or so, shared a room off Grub Street with a shoemaker who possessed a tattered library of Milton, Shakespeare, Goldsmith, Cowper, Gay, Gray, Bloomfield, etc., and translations of Homer, Virgil, and Ovid. 'Of all these works I had heard more or less,' Brown wrote; 'for to me reading was the greatest luxury of which I had any conception.' On their first evening together he and his new companion started reading Shakespeare together.[26] The Gloucestershire-born shoemaker-poet Allen Davenport learned shoemaking in the army. With no schooling whatsoever, he taught himself to read and write by learning songs and matching their words to their printed texts, and eventually began to write poems of his own. He moved to London in 1805 and became a Spencean active in Wedderburn's 'chapel', wrote for Carlile's *Republican,* and wrote among other pieces a poetic drama, *Kings, or, Legitimacy Unmasked* (1819), as well as a biography of Spence and a substantial autobiography. The Chartist shoemaker Thomas Cooper learned his trade in a garret where 'the conversation ran on the poetry of Shakespeare and Byron': he produced his first poem when he was fifteen.

SHOEMAKER RADICALISM

Shoemakers' careers don't promise the most exciting reading, but one effect of their condition was that their experiences were as intense, mobile, and varied as their politics were dissident. Most, including our men, had at one or another point in their lives been 'on the tramp', walking vast distances in search of employment until trade recovered at home or disputes were resolved. Moreover, as their clubs debated wages and craft controls, or donated 'tramping money' to help unattached men, they turned easily to politics. In 1792 nine craftsmen gathered in the Bell tavern in Exeter Street to hear the views of the Scottish shoemaker Thomas Hardy and to establish the London Corresponding Society – 'corresponding' with the French radicals, that is:

> After having had their bread and cheese and porter for supper, as usual, and their pipes afterwards, with some conversation on the hardness of the times and the dearness of all the necessaries of life, which they, in common with their fellow citizens, felt to their sorrow, the business for which they met was brought forward – *Parliamentary Reform.*[27]

A spy reported in 1792 'that all the divisions [of the LCS] I have seen are attended by the very lowest tradesmen, and the most of them seem Scotch shoemakers'. The Crooked Billet in Little Shire Lane near Temple Bar was the LCS's chief venue in 1798, its last year.[28] The Crooked Billet was also where a major shoemakers' strike for higher wages was organised in 1808. Strikers were allowed seven shillings provided they left London to tramp 'into the country'; allowances were given to wives and children. Seventeen of the leaders were convicted of unlawful conspiracy.[29]

The continuity in these venues was remarkable. In 1792 the Scotch Arms was listed as one of twenty-nine taverns in which clubs met to disseminate seditious principles; a hundred LCS members had just met there.[30] A quarter-century later the same pub was the centre of London's shoemaking unionism. In 1820 Ings, William Davidson, and Hiden attended shoemakers' meetings there, and Davidson, though no shoemaker, chaired one or more of their meetings. There too George Edwards tried to persuade an innocent man to take home a grenade and a pike, comparing the government to 'bloody vermin'.[31] Well might the conspirators' defence counsel refer axiomatically to a 'member of a shoemakers' club, that is, in plain language, of a seditious club'.[32]

The trade hierarchy of eighteenth-century shoemaking extended from the humble *cobbler* who mended old shoes on his own account, often from a pavement shed; up to the *clicker* who, usually on the master's premises, cut the leather for putting out; up again to the shoe- or boot-*closer* (of men's shoes) or -*binder* (of women's shoes), who 'closed' the uppers; then to the *shoemaker* who joined the uppers to the sole; and finally to the *cordwainer* who made new shoes from new leather. The apprenticeship system secured the hierarchy. After apprenticeship the journeyman worked for a master, hoping to become a master himself. The system was fast weakening by our period, but every shoemaker knew his and others' places in it:

> *What is Hooper?* – a shoemaker.
> *Is he not a cobler?* – I don't know what he is.
> *Is Preston a cobler?* – He is a shoemaker.[33]

Urban masters employed their men in workshops, but shoemaking was also a domestic process, and in some places had been a prosperous one. In eighteenth-century satirical prints humble cobblers were typecast as fat and contented as they worked in spacious lodgings with pleasantly domesticated wives, the common joke being that they were easily cuckolded. But in the new century jokes about shoemakers' prosperity lost credibility. John Brown knew why:

> The long war in which the country had been engaged had raised all articles
> of consumption up to famine price, so that men having large families
> could not earn sufficient to buy them food. Hence a feeling of

discontent arose in most trades, and a general 'strike' was the result in our own. I attended meetings at the different public-houses where they were held, and heard the great orators of the craft, men in ragged habiliments and of squalid looks, pour forth in touching and eloquent language their appeals to the unmarried men, to support them in the death struggle.

The major strike of 1812 collapsed when wholesalers retaliated by sending uppers to be stitched in Northampton where labour costs were lower, which marked a decisive shift in the production process. A further strike united the masters, from which 'fatal strike', Allen Davenport wrote, 'I date the downfall of the power of the men, and the commencement of despotism amongst the master shoe-makers'. Since club funds were exhausted, some hundreds of pounds were borrowed from the farriers, carpenters, and other trades to support the strike. Brown described the outcome: 'Nearly all the single men packed up their kits and went on tramp as they were not allowed any relief':

> Thus week after week passed on: the pawnbroker's store-rooms were crowded; families were reduced to the greatest misery, having parted with their beds, furniture, clothes, in fact anything and everything that would fetch money; the men were reduced to mere shadows ... and mothers were crying over their starving children ... Such scenes of indescribable misery I hope never to witness again!

After ten weeks Brown gave up. He packed his tools and two shirts, and with tenpence-halfpenny in his pocket walked along Oxford Street to the country, gazing moodily at the shops and carriages and well-dressed people as they passed by. Near starvation, he saved himself at last by accepting the king's shilling, though he was so ashamed of becoming a soldier that he told none of his friends. Within a few weeks he had deserted, and for a time survived as a travelling player.[34]

With the high price of bread in the 1810s already eroding real wage income, shoemakers were wounded further when in 1814 parliament repealed the Elizabethan statute that required skilled men to train through a seven-year apprenticeship. And with the Peace of 1815, the collapse of the army and navy's demand for footwear made things worse. The trade recovered a little by 1820, but the growth of subcontracting and the incursions of cheap unapprenticed workers, especially of women and children, meant that over the first half of the nineteenth century shoemaking wages fell steadily; in the 1820s fewer than one in twenty shoemakers belonged to their trade society.

Every one of our Cato Street shoemakers was affected by the crisis, for it was this experience that underpinned shoemaker radicalism in our period. Like Brown, some simply gave up. '*What are you?* – I was brought up a shoe maker, but I am articled to a cow-doctor,' one testified.[35] Just as Wilson became a tailor and then a milkman, so Strange became a boot-maker's shopman and then a tinker. Others went on the tramp. Thomas Preston made it to Ireland before returning to London in 1794, while Tidd served his apprenticeship to a shoemaker in Grantham before travelling around England, Ireland, and Scotland, finding such work as he could. If Kelleher's *Lives* is to be believed, he worked five years in Scotland 1803–8, then nine years in Rochester before returning to London in early 1818.[36]

Brunt's was the most extraordinary story. His father was a tailor who had apprenticed him at the age of fourteen to a lady's shoemaker off Oxford Street, but his father died four years later and his mother had to buy him out of his time so that he could support her. He managed to article himself to a boot-closer, and a couple of years later married a young woman who gave birth to their son in 1806.[37] For a time things went well enough, but with the war's end his income fell, so he took his son with him to look for work in Paris, walking most of the way. There he assumed the name 'Thomas Morton', possibly for criminal reasons, since he seems as yet not to have been politically opinionated.[38] In 1816 he found work in the Coldstream Guards barracks at Wellington's head-quarters in Cambrai, and there met Adams, a discharged soldier and would-be shoemaker who was as yet without 'judgement in the trade'. Brunt cut out boots for the officers and taught Adams how to close them. When Adams caught Brunt flirting with his wife, 'the man became jealous of me', Brunt told the court, 'and threatened to take my life: and declared to his wife, if she did not make an open declaration to me, that if ever she spoke to me her life was not safe, he would be the death of her; accordingly, I was obliged to leave the house'. He went to Lille for eighteen months to work for an English master before returning to London.[39]

In London Brunt found 'trade was very bad, extremely bad indeed'. He lodged with his wife and son in Shoe Lane and was given work by a Mr Hale whose shop was in Castle Street between Fetter and Chancery Lanes. Hale supplied families in the West Indies. When Hale asked Brunt to take on a relative as his apprentice, Brunt couldn't refuse 'without losing my bread'. Hale cut his wages nonetheless: 'I put up with it once; he wished to curtail me again, which I could not put up with any longer. I was obliged, my lord, to leave my work.' So he, his wife, his son, and Joseph Hale the apprentice moved to a cheaper two-room lodging in Fox Court, a few minutes' walk away on the northern side of Holborn. They worked in one room and slept in the other. Relations were difficult. His wife had been in the asylum not long before, and young Hale had a taste for thieving. Two years into his apprenticeship, the youth gave evidence against Brunt by reporting every detail of the conspirators' meetings in Fox Court.

Meanwhile Adams turned up like a ghost from the past. He was in a bad way, and close to begging. In September 1819, carrying pieces of leather to identify himself as a shoemaker, he accosted Richard Carlile near the Islington skin market off Northampton Square to ask him if he might share a drink. With no idea who Adams was (though he was himself known after Peterloo), Carlile replied that he didn't drink, but politely listened to Adams's explanation that he had 'lately' left the Horse Guards (in fact he had been discharged in 1802), and that friends at home 'in Yorkshire' had told him about the distress of the country and the disposition of the people. Now, therefore, he 'wished to find out a society of good fellows'. Carlile took his leave after a few minutes and never saw him again, so the point of the encounter rather mystified him.[40] In truth Adams was at his wits' end. Eventually he came to Brunt 'in the greatest distress, and begged a shilling of me, as I was a little better off than himself, though not much, to get his family a supper'. So he joined Thistlewood's group. 'Now,' Brunt added sourly, 'he comes forward to this bar [as king's evidence] and swears my life away.'

Brunt's last statement left no doubt that his enthusiasm for the assassinations of the men who governed him was forged in hardship:

I have been in the habit of earning three or four pounds a-week, and then I never troubled myself about government; but when I came to earn, perhaps, not ten shillings, I began to inquire why I had a right to be starved; the Creator of the world, who made the world, gave every man a right to live in it; and why it was taken from the people, and I and thousands more should be starved, why men who toiled should not enjoy a little, and why millions should toil and some few should dissipate it; and this brought me to the conclusion of being an enemy to those men [the ministers]. After the massacre of Manchester, but not before, when I considered there was not sufficient, with heaping up all the treasure in the country, to relieve the country, but that these men were starving them to death, literally starving them to death, and that yet they were not satisfied, but they must call in ruffians, not men, to murder them, for I am a descendant of the ancient Britons, I thought nothing could be too bad for those men, and there would be men in the country who would come forward and join me.[41]

'With pleasure would he die as a martyr in liberty's cause,' he added. As two days later he did.

CHAPTER 14

Wives, Marriages, Children

MARRIAGES

In November 1819 the wife of a journeyman tailor named Hill complained that after her husband became a radical he became 'very cruel to her'. His latest offence was to introduce to a meeting in the White Lion a female reformer from Manchester who had 'come up to Town for instructions'. After the meeting

> he ordered his wife to dress a good dinner for her which was done and in
> the evening the husband and the female reformer walked out together –
> and Mrs Hill not being very well pleased left the house also; but, returning
> at night, she found her husband and the radical female in bed together,
> which caused a violent dissension – and the consequence was the poor wife
> got a violent beating and exposed her husband and his reforming pursuits
> [to the magistrate] which were such as to render him liable to prosecution
> and he had fled to Manchester.[1]

Among radicals, the stresses of living a semi-clandestine (or an imprisoned) life doubtless often caused marital difficulties. But not invariably. It had been before the men were politicised that Preston's and Watson's wives deserted their husbands, that Brunt flirted with Adams's wife, and that William Davidson was serially unfaithful. Nor was disaster the norm. Couples like the Thistlewoods, Evanses, and Carliles lived as harmoniously as their vulnerability permitted, the women's support indispensable to the men. And family support mattered deeply to radicals' survival. After the arrests, the Cato Street wives met together in Preston's lodgings on 8 March to concert a defence committee.[2] And after the executions they petitioned the home office for the return of their husbands' bodies and heads for decent burial. The signatures of Sarah Davidson, Celia Ings, and Mary Brunt were cramped and awkward but showed literacy. An unknown Ann Dolland signed on behalf of Susan 'Thiselwood', and Mary Brunt signed for Mary Tidd, perhaps because Mrs Thistlewood and Mrs Tidd were absent or ill, or in Mrs Tidd's case unable to cope with the frightful business. She was the only wife who seems not to have visited her husband in prison. The wives also talked of exhibiting the bodies to raise funds 'for the benefit of the poor families, which are literally starving'. They knew that the body of the wrongly hanged servant-girl Eliza Fenning had been exhibited for three days in a picture cleaner's house off Red Lion Square. People had queued to see her as she lay in her coffin 'seemingly as in a sweet sleep, with a smile on her countenance', presumably paying to do so.[3]

On the last matter the wives hadn't a chance. A sweet smile on the face of a wronged girl was one thing, an inflammatory display of headless relics another. The home office wanted at all costs to avoid any celebration of the conspirators, for the aftermath of Despard's burial was well remembered. In 1803 people had applauded Despard as he spoke his last defiance on the scaffold; they hissed the executioner, doffed their hats as he hanged, and later burnt one of the witnesses in effigy. Then in numbers 'beyond belief' a crowd attended his body to the grave 'as if giving him the honours of a public funeral'.[4] On a hearse drawn by four horses and followed by mourning coaches for his friends, his coffin was borne from Horsemonger Lane gaol across Blackfriars Bridge to St Paul's churchyard, where he was buried in a grave fourteen feet deep to deter bodysnatchers. His co-conspirators' remains were followed by lines of mourners to Harper's Chapel in London Road. No surprise, then, that Sidmouth dismissed the wives' plea for the Cato Street bodies. In coffins filled with quicklime, their husbands were buried under stone slabs in the tunnel between the Newgate cells and the Sessions House. Their initials were carved into the walls to mark their locations.[5]

The wives had no choice next but to mount a public appeal for subscriptions to relieve them and their children from 'famine and despair'. 'They are at this moment actually destitute of the means of subsistence, and dying for want of food,' their circular said. The dependent children were listed. If we exclude Preston's four children, correct the figure for the Tidds' children, and add the Ings' four, we find that seven of the ten men who were hanged or transported had fathered twenty-six known children between them:[6]

> Mary Brunt, [signing] for herself and one child
> Mary Tidd, and eight children [the Tidds had one child]
> Amelia Bradburn, and eight children
> Mary Strange, and two children, another near birth
> Charlotte Preston, and three sisters
> Susan Thistlewood, one child
> Sarah Davidson, and six children
> Caroline Harrison, and three children.
> [Celia Ings, not signing here, had four children.]

The Tidds had one daughter and cared for that daughter's two 'orphans', their father or fathers having died or absconded. On the Sunday before the executions Tidd's daughter wrote humbly to Sidmouth to point out that she had been 'unkindly excluded' from visiting her father since his arrest. Tomorrow she would be 'left destitute with two orphan children and no support for them. O my lord let me again appeal to your feelings and let me and my infant children see my father before it is too late.' For once the plea was granted.[7]

Finally, on 20 May after the failure of Alderman Wood's efforts in the Commons to bring Edwards the spy to book, Susan and Julian Thistlewood, Mary Brunt, and the duplicitous Abel Hall and Robert George brought a bill of indictment for treason against Edwards, but the villain had left the country and the case collapsed.[8]

Celia Ings and her children had returned to Hampshire because they had nothing to eat in London; but she came back with an infant at her breast in early March to see her husband, and stayed for the trials and their aftermath. Her inheritance of 'a little freehold in Portsea of about £26 p.a.' helped her. The 1841 census shows her living in the village with three unmarried seamstress daughters; never remarrying herself, she died as the landlord of the same small house in 1874, aged eighty-two.[9] Other widows' burdens were insurmountable. Sarah Davidson's two children by William were aged one and three years when their father was executed; she also had four children by her previous husband. Mary

Brunt had gone 'out of her mind' in 1817 when falsely told that her husband and son had been killed in France. Her sad entry is still recorded in the Curable Patients Book of St Luke's Hospital for Lunatics: 'Mary Brunt of St Bride [parish], admitted 28 March and discharged 25 July 1817. On parish support. Reason of discharge, Cured.' According to Brunt she never recovered, and in 1818 had to be boarded 'out of town'. Perhaps so, but along with Susan Thistlewood she had courage enough to spy on Harrowby's mansion in January 1820. All the wives were helped by a support committee, and shoemaker solidarity was significant in this. When the Brunts' son was apprenticed to a boot-closer, shoemaker clubs raised the premium.[10]

Five of the Cato Street husbands had their death sentences commuted to transportation. They did well in New South Wales, after initial ill-treatment. They stayed in touch with each other, and remained unrepentant to the last. The wives had less luck. The transportation of married men usually preceded their desertion, so the women knew what to expect. Told of the verdicts, Charles Cooper's wife 'was seized with a fit of phrenzy, and lies in a dreadful state, at her lodgings, near Montague-street, Whitechapel'.[11]

Between them the transported men left wives with seventeen children to care for. Mary Strange was in late pregnancy, so she had three to look after. In 1822 her husband John Shaw Strange petitioned for her to join him, but the petition was rejected and she never saw him again. Two years later he was living with a woman in Sydney, and in 1829 he married a sixteen-year-old girl in the tiny settlement of Bathurst and fathered seven more children. In a single-handed struggle he had captured one Robert Story, the most notorious bushranger of his time, so the governor rewarded him first with a ticket of leave (a form of parole) and then a conditional pardon in 1833 and an absolute pardon in 1842. By then he had become Bathurst's chief constable – of all things, one might think, were it not that the 1828 New South Wales census shows that all eleven of Bathurst's constables were transportees; five had been transported for life, Strange included. In due course Strange headed 'a patriarchal home on the banks of the Fish River at Bathurst, surrounded by children and grandchildren, all industrious persons, in the enjoyment of a comfortable competence'.

He died in 1868. In Bathurst too, Wilson served as a constable before marrying and becoming a fashionable tailor. And, despite his ferocious appearance and allegedly challenged intellect, Harrison, 'well conducted', became Bathurst's leading baker, while Bradburn, despite a brief but spectacular escape from surveillance, was employed as chief carpenter in Port Macquerie.[12]

Then most of the women and children disappear from history. There were two exceptions: Arthur Thistlewood's wife Susan and his illegitimate son Julian.

SUSAN THISTLEWOOD AND JULIAN

Women of radical views in London were more numerous and active in this era than the record shows. This truth was obscured by the fact that Bow Street police and spies targeted the supposedly dominant males, and also by the absence in London of big set-piece confrontations like that mounted by Manchester's female reformers, dressed in white, who were conspicuous on the platform at Peterloo and suffered for it. Nor were women recorded at tavern meetings. When that Manchester female reformer arrived in London after Peterloo 'for instructions' in the White Lion, the spy noted her as exceptional.[13]

In that patriarchal world, wives, mothers, sisters, sons, and daughters usually shared, or had to share, the opinions of the male head of the family. No doubt most therefore waved loyalist flags alongside loyalist husbands and fathers, and went to church or chapel on Sundays. But among the radicalised minority their support helps explain the longevity of insurrectionary dissidence in these decades. Assemblies and riots were often neighbourhood and therefore family affairs in which women and children participated. Women attended the great assemblies at Spa Fields and Smithfield, and they helped the law's victims also. Over 20 per cent of subscribers to the Carliles' support fund in 1820 were female. Henry Hunt's triumphant progress through London after Peterloo was noted for the thousands of admiring and handkerchief-waving women along the route. And the new king's oafish treatment of Caroline in 1820–1 mobilised very large numbers of women in her support.[14]

In what appear to have been marriages of equals, Janet Evans, Jane Carlile, and Susan Thistlewood were each supportive of their husbands – and of each other. It was Susan and Janet who bonded their families in friendship over 1814–16. Janet looked after young Julian Thistlewood when Susan returned to Lincolnshire, while Susan and Janet jointly cared for sixteen-year-old Charlotte Watson while her father awaited trial in 1816.[15] It was Jane Carlile rather than Richard who refused to admit the spy Edwards into their house; and when Richard and Jane were imprisoned, it was Richard's sister Mary-Ann who kept their shop going. When Thomas Davison the printer was put in Oakham gaol for two years, his most active supporter was a female printer named Rhoda Helder, who took over his Duke Street premises. The support of the next generation was fostered by women too. Richard and Jane Carlile named their son Thomas Paine Carlile; and Janet Evans persuaded Arthur Thistlewood to take young Thomas Evans to Paris for his political education. The political unanimity of fathers and sons in the Evans and Watson families was striking. And in 1819 several father-and-son booksellers and printers were arrested together for seditious publication.

Susan Thistlewood was a fine example of this feisty female effect. Born c. 1787 and thus a dozen years younger than Arthur, she was first mentioned in the spy reports in December 1816. Castle wrote that in Southampton Buildings she helped prepare for the Spa Field meeting by making tricoloured cockades and '20 or 30 small colours' for young women to carry before the radicals' flag, and also folded newspapers advertising the meeting, which Arthur then posted to safe public houses in the manufacturing districts.[16] As we have seen, she next appears as an active go-between in the plans for the fugitive family's escape to America after Spa Fields when she touched her father for £200 travel money. Then on 3 January 1820 she was reported as one of the company that discussed which minister each most wished to kill.[17] In late January, in anticipation of an attack (aborted) on a cabinet dinner at Lord Harrowby's, she and Julian and Mrs Brunt and her son walked around Grosvenor Square to survey the house and report back on movements inside and around it.[18]

When officers duly arrived to search the Thistlewood lodgings, Susan showed none of 'that alarm which, in a female, might be considered natural'. Calm and dignified, she demanded proof of their authority.[19]

We next meet her visiting her husband in prison in 1820 and enduring body searches for weapons or letters, 'even to the removal of her stays and cap'. She bore this with dignity. Reporters referred to her as a 'very interesting woman', a 'smart, genteel little woman', and 'very elegant and accomplished'. Finally she and the other wives petitioned for their husbands' bodies and cooperated with Alderman Wood in May in the attempt to bring Edwards to justice.

During Thistlewood's trial and after his execution, Susan found asylum with William West, the radical wire worker of Wych Street. When the Manchester radical Samuel Bamford met her there he was struck by her looks if not her character. 'She was rather low in stature; with handsome regular features, of the Grecian cast; very pale, and with hair, eyes, and eyebrows as black as night. Still she was not what may be called interesting: she had a coldness of manner which was almost repulsive. She seemed as if she had no natural sensibilities, or as if affliction had benumbed them.'[20] Henry Hunt didn't like her either. He spread word that she had had an affair with West. Bamford denied this, noting that Hunt's vanity was wounded by the conspirators' fame and that he 'would have said anything of anyone, against whom he entertained a pique'.

But the informer X.Y's reference to Susan's 'giddiness' suggests something more interesting than coldness of manner. She had feeling enough, and courage. A provincial newspaper gives us an extraordinary vignette. It described her as a 'smartly dressed and jaunty little woman' when she and young Julian called on the Bow Street chief magistrate Sir Nathaniel Conant two days after the Cato Street arrests. In mockery she gave the magistrate 'a milk-maid's curtsey' and pertly asked for the return of possessions which 'your people' had taken from Stanhope Street after the arrests. She listed pamphlets, bills, receipts, newspapers, a penknife, and (sarcastically) the ropes and strings that had been tied round her husband's trunks when he was arrested at Gravesend in 1817. As a heavily pointed joke she added to her list two imagined portraits of one Richard Gathorne Butt who a year previously had sued Conant for assault and false imprisonment. When Conant refused her request, her amusement at his discomfiture made onlookers laugh. Laughing loudly as well, she left the office 'highly pleased with herself'.[21]

After Arthur's conviction the *Times* reported that Susan's levity 'seemed to have deserted her, and she gave way to the full tide of her feelings'. Her plea to the new king for Thistlewood's body on the day after execution referred to 'her late beloved, faithful and affectionate husband'. She asked for a lock of his hair so that she might 'perform the last mournful duties', but of course didn't get it.[22] Her young stepson Julian was also 'in an agony of grief'.

Three months after Arthur's execution, life in London had become grim enough for her to return to her birthplace in Horncastle, taking Julian with her.[23] There she retained credit and presumably money enough in 1824 to marry Henry Turner, a corn and coal merchant who was the land agent of a Sir Henry Dymoke of Scrivelsby Court. After her earlier experiences such a marriage must have been dull, though not the worse for that. The censuses show that the couple employed two female servants and a groom and had a daughter together in 1836. By the time of her death in April 1856 she was 'generally respected in the respectable sphere in which she moved' – which speaks unexpectedly for that sphere's tolerance and forgiveness of a traitor's widow.[24]

Thistlewood's illegitimate son Julian's progress was even more remarkable. He was 'a genteel ingenious youth', despite a childhood and youth of fearsome difficulty. When his father gambled away the family money, Julian much later told his daughter that he remembered Susan 'crying when books and furniture were sold' to recoup it. In early 1817 his father, Susan, and he were in hiding after Spa Fields. Then Arthur corralled the family to flee to America, only to be arrested as they embarked on their ship at Gravesend. The boy had to cope next with his father's imprisonment as he awaited the trial for treason, and yet again with his imprisonment in Horsham after challenging Sidmouth to a duel. In his fourteenth year, father and son had to say goodbye in the Newgate condemned cell on the day before Arthur's execution.

This memory haunted Julian ever after. 'His heart was half broken by the remembrance,' his daughter Sophie recalled: 'He wrote it down for me, but through his whole life he would hardly speak of it. On [each] 1st May we children stayed quiet, looking tenderly on our dear father's face, so sad and severe. No noise was made; no play. We felt for him. He must have inherited his mother's character, so gentle was he.'[25]

Wrenched finally by his mother from his London haunts and taken to Horncastle, Julian had to suffer her marriage to a provincial coal merchant. No surprise that he found peace at last by leaving England and going to Paris.

Some familial metamorphoses invite a cheer for human resilience, and this is one of them. Funded by his uncle John (Arthur's well-heeled Lincolnshire brother) and armed with letters of recommendation, the seventeen-year-old went to left-bank Paris to study medicine and take his degrees while teaching drawing and English. Calling himself Julian Thornley-Thistlewood, he became a French citizen and in 1841 married 'for love' one Adèle Victoire Petit. (The couple already had illegitimate children.) He gave up medicine, his daughter wrote, worked hard all his life, and became a practised artist. He earned 'much money' before dying in his eighty-sixth year.

Not the least sign of the family's recovery was the success of one of Julian's sons. Born in 1857 as George William Thornley-Thistlewood, he later dropped the name Thistlewood, was taught by Puvis de Chavannes and Eugène Cicéri of the Barbizon school among others, and turned himself into a skilled lithographer. In the 1880s and '90s he produced a series of now valuable lithographs of paintings by Boucher, Puvis, Corot, Degas, Pissarro, and Monet, and then embarked on his second career as an over-prolific landscape and seascape painter in oils. He exhibited at the Salon and at the Galerie Georges Petit, the home of impressionism. He died in 1935, and today has a museum to himself in the Château de Grouchy in Osny – at 14 rue William Thornley, no less.[26]

George William discarded the Thistlewood surname less in shame than because *th* is difficult for French people. It hints at his loyalty to Arthur's memory that he produced very few lithographs of long-dead artists, but did, oddly, produce a lithograph of Géricault's *1821 Derby at Epsom*. Géricault had painted the famous original for his friend the horse-dealer Adam Elmore, with whom he lodged on his second visit to London in 1821. Elmore's house and stables were in John Street directly opposite the entrance to Cato Street, so Géricault knew all about the drama, as we'll see in our last chapter. Was it familial piety that explains Thornley's choice of the Epsom painting as subject? It would seem a distinctly off-beam choice if not.

George's sister Sophie certainly expressed a surprising affection for their grandfather. He was 'the hero of my life', she wrote in her 1907 reminiscence. She treasured his prayer book (!?), along with the *Observer*'s report of his trial and execution, and a 'beautiful oil painting' of Arthur which Julian had painted from Wivell's lithograph. She was also delighted to learn that her correspondent's husband, George Thistlewood, had been 'proud of his historical connection'. Either the family saw straight through the cynical political expediency of Arthur's execution, or else the truculent man simply left fonder memories than outsiders could have expected.

LOVE, FAMILY, AND JAMES INGS THE BUTCHER

Some of the Cato Street marriages were close and affectionate, and of them all we have the fullest sense of James Ings's. 'I married a girl that I loved,' the butcher declared in his mercy petition to the king. His last letters to her and his children confirm it. Indeed, nothing in Ings's letters – or in his portrait by Wivell – prepares one for repeated reports of his readiness to hack off Castlereagh's and Sidmouth's heads with his butcher's knife and to parade them on pikes through London. He announced this intention noisily at every meeting he attended and behaved so noisily on the scaffold that Thistlewood had to calm him. In today's terms he was another who might be suspected of a bipolar disorder. Although he seems to have been physically fit, 'poor Ings' was 'ill', it was stated after his death.

The Peace had ruined the butcher's trade in the Portsmouth ship-yards, but Ings found butchering no easier when he brought the family to London. The butcher's stall he opened there failed as well, and he had to send his wife and children back to Hampshire, where the family retained a small freehold. He lodged in 20 Primrose Street, off Bishopsgate. Several blocks to the east of that, at 9 Old Montague Street in Whitechapel, he opened in September 1819 what he called 'the Republican coffee-house'. A photograph taken just before the street's demolition in 1961 gives an idea of the territory; the houses dated from

14.1. *Old Montague Street, Whitechapel* (1961, before demolition)
(© London Metropolitan Archives)

Ings's time (Fig. 14.1). From the coffee house he tried to sell deistical and Spencean pamphlets which he had acquired from Carlile's bookshop at 55 Fleet Street. He read these so avidly that 'from being a churchman, [he] became a confirmed deist'.[27] But his own enterprise failed since the neighbourhood was too poor to buy pamphlets. The coffee house's main effect was to expose Ings to Edwards's blandishments. Edwards allegedly met him in Carlile's shop, recognised his vulnerability, and wooed him by buying him food and drink.

In his younger years Carlile had experienced the same setbacks as Ings, and had also married his wife Jane in Gosport, across Portsmouth harbour from Ings's home in Portsea. So his account of Ings was sympathetic:

> Although [Ings] has been described in the papers as the most ferocious [conspirator] in conduct and appearance, yet I have not a doubt, but that on his trial he will be found to have been lately entrapped into this gang, and to have been quite a misled man, and ignorant of the men he was acting with; that he has not been connected with or known to them many weeks. .... He called on me in the Bench [King's Bench prison], quite in despair as to his own prospects, and melancholy to reflect that his wife found it necessary to return to Portsmouth, where it was impossible that he could do anything for himself and his family. I have

every reason to believe that up to this moment, the middle of November, Ings had no knowledge of, or connection with Thistlewood. ... His whole demeanour to me was that of a strictly sober and moral man, lost in despair, because he could not support his wife and family as he could wish.[28]

Ings's petition for mercy after his death sentence announced that he had arrived in London in May 1819 and that he 'never was at a political meeting in my life not before this time'. In court he declared that he had first met Thistlewood in late January 1820 when Edwards introduced them.[29] Actually spy reports showed that he had attended a Thistlewood meeting at the White Lion just before the Smithfield meeting in July 1819, and that his first full meeting with Thistlewood was on 22 December, when Thistlewood was chairing a closed meeting at the Scotch Arms in Round Court. According to Edwards, Ings there stood up in the audience and dramatised his outrage:

> He said much about not being able to keep his family and that he was willing to go to any length he would go to the house of Commons and destroy any of them he then drew a loaded pistol from his pocket and said he would shoot Lord Sidmouth and concluded with oaths etc. declaring he had made up his mind to destroy some of the ministers.

The crown witness Adams testified that 'when anything occurred, [Ings's] whole blood and soul boiled for murder'.[30]

When Ings spoke in his own defence in court, the first question he asked was why Edwards wasn't in court also.

> Early in January, I met [Edwards] in Smithfield, and he went and gave me victuals and drink; ... and in my anxiety of mind, for I could not keep my family, it was, that I was induced for the sake of these things, to keep company with him, and it is through him I shall lose my life; I do not mind dying, if you will let that man come forward, and die with me; he was the instigator and author of all the atrocity I was going to commit. The murdering his majesty's ministers, I admit, was a disgrace to human nature; but those ministers meet and conspire together, and pass laws to starve me and my family and my fellow-countrymen; if I was going to assassinate those ministers, it is [would not be] so bad as starvation, in my opinion, my lord.

The people at Peterloo, he continued, had been 'under the protection of the great charter of England, which our forefathers bled and fought for'. Despite this, the Manchester yeomanry had had their swords ground in readiness before the meeting; then they 'cut down unarmed men, women, and children; that was a disgrace to the name and character of Englishmen'. 'I hope my children will live to see the day that there will be justice administered in the country; that they all will be freemen, and live like men: I had rather die like a man, than live like a slave. I am sorry I have not got abilities to address you, but I have not, and therefore I must withdraw.'[31] As he mentioned his family's distress he burst into tears. At one point he complained about Edwards's entrapment in a phrase natural to his calling: 'I am sold as a bullock that is driven into Smithfield-market, depend upon it, gentlemen, I am sold like a bullock driven to Smithfield-market'. This image is hard to beat, as epitaphs go.[32]

We are at the mercy of unreliable reporting so far as Ings is concerned. While his enemies might have lied about him, Ings might have lied about them, and especially about Edwards. Edwards certainly affirmed this. On 11 March Edwards had to swear a statement of some 24,000 words before the Bow Street magistrate Baker, and in it he denied great swathes of Ings's statement. Edwards added that Thistlewood told his men 'to lay their misconduct on me to remove from himself the just odium he so justly deserves'. It's impossible now to unravel the truth of the matter. None of Edwards's reports showed that he and Ings had private meetings. On the other hand, Carlile confirmed their relationship, and Edwards might have been concealing one of his own secret forays into extortion. Nearly all the evidence about Ings's bloodthirstiness depends on Edwards's and Adams's say-so.

In Ings's last letters to Celia we meet a gentler man than the wild firebrand described by his enemies. The letters were written on the Sunday afternoon of 30 April after Celia had said goodbye to him before the next morning's execution. Published in the newspapers a day or two later, their punctuation, spelling, and grammar were obviously corrected; probably some phrasings were suggested to him too. Yet their racing prose confirms their authenticity.[33] Uppermost in his message to Celia was his insistence that she should remarry for the sake of the children:

> My dear Celia, – I hardly know how to begin, or what to say, for the laws of tyrants have parted us for ever. My dear, this is the last time you will ever hear from me. I hope you will perform your duty [to remarry] without delay, which is for the benefit of yourself and children, which I have explained to you before. My dear, [out] of the anxiety and regard I have for you and the children, I know not how to explain myself; but I must die according to law, and leave you in a land full of corruption, where justice and liberty has taken their flight from, to other distant shores. . . . I thought I should have rendered my starving fellow-men, women, and children a service. . . . My dear, it is of no use for me to make remarks respecting my children. I am convinced you will do your duty as far as lies in your power. My dear, your leaving me but a few hours before I wrote these few lines, I have nothing more to say. Farewell! farewell, my dear wife and children, for ever! Give my love to your mother and Elizabeth. I conclude a constant lover to you and your children, and all friends. I die the same, but an enemy to all tyrants. James Ings

To this he added a postscript to his wider family to beg them 'to think nothing of my unfortunate fate; for I am gone out of a very troublesome world, and I hope you will let it pass like a summer cloud over the earth'. Then he wrote to his daughters:

> My dear little girls, receive my kind love and affection, once more, for ever; and adhere to these my sincere wishes, and recollect, though in a short time you will hear nothing more of your father. Let me entreat you to be loving, kind, and obedient to your poor mother, and strive all in your powers to comfort her, and assist her whilst you exist in this transitory world; and let your conduct throughout life be that of virtue, honesty, and industry; and endeavour to avoid all temptation, and at the same time put your trust in God. I hope unity, peace, and concord, will remain amongst you all. Farewell, farewell, my dear children. Your unfortunate father, James Ings.

And at eight o'clock on that last night he sent this bleak, blunt advice to his son:

My little dear boy, Wm. Stone Ings, I hope you will live to read these few lines when the remains of yr. poor father is mouldered to dust. My dr. boy, I hope you will bear in mind the unforte. [*sic*] end of your father, and not place any confidence in any person or persons whatever; for the deception, the corruption, and the ingenuity in man I am at a loss to comprehend – it is beyond all calculation. My dear boy, I hope you will make a bright man in society; and, it appears to me, the road you ought to pursue is, to be honest, sober, industrious, and upright in all your dealings; and to do unto all men as you would they should do unto you. My dear boy, put your trust in one God; and be cautious of every shrewd, designing, flattering tongue. My dear boy, be a good, kind, and obedient child to your poor mother, and comfort her, and be a loving brother to your sisters. My dear boy, I sincerely hope and trust you will regard these, my last instructions. Yr. loving and unforte. father,

William Stone Ings returned with his mother to Portsea, became a butcher like his father and then a ginger-beer maker, married, had a son and two daughters, and died locally in 1896 in his eighty-sixth year.

In Ings's petition to the king for mercy he abbreviated the account of himself that he gave in his final speech in court. Written on the day before his execution, he described the common experience of hardship in those years, and spoke with a simple directness about a poor man's life that needs no commentary. It is one of this story's most poignant documents.[34]

... I married a girl that I loved, and she had a little property, and I continued working till I could get nothing to do, and I went into business, and it turned out very unfortunately, and I lost a great deal of money, not through drinking and gambling, for I never went to a public-house in my life but to smoke my pipe, or for the sake of company. I can assure your most gracious Majesty, that I never was tipsey but three times in my life, and that was not through the love of liquor.

... I can assure your most high and mighty and gracious Sovereign, that I have been a true and faithful subject till now, but being in distress, and hearing the language I did, when irritated, took advantage of my distressed situation.

I know not what to say or how to address a King, but I hope your most gracious Majesty will spare my life – for sake of family – for I was not the inventor of this plot. I shall in future, if your most gracious Majesty spare my life, be a true and faithful subject.

James Ings.

CHAPTER 15

Men of Colour: Wedderburn and Davidson

RACIAL PREJUDICE

One sometimes meets the argument that since poor black and poor white people were equally oppressed in eighteenth- and early nineteenth-centuries Britain, black peoples' situation was softened by the fact that class solidarity in plebeian communities outgunned colour prejudice. Recent efforts to knit the history of slavery into a history of a multi-ethnic and exploited 'Atlantic working class' has deepened this emphasis. But all this badly underplays the power of the long eighteenth century's everyday racism. Being black, and a black radical in particular, indicated otherness, and both Robert Wedderburn and William Davidson paid the price for it.[1]

There were exceptions to this rule. One of the unsung heroines of the age was Marcus Despard's Afro-Caribbean wife Catherine, whom he married while he was superintendent of Honduras. When her husband was imprisoned in Cold Bath Fields for his relations with the United Irishmen and the United Britons, she joined Sir Francis Burdett in a well-publicised campaign against the horrors of 'the English Bastille'. And she composed Despard's gallows speech when he was hanged and decapitated for treason in 1803. Adverse comments were about her female presumption in these actions rather than her colour.

In Wedderburn's and Davidson's cases, likewise, one is at first struck by the apparent ease of their networking. Davidson declared that he had no friends in England, but on arrival in London he quickly found a journeyman cabinet-maker's job and established intimacies with the ladies of the local methodist Sunday school; and he was smoothly intro-duced to Edwards the spy by the soldier John Harrison. Edwards's reports on Davidson sometimes calls him 'the black' but betray no individualised hostility to him. Wedderburn similarly would not have left any mark had he not established friendships with Spence, the Evanses, and Thistlewood before 1820, and with the radical pornographers Cannon and Dugdale after it. Thistlewood thought of both men as indispensable to his cause, and apparently never mentioned colour.

On closer enquiry, however, what suggests itself in the wider culture is a reflexive racism that was so taken for granted that spies wouldn't have thought it worth noting. As Jamaicans of mixed race with slave blood in them, both men were guaranteed difficult lives – Davidson particularly, because he had well-publicised sexual relations with white women and married one of them.

There were 10,000 or so people of colour in the metropolis around 1800, and none would have escaped insult and exclusion for his or her skin and presumed past enslavement. Ignatius Sancho was a rare case of a black who was assimilated into respectable London society, but even he wrote that although he had lived in Britain since he was two, he felt he was 'only a lodger, and hardly that'; and he was never unaware of the whites' 'antipathy and prejudice towards their woolly headed brethren'. Edward Long's *History of Jamaica* (1774) classically announced that black people displayed bestial manners, stupidity, and 'every species of inherent turpitude'. Another protested that English towns were plagued by 'a little race of mulattoes, mischievous as monkeys and infinitely more dangerous', and added that if black people must live among whites they should 'be compelled to marry only among themselves ... There is not on earth so mischievous and vicious an animal as a mule, nor ... a worse race of men than the negroes of Africa'. Radicals like Cobbett agreed:

> Who, that has any sense or decency, can help being shocked at the familiar intercourse, which has gradually been gaining ground, and which has, at last, got a complete footing between the Negroes and the women of England? ... Amongst white women, this disregard of decency, this defiance of the dictates of nature, this foul, this beastly propensity, is, I say it with sorrow and with shame, *peculiar to the English.*

By 1829 Carlile was also venting 'out-and-out anti-black racism' in his writings and was selling pro-slavery pamphlets not long after.[2]

Britain abolished the Atlantic slave trade in 1808, but as black beggars multiplied on the streets after the wars, public sympathy was low. The radicals' notion that the African slave was better off than the English commoner was to distort views for decades yet. The slave's 'confinement is not so strict [as that of the English poor],' Cobbett believed; 'his discipline not so severe, his sustenance full as good, and his labour, upon the whole, less harsh and burthensome'.[3] Most radicals would refer to slavery to prescribe how Britons should *not* live, rather than to describe a condition that should nowhere be.

Mulattos, lascars, and freed or runaway West Indian slaves who made it to Britain usually had little choice but to join the army of poor people who lived by their wits and who year after year tramped the country in search of work. Large numbers served in the navy and had to thieve or beg in London when they were injured or discharged. Davidson was as poor as any of them, and knew everything about a black man's adversities. By his own account he had had no master for five years and picked up such furniture repair work as he could from auctioneers. With six mouths to feed by January 1820, he begged in the streets, and looked bedraggled enough to persuade the Mendicity Society to grant him thirty shillings. In pursuit of self-validation both Wedderburn and Davidson had to tell or invent elaborate life stories. Both were chancers, but how else to survive? It proved uncommon resilience that, despite all, both men did join the ultra-radicals, did go to meetings, and did learn about Spence and Tom Paine. No surprise either that Davidson picked up a grievance or two. Once employed by Harrowby to mend furniture in the Grosvenor Square mansion, he felt no gratitude for the employment. He had 'long been endeavouring to kill the Earl of Harrowby and ... knows every part of the house', said Thistlewood.[4]

In the late regency years Wedderburn caused government more anxiety than Davidson. Twenty-five years older than Davidson, he became something of a father figure to the other. An ardent Spencean until he quarrelled with Thomas Evans's moderation in 1819, he might well have stood on the scaffold with the Cato Street men had he not then been imprisoned for blasphemy. His eventual prominence as a slavery abolitionist owed everything to his unspeakable Jamaican childhood and miserable life thereafter. He was one of the few radicals whose views enabled him to overlook William Wilberforce's reactionary politics. Although relatively fair-skinned, he knew all about racial abuse. A newspaper report of 1823 mocked him as 'Robertus Wedderburn, as he delighteth to designate himself, . . . a man of colour – something the colour of a toad's back; plump and puffy as a porpoise, and the magnitude of his caput makes it manifest that nature cut him out for a counsellor, had not the destinies decreed that he should cut out cloth' (as a tailor).[5]

Wedderburn was racially targeted in two of George Cruikshank's prints. One was *A Peep into the City of London Tavern. . . . – on the 21st of August 1817.* This picked up on newspaper outrage at Wedderburn's interruption of a meeting of London's radical stalwarts (Place, Cobbett, Cartwright, Burdett, Wooler), who had gathered to hear the cotton manufacturer Robert Owen lecture on his blueprint for a co-operative reformation, his *New View of Society* (Fig. 15.1). Wedderburn intervened with the opinion that slave-masters and cotton-masters like Owen were as bad as each other, here echoing Cobbett's representation of Owen's 'villages of cooperation' as so many 'parallelograms of paupers'. A newspaper reported that he looked 'most wretched' and alarming to the ladies nearby, not least because he delivered his views after mounting a table in stockings, 'if such they might be called, that ill concealed his brawney legs and feet'.[6] Cruikshank followed these cues by having an inaccurately black Wedderburn shake his fist at Owen and declare that the latter's 'New View of Society' proposed slavery for the poor: 'I understand Slavery well! my mother was a slave! This would be an improved system of Slavery – & without the solace of Reveal'd Religion and Faith.' In his pockets are a New Testament and a paper entitled 'Wilbeforce [*sic*] on the Slave Trade'. A Quakeress next to him flinches in alarm.

Cruikshank's second satire put at its centre an unnamed black man who probably stood for Wedderburn. In one of the most elaborately composed and by modern standards noxious satires of the century, the print mocked the anti-slavery movement.[7] Its subject matter had been suggested by Cruikshank's friend Captain Frederick Marryat, the son of the leader of the West India interest in Parliament. *The New Union-Club: Being a Representation of what took place at a celebrated Dinner, given by a celebrated – society,* dated 19 July 1819 (detail, Fig. 15.2), depicted an

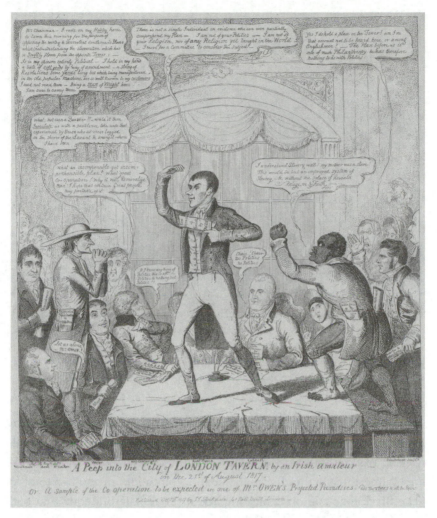

15.1. George Cruikshank, *A Peep into the City of London Tavern. ... – on the 21st of August 1817* (Stockdale, October 1817) (© The Trustees of the British Museum)

imagined public dinner held by the African Institution. Its lampooning of the abolitionists Wilberforce, Stephen, and Macaulay was vicious, and its visual puns and textual and pictorial references played with a range of stereotyped black people, drunken and promiscuous, before whose disorder the whites appear bemused and submissive. The sexes and races mix lasciviously, and the pictures on the walls underscore the satire. The black women are obese grotesques; an infant born of mixed parentage is

15.2. Detail from George Cruikshank, *The New Union Club: Being a Representation of what took place at a celebrated Dinner, given by a celebrated – society* (Humphrey, 19 July 1819) (© Chicago Art Institute)

vertically divided into black and white halves; Billy Waters, a well-known black beggar, fiddles in the background; and the central figure is a well-dressed Wedderburn who speechifies on the table. To the left an emaciated Wilberforce in the chairman's seat (a commode) proposes a toast to 'The Black Joke', an obscene song about the female pudenda that had once featured in Hogarth's *Rake*.

WEDDERBURN

The son of a Scottish plantation owner and an African-born slave-woman, Wedderburn was born in Kingston, Jamaica, *c.* 1761. His sole known portrait (in his 1824 autobiography) shows him as European in feature, though the Dorchester prison records described him as 'a man of colour, broad nostrils, a cut on the left side of the forehead, a slight cut across the bridge of the nose. Lusty.' He was granted his freedom at birth and was briefly schooled in the Bible, but he lost his mother when he was four. He last saw her 'stretched on the ground, tied hands and feet, and FLOGGED in the most indecent manner, though PREGNANT AT THE SAME TIME!!! her *fault* being the not acquainting her mistress that her master had *given her leave to go to see her mother in town!*' She was sold to another owner, so he was brought up by his grandmother Talkee Amee. When he was eleven the boy had to watch her flogged for bewitching her master's smuggling ship.[8] Wedderburn's 24-page autobiography, *The Horrors of Slavery* (1824), testified to all these horrors, as well as to his father's cruelty and rampant sex life. Like countless plantation owners (including Arthur Thistlewood's uncle), this man

> ranged through the whole of his household for his own lewd purposes; for they [his slaves] being his personal property, cost nothing extra: and if any one proved with child – why, it was an acquisition which might one day fetch something in the market, like a horse or pig in Smithfield. . . . From him I have received no benefit in the world. By him my mother was made the object of his brutal lust, then insulted, abused, and abandoned.

How Wedderburn survived he didn't explain; child abuse on the plantations was so taken for granted that it was unnoticed. All he tells us is that he escaped the nightmare by joining the Royal Navy, and came to London in 1778, his seventeenth year.

Initially he lived precariously as a petty thief among fellow 'blackbirds' in St Giles and Covent Garden. He might have married one of them. He was almost certainly the Robert Wedderburn recorded in the Middlesex Sessions Papers in 1794 who 'did unlawfully run away' from his wife, leaving her to be maintained by the Shoreditch workhouse. Charged as a rogue and vagabond, he claimed that he was a journeyman tailor and was legally settled in Shoreditch. In 1781 he signed his marriage certificate with a cross, and did the same with his settlement claim in 1794.[9] Crushingly poor, he travelled to Scotland in his twenties to beg relief from his father. He was turned away from the door, though 'from his cook I had one draught of small beer, and his footman gave me a cracked sixpence'. An Edinburgh charity and a Berwick fishing-smack captain helped him return to London. According to McCalman, thieving put him inside Cold Bath Fields prison for a spell. He made some kind of living as a tailor, but he earned more from patching clothes and selling pamphlets from a wooden stall off St Martin's Lane.[10]

Wedderburn's developing literacy is puzzling. Despite the cross on his settlement claim, he published his first pamphlet *Truth Self-Supported; or, a Refutation of Certain Doctrinal Errors* in 1790; it recounts his conversion by a methodist preacher he heard in Seven Dials. We know that his later publications in the 1820s were dictated to and ghosted by the radical lawyer George Cannon, so this and subsequent pamphlets were probably ghosted also. Still, the pamphlets he sold from his barrow fired his curiosity, and he learned to read well enough to ingest a mixture of deistical ideas and to have himself licensed as a unitarian preacher. He joined Evans's Spencean Philanthropists, which Thistlewood joined too. In 1817 he published six issues of a journal, *The Axe Laid to the Root*. Addressed 'To the Planters and Negroes of Jamaica', it recommended Spence's Land Plan as a way of emancipating the slaves: henceforth his preaching against slavery was impassioned and frequent. As his millenarian convictions strengthened, Evans's weakened, and after the latter's release from gaol each accused the other of stealing their society's property. Since Thistlewood had also quarrelled with Evans, he and Wedderburn drew closer.

In April 1819 Wedderburn opened his own Spencean venue in Hopkins Street, Soho. It was once a French Huguenot chapel, and had lately housed an unlicensed theatre that could seat 350 persons. Here, months before Peterloo, he announced that he had had 'sleeping visions' of the blood that would soon be spilled in England, so after the Manchester massacre his followers regarded him as a prophet. As attendance at the chapel swelled, Carlile regarded its congregation as the 'most vehement group in London'.[11] Spies put it less gently: those who attended were 'persons of the lowest description', with the Watsonites Allen Davenport and Davidson prominent among them. They added that 'Thislewood [*sic*] says he depends more on Wedderburn's division for being armed than all the rest'. After Peterloo the chapel encouraged armed drilling. Early one morning on Primrose Hill a 'man of colour', Wedderburn or Davidson, was seen drilling sixteen or so men by 'marching, wheeling and shouldering sticks', and lamenting that the cold weather had stopped more attending. Several wore shoemaker's aprons.[12]

Admission to the twice-weekly evening debates and Sunday evening lectures at Hopkins Street cost sixpence, so only craftsmen in work could afford it (Davidson's attendance was irregular). Debates catered to all tastes, especially shoemakers'. The subject for debate on 27 October was whether 'loyal cordwainers' would become radical reformers because the regent's boot- and shoe-maker paid irregular wages and got his work done in poorhouses.[13] One evening a spy reported that Wedderburn brought in two 'west Indian blacks' to denounce Wesleyan ministers in the West Indies as 'vipers' who were 'sent from London by the secretary of state for the home department' to 'preach the gospel to poor devils and passive obedience to the planters there marsters [sic]'.[14] A meeting in early August voted positively on the question, 'Has a slave an inherent right to slay his master, who refuses him his liberty?' The spy noted the implication that the English poor should kill their oppressors too.

Another discussion was whether 'Religion is necessary for the preservation of Christianity and good in society – or a crafty design of the ministers and priests to preach up passive obedience to the people with a view the more easy to enslave them.' In October 1819 they discussed whether in Carlile's trial for blasphemous libel chief justice Abbott refused to allow the accused to read passages from the Bible because they would expose the Bible's absurdities. Another was whether the English people had a right to bear arms. Yet another, on 29 November 1819, was elaborately ironic:

> Seeing that his majesty's ministers have ordered all pieces of ordinance and military stores which are in the possession of private Individuals, to be deposited in their own depots; would it not also be advisable for them to take down all the iron pallisading throughout the empire, and to destroy the gas-works, to prevent the radicals making use of them in case of civil war?

At this last debate a spy reported that some 200 young men attended, and, worse, that they applauded Wedderburn's stunning pronouncement

> that there was no God at all and that we were a pack of hobgoblin and ghost believers and that Carlile would not have been guilty if there was not such a pack of ghost believers for a jury ... and that he had rather be in hell than

sit in heaven with such a mollock of a God as ours was then ... He then spoke about the 10th Joshua in which [Moses] commanded the sun to stand still he said that Joshua was a liar and Newton proved him to be so ... He was nothing but a murderer that wrote [the Bible] ... as for Jesus being able to forgive sins it was a lie for none but Herod could at that time forgive sins.

In England, he elaborated, it was the king or regent who forgave sins – or 'if [the regent] is drunk or sleepy as he generally is he authorises Lord Sidmouth in his stead'. Then he condemned Peterloo and the regent's thanks to the Peterloo murderers, expatiated on the wicked treatment of blacks in Jamaica, equated slavemasters with cotton-masters and enslaved blacks with oppressed Britons, and compared himself to the millenarian preacher Richard Brothers. Adding that Sidmouth and Castlereagh might 'look big' but 'were frightened', he ended with the prophecy that 'government were looking at him open-mouthed ready to devour or imprison him'.[15]

On the last point Wedderburn was only too right. In November 1819 he was arrested on an *ex officio* information for publishing a blasphemous libel 'dedicated to the high priest of the Jews'. The continued suspension of habeas corpus and the updated Blasphemous and Seditious Libels Act allowed his detention without trial in Newgate for two months. Then he was indicted for 'certain wicked, blasphemous, and impious words, tending to bring the holy scriptures into contempt, and to encourage irreligion and impiety in the minds of his majesty's liege subjects, to the great scandal of the king and his laws, &c.' He had to wait a further month until his trial opened on the day after the Cato Street arrests. The judge allowed no levity in court. Someone who laughed at one of the offending passages was ordered out.[16] Wedderburn was convicted a few days after his friends were hanged and decapitated. Since the jury mercifully believed that he had 'erred out of ignorance' and 'for want of personal care' in youth, he was sentenced to live for the next two years on grey pease and barley broth in Dorchester gaol, alongside Richard Carlile. In 1831 he was imprisoned for brothel-keeping before fading from history.

DAVIDSON AND SELF-INVENTION

In trials, newspapers, and common conversation William Davidson was referred to as the 'man of colour' and in spy reports as 'the black' or as 'Black Davidson'. Kelleher's *Lives* describes him as 'of a tawney complexion, ... or what is usually termed in the West Indies, a quadroon'. The prosecuting counsel called him 'nearly a black'. Wivell's two etchings do justice to his good looks and in one to his braided hair, unprecedented in black people's portraits of the time (see Fig. 13.5).

Unsurprisingly, he was as much the victim of racist attitudes as Wedderburn – and from his fellow radicals too. When Carlile first set eyes on Davidson in the Crown and Anchor he disliked his 'free and open manner' and his ability 'from his vivacity to keep the whole company alive'. He suspected that Davidson's exuberance was affected to hide his spying, and on another occasion found it singular that 'a man of his complexion' should be on the committee to welcome Hunt's return to London after Peterloo.[17] In December 1819 a meeting in the White Lion laughed at Davidson as he took the chair. Protesting that his audience 'would rather joke and laugh than fight', he rebuked them by stating grandly (in the spy's transcription) that

> since for my part I may not live till tomorrow night it is therefore proper to be serious when a man is so near his last as this for I mean to fight tomorrow and I wish to know if I am to die alone for fight I will and if I am to be opposed to a Life Guard man by myself so it shall be (*Cries of No Davison* [sic] *you shan't be alone while I am living resounded from several persons*). ... It would be gratifying to me in my last moments to see my fellow creaters fighting in the same cause for which I am bleeding but should I in my last moments when my eyes are closing behold myself forsaken and the cause abandoned this would give me more pain than my enemies could inflict.[18]

Davidson's difficulties with the court that tried him were just as irk-some. He must have sensed its antipathy because at the end of his trial he challenged its prejudices frontally:

If my colour should be against me, which perhaps, gentlemen of the jury, you may suppose it to be, and think that because I am a man of colour I am without an understanding or a feeling, and would act the brute; I am not one of that sort; I would wish to wipe off those impressions from those learned gentlemen who have so prosecuted me.

Stunningly, the presiding judge met this head-on. When Davidson asked for a drink of water, Garrow replied:

Oh, certainly, take your refreshment, sit down and compose yourself, and address the jury again, if you desire it, when you are composed, there is no impatience on the part of the Court, take your own time. I would observe to you, upon that which you have said, that you may rest most perfectly assured that with respect to the colour of your countenance, no prejudice either has or will exist in any part of this Court against you; a man of colour is entitled to British justice as much as the fairest British subject that ever came into a court of justice, and will always be sure to obtain it, and this case will be decided upon the facts given in evidence; God forbid that the complexion of the accused should enter, for a single moment, into the consideration of the jury.[19]

Notwithstanding Garrow's courtesy, Davidson's head came off two days later.

Davidson's life story is as perplexing as those of his associates. As already noticed, a week after the executions the *Observer* published the conspirators' lives from 'various sources' unnamed; these were recycled in Kelleher's brief *Lives* and thence by Wilkinson in *Authentic History*. All these sources stated that Davidson's father was Jamaica's attorney general. Claims like this have been recycled ever since, both by scholars of independent mind and by website authors in search of Britain's black heroes. Since Fryer's *Staying Power* (1984), Davidson has been the most pedestalised of all the Cato Street men.[20]

Davidson was reticent about his paternal origins. The most we hear from him is that he had an English father and that he himself had a sense of his own distinction. Invited to a drink by a man who claimed to be his countryman, 'I said, "what do you mean by a countryman?" . . . he says, "a man of colour." I had an objection to going in, for though I am a man of colour, I have never associated with any of them. I was very well brought up. I found them all very ignorant.'[21] In his final appeal to the court he affirmed: 'I am a stranger to England by birth, but I was educated and brought up in England; my father was an Englishman and my grandfather a Scotchman; I certainly have a little prerogative for claiming to be an Englishman, being here from fourteen years of age.'

But why didn't he say who his father was? Neither in spy reports nor in court do we hear a word about a father who was a Jamaican attorney general, nor for that matter do we hear anything about Jamaica. He is given a Jamaican attorney general father named Davidson only after his execution. Such a man is unknown to the list of all Jamaica's attorney generals in Cundall's *Historic Jamaica,* or to the *Jamaica Almanac,* the *Imperial Calendar,* and the draft patents for that post. The attorney general in the year of Davidson's birth was one Thomas Harrison. Tales about Davidson's ancestry might have had no firmer basis than Thistlewood's claim to have seen action in 'several revolutions'. Indeed, it comes as a shock to read Cobbett's firm statement, dated a day after Davidson's execution, that Davidson was born in *Liverpool.* Cobbett didn't substantiate this (the embroidered life stories hadn't spread as yet); but he got the birthplaces of Thistlewood, Tidd, and Ings right, and he was well informed and honest.[22]

This awkwardness taints other elements in Davidson's life story. It didn't help his trial that he could muster only two character witnesses in his favour, and they said nothing more about his past than that he had spent his youth in Scotland. Neither mentioned a distinguished father or a Jamaican past. Robert M'William, a Scottish architect living in Lyon's Inn, had known him in 1800–1 'from reading mathematics with him at Aberdeen'. He had 'a gigantic mind', M'William remembered. Davidson had then been working as a cabinet-maker, he added – contradicting later tales that he was apprenticed to an attorney. M'William had met him in the streets of London only two or three times since then, most recently in 1816. 'I was rather surprised at his sending to me [to testify to his character]; it is so long ago since I have known much of him'. The second character witness was Isaac Cook, who in 1814 had employed Davidson as a journeyman 'in the cabinet line' at his workshop at 24 Charlotte Street, off Surrey (now Blackfriars) Road. At that time Cook thought him 'a very honest hard-working industrious man', but could say nothing about his life before or since.[23]

Nonetheless, quixotic stories multiplied apace, became more elaborate, and are still repeated. Thus (following Kelleher as well as modern writers) in 1800 Davidson's father is said to have sent the fourteen-year-old boy from Kingston, Jamaica, to Glasgow to study law. For unexplained reasons he studies mathematics in Aberdeen instead, and somehow also attends Edinburgh University. Apprenticed to a Liverpool attorney for three years, he tires of the law and runs away to sea. Allegedly, he joins a merchant vessel, but is lifted off it by a naval press gang. He deserts the navy in the West Indies, joins a privateer, and is wounded in skirmishes. Two years later he returns to Liverpool, and his surprisingly tolerant father *then* apprentices him to a cabinet-maker. He decides to visit his parents in Jamaica, but on the way is again pressed into service by a naval ship. He deserts in St Domingo, returns to Liverpool, moves to Birmingham, and does well at his trade. Countless West Indian blacks found service in the navy a good way to escape their pasts. Indeed, this was an age of enforced travel and picaresque adventure among all marginal and rootless people. Davidson claimed to have shared this experience, but dates and sources aren't supplied, and the many strands in the story are tangled. His well-off mulatto mother, still in Jamaica, allows him two guineas a week, and at one point via her 'agent' sends him £1,200. (If true, this would have set him up for life.) At this point his well-heeled parents suddenly disappear from the narrative, for reasons neither noticed nor explained.

Only then does he enter the record more reliably. There is no question that he has had some serious schooling. His autograph for the defence counsel Adolphis before his execution is written in immaculate copperplate script (see Fig. 16.2). Nonetheless, in poverty, he comes to London *circa* 1814 to work for the carpenter Isaac Cook in Walworth, south London. He marries an illiterate widow, Sarah Harris, in the same year. On 12 August in Christ Church, Spitalfields, he signs the banns and she marks with a cross. He takes on her four children and has another two boys by her, so they have six children to bring up on fragile incomes. For some reason Cook dismisses him. By 1819–20 the family occupy a 'hovel' at 12 Elliot's Row, Marylebone, one of many such in Paddington which the parish vestry deplore as leaking and undrained, and productive of 'disease, filth, and wretchedness'.[24] Here Davidson scratches the barest of livings and is reduced to turning the mill in the Marylebone workhouse for three shillings a day. He is unpopular. He sings radical songs to his neighbours, and one day he shoots a neighbour's dog in anger. Two neighbours, a smith and a whitesmith, dislike him enough to appear on the list of witnesses against him in the Cato Street trials, though they aren't called.[25]

In this tangle we hear a great deal about Davidson's erratic sex life, although the more lubricious tales are probably inflated by attitudes akin to Cobbett's disgust at the beastliness of black men's going with white women. Strong and good-looking, he is said first to have won the heart of a fifteen-year-old Miss Salt, a shopkeeper's heiress in Lichfield. The girl's father is cool to a black suitor and puts a bullet through his hat. She finds another man, and the loss of her £7,000 dowry supposedly prompts Davidson to attempt suicide in despair. Next, in London, while married and working for Cook in Walworth, Davidson teaches at the Sunday school of the methodist chapel in Blackfriars Road. Established by Rowland Hill and associated with the anti-slavery London Missionary Society, the chapel is a magnet to black Jamaicans new to London. It was built in the round so that the devil wouldn't find corners to hide in. This precaution fails to protect Davidson from making 'an indelicate attack' on one of the female teachers and 'attempts of a gross and indelicate nature' on the children in his care.

Nobody found these last offences worth mentioning during the trials, but in his final speech Davidson raised them himself, in his own defence. He denied the crimes because he wanted to show that men of colour like him were easily mistaken for each other and that accusations like this one were often based on false identifications. Quoting the sixteenth chapter of Deuteronomy on false witnessing, he pointed out that his wife believed in his innocence, and that the Sunday school lady who had accused him of impropriety had apologised to him when she realised her mistake. However, Wilkinson later investigated the allegations for his *Authentic History* and dismissed Davidson's excuses outright. 'The outward sanctity of the man screened him from suspicion, and the indelicate nature of his attacks' silenced the women concerned. The Sunday school had expelled Davidson after an enquiry that resulted in 'the most perfect unmasking of the hypocrite'.

In December 1818, the narratives continue, he wrote self-pitying letters to an unknown Eliza. He wooed her passionately until the lady's cousin discovered that he was married and had a two-year-old son. Davidson denied his marriage and threatened that if Eliza didn't yield he would hang himself from the lamp post outside her front door, 'for which purpose', he informed her, 'I have already purchased a rope'. In the event he didn't use it.[26] After this, Kelleher's *Lives* give him three wives, two of whom live with him under the same roof. In bed with his first wife, he almost bites her finger off in anger. On another occasion he sends her out at midnight into a snowstorm when she is in advanced pregnancy. He breaks his second wife's jaw, and sends out two of his first wife's offspring as chimney-climbing boys 'the moment they were able to crawl'. He boasts of having five or six affairs at the same time.[27]

In the real world, Davidson's only surviving letter to his wife was business-like and posturing rather than affectionate and sorrowful, and in court he spoke of her without gallantry: 'I have a family of very little children, and a wife that never earned a penny for me since I have had her.' But at the couple's last meeting he had kissed her and, either for effect or honestly, told her, '[I]f I should betray a weakness when I come out on the scaffold, I hope the world will not attribute it to cowardice, but to my intense feelings for you and my dear children. Farewell, love! pray that God will take mercy on me, and receive my soul.'[28]

Nor was the domestic realm unimportant to him. A week before the arrests, he invited some of his radical friends to supper in Elliot's Row. Preston and his three daughters came, as did Robert George and his two-year-old child, and Wilson who flitted 'in & out', and Walker from Manchester who 'drank a draft of porter & and read aloud' to the company.[29] Davidson cared for his children. From prison he petitioned for his three-year-old son to be allowed to 'stop with me occasionally from one visit to another of his mother'. And his last words to the court were affecting: 'I can die but once in this world, and the only regret left, is that

I have a large family of small children, and when I think of that, it unmans me.'[30]

In court Davidson deployed his defence of mistaken identity. A black man like him, he said, simply couldn't have been in the conspiracy: 'I must have been a silent spectator from the nature of my colour. I should have been immediately remarked if I had taken an active part.' It was by the purest mischance that he was walking by Cato Street when he was arrested.[31]

Alas for him, the home office knew that he had carried a black flag with a skull on it at the Covent Garden hustings in 1818,[32] that he was on the White Lion committee that planned Hunt's grand entry to London after Peterloo, that he first met the spy Edwards there, and that at the ultras' public meeting in Finsbury Market on 1 November 1819 he carried a black banner bearing the words 'Let us die like Men and not be sold like Slaves'. On this last occasion Davidson urged people to go armed to public meetings, and read out the addresses of gunsmiths and sword cutlers so that the crowd might loot them if the opportunity arose. Thistlewood was reported as saying that Davidson 'would have killed right and left' to defend the flag.[33] Edwards wrote that Preston wanted Edwards to be put on the Committee of Five 'to oppose the Black as he [Davidson] was too rash and violent'.[34] On 26 December Thistlewood, Bradburn, and the spy went to Davidson's in Marylebone, presumably to check on his *bona fides* as well as his weapons. He showed them his flintlock and cartridges, his belt, cartouche, and bayonet, and declared that he would shoot the first who came to his house to search it. Thistlewood gave Davidson's child a shilling.[35]

It was also sworn in court that Davidson had joined the Marylebone Union Reading Society in order to read Tom Paine and Spence, that he was secretary of a shoemakers' club in the Scotch Arms,[36] that at Wedderburn's invitation he attended the Hopkins Street chapel, that at meetings at the White Lion in Wych Street and the White Hart in Brook's Market he was a committee member and once a chairman, and that he had old files sharpened into pike-heads which he said were 'for turning men's guts out'.[37] In October 1819 he was accused in a White Lion meeting of appropriating collection money for his own use, and in February 1820 he conned thirty shillings out of the Society for the

Suppression of Mendicity. He said he wanted to redeem his pawned tools, pleading that he had not earned a penny in the last eighteen weeks. He used the money to redeem a pawned blunderbuss instead. In court he claimed that the weapon belonged to someone else and that he was about to clean it before it was auctioned.[38]

Davidson was poorer than Wedderburn, but better educated. His written style achieved heroic flourishes or suicidal ones when it suited him, and he was a gifted melodramatist in a culture that looked kindly on theatrical posturing. (When he worked at cabinet-making off the Blackfriars Road, he was minutes away from the home of English melodrama, the Surrey Theatre at the Obelisk.) It was in this mode that Davidson wrote to his wife soon after his arrest. Aware that his letter might be published, he stretched the poor woman's credulity by announcing that he would never betray the proud spirit that 'had so long been in possession of the ancient name of Davidson' – a trope which referred to the heroism of Clan Davidson's medieval provost of Aberdeen, who was killed in a clan massacre in 1411. 'Death's countenance is familiar to me,' he expanded; 'I have had him in view fifteen times, and surely he cannot now be terrible.' More fine moments adorned his last speech in court, when he expatiated on Magna Carta and the people's practice 'with arms to stand and claim their rights as Englishmen':

> And our history goes on further to say, that when another of their majesties the kings of England tried to infringe upon those rights, the people armed and told him that if he did not give them the privileges of Englishmen, they would compel him by the point of the sword. ... Would you not rather govern a country of spirited men, than cowards?[39]

It was a fine display, but Davidson's defiance evaporated as he wrote a private and self-abasing letter to Harrowby to beg for mercy on the grounds that he had once worked for him as a furniture repairer – forgetting Thistlewood's comment that Davidson wanted more than anything to kill Harrowby. And though one or two reports stated that on the scaffold his step was firm and fearless, most had him trembling, weeping, and contrite. On the day before his death he asked for the ministrations of a man called Rennett, a journeyman tailor who had once preached 'among the Wesleyans'. The officials decided that Rennett 'was in a situation in life not well adapted to reveal the holy tenets of salvation to a dying man', so Davidson had to endure the Rev. Cotton's consolations instead. Cotton spent the night in prayer with Davidson and skilfully reduced him to the state of sobbing self-abasement that the clergyman thought of as 'penitence'. The other four condemned men kept aloof from his submission.[40]

PART FIVE

THE EXECUTIONS

CHAPTER 16

Trials and Verdicts

THE TRIALS

At 6.30 in the morning of 14 April 1820 the authorities transferred to Newgate seven of the eight state prisoners in the Tower: Thistlewood, Ings, Tidd, Brunt, Davidson, Harrison, and Wilson. Monument was left in the Tower for later use as an informer. There had been some anxiety that Newgate was too full to hold them. The ritual reading of the recorder's report on the verdicts delivered at the last two Old Bailey sessions would normally have emptied a few cells by sorting which of the people condemned should hang and which should be transported; but the report had been delayed by the Cato Street arrests.[1] With the report read at last, some cells were cleared; so the City sheriffs and marshals in full uniform arrived at the Tower followed by strong detachments of Guards and Bow Street officers. Each prisoner was handcuffed and put into his own coach with three Bow Street men for company. Thistlewood was 'greatly agitated and trembling exceedingly'. The procession was led by the chief marshal in his carriage, the sheriffs in their two carriages, and a troop of Life Guards. The coaches were flanked by Horse Guards in single file, and Life Guards followed. The whole proceeded through the streets at a brisk trot that drew admiring attention from pedestrians, as it was meant to.

At Newgate, constables and the marshal's men formed a half circle round the felons' door, with Horse Guards behind, as the chief turnkey received the prisoners. Thistlewood, Ings, Tidd, and Brunt seemed 'greatly dejected' as they mounted the steps; Davidson, Harrison, and Wilson seemed calm. Thistlewood they put in a small cell of his own, with a fireplace and chamber pot. The other six were kept together, with

343

access to the press-yard. In each cell one officer sat by day and two by night. Later that day the four prisoners in Cold Bath Fields were brought in and put into cells of their own.[2]

Next, with a great clanking of irons, the men were brought into court for their arraignment. Unshackled but closely guarded, they pleaded not guilty to the charges of treason, murder (of Smithers), and the attempted murder of other constables. When asked how he would be tried, Ings answered 'By the laws of reason'. Rebuked, he amended his answer to 'By God and my country – the laws of reason are the laws of my country.'

There would be four separate trials: Thistlewood's, Brunt's, and Ings's singly, and then Davidson's and Tidd's jointly. After each day's proceedings the prisoners – never then called 'the accused' – were shackled and returned to their cells. The cross-examinations and arguments lasted ten days, from Monday, 17 to 27 April. The summings-up and sentencing took the whole of Friday, 28 April. Throughout, a detachment of the London Militia kept order outside. Executions followed on Monday, 1 May – May Day.

The trials inflicted taxing ordeals on both sides, even if on one side more than the other. Juries had to listen to examinations and legal arguments for up to ten hours a day, and in Thistlewood's case this over three successive days. By the third day jurors were so exhausted that Ings's trial had to be postponed while a new jury was chosen. Then Ings's and Brunt's trials, followed by Davidson's and Tidd's, each took two days.

Trying five men over ten days was then a generous pace of proceeding. In 1803 it had taken only a day to send Colonel Despard to his doom, and another day to send six associates after him. Judges were impatient with juries that took their time, so in most felony cases juries announced their verdicts after a brief public huddle in court. A jurist noted that a felony trial at the Old Bailey lasted on average five minutes, so that 'a man there may be sent to the gallows before he knows his trial has commenced'. By 1833 Old Bailey trials each took on average eight and a half minutes, though capital trials took longer. Even so, 'full two-thirds of the prisoners, on their return from their trials, cannot tell of any thing which has passed in the court, not even, very frequently, whether they have been tried'.[3] It surprised nobody, therefore, that at the end of the first day of Thistlewood's trial the Sessions found time to squeeze in a bit of what it called 'ordinary business'. This was the five-minute trial of one Gilbert Hayes, who was sentenced to death for stealing sixty pounds from a dwelling house, and the ten-minute trial of one Daniel Evans, who was sentenced to death for stealing six silver spoons and six forks. All Evans said when asked to defend himself was 'I can say nothing'. As was usual in felony cases before 1836, neither man had counsel.[4] Both were granted the king's mercy and sent to Van Diemans's Land without more ado.

As early as seven o'clock on the first day a crowd assembled outside the Old Bailey Sessions House next to Newgate. As the crush thickened, policemen were stationed at strategic places, and rails at each end of the Old Bailey kept out all wheeled traffic except the carriages of the great and of those with business in court. The crown witnesses were divided into two parties. The respectable ones were accommodated in the grand jury room and 'those of an humbler class' in a room adjacent. The crown witnesses Monument and Adams were put in rooms by themselves. Then came a clamour of ticket holders awaiting admission as spectators. At 8.30 Thistlewood was brought to the bar, and the judges took their places at 9. Three hours later they allowed Thistlewood a chair to sit on. At one point a man approached the dock and laid his hat in front of Thistlewood. It contained five oranges, which Thistlewood put in his pocket. They were confiscated lest they contain poison. The rest of the day was spent in examining Adams.[5]

The court filled daily with paying audiences. High admission prices were charged for Thistlewood's trial. During the following trials, prices were reduced and half-price was charged after two o'clock to keep the court full. The prisoners' friends attended, and the prisoners would nod to them from the dock.[6] Ladies were directed to boxes of their own. They cried out in alarm on the first day when they saw pikes, swords, pistols, grenades, and ammunition laid out on a table. Finer people were separated in the private galleries. They coped with the spectacle equably. The Austrian ambassador's diary shows that he was less moved by the trials than by the personal charms of Lady Georgiana Stanhope and the Countess St Antonio's niece in the ladies' boxes. After Brunt's trial some days later he adjourned to Count Palmella's to enjoy a reception with Ladies Granville and Harrowby and Princess Lieven. But he did visit the Cato Street stable; his diary describes it.[7]

It was thought to measure one of the many perfections of the English criminal law that counsel was provided for those tried for treason, but in this the Cato Street men were poorly served. The crown wheeled out its heaviest guns against them: Robert Gifford the attorney general, John Copley the solicitor general, and four further barristers of note. These had time and funds to prepare their cases. By contrast, the prisoners' defence had to be organised in prison while they were still ignorant of the charges and witnesses against them. One result was that the juries heard far less evidence for the defence than for the prosecution. In any case, the prisoners had no powerful interest to help them. The defence counsel Adolphus told the court that 'other prisoners in the same situation have been allied by party, connexion, or other means, with some considerable number of men of influence, weight, and reputation in the state'. Here he was referring to Horatio Nelson's testimony on behalf of his one-time officer Despard. 'This poor man [Thistlewood] and his associates are deserted by every one,' Adolphus continued: 'My clients are too poor to get together the necessary witnesses; they are too poor to support their wives and children while they are in prison; they come therefore naked amidst all these perils.'[8]

It helped the men a little that the attorney James Harmer served them without payment. He had already served Thistlewood, Watson, Preston, and Hooper in the 1817 treason trial. Famous for his labours on behalf of the poor and the unjustly treated, he had 'amongst the classes whose natural destination was the Old Bailey an immense reputation'. He campaigned ceaselessly against the criminal law's casual corruptions and wrongful imprisonments or death sentences. He was active in efforts to prosecute the Peterloo magistrates and yeomanry cavalry and acted as the Peterloo radical Samuel Bamford's attorney. He gave evidence against the capital code to both the 1819 Select Committee and the 1836 Royal Commission on the criminal law. The 1819 committee pointed out that Harmer had dealt with more than 2,000 capital prisoners and that his arguments against the death penalty were authoritative.

In the present case Harmer organised a committee to collect subscriptions for the Cato Street men's defence. Thomas Evans, Wooler, Hone, several past Watsonites, and the London and Westminster divisions of shoemakers gave fifty pounds each. It was probably Harmer who mobilised the support of Alderman Wood, ex-sheriff Philips, and sheriff Parkins to mount the wives' attempt to charge Edwards with treason in mid-May. He offered £100 of his own money for Edwards's arrest. If anyone in that age exposed oligarchical law at its most brutal it was Harmer, though today his achievements are forgotten.[9]

Yet Harmer's efficiency hardly offset the fact that Adolphus was appointed only a day before the trial opened. 'I never heard of his case till Thursday last; I was out of town in Friday; I had not my instructions till Saturday night, and I had to appear before you on Monday.'[10] Taken by surprise, he had to stay up all night to brief himself. Nonetheless, his summing up for Thistlewood took five hours and was the most admired of all the trial speeches. His case rested on the absurdity of regarding so half-baked a conspiracy as treasonable. Less carefully selected jurymen might have been persuaded by his eloquence, but not these ones, so carefully chosen.[11]

ADOLPHUS'S DEFENCE

When all is said and done, the Cato Street men did propose the most violent and precisely aimed assault on the British political order since Guy Fawkes and friends had tried to blow up parliament in 1605, and then since the Cromwellian regicide. Although they had not the least chance of overturning the state, no other plot over the ensuing century and a half was to be as ambitious as theirs, nor did any other so accurately target the most powerful figures in the nation.

That said, it is right to be suspicious of much of the evidence about the conspiracy's treasonous intent – and not merely because the trials were skewed by 'the quirks, quibbles, tricks, and shuffles of both the bar and the bench', as Henry Hunt described their arcane procedures. Hunt had in mind the selection of the jury, the exclusion of key defence witnesses, and the hiding of Edwards's entrapment. We should add the incessantly hostile commentaries on the prisoners in the weeks before and during the trials. 'From the moment of their apprehension to the day of their trial,' Cobbett wrote to his son,

the daily press had been teeming with the most shocking abuse of them …
as *murderers, assassins, blood-thirsty monsters*, … while no man, who had the
smallest regard for his own safety, dared to utter a syllable … to stem this
torrent of cruel calumny; or even to hint at the *possibility* of the
calumniated persons being innocent of wicked intention.[12]

Already in March the tory *Courier* was attacking the *Chronicle* for not being
harsh enough in damning the conspirators, while the *Times* called for
their speedy punishment and a 'purification of society'.[13]

Yet intelligent people knew only too well that ministers, prosecutors,
and judges had a self-preserving political project to fulfil – and that
Sidmouth had connived at and steered the conspiracy towards its prosecutable outcome in order to frighten would-be revolutionaries, justify
repression, and impress conservative voters. After the executions Carlile
was certain that 'if the manner in which this Cato Street conspiracy has
been made to burst and to petrify the minds of the public had not raised a
strong prejudice against the accused, the juries would have rejected the
evidence adduced by the crown with indignation'. On 3 March his
headline could proclaim 'Another Plot Manufactured by Ministers':
'We have been so much accustomed to these imaginary Downing Street
plots of late, that they appear to be essential to the support of the present
system.' On the day the death sentences were delivered he wrote that
there was 'something too black between the ministers and Edwards, to
have him produced as a witness':

the ministers have been playing with Thistlewood, and … they have
reserved him for some time with the hope of drawing in some character
of more importance with him [Hunt or J. C. Hobhouse]; but finding that
hopeless, they brought the Cato-street affair to maturity, just to answer
their purposes for striking terror into the minds of the people on the eve of
a general election … The ministers have many a time sallied forth their
military with the hopes that Thistlewood would commence some of his
projects, but they never attempted to stop his career, whilst they had any
further hope of making him useful.[14]

In similar spirit the LCS veteran John Thelwall risked imprisonment by
addressing open letters in his *Champion* newspaper to chief justice Abbott

both before and during the trials. Invoking the legal wisdom of 'our venerable ancestors', he condemned the use of spies and defended the rights of 'citizens' to fair trial. He suspected that 'the moment for the detection or development of the plot … [was] determined upon for a grand theatrical effect – as a dashing, electioneering manoeuvre'.

Byron's friend John Cam Hobhouse had no doubt of this. Imprisoned in Newgate between 14 December 1819 and 29 February 1820 for breaching parliamentary privilege, but winning his seat at the Westminster election shortly after his release, he was 'certain that Edwards, a government spy, was the chief instigator of the whole scheme. The people cried out for him during the execution.' Later he told the Commons that 'there is a very general feeling abroad that the plot for which the unfortunate men have lately suffered, has been got up by the agents of our police departments'. William Cobbett, too, had observed to Hunt as early as 1816 how 'the sons of corruption' simply 'sighed' for the evidence of 'a PLOT': 'Oh, how they sigh! They are working and slaving and fretting and stewing; they are sweating all over; they are absolutely pining and dying for a Plot!' After the executions he wrote,

> The judge, you see, said a good deal against conspiracies; against assassination, and against seditious and blasphemous publications: but not a word did he say against spies, or against the hirers of spies. … It was observed by the judge, that the object of the conspiracy was without a parallel in the annals of this country, and that he trusted in God it would remain without a parallel. Very good; but so was the Manchester attack without a parallel: the Six Acts are without a parallel: the Clergy Indemnity Act is without a parallel: banishment for libel is without a parallel: bail beforehand, to pay libellers' fines, is without a parallel: punishment for publishing cheap pamphlets is without a parallel: the Bank protecting Acts are without a parallel: the Ellenborough Act, under which Maggenis was tried and executed, is without a parallel: nay, the very Act, under which the Conspirators were convicted, and for which they suffered death, is without a parallel: [the spies] Oliver, Castles, Edwards, and their acts, are without a parallel: all these, and numerous other things that we behold and endure, are without a parallel in this country.[15]

Thistlewood's defence counsel John Adolphus knew all this too, but he had to stay with the evidence in court. His speech in Thistlewood's defence could do little more than hint at prior 'communications' between Bow Street and the home office, and at the authorities' feeling that 'something must be done to force the plan forward a little'. He did repeatedly note the oddity that Edwards hadn't been called despite his inclusion in the witness list, and he commented meaningfully on the fact that Edwards had discovered the advert for the cabinet dinner in the one paper that had published it.[16] But he could only mention these matters in passing. On the third day of Thistlewood's trial his main effort was to undermine Robert Adams's evidence. Adams provided the prosecution with the primary narrative of the conspiracy's later stages, and this was the backbone of the case against Thistlewood. Under the stress of interrogation his evidence was at points confused, but most of its details were too sharply observed and consistent with other evidence to have been fabricated. At nearly every point it was consistent with Thistlewood's track record since 1816. Still, in his long and brilliant speech, Adolphus ran rings round him.

Adolphus first accepted that the conspirators assembled in Cato Street in order to assassinate the cabinet, and also that trials for Smithers's murder and for attempted murder would follow in due course.[17] But for the moment, he said, murder wasn't at issue; the issue was whether treason was committed. In truth, he said, the court had heard 'nothing which could be called a political motive, or be put in question as endangering the government at all'. The conspirators' immediate intent had been simpler: 'Poverty was their goad, and plunder their aim.' And such evidence to the contrary as Adams offered was duplicitous and fictitious:

> Is it to be endured, that a man shall come with these crude and rash inventions to swear away the lives of eleven men, upon testimony which would, in another place, weigh nothing in proving a milk-score or a washerwoman's bill? Can such idle dreams and dotages be received in a court of criminal judicature, or should they not rather be dismissed with the scorn and contempt so eminently their due? ... The question then came to this point, whether a charge of high treason ought to be considered as made out, which rested solely on the testimony of an

accomplice, and an accomplice, too, like Adams; ... if Adams were
believed, no witness could hereafter be rejected as unworthy of credit,
and consequently no man's life or honour could be considered secure.

To establish his case Adolphus bypassed the conspirators' hatred of
the ministers, their wish to avenge Peterloo, their stockpiling of weapons,
their moves to replicate the attempted insurrection of December 1816,
their inflammatory speeches, and their emulation of Despard and friends
(who had also planned to capture the Bank and Mansion House). Instead
he stressed the pathetically casual, impromptu, and impoverished nature
of the conspiracy, and its absurdity when measured against the planning
and support that would be required for effective treason: 'This, gentlemen, is not the way that kings are destroyed, and governments overthrown.'[18] At one point he pointed to the table littered with rusty
swords, homemade pike-heads, pistols, and blunderbusses: 'Here is the
whole arsenal of the conspirators: with this they were to do – what? To
overset a mighty empire.' This, he kept banging home, was a revolution
without resources. Even 'the magnificent Mr Brunt' could offer only a
one-pound note to pay his men:

> If he gave them only a slice of cheese and bread, and porter or gin, the
> fund [the pound note] would be exhausted on forty men, and there is an
> end of the ... revolutionists. For the most money produced was on one
> occasion six shillings, on another a shilling, on another seven-pence; this
> was all the treasure that astonished the eyes of the gazers, and one pound
> note was talked of, that they might see on some future occasion if he
> possessed it ... ; I ask again, is it credible, that twenty-five men, from the
> dregs of society, could be allured by sharing in one pound to overturn a
> state? Or is it not probable they had some other view? ... the hope of such
> plunder as confusion and uncertainty might assist them in obtaining?[19]

Adolphus questioned Adams's evidence on small points as well as big.
He pointed out that Furnival's Inn was the biggest building complex in
Holborn and a few minutes' walk away from Fox Court, so everyone knew
it, but that it had no strategic significance. It wouldn't burn down anyway,
because it had lately been rebuilt in stone with strong party walls. Only
'idiots and drivellers' would think Furnival's Inn could be burned. (In

fact Edwards's reports confirmed that Furnival's Inn really was a target. Easily entered through the palings in Leather Lane, it was full of wooden lathes and building materials 'which if fired will be likely to destroy the whole of that fine new building'.)[20]

As for a treasonable plot to kill the king, the evidence was scanty. As we have seen, the conspirators dodged all discussion of monarchy and instead put their faith in a vague and unpredictable form of social unravelling which might work to the peoples' advantage. By late December they had agreed that the best way forward was to assassinate the ministers either in their own houses or collectively at the next cabinet dinner. But the only hint at regicide came in a conversation in Fox Court ten days before George III's funeral in Windsor on 16 February.

Adams's story was that Harrison had then passed on to Thistlewood, Brunt, Ings, and himself a Life Guard's suggestion. The man had mentioned to Harrison that on the day of the funeral all soldiers and police officers who could be spared would be twenty miles away in Windsor. This 'would be a very favourable opportunity to kick up a row, and see what they could do that night'. Thistlewood agreed that when the military heard of a rising 'they would be so tired when they got to London they would not be able to do anything'. He added that once the insurrectionists and their cannon had seized London, they should 'go to the telegraph [station], over the water [Thames], to prevent any intelligence being conveyed to Woolwich'. Then they should form a provisional government and 'send down to the sea-ports to prevent any gentlemen being permitted to leave this country without a passport from the provisional government, he particularly mentioned Dover, Brighton, Ramsgate and Margate'. They should send a force to take Brighton and prevent anyone leaving. 'As to the prince regent or the king,' Thistlewood allegedly said, 'we cannot think of his ever wearing the crown, the present family have inherited the crown long enough. ... it is no use the new king ever thinking of wearing the crown.'[21]

This was the essence of the treason: but it didn't go far, and it was reported only by Adams. As Adolphus put it, 'If high treason in this case comes entirely from the mouth of an accomplice, you cannot receive it. It is the whole of the charge; and if in that the accomplice is not confirmed, that charge is unsupported; for, if you strike out the evidence of Adams, there is not one word to prove treason.' No other interest in regicide was reported in the trials, and this one was reported unreliably.[22] He added later, when defending Ings: 'Suppose they had seized the cannons, that would not be a levying of war; for they are not the king's, but the property of private individuals. The Mansion-house and the Bank were not the king's. The only title to support the treason was the absurdity of a "Provisional Government"'.

Adolphus's final defence rested on the plot's absurdity. He derided the notion that the military and police would be too fatigued in Windsor 'to come to rescue the metropolis and the kingdom from a handul of desperate ruffians'. As for 'kicking up a row', he added, 'the very phrase explains the whole design!' 'Thus far ... there has not been a word about overturning the State': they aimed not to overthrow government but simply to steal and 'commit depredation'. In any case, it was ridiculous to think that two cannon from Gray's Inn Lane and six from the Artillery ground would give twenty-five men possession of all London, as well as the road to Windsor and 'all the avenues!':

> The possession of London! I should have thought that any man with a military education ... who had seen the march of a single regiment, would have said at once, there is nothing less probable than that you would have taken possession of any one parish in London – of any one populous street in London ... [let alone] of Oxford-street. Of Oxford-street! It would not give the possession of a street of half its importance, because there are avenues that would require the guard of four or five hundred men and much more artillery than these conspirators proposed to have ... and Harrison and Adams, with all their military experience, said nothing against the plan!

Some of the conspirators were to drag the cannon (no horses were thought of, he noticed) to seize the Bank of England and the Mansion House. 'The Mansion House!' he exclaimed: 'twenty-five men would have been completely lost in the passages: they might as well have gone to take the Tower of Babel'. Nonetheless there they proposed to set up a provisional government with none other than Ings the butcher as secretary.

The conspirators who could devise such a plot might well be considered as mad; … Thus were roads to be commanded in this direction; important diversions operated in that; telegraphs secured over the water; a metropolis like London secured, and an army paralyzed, by a band of five-and-twenty paupers. … That a [single] wicked man may have invented [these plans], I can well understand; but that seven or eight men, two of them soldiers, should have met to act on so ridiculous proposal, exceeds all human credibility. If this can be credited, there is nothing in oriental fiction – nothing in ancient or modern poetry – nothing in the legends of the fathers, or the lives of the saints, but may be received as history and credited as truth.[23]

It was Adolphus's job to argue this way, and he overstated the conspirators' ineptitude by presenting the plot as a 'dream of delirium' or an 'illusion of frenzy' in whose strategic seriousness he disbelieved. But his sarcasm was so withering that a jury that hadn't been carefully filtered might easily have agreed with him – as, with a qualification or two, we must.

VERDICTS

The government was not to be thwarted. Both the treasury solicitor's speech and Abbott's summing-up insisted that much in Adams's evidence was confirmed elsewhere. Adams was a contaminated witness, but his character was unimpeached in court and his testimony was supported by Monument, Hyden, and Dwyer. The crown witnesses were unknown to each other, yet independently confirmed a plan to assassinate the cabinet, seize cannon, stockpile arms, capture the Bank and Mansion House, and establish a provisional government. Brunt's apprentice, Brunt's landlady, Tidd's daughter, the Bow Street officers, and a dozen lesser players spoke to points 'trivial in themselves' but all 'dovetailing with the most minute parts of [Adams's] story … Each formed a link in the general chain, which was complete in all its parts'. The whole plan might seem ridiculous, but it was 'formed on some vain expectation, that, if the blow were ever struck, there were a great number of people in the metropolis who would readily join in the scheme, and levy war against his majesty'. On these grounds Abbott directed the jury to consider whether the assassination of the cabinet were not 'part of a scheme, having for its object a general and tumultuous rising of the people, to levy war against the king; or whether they conspired to effect that assassination alone?' He added that they should notice the arms the conspirators had collected: 'They certainly were far more in number than could have been wanted, or used in the abominable attempt that was to be made at Lord Harrowby's. Some of them could not have been used there at all.'

The chief justice concluded by reading out the clause in the Treason Act which made it treason 'to compass, imagine, invent, devise, or intend to deprive or depose the king from the style, honour, and kingly name of the imperial crown of this realm; or to levy war against him within this realm, in order to compel him to change his councils'. Counsel on both sides, he continued, agreed that if the project stated by the prosecution were proved, it fell within the meaning of the Treason Act; 'for, if a provisional government were formed, the royal style must of necessity cease'. Nor did the levying of war 'require soldiers drawn up in military array. It was sufficient if a number of people met to do some public act, in which they had no private interest, but which affected the country at large. Devising to force the king to change his measures was always considered a levying of war, under the old statute of Edward III.' The assassination of the cabinet was not the conspirators' only purpose; they counted also on a rising in the metropolis that would put the country into their hands.[24]

Directed by the judge, Thistlewood's jury delivered a verdict of guilty on the counts of conspiring to levy war and of actually levying war against the king. Where his case led, Brunt, Ings, Tidd, and Davidson, on the same evidence, were found guilty also. Thistlewood's guilty verdict took the jury fifteen minutes to decide upon, Ings's twenty-five, Brunt's twenty, and Tidd's and Davidson's forty. For their time these speeds were generous.

Many in the court thought that Adolphus's speech would win Thistlewood an acquittal. Thistlewood might have hoped so too – except that Adolphus anticipated a guilty verdict for murder if the treason prosecution failed. He maintained his composure throughout the trial. Taken back in shackles to his cell, he spoke scarcely a word. Throwing himself into a chair and brooding, he ignored the guards around him. Outside the Old Bailey the prisoners' friends had been set to cheer if the verdict was favourable. When it proved otherwise 'they departed with strong manifestations of disappointment'.[25]

THE DEATH SENTENCES

On the day before their sentencing, the defence counsel John Adolphus asked the ten men who were sure to receive death sentences (including the five who in the event were to be transported, but excluding Gilchrist) to provide him with autograph mementos to distribute among his friends. Facsimile copies duly went to Lord Liverpool and the duke of Wellington, and doubtless to other ministers.[26] Adolphus's request said little for his sensitivity, but the men raised no objection. Their poignant last writings are copy-book sententious, but they eloquently express their character, literacy, and feeling (Fig. 16.1).

Tidd was the only one lost for words: 'Sir I Ham a very Bad Hand at Righting,' he wrote with some difficulty, and left it at that. Thistlewood's and Brunt's scripts were mature and well practised; Davidson's and Cooper's deployed schoolroom copperplate. Cooper's was signed with elaborately curlicued flourishes; it also conscientiously acknowledged its source: 'Affliction's sons are brothers in distress / A brother to relieve how exquisite the bliss. Burns.' Bradburn, Strange, and Wilson battled with spelling. 'Wanst [once] i was blind and could not / see but now providence directed me,' wrote Bradburn, while John Shaw Strange wrote, 'Though sad misfortun's hunts me from the land / all ^{though} [inserted] my utter ruin seems at hand / Composed and self-colected I remain, / near ['ne'er] start at perils nor of ills Complain.' Wilson turned to history: 'the cause wich nerved a Brutus arm / to strike a Tirant with alarm / the cause for ^{wich} [inserted] brave Hamden died / for wich the galant [William] Tell defied / a Tirants insolence and pride.'

Ings the butcher, indignant to the last, repeated his assertion in his last speech: 'If my life is destroyed in this conspiracy, I shall consider I ham a murdered man the reason is I was not the Inventer of the conspiracy & I should never know the party if Mr Edward had not come to my house & got a quainted with me,' he added, 'and it was through him I was drawn a one side in my distress and unfortinate situation, because I could not keep my Wife and children.' John Harrison briefly agreed: 'A Fals Witness as [is] a Cars [curse] that Cannot be for Given.'

The other contributions were poetic. Thistlewood cited a melodramatic exclamation from George Sewell's *Tragedy of Sir Walter Raleigh* (1719):

> Oh! what a mine of mischief is a Statesman!
> Ye furies, whirlwinds and ye treacherous rocks,
> Ye ministers of death, devouring fire,
> Convulsive earthquake, and plague-tainted air,
> All you are merciful and mild to him.

He probably lifted it from *The Manual of Liberty, or Testimonies in Behalf of the Rights of Mankind* (1795), a compendium of radical texts of the kind he might have owned. For his contribution Davidson transcribed three biblical saws. Two expressed his sense of his foreignness and colour: 'Thou shalt not Oppress a Stranger in a Strange Land' and 'Thou Shalt not Pervert the Judgement of a Stranger'. Finally, Brunt displayed his versifying skill in a version of 'Death or Liberty':

> Tho' in Newgate Close Confind
> No fears alarm the Noble mind
> tho death itself Appears in View
> Daunts not the soul Sincerely true
> Let S—h and his Base Colleagues
> Cajole And Plot their Dark intrigues
> Still Each Britton's Last words shall be
> *Oh give me Death or Liberty.*

He left a copy for his wife and added his last shilling to the envelope, asking her to keep the coin as long as she lived.[27] The pathos didn't check Adolphus's amusement at Brunt's delicacy in writing 'S—h' for 'Sidmouth' when he was about to die.

In court on sentencing day, 28 April, the clank of irons was heard as the eleven convicted prisoners were brought in. All were double-ironed except Ings, who was 'indisposed', though how and why he was

16.1 (a–b). The convicted conspirators' autographs, 27 April 1820: (a) Thistlewood, Ings, Brunt, Davidson, Ings (hanged); (b) Cooper, Strange, Wilson, Harrison, Bradburn (transported) (© Wellington Papers, University of Southampton Library) 'f My life is destroyed in this conspiracy I shall consider I ham a Murderd man the reasons is I was not the Inventer of the conspiracy & I should never known the party if Mr Edward had not come to my house & got a quainted with me & it was through him I was drawn a one side in my distress & unfortunate Ntuation because I could not keep my Wife & children   *James W...*

Afflection's sons are brothers in distress
A brother to relieve how exquisite the bliss
                                        Budaus
                    Cha: Cooper

Though sad Misfor'un's Hunto me from the Land
all, though, my utter ruin seems at hand
Composed and self colected I remain
near start at perrils nor of ills Complain
                    Jn Chas Strange

---

the Cause wich nerved a Brutus arm
to Strike the Tyrant with alarm
the cause for brave, wich, Hamden died
for wich the Galant Tell defied
a Tyrants insolence and pride
                    James Wilson

A False Witness as a Cars that Cannot be for
Given   *John Harmon*   Newgate 27 Aprill
                                        1820
wanst i was blind and could not
see but now providence Directed
me   *Richard Bradburn*

16.1 (a–b). (cont.)

indisposed wasn't explained. Tidd complained that his irons were 'so heavy that I cannot step; my legs are very tender, they have been very bad for some time'.[28]

Gilchrist, the unemployed Scot who had come for his bread and cheese, was so obviously ignorant of everything except his own starvation that his death sentence was fully respited after enquiries into his 'character' – though he had to wait months for his release. Since the preceding trials had made their guilty verdicts inevitable, Cooper, Bradburn, Harrison, Wilson, and Shaw Strange were advised to change their pleas to guilty, thus to forego a trial and throw themselves on the king's mercy.

In this advice they benefited less from the attorney general's compassion than from the calculation that juries and witnesses were so exhausted by the preceding trials 'that witnesses might trip in repeating the same tale so many times, and that one adverse verdict might affect those already obtained'. During Tidd's and Davidson's trials the treasury solicitor George Maule warned Hobhouse at the home office that 'too frequent a repetition of the same facts [would] not only lessen the interest that they have exerted, but perhaps create a sort of reaction in men's minds in favour of the prisoners, particularly as the proof against the individuals as we go on will weaken'. (What a dirty game this was!) The men followed the advice and were 'pardoned' for transportation. Strange, Cooper, Bradburn, and Gilchrist expressed gratitude, but Wilson and Harrison 'persisted in the most obstinate indifference to the mercy which had been so graciously extended towards them. During the night and morning … they wept for the ignominious fate of their companions, [and] expressed a wish that they might have been participators in its consequences, horrible as they were.'[29]

On the night of 1 May the five transportees were heavily ironed and under armed guard placed in the Portsmouth coach for transfer to the *Guildford* at Spithead. When on the Tuesday morning their wives applied at Newgate to say goodbye, they were brusquely informed that their husbands 'were gone'. Most of the men were in their twenties and all had children. Harrison's and Wilson's wives went to Portsmouth to say goodbye, bearing with them the news that Hall had betrayed them.[30] The boat took the men and 200 other convicts to Botany Bay. Landing in September, Wilson was sent to Van Dieman's Land (Tasmania) on a sentence of twenty-one years; the other four went for life to New South Wales.

That left Thistlewood, Brunt, Ings, Tidd, and Davidson.

The traditional sentence for treason was horrific. It had been enunciated in full and its symbolism explained by Sir Edward Coke in his Gunpowder Plot judgement of 1606. The meaning of the crown's disproportionate attack on the traitor's body was established through bodily symbols and metaphors. Since it was 'the physic of state and government, to let out corrupt blood from the heart', it followed that the traitor should be 'drawn' to execution on a sledge across bare ground

> as being not worthy any more to tread upon the face of the earth whereof he was made: also for that he hath been retrograde to nature, therefore is he drawn backward at a horse-tail. And whereas God hath made the head of man the highest and most supreme part, ... he must be drawn with his head declining downward, and lying so near the ground as may be, being thought unfit to take the benefit of the common air.

Then he should be 'strangled, being hanged up by the neck between heaven and earth, as deemed unworthy of both, or either'. Cut down alive, his privy parts were to be cut off and burnt before him 'as being unworthily begotten, and unfit to leave any generation after him. His bowels and inlay'd parts taken out and burnt, who inwardly had conceived and harboured in his heart such horrible treason. After, to have his head cut off, which had imagined the mischief.' The then quartered body was to be set on high 'to the view and detestation of men, and to become a prey for the fowls of the air'.

By the 1790s one element in this ritual was regarded as intolerable. The quartering of the traitor's body was remitted for the Irish rebels James O'Coigley in 1798 and Robert Emmet in 1803, for the seven Despard conspirators in 1803, and for the Pentrich luddites, Brandreth, Turner, and Ludlam in Derby, in November 1817. The ignominy of being 'drawn' to the scaffold on a hurdle was also remitted for the Cato Street men, though only to avoid what the home secretary demurely termed 'inconvenience'. He had rescue attempts in mind.

The removal of the heads which had 'imagined the mischief' was another matter. Decapitation also had its critics by now. 'Men could not be accustomed to look on such horrid sights without becoming hardened and insensible,' the whig Samuel Romilly said in parliament in 1814, as he and Samuel Whitbread tried to limit the treason punishment to hanging alone. Alas, their bill was torpedoed by the timeless law-and-order riposte of the Pittite MP Charles Yorke. How extraordinary it was, Yorke exclaimed, that men 'should feel all the pity for those culprits whom the [Treason Acts] meant to curb and control; and none at all for the evils which the public might suffer if they were not in existence. … How many houses would be burned – how many murders perpetrated – how many rapes committed', if men got away with treason? These costs should not be forgotten out of 'commiseration of the criminals'.[31]

Abbott would have agreed. This entity was an archetype of the 'sable bigots' and 'furred homicides' that the whig Dr Parr referred to when he described the judges.[32] 'Cold, slow, parchment and precedent men without passions or *praecordia* [heart]' was the whig wit Sydney Smith's view of his kind. Abbott's friends described him as sour, pedagogic, overbearing, harsh, morose, and violent. He was said to hate the self-indulgence of Romantic poetry, and would have no regrets about what ensued. Deep into the age of sensibility and reason he wanted still to degrade the traitor by fully enacting the body metaphors of past times.

On Friday, 28 April, with a rare show of emotion, which might have expressed sadistic excitement, he explained why and how the remaining five conspirators must die. They had intended 'to have steeped their hands in the blood of fourteen persons, to many of them unknown – a crime of a character so black, that it was hitherto without parallel in the history of this country – (*his lordship here seemed considerably agitated*)'. It remained only to pronounce sentence on Thistlewood, Brunt, Ings, Tidd, and Davidson in the old-fashioned way:

> that you, each of you, be taken hence to the goal from whence you came, and from thence that you be drawn on a hurdle to a place of execution, and be there hanged by the neck until dead; and that afterwards your heads shall be severed from your bodies, and your bodies divided into four quarters, to be disposed of as his majesty shall think fit.

This anachronistic pronouncement was a wretched protest at modernity. It obliged the new king next day to go through the formality of respiting a public quartering that everyone knew couldn't happen. His majesty would, however, be required to order the heads off and held up to the crowd.

As it happened, the king's one and only virtue was that he didn't like ordering convicted felons to be killed. At the last recorder's report in March, at which meeting the monarch and his privy council ticked off who to hang and who to 'pardon' (i.e. transport), the king had to take laudanum before proceeding to business, and then he proposed that everyone be pardoned. Sidmouth had protested at this so vehemently that the king allowed six of the seventy-seven death sentences handed down to be ticked off for execution – decisions of this kind usually taking a minute or so each. The king didn't think twice about despatching the Cato Street men, however, though it took two hours on Saturday afternoon before he signed his warrant dispensing with the quartering but allowing the beheading.[33]

A few days after the sentencing, an unsigned satire entitled *A May Day Garland for 1820* was published by Fores of Piccadilly (Fig. 16.2). It looks like one of the Cruikshanks' works. Ministers, judges, and a masked executioner (his back to us and a surgeon's knife between his teeth)

16.2. Anon., *A May Day Garland for 1820* (Fores, May 1820) (© The Trustees of the British Museum)

dance with joy round a maypole on which are impaled the five conspirators' heads, two recognisable from side-whiskers and skin colour. On the
hangman's right Castlereagh cavorts with the attorney general Gifford
(in black robes and wig). Sidmouth is on the hangman's left, facing
Canning and Abbott (in wig and robe). On a hill behind, Edwards fiddles
and cries 'Dance away my Friends, I have been the cause of all this fun by
your Help and Money – Edwards the Instigator!!!' The artist's attitude is
unclear. A grim joke at the radicals' expense may be intended, since the
print quotes ironically from one of Spence's satirical tokens of the 1790s
(see Fig. 5.2). This shows four radicals dancing round a king's head
impaled (on a 'TREE OF LIBERTY'. On its reverse the token states, 'WE
WERE BORN FREE AND WILL NEVER DIE SLAVE[S]'.

CHAPTER 17

May Day at Newgate

THE CROWD

After chief justice Abbott had delivered their death sentences on Friday, 28 February, the five condemned men were shackled and taken from the Old Bailey courtroom, along the enclosed passage to Newgate, across the prison's quadrangle for male felons, and down a further passage to the condemned cells at the rear of the prison, where they would live two days longer. The Rev Cotton got to work on them but was rebuffed by all but Davidson. On the Sunday afternoon the wives were allowed an hour each for a last visit.

Cobbett described the accommodation:

> The cells are by the side of a long, dark, arched passage, which has a feeble lamp glimmering at each end of it. Out of this horrid cavern you go to each cell, which is very small, which is lighted by a little faint lamp, and which has a little hole in the wall against the passage, to let in air. The walls are several feet thick of stone, bound together with iron. The door [is] of massy iron.

The cells were 'beastly', the radical freethinker Haley wrote from inside knowledge in 1824: the food was bread, water, and gruel, and the condemned were 'half devoured by vermin of the most loathesome description'. By day the condemned had access to the press-yard, a gloomy space flanked by blank stone walls topped with spikes, where a century earlier felons had been forced to plead by pressing them with weights. A gate of iron bars permitted prisoners to communicate with friends across a short passage terminated by another barred gate, guarded by turnkeys.[1]

Outside Newgate a triangle of open ground had been opened up in 1770 when 'Little' Old Bailey and its houses were demolished for the prison's rebuilding. In 1783 executions were moved from Tyburn to the Newgate debtors' door facing this space. On Sunday the Cato Street condemned could hear carpenters hammering the scaffold together and setting up barricades round the platform. This was to control the crowds and to ensure that they wouldn't hear the conspirators' last speeches. The standard scaffold had to be enlarged to make space for the decapitations.

Tumult and riot were expected. In 1803, recall, an 'immense crowd' outside Horsemonger Lane prison south of the Thames had applauded Despard as he made his last speech on the scaffold. 'Those who had been in dry situations were pushed into the middle of the road, where they stood up to their knees in mud. . . . While the heads were exhibiting, the populace took off their hats.' The crowd had been ringed by soldiers and Southwark had swarmed with constables and Life Guards. The keeper of the prison had a 'sky-rocket' to let off as a signal to the military in case of disturbance. Similarly, when Bellingham was hanged for assassinating the prime minister Spencer Percival in 1812, some of the watching crowd had cried 'God bless you!' Five thousand troops were held ready near Lambeth and several country regiments advanced towards London. When Turner, Ludlam, and Brandreth were hanged and decapitated for the Pentrich rising in 1817,

> troops of horse, with keen and glittering swords, hemmed in the multitudes collected to witness this abominable exhibition. When the stroke of the axe was heard, there was a burst of horror from the crowd. The instant the head was exhibited, there was a tremendous shriek set up, and the multitude ran violently in all directions, as if under the impulse of sudden frenzy. Those who resumed their stations, groaned and hooted.

And when James Wilson was hanged and decapitated for treason in Glasgow in 1820, the crowd of 20,000 was ringed by one of the biggest military displays the town had seen (but still the crowd cried 'Murder!' and 'Shame!').[2]

So shortly after dawn on May Day morning 1820, soldiers with six light artillery fieldpieces were stationed on the Surrey side of Blackfriars Bridge, ready to move forward as the ceremony began. 'Helmets, bayonets, and falchions gleamed on every side,' the *Black Dwarf* reported.

A troop of Life Guards was stationed next to the scaffold and two more troops were lined up in Ludgate Street and Bridge Street, and a detachment occupied Giltspur Street Compter (gaol). The City Light Horse were kept under arms in their Gray's Inn Lane barracks, and a civil force of 700 men from the City wards was mustered. Placards were prepared to announce that the Riot Act had been read, should they be needed.[3]

A crowd began to assemble from five in the morning and gradually swelled into one of the biggest London had seen. 'All the house-tops were covered with spectators,' wrote the dandy Thomas Raikes from his privileged viewpoint; 'and when we first looked out of the window of the sheriffs' room, there was nothing to be seen but the scaffold, surrounded by an immense ocean of human heads, all gazing upon that one single object.'[4] Estimates were unreliable, but every account put the crowd at 100,000. The space before the debtors' door couldn't have held such numbers, but spectators stretched far distant from the scaffold – from Ludgate Hill to the Old Bailey and then Giltspur Street, back down Fleet Lane, and along Newgate and Skinner Streets. Every suitable window and rooftop was paid for and occupied, and distant streets were lined with wagons and carts on which people paid for standing room that gave the merest glimpse of the scaffold. At Holloway's and Haggarty's hanging for murder in 1807 thirty spectators in a crowd of 45,000 were crushed to death. On the present occasion the barriers prevented a similar catastrophe, but women were brought out fainting and the railings of St Sepulchre's church collapsed under the weight of people standing on them. Sixteen people were injured; two with arms broken and one with a broken leg.

The most dynamic image of the Cato Street executions was produced on 16 May by George Thompson of Long Lane (Fig. 17.1). Like his similar prints of the Smithfield meeting and of Peterloo, it draws on the broadside tradition. Architectural and human detail is symbolically handled and the remote crowd crudely sketched. But it quivers with noise and energy. Stave-wielding constables surround the scaffold, dragoons on horseback control the centre, the roofs are thick with people, and each of the hanged is named and labelled. Thistlewood's side-whiskered head is held up by the hangman at the front of the scaffold.

17.1. *The Execution of Thistlewood Ings, Brunt, Davidson and Tidd for High Treason* (Thompson, Long Lane, 16 May 1820) (Guildhall Library & Art Gallery/Heritage Images/Getty Images)

In respectable circles the plebeian crowd was unfailingly vilified for its barbarism. And it was true that fellow feeling for scaffold victims was easily numbed in a citizenry as familiar with cruel punishment as London's was. Between 1801 and 1820 anyone hungry for morbid sensation could have witnessed 311 hangings at Newgate and a few more at Horsemonger Lane in Surrey.[5] Some thought the 'mob' so accustomed to hangings that on May Day 1820 half of them came only for the beheadings.[6]

But elite commentators needed to peddle misinterpretations and projections of this kind. The crowd deployed far more diverse languages than its betters could understand – let alone achieve themselves. In most if not all cases, its hisses, cries, protests, silences, and profanities had critical meanings, like those of a Greek chorus. They didn't speak in assent. It says something about the complexities of popular feeling that within an hour of the Cato Street beheadings masked chimney sweeps and milkmaids made rough music as they cavorted round a walking hedge or 'Jack-in-the-Green' to celebrate their annual May Day festival. Princess Lieven was astonished that the streets around Newgate filled with 'drums and people in masks ... dancing at every corner'. Far from signifying insensitivity, however, these antique displays might be better read in context as cynical or parodic comments on the carnival just staged by the high people – a ritual of urban purification and a return to normality on the street people's terms.[7]

Spectators at executions weren't all plebeian. The crowd Thackeray described at the murderer Courvoisier's execution in 1840 included 'mechanics, gentlemen, pickpockets, members of both Houses of Parliament, street-walkers, newspaper-writers' – and novelists like himself and Dickens. He saw 'many young dandies ... with mustachios and cigars, some quiet, fat, family parties of simple honest tradesmen and their wives'. Children too. On May morning 1820 young Renton Nicholson played truant from school and paid fourpence for a space on a coal wagon by St Sepulchre's church. 'We had a good view,' he wrote. He remembered the dripping heads held up by the hangman and claimed that they 'saddened and sickened' him; but he 'made holiday all the morning' nonetheless.[8]

Privileged gentlefolk attended the Cato Street men's demise as well, driven by what Thackeray regarded as 'the hidden lust after blood which influences our race', but which they thought of as manly curiosity. Byron had watched criminal decapitations in Rome because he was 'determined to *see* – as one should see every thing once – with attention'.[9] In this spirit young aristocrats like Lord Alvanley, friend of the regent and Beau Brummel, claimed the best views of the Cato Street executions from inside Newgate itself. As practised surveyors of form they were granted the right to follow the sheriffs to the condemned cells and to assess the demeanours of the condemned as their shackles were removed in the press-yard (Fig. 17.2). Then they would adjourn to the keeper's or sheriff's windows for the best view over the scaffold.

Thistlewood was brought into the press-yard first. He bowed to the aristocrats and said that the weather appeared fine and that he had never felt better. Alderman Wood stepped forward and asked him when and how he first met Edwards and what he thought of him. Ignoring the sheriff's

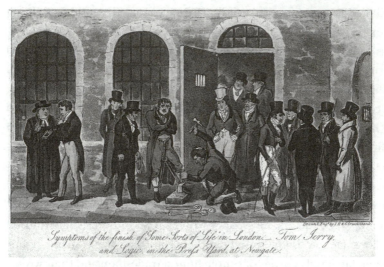

17.2. George and Isaac Robert Cruikshank, *Tom, Jerry and Logic in the Press Yard at Newgate* (1821) (Ann Ronan Pictures/Print Collector/Getty Images)

protest, Wood took detailed notes. Richard Tidd came next. 'Well, Mr. Thistlewood, how do you do?' he asked as his irons were knocked off. 'Never better,' Thistlewood replied as they shook hands. Then James Ings. He wore his butcher's slaughtering clothes, 'a rough pepper and salt coloured worsted jacket, and a dirty cap' – this to prevent the hangman from collaring his best clothes once he was dead. In the condemned cell the night before he had 'wished that his body might be conveyed to the king, and that his majesty, or his cooks, might make turtle soup of it'. Now he danced into the press-yard as best his shackles allowed, fell silent for a while, then began to laugh and shout. He wasn't drunk, we're informed. Someone told him to be firm. 'Firm!' he exclaimed: 'I am firm; but we have children, Sir!'[10] Brunt came next, subdued and composed. 'All will soon be well,' he said to his companions. Davidson came last, weeping and praying.

Thistlewood refused the wine offered to him, but Tidd and Brunt each took a glass. Tidd asked for an orange to suck; the others got one too. They clasped them in their pinioned hands as they were led onto the scaffold. All except Davidson dismissed the Rev. Cotton when he offered his spiritual assistance. Four declared themselves deists to the end, and Ings refused to 'have anything to do with any man who feared God or the devil, heaven or hell, or who went to church and chapel'. Then the high-born spectators adjourned to the keeper's and sheriffs' rooms. Lord Alvanley had invited Thomas Raikes to join him. It was Raikes's first ever execution. Afterwards, shocked, he swore he'd never go to another.[11]

Outside, the rooms and windows overlooking the scaffold were rented by monied people for two or three guineas each. The French artist Théodore Géricault and friends were almost certainly at one window, the tragic actor Edmund Kean at another. Géricault was sketching, and Kean was preparing for his role as Richard III on the following evening. 'I mean to die like Thistlewood tonight,' he said just before he next took the stage; 'I'll imitate every muscle of that man's countenance.'[12] Mrs Arbuthnot, the presiding dame of high tory society, wrote that her brother Cecil Fane took his window from 'curiosity', wishing 'very much to see how [the men] w^d behave'. In the event he couldn't bear to watch, and this 'excited great contempt in the people who were in the room with him'. The more typical reaction, Mrs Arbuthnot reported, was that of the pretty young lady who 'kept her eyes fixed on it all the time &, when they had hung a few seconds, exclaimed, "There's two on them not dead yet!!"'[13]

The scaffold outside the prison was hung with black cloth. Five rough-hewn elm coffins were lined up behind the waiting nooses, and a block of wood at the head of the first coffin awaited the first head. Heaps of sawdust were levelled out to absorb the blood. Then one by one each man was led onto the scaffold to his allotted place under the beam, and the noose was put over his head and his hands tied behind him.[14]

Thistlewood was led to the beam first and alone. The *Examiner* reported:

> He walked up the ladder with a firm step. His appearance had not changed
> since his trial. The same evidence of a dissatisfied mind was observable in
> his countenance. He looked around without curiosity. The executioner
> proceeded to fasten the rope round his neck, and Thistlewood assisted,
> but without ostentation. Mr Cotton approached, and spoke to him upon
> the religious subject. Thistlewood shook his head, and said he required no
> earthly help upon that subject. He then sucked his orange, and looking
> down at the officers who were collected about the scaffold said, in a firm
> voice, 'I have but a few moments to live, and I hope the world will be

convinced that I have been sincere in my endeavours, and that I die a friend to liberty'.

In his *Authentic History* Wilkinson confirmed that he showed no fear of death and looked as he always looked: 'Thistlewood with the rope round his neck was the same Thistlewood that appeared so conspicuous at Smithfield.' He refused to have the cap pulled over his face.[15]

Tidd, next, *ran* up the ladder. He was greeted with applause and 'huzzas!' He bowed to the people, smiled at the coffins, and instructed the hangman that the noose's knot would be better on the right of his neck rather than the left, since the pain of dying might be less there. To Thistlewood he complained about Cotton's 'breaking in upon their last moments.'

Then Ings 'bounded onto the platform'. His showy defiance parodied the great gallows tradition of the 'game' death, but there was hysteria in it. As he crossed to his place he laughed, taunted, cavorted, and bowed to the crowd, shouting to someone taking notes, 'Mind, I die an enemy to all tyrants. Mind, and write that down!' – then bellowing, 'Each true-born Briton's song shall be, O give me death or liberty!' He laughed at the coffins and said, 'I'll turn my back upon death! Is this the gallows they always use? Those coffins are for us, I suppose.' Tidd rebuked him: 'Don't, Ings. There is no use in all this noise. We can die without making a noise.' But as the executioner approached him with his noose, Ings called out, 'Do it well – pull it tight!' – 'give me a better fall' – adding that 'the others won't have fall enough'. 'Here I go, James Ings!' he shouted near the end, 'and let it be known that I die an enemy to all tyrants. Ah ha! I see a good many of my friends are on the houses.' Then he laughed and said to the ordinary, 'Well, I hope, Mr Cotton, you'll give a good character of me when I am off.' He called to Tidd: 'Come my old cock-o'-wax, keep up your spirits; it all will be over soon.'

When Davidson was brought up his step was steady; after bowing to the crowd he joined Cotton in prayer. Brunt arrived calmly and ignored Cotton. 'His eyes sent forth glances of great keenness; his lips were firmly compressed together; not a tear trickled down his cheeks; there was no quaking of the members.' He commented in mock surprise only on the number of soldiers before him: 'What! Soldiers! What do they here? I see nothing but a military government will do for this country.'

As they awaited their moment, a well-dressed man on one of the roofs opposite shouted to Thistlewood, 'God bless you! God Almight bless you!' 'Thistlewood slowly turned his head ... without moving his body, and as slowly reverted to his former position, always with the same fixed impassible countenance.' His last words were: 'We shall soon know the last grand secret.' 'Aye, to be sure,' Brunt said: 'It is better to die free, than to live as slaves!' 'Come, old man, finish us tidily,' Ings said to the executioner. The caps were pulled down, the executioner left the scaffold, the crowd was hushed, the drop fell.

> Thistlewood struggled slightly for a few minutes, but each effort was more faint than that which preceded. Tidd scarcely moved after the fall. The struggles of Ings were great. The assistants of the executioner pulled his legs with all their might; and even then there were vehement efforts on every part of the body. Davidson, after three or four heaves, became motionless. Brunt suffered extremely; but in the course of five minutes all was still.[16]

Women shrieked and men groaned. 'God bless you,' and 'Bring out Edwards!' and 'It was Monument brought you to this!' they shouted. And to the hangman: 'Shoot that—murderer!'

The bodies were left to hang for half an hour before the drop was returned to its closed position. The executioner returned and placed the dead men, still suspended, in a sitting position. He cut down Thistlewood first and laid him in his coffin with his shoulders resting on its upper end. The cap was removed from the face: 'the last convulsions had thrown a purple hue over the countenance, which gave it a most appalling appearance, but no violent distortion of feature had taken place' (*Examiner*). Then a masked man stepped forward. He had a handkerchief over his lower face and a black mask over his eyes, and he wore a sailor's jacket and trousers. The *Black Dwarf* thought he was the man who had beheaded Despard in 1803; others said he was a resurrection-man. He might have been the Mr Webb, surgeon of Cold Bath Fields prison, who after the executions was listed in the treasury solicitor's account ledger as having been paid £25 7s 6d for unexplained services.

According to the *Examiner* the executioner offered the man a new axe.[17] Fairburn reported that 'he declined using it, and cut off the head with a large knife in about four cuts'. He bungled the first operation: the knife was turned by Thistlewood's vertebrae in a replay of Despard's similarly bungled decapitation in 1803.[18] 'When the crowd perceived the knife applied to the throat of Thistlewood, they raised a shout, in which exclamations of horror and of reproach were mingled.' The head was handed to the executioner, who held it up and proclaimed, 'This is the head of Arthur Thistlewood – a traitor.' 'A thrilling sensation was produced on the spectators by the display of this ghastly object, and hissings and hootings of a part of the mob were vehemently renewed.' Or as the *Courier* put it, 'the crowd proved its evil spirit by hissing, groaning, and crying out, "murder, murder, murder"'. Tidd's head followed. It was held up by the cheeks because it was bald. Davidson's head 'remained in death exactly what it had been while he lived'; but as blood fell from it 'the hisses and groans of the crowd were repeated'. 'The rush of blood at each decapitation was so great, that the end of the scaffold had the aspect of a slaughter house.'[19] Men cried out 'murder, murder, murder'. The five heads and bodies were crammed into the coffins behind, and taken into the prison for burial in quicklime.

An hour later the lord mayor sent word to the home office that although there had been a little shouting and some 'transitory dissatisfaction expressed at the decapitation', the executions had 'for the most part taken place in perfect quietness', and 'on the whole there has seldom been a more tranquil execution witnessed'. This evaded the condition that might have explained it: 'the Troops were so dispersed that in whichever way the populace approached to the Old Bailey, they must be seen in force sufficient to deter any attempts at rescue'.[20]

The Cato Street trials and executions dealt revolutionist radicalism a death blow, though not radicalism itself. When first announced, the arrests had amplified the trauma of Peterloo and reverberated across the West Riding of Yorkshire and the Scottish border and midlands, where a general strike ended in more hangings and decapitations. In London, Abel Hall reported that although 'the people' hoped something might be done, they were 'out of spirits [and] all think it is over'. Thistlewood's fate and Hunt's conviction and imprisonment after Peterloo had 'stagnated them and there is no leader among them now'.[21]

What was left was a seething resentment. As the repeated calls for Edwards showed, many and perhaps most in the crowd perfectly understood the iniquity of the killings. Three weeks after the executions two medical students were seen carrying a severed head from St Thomas's hospital to dissect at their lodgings. It was assumed that one had to be the knifeman. 'Both were beat most dreadfully, and it will be months before thay can leave their lodgings, as the villains attempted to cut off their testicles'.[22]

Dozens of anonymous letters were sent to Sidmouth as well, both before and after May Day:

> My Lord your end draweth nie the morning of execution is not far off you have hired spys and now there are spyes upon the look out for the heads of two or three of the greatest monsters that ever disgraced human nature you may think perhaps to elude the vigelance of the persuers but you shall fall as sure as that the Globe on which we live shall desolve and your impious heads shall be exebited to an infuriated populace.

And:

> Thomas Keneadey and Company declares that they will take the first opportunity to put an end to Lord Sidmouth and Lord Castlereagh and the king as they are a damnable set of raskels . . . [they] gave Edwards, their damnable spy, twenty pounds a piece for the light [life] of Thistelwood and we have about eighty of us in the gang and we declare that the first opportunity that there is we will do the job as we don't mind dying as we can die but once, so beware of your guard as we are in strict watch for you all.

As has been well put, decapitating conspirators was one thing, but dismantling a deep-rooted radical culture was a more difficult thing entirely, as the rest of the century would show.[23]

A BRIEF HISTORY OF SYMPATHY

How past people felt and how we might feel about the outcome of Cato Street's history are questions not easily answered in a summary. The Cato Street executions occurred on the cusp of that great cultural or attitudinal shift whose sources, timing, and ambiguities I discussed in my book, *The Hanging Tree*. Compassion for the cruelly dead has as ancient a history as the sadistic excitement of the aristocratic barbarians who went to executions. But socially induced and approved emotions aren't static entities; they have histories, so that past attitudes sometimes seem those of a foreign country, while present-day emotions and attitudes would be unintelligible to past people. Not every social group acquires empathy; many cultures couldn't and can't afford to do so. But today, at best if not worst, a learned capacity to feel the suffering of others combines with bodily squeamishness to make even reading about, let alone watching, cruelties like that May Day horror next to unbearable.

On May Day 1820, however, there was little public evidence of any such response in polite culture. Only the whig-radical *Morning Herald* denounced 'the barbarous and inhuman butchery of the lifeless corpse' as 'the offspring of irrational barbarian vengeance, ... a horrid anomaly in the escutcheon of a humane and civilised nation, ... a relic of that heathenish spirit of revenge, so contrary to the genius of the Christian faith'. How could it be supported 'by men who can think and feel'? The dominant opinion pointed elsewhere. The *Morning Chronicle* hoped never again to witness such a spectacle, but was chiefly disappointed to see women among the spectators. The tory *Morning Post*, silent about the violence, instead eulogised the ministers whom the 'monsters' had planned to slaughter and stressed the crowd's acquiescence in the traitors' deaths and the 'unheroic' grimaces of the dying men. In his *Authentic History*, G. T. Wilkinson ground out the view that the radicals were 'sanguinary and designing men, who traverse the country, intruding themselves into all classes of society, with specious plans of reform in their mouths, but, in reality, with revolution, massacre, and plunder in their hearts'. He added that 'the abandonment of the duties of our holy religion alone' explained why some were 'wicked enough to conceive, and others so weak as to assist in, such preposterous and atrocious schemes'.[24] All the polite papers ritually deplored the 'thoughtless levity' of the 'mob', even though it was the mob whom the spectacle upset most, levity being the last thing it felt, except hysterically. This strange projection of guilt onto the populace was repeated by the respectable all the way down to the abolition of public execution in 1868. The mob got the blame, not the comfortable people who endorsed the procedure. This is still true.

Gentlewomen's reactions followed these cues. The tory hostess Mrs Arbuthnot thanked God that 'the world was rid of such monsters' – 'monsters' a fashionable word after *Frankenstein*'s publication two years earlier. 'Horrible' was what Mrs Piozzi thought of the men's behaviour on the scaffold: 'a fearful exhibition of black-guardism and brutality exceeded only by that of the mob that cheered them'. This from the lady who, after the aborted Spa Fields trial in 1817, opined that only gentlemen should be treated as traitors: 'What a piece of work has been made with these housebreakers and street ruffians, to turn them into gentlemen, and try them for high treason!' Princess Lieven nearly broke ranks. She thought the conspiracy 'monstrous' when she first heard about it, and might even have attended the execution. Immediately afterwards she wrote to Metternich: 'Do not imagine that I regret the fate of Thistlewood', but then added,

I feel pity for these poor human beings, for these aberrations of mind and imagination. I do not believe in the existence of a human being evil at heart; that would be to doubt the Creator. A false exaltation – such is the motive of crime. Why did Brant [she meant Ings] die crying, 'Long live liberty!'? Why did that emotion dominate him at the moment of saying good-bye? Even in him the emotion is not criminal.

Still, it was predictable that a high-born woman who was happy about Thistlewood's death and puzzled why Ings called for liberty should write to her brother a few days later that she and her friends were 'one and all going on well here: at any rate nobody is conspiring, and everyone is on amusement bent'.[25] So much for the delicacies of Jane Austen's England.

One who did break ranks was a humbler man, a Manchester weaver with a political interest in doing so. About to be imprisoned for encouraging 'riotous behaviour' at Peterloo, Samual Bamford, then in London, was disgusted by the executions and kept his distance from them. On the fatal morning 'I remained in my room, earnestly praying God to sustain them in their last hour. . . . At noon, when it was all over, I came down stairs. The execution was soon the subject of conversation in every place, and I soon heard . . . the particulars of the disgusting trans-action.' Two of his friends had hired a window to watch it. Bamford told one of them that 'he was welcome to the gratification such a scene could afford; for my part, I would not have gone on any account'. The friend replied that 'he went merely from curiosity, to see how such things were done'.[26]

Countless voices as sympathetic as Bamford's doubtless pass unre-corded, but the public evidence of a shift in emotional repertoires was smothered by commentators' political interest or ability to dissociate themselves from the horror. For the strongest evidence of movement in the history of feeling at this point one must turn to a different kind of source, an artistic work which betrayed new attitudes more clearly.

Regard what follows as an epilogue, because it alters the book's register and breathes air into our stifling subject. It is with Géricault's drawing of the Cato Street execution that we end.

CHAPTER 18

Epilogue: Géricault Goes to Cato Street

At an early point during Théodore Géricault's first visit to London in 1820, he sketched a scene in pencil and sepia wash which he valued enough to preserve but not to finish or protect (Fig. 18.1). It's now stained by spilled water. Unknown in its own time and hardly known in ours, it extends what was artistically thinkable in that era, and in that sense it was the most interesting work he attempted in London. For the first time in western art history a drawing engaged honestly with the frightful intimacies of a public hanging without moralising or piety, or making the punishment symbolise something other than itself. It sketched the last minutes of three of the Cato Street conspirators. The other two men, we must imagine, would follow them onto the platform within minutes.

Behind the two men facing us on the left is the faint silhouette of the dome of St Paul's; so the scaffold is outside Newgate. Their hands are tied and nooses encircle their necks. A white-haired clergyman and a top-hatted hangman attend them, both seen from the rear. On the far right, lightly sketched, a grieving woman is supported by officials. The hangman pulls a hood over the head of one of the condemned; his eyes are closed and his lips open. Above and behind him the shadowed shape of the assistant hangman adjusts his noose on the beam. In the middle of the three a neatly dressed man is already noosed and hooded. He stands demurely, hands before him. The man on the left gives the drawing its emotional force. His cap has yet to be rolled down over his face. Wearing

18.1. Théodore Géricault, *Scene of a Hanging in London* (1820)
(© Musée des Beaux-Arts de Rouen)

a long coat and wide pantaloons, he parts his legs to steady himself. His bound hands are clasped as if in prayer, but he isn't praying. He ignores the clergyman's exhortations and stares past him, at us. His face is swarthy, his eyes deep-set and darkly circled. His stare draws us into his experience. The sheet on which this is drawn is too big to handle in an excited crowd. At 408 by 322 millimetres it is larger than modern A3 paper. It was probably drawn from a window a hundred or more yards away, even though it is imagined close-to. Unfinished, it was an artist's pencilled note to himself; brown washes were applied later.

There has been doubt about its subject matter. Géricault failed to date the drawing, or give it a title, or develop it further. His few surviving letters mention neither a London hanging nor Newgate. He merely added it to the sketches and notebooks he took back to Paris. When he fell off his horse and died from a tubercular infection in his thirty-third year, in 1824, the chance of further information died with him. It was his pupil P.-F. Lehoux who much later inscribed his own title on the drawing, 'Le supplice' (the 'torment' or 'agony'), adding the catalogue number given to it by Géricault's first biographer Charles Clément in 1867. Neither Lehoux nor Clément identified the doomed men, and Clément's catalogue raisonné dated the drawing vaguely: '1820–1824'. Only after Lehoux had bequeathed the artist's notebooks and drawings to the Rouen Museum of Fine Arts in 1882 did someone date it '1820' and name it in French as *Scene of a Hanging in London, or the Hanging of Arthur Thistlewood and his Accomplices*. Géricault's most recent and voluminous biographer, Germain Bazin, ignores this when he discusses the drawing; he mentions neither Thistlewood nor Cato Street. Still, if the Rouen curator's reference to Thistlewood was a guess, it was a good one.[1]

The obvious difficulties are that the drawing showed only three, not five, condemned men on the scaffold, and that it omitted the waiting coffins and noisy crowd.[2] Compare the sketch with Géricault's earlier works, and it can only be called reticent. This is odd because Géricault was the last man to shrink from the full horror of decapitation. He drew classical and coolly disengaged cameos of judicial beheadings in Rome in 1816–17, and in 1819 he collected ghastly hacked-off limbs and guillotined heads from the mortuaries and dissection rooms of the Beaujon and Bicêtre hospitals, and drew and painted them to prepare for his *Raft of the Medusa*.[3] If the drawing did depict the Cato Street men, popular prints recorded the scene more informatively.

But the last thing Géricault was interested in was factual reporting. His faint sketch of the grieving woman, for instance, may suggest that she is about to be hanged too, but it is more likely to be a fiction designed to deepen pathos in a later painting. (No woman was hanged at Newgate between April and July or November and December during his two London visits.) As for showing three men as distinct from five, no male threesome was hanged in 1820 (though four were in December). Each of the Cato Street condemned was brought out alone for his noosing and had to wait as the others followed. So there really was a moment when only Thistlewood, Tidd, and Ings were on the scaffold. The right-hand side of the drawing allows for the additions since the full extent of the gallows beam is not depicted. The clincher, however, is that if Géricault was to watch and sketch any execution in these months, it had to be this one.

He landed at Dover on 10 April 1820, and returned to Paris in June. He came back to London in November or December 1820, and stayed a year.[4] On his first visit he brought to London, rolled up, his great history painting *The Raft of the Medusa* – literally great: it measures five by seven metres.[5] Displayed at the Paris Salon in July 1819, its reception had been mixed. Its exposure of French naval incompetence was thought unpatriotic, and its Romantic agony and exuberant painterly manner defied the stranglehold in France of David's chilly classicism. It also made critics ask whether an unpleasant subject could ever result in great art – whether one could have a heroic painting that lacked a heroic subject, for 'the goal of painting is to speak to the soul and the eyes, not to repel', as one wrote.

Géricault was depressed by this reception. At the same time he was recovering from the scandal that had erupted over his affair with his thirty-year-old aunt and the birth of their child in 1818. He suffered a nervous collapse and spent time in a Paris clinic. In London, his friend Charlet reported (unreliably) that he tried to commit suicide.[6] True or not, it was in a fragile mood that he arrived to exhibit *The Raft* in William Bullock's Egyptian Hall in Piccadilly. Bullock claimed that some 50,000 people paid a shilling each to see it, not least because it reminded the English that their navy was more competent, brave, and honourable than the French one. A 'tremendous picture of human suffering' with something of Michelangelo's severity and Caravaggio's gloom, the London critics said. Turner appropriated some of its elements in his *Battle of Trafalgar* and *Disaster at Sea*, and William Moncrieff staged a dramatic version at the Coburg Theatre. The exhibition netted the artist near on twenty thousand francs, a serious sum.[7]

Why, then, with the *Medusa* on his mind, should Géricault bother with Cato Street? The better question is, how could he not? His first visit began just over six weeks after the Cato Street arrests, a week before the trials opened in the Old Bailey, and three weeks before the executions. English treason executions were exotic and rare spectacles, quite as bloody as French guillotinings; and for curious people, as they were called, they were worth going to see. Moreover, the Cato Street trials and executions were more heavily reported than any of their predecessors. Géricault was exposed to a wealth of information about the drama – in Paris before his Dover landing on 10 April, and in London after it.

In Paris the *Journal des Débats Politiques et Littéraires* reported the Cato Street story extensively. It was the most widely read of the restoration newspapers. A very few days after the arrests the publisher Langlumé reproduced an English lithograph that illustrated the arrests above twenty-five lines of explanation in French.[8] Arriving in London as the trials began, Géricault would have seen more images. In the two months following the arrests a dozen or more prints of the Cato Street stable were published, and the conspirators' engraved portraits sold widely. Cruikshank's iconic depiction of the police attack appeared on 9 March (see Fig. 2.1). Géricault would have seen all or most of these prints. He habitually consulted popular prints for artistic cues and subjects. Since he would have read the newspapers too, it would have been impossible for him to ignore the Cato Street story, even with other matters in mind.

Géricault was in quest of a new and politically and emotionally supercharged subject, and Cato Street might have tempted him. In early 1818 he had produced sketches for a major painting on the apparently political murder of the liberal magistrate Fualdès, a brutal but puzzling case that had filled French newspapers for weeks and was reported in London too. When those plotters were convicted as thieves rather than as ultraroyalists, Géricault replaced the project with the *Medusa*.[9] One of his sketches for the Fualdès work had imagined the murderers conspiring before the crime, and a popular print had depicted the battered Rodez brothel in which Fualdès had been murdered. The Cato Street story echoed this. Like everyone else of his standing, Géricault would have regarded the conspiracy as atrocious, but he would also have known that it was moved by hunger and injustice and was probably broken by government spying and provocation. Cato Street was a liberty lover's subject.

Love of liberty and hatred of privilege and corruption were the political values that tied Géricault's art to its time.[10] Although he was the son of an affluent royalist, and had even served a couple of months in the royal musketeers after the Bourbon restoration in 1815, he fought to free himself from ancestral attitudes and regretted his moment of military folly when the Bourbons' despotic instincts revealed themselves. He had brief spells of training in the studios of Carle Vernet and Pierre Guérin, but private income allowed him independence, and he developed his classical style through his own study of antique and Renaissance models rather than David's fashionable neoclassicism. Even his own classicism he soon discarded in favour of 'natural' subjects with liberal subtexts. From 1813 onwards he repeatedly portrayed wounded or defeated soldiers in preference to heroic and victorious ones. He mixed with the Bonapartist artists and politicians in his friend Horace Vernet's circle, and Vernet at one point joined him in London, as did the artist Jean-Baptiste Isabey when the French police were after him for circulating seditious drawings. His *Medusa* became an icon of the liberal opposition.[11]

Either in London or later in Paris he sketched ambitious if aborted ideas for works on the slave trade and the liberation of the prisoners of the Spanish Inquisition. His expanding sympathies also shaped his erotica. Moving from the classicised mannerism of his Roman drawings towards a lusher and more explicit realism, they present a young man of passionate instincts and transgressive sexual experience.[12] In London, further, he was cared for by William Bullock. Bullock was a showman but also a man of enlightened views, a natural historian in his own right and a fellow of several learned societies. In London, too, Géricault's companion and friend, the artist Nicolas-Toussaint Charlet, was a declared republican. Charlet introduced Géricault to a fresh subject, London's street people. In 1821 both men produced lithographs illustrating the plight of the poor. Géricault's are the most humane of his English works. Altogether, Thistlewood's tragedy had the ambiguities and political loading he had been looking for, and what he learned about Thistlewood's tortured but not ungentlemanly soul might have reminded him of his own. If there was madness in Thistlewood there was madness in Géricault and his family also, and the subject fascinated him. In 1822 he was to paint ten portraits of inmates of the Salpêtrière asylum in Paris.

It's likely that he soon gave up the Cato Street theme, however. His hunger for a new heroic subject waned after the *Medusa* was completed, and the conspiracy's delusional nature became more apparent as the trials unfolded. Before coming to London he was already favouring small-scale works undertaken in what his biographer Eitner calls his 'little manner'. In London his notebooks filled with sketches of street people, horses and carriages: the hanging sketch stands out as an exception. He also planned to practise in London the new art of lithography, the secrets of which had been published in 1818. By 1821 he was dismissing history painting as 'beggar's work'.[13]

In any case London's high art world hardly encouraged flirtation with a story like Cato Street. There was no money in so contentious a subject. Other than Géricault and David Wilkie,[14] no artists of note gave it (or Peterloo) the slightest attention. The artist Joseph Farington dismissed the conspiracy as 'atrocious' when he and Smirke the architect discussed it on the day after its exposure. A few months later Farington and Sir Thomas Lawrence agreed that the times were fearful and that the 'object was revolution'; rumbustious popular support for Queen Caroline against her husband made Lawrence fear what the strumpet might do when supported by a headlong mob.[15] As president of the Royal Academy, Lawrence was wallowing in royal and aristocratic commissions. Soon to be taken up by Lawrence and his circle, Géricault would have checked all further thoughts about working on Cato Street, even if he hadn't done so already.

But that lay ahead. At the beginning there remains the extraordinary possibility, nowhere so far noticed, that he went to London not only to show the *Raft of the Medusa* but also to engage with the Cato Street drama. A report in the 6 May issue of the Paris journal *Le Conservateur littéraire* stated that he went to London to produce portraits of the country's 'most illustrious radicals'; it then mused that thanks to their executions he had been too late to portray Thistlewood and his 'honourable colleagues'.[16]

This report is endorsed by Géricault's eccentric choice of location for his lodgings. Continental artists visiting London after the 1815 Peace were most likely to lodge along the axis of the artistic city – either in Covent Garden or Soho, or above and below eastern Oxford Street, or if they could afford it in Pall Mall, Piccadilly, and St James's.[17] Yet Géricault chose to lodge off the beaten track in the terraces newly built on the eastern side of the Edgware Road. The district's expansion had been accelerated by the opening of the Paddington basin on the Grand Junction Canal in 1801, and its gentility was guaranteed by the planned estate of 'Tyburnia' and Connaught Square. It's possible that in the eyes of an artist with Géricault's interests coming to London in mid-April 1820 the neighbourhood would be distinguished partly by the availability of horse-riding in Hyde Park (Géricault's passion) – but also by the fact that it lay within Cato Street's force field.

Géricault lived as near to Cato Street as he could. At first he lodged at 39 Edgware Road with a master bootmaker and his family, who were genteel enough for him to make a delicate drawing of the wife and children which he later turned into a lithograph.[18] The house was three minutes' walk away from Cato Street, and Géricault was almost certainly living in it when he went to Newgate to watch the men lose their heads. It's unthinkable that he didn't know every last detail of the tragedy. On his second visit to London, in 1821, he even lodged with the fashionable horse-dealer Adam Elmore at 3 John Street.[19] Elmore's substantial house and stables were directly opposite Cato Street's narrow entrance and a stone's throw from the conspirators' stable. His host played a marginal if unwitting part in the Cato Street story. Thistlewood had visited Elmore's stables in early February 1820 to recruit the distressed Irish bricklayer Thomas Dwyer whom Elmore employed. Dwyer later testified that he had met Thistlewood and Davidson 'the black' in the Elmore stables and at the Horse and Groom opposite.[20]

Géricault and Elmore had horse-love in common. Elmore was England's greatest patron of steeple-chasing and had prospered by horse-dealing 'with the foreigners'.[21] Géricault designed a signboard for the Elmore stables, several times sketched Mr and Mrs Elmore on horseback, bought three expensive horses from Elmore, unpaid for when he died, and for Elmore painted his famous *Epsom Derby* (which Thistlewood's grandson engraved decades later).[22] Mrs Elmore was from a well-connected French family with artistic associations in Paris: Géricault's friend Delacroix lodged with the Elmores when he came to London in 1825.

Either way, Géricault must have known all about the Cato Street sensation while living with the Elmores opposite Cato Street. Since out of his thousand affordable options in London he twice lived next to Cato Street, he could hardly not have been moved, as we are all moved, by the pleasing illusion and quasi-mystical sense that engagement with past people's topographies helps one to understand their otherwise mystifying lives.

The final confirmation that Géricault attended and drew the Cato Street executions lies in the figure who stares out at us so terribly on the left of his drawing. Heavy-browed, with eyes dark-ringed and sunken eyes, and in overcoat and pantaloons – these distinctive features confirm the subject absolutely. Géricault knew that Thistlewood looked something like this even without setting eyes on him. Sidmouth's notice of 24 February, offering £1,000 for Thistlewood's capture after his escape the night before, described him as having dark eyes and heavily arched eyebrows and usually wearing 'a blue long coat and blue pantaloons', as in the drawing.[23] Géricault is likely also to have seen Wivell's portraits.

Thistlewood's staring eyes are the focus of the drawing, and carry its whole significance. The sketch's originality might have been more widely acknowledged had he engraved or painted it more fully. As it is, later commentators have belittled or ignored it. Eitner thinks that never before had the horrors of an execution been recorded 'so prosaically'. Another dismisses the drawing as 'somewhat detached and objective'; she prefers the 'sympathetic approach' of Géricault's London lithographs; only there, she thinks, does he 'border on involvement'. Bazin briefly noted that it wasn't the artist's best work.[24] None of these comments shows the slightest sense of context. Our tale points to a more positive meaning. Géricault here presents us with an icon of all people numbed and incredulous at their imminent endings, and also one that demonstrates the possibility in that unthinkable crisis of defiant personal strength.

Countless previous artists had depicted executions in high-flown history paintings of saints or martyrs flayed, pierced, or roasted in the grand manner, their piety inscribed on their radiant countenances. But these images had referred extraneously to belief systems that lay beyond the event, in an iconography of martyrdom in which the human pain, terror, and horror were negated. Even in secular works like Callot's horrific etchings in 1633 of the *Miseries of War* (and the eleventh plate's mass hanging from a tree), it was the collective horrors of war that were addressed rather than the agony of the individual hanged. This evasion was true of all the English execution images from Hogarth's down to Thomas Rowlandson's in the 1790s to 1810s. None was interested in the sufferers' emotion or knew how to convey it. Rowlandson drew hangings as quasi-comic episodes in the theatre of manners: he was more interested in the watching crowd, stereotypically and comically rendered, than in the victims.[25]

So far as intention goes, Géricault's uncompromisingly intimate drawing has only one equivalent in contemporary European art. It is Goya's *The Third of May 1808* (Fig. 18.2). Painted in 1814, this depicts the staring

18.2. Francisco Goya, *The Third of May 1808* (1814) (Prisma/UIG via Getty Images)

incredulity and terror of Madrileño rebels as they face a French firing squad after their 1808 rebellion. The critic Robert Hughes described it as the work 'against which all future paintings of tragic violence would have to measure themselves'. It had no influence on Géricault (or on any other work before Manet's *Execution of Maximilian* in 1868–9) because the Bourbon dynasts thought it so inflammatory that it was kept in storage for forty years.[26] Yet despite the yawning differences between Goya's finished work and Géricault's sketch, similarities in tone and purpose are unmistakable.

Two artists, geographically remote from each other but each shadowed by the greatest war then known to the western world, are appalled by the brutalities of power. Each turns voyeurism into honest witnessing, harnessing a cultivated sensibility to his task and achieving empathy with power's victims. In both works the agents of punishment – clergyman, hangman, firing squad – are seen from behind, both to diminish them and to reveal their emotional detachment. The victims are depicted face-on, their terror, contempt, or incredulity the dominant and empathetic point of each picture.

This inversion of the traditional pedestalisation of the general, statesman, or priest and devaluation of the sufferer is the key to both images' modernity. 'No glory; only pity and loss, and the defiant humanity of the victims,' as Hughes puts it. And if, as Hughes claims, Goya's was 'the first truly modern image of war, the first to register the machine-like efficiency of oppression', then Géricault's *Hanging* was the first intimately to confront and to feel the violence delivered on those who challenged the sovereign's might and law.[27] In that war-torn world grown so familiar with violence, each artist sought to see truly and to avoid cant. However mad, wicked, or misguided the suffering-other might be, both believed that sympathetic engagement with his or her plight was part of the artist's and indeed everyone's business.

The People Listed

(1) **1816–17** After the *Spa Fields insurrection* (2 December 1816), four
men are arrested and arraigned for treason; Watson's son escapes.
'Old' Watson is tried on 9–17 June 1817; he, Thistlewood, Preston,
and Hooper are discharged when the crown witness John Castle is
exposed as a spy.

'Dr' James Watson ('old' Watson) (1766–1838), apothecary, trained
as surgeon, born at Kirton, near Boston, Lincolnshire. Wife leaves
him. In London lives with four daughters and son ('young' James
Watson). Leading ultra-radical; avoids arrest in 1820 because
imprisoned for debt in Whitecross Street prison.

Arthur Thistlewood (1774–1820), son of tenant farmer, baptised in
Tupholme, near Horncastle, Lincolnshire. Leader of Cato Street
conspiracy. Married to Susan Thistlewood; one illegitimate son,
Julian.

Thomas Preston (1774–1850), born in London; shoemaker; wife
leaves him; lives with daughters; arrested February 1820 but discharged for want of evidence.

John Hooper (?–1817), shoemaker, dies of 'exhaustion' seven
months after arraignment for Spa Fields insurrection.

'Young' James Watson (1797–1823?), son of Dr Watson; surgeon-
apothecary; escapes to America after Spa Fields riots; *Observer*
(unreliably) reports his death in Kentucky from 'bilious fever'
in 1823.

(2) **1 May 1820** Five men are hanged and decapitated for treason:[1]
Arthur Thistlewood (as above); age forty-five at execution.

390

John Thomas Brunt (1774–1820), boot-closer, born in Retford, Nottinghamshire (or Union Street, London?); married to Mary, one son; age thirty-six at execution.

William Davidson (1787–1820), cabinet-maker, born in Kingston, Jamaica, or (according to Cobbett) Liverpool; married to Sarah, six children; age thirty-three at execution.

James Ings (1794–1820), butcher, born in Waltham, Hampshire; married to Celia, four children; age twenty-six at execution.

Richard Tidd (1773–1820), shoemaker, born in Grantham, Lincolnshire; married to Mary, one daughter; age forty-six at execution.

(3) Five Cato Street conspirators are sentenced to death but transported for life to New South Wales:

John Harrison (1786–1839), ex-Life Guardsman/baker, born in Derby; married to Caroline, three children; age thirty-four when transported.

Charles Cooper (1790–1866), bootmaker, then seaman, born in Durham; age thirty when transported.

Richard Bradburn (1791–1835), carpenter, born County Neath; married to Amelia, eight children; age twenty-nine when transported.

James Wilson (1793–1857), shoemaker/tailor/milkman, born in London; age twenty-seven when transported.

John Shaw Strange (1792–1868), shoemaker, born in Warwickshire; married to Mary, pregnant, with two children; twenty-eight when transported.t

(4) One Cato Street man has his death sentence respited and walks free several months after trials:

James Gilchrist (1787–?), shoemaker, born in Dundee; age thirty-three at trial.

(5) Arrested in 1820 but not tried for want of evidence; freed at end of the trials:

William Firth, cow keeper, member of Marylebone Union Reading Society; rented out Cato Street stable.

Robert George, seaman, arrested as about to escape to East Indies; becomes a government informer.

William Hazard (1760–?), schoolmaster; hosted Marylebone Union Reading Society in Queen Street next to Cato Street.

Thomas Preston (as above); 'was too late for the meeting in Cato Street' (spy report).[2]

(6) Not arrested in February 1820:

Dr James Watson (as above); in debtors' prison from early December 1819.

Robert Wedderburn (1762–1835/6?), Jamaican-born Spencean; imprisoned under Sidmouth's Six Acts, December 1819 – April 1820; then tried for blasphemous libel and sentenced to two years in Dorchester gaol.

Thomas Chambers, bootmaker, witness for the defence.

— Harris, typefounder, Finsbury; made bullets and pike-heads for Thistlewood; he and wife provide Thistlewood with hiding place on night of 23 February; Thistlewood arrested there in bed next morning.

(7) Conspirators arrested but who gave information or turned king's evidence and so not tried:

Robert Adams (born Ipswich, 1775), ex-Horse Guardsman and shoemaker, arrested 25 February; four children.[3] His information is the backbone of the prosecution's case.

Thomas Dwyer, Irish bricklayer, Gee's Court, Oxford Street, recruited by Davidson on 4 February; informed on the conspirators, 22 February.

Abel Hall, journeyman tailor, gave information in prison and became a government spy.

Thomas Hiden, milkman/cow keeper; a late recruit to the conspiracy.

John Monument, shoemaker, arrested in the hayloft and turned king's evidence.

William Simmons, footman, gave information.

(8) Cato Street conspirators known to have escaped:

John Palin, aged forty; arrested November 1820, interrogated and released.

William Cook, shoemaker; never found.

— **Potter**, never found.

(9) Spies:

'Oliver the Spy', real name W. J. Richards (?1774–1827), carpenter, builder, surveyor; informer and *agent provocateur* helpful in arrests of the Pentrich luddites, June 1817. Takes refuge in Cape Town; became inspector of buildings; buried in Green Point cemetery.

John Castle, born Yorkshire *c.* 1785. Met Watson 1816; joined Spenceans; prosecution witness in Watson's trial, June 1817, until exposed as pimp and spy: Watson acquitted, and prosecutions of Thistlewood, Preston and Hooper dropped.

George Edwards (1786?–1843), born in London, plaster-model–maker in Eton; in poverty returns to London in winter 1817/18; in 1818 becomes home office spy. Watson introduces him to Thistlewood in June 1819. After the trials he takes refuge in Guernsey and then in Cape Town, where he too is buried in Green Point cemetery.

(10) Government ministers:

George Canning (1770–1827), president of board of control 1816–22.

Viscount Castlereagh (1769–1822), Irish secretary 1798–1801; foreign secretary and leader of Commons.

Earl of Harrowby (1762–1847), lord president of privy council, 1812–27.

Earl of Liverpool (1770–1827), prime minister 1812–27.

Viscount Sidmouth (1757–1844), home secretary 1812–22.

[**Henry Hobhouse**, undersecretary at the home office and solicitor to the treasury 1817–27: not to be confused with John Cam Hobhouse, radical MP for Westminster 1820].

Duke of Wellington (1769–1852), victor of Waterloo 1815; master-general of the ordinance, 1819–27.

(11)   Key Spenceans and radicals:

Thomas Spence (1750–1814), born in Newcastle upon Tyne; moves to London 1788; agrarian socialist, radical writer and publicist; his writings more influential on some Regency ultra-radicals than Tom Paine's.

Richard Carlile (1790–1843), born in Devon, father a shoemaker; radical publisher and writer, edits *Weekly Political Register*, renamed *The Republican* August 1817; opens printshop at 55 Fleet Street, February 1819; on platform at Peterloo, August 1819; October 1819 tried for republishing Paine and sentenced to six years in Dorchester prison; returns to free-thinking publishing in London in 1825.

Thomas Evans (1763–1831); member, then secretary, of London Corresponding Society (LCS) 1793–8; imprisoned without trial 1793–1801 and again 1817–18; forms Society of Spencean Philanthopists upon Spence's death; supported by wife Janet and son; becomes a moderate radical.

Robert Wedderburn (1762–1835/6); born of slave mother in Jamaica; a radical Spencean, his Hopkins Street 'chapel' a centre of insurrectionary activity in 1819; imprisoned under Sidmouth's Six Acts, December 1819 to April 1820; then imprisoned for two years for blasphemous libel.

(12)   'Respectable' radicals:

Sir Francis Burdett, MP (1770–1844), whig-radical MP for Westminster 1807–37; parliamentary reformer.

William Cobbett (1763–1835), supports Burdett 1807; his *Political Register* published weekly 1802–35 (popular edition from 1816); flees to United States to avoid prosecution May 1817; returns in October 1819 bankrupt and out of favour with Henry Hunt, once his ally. Recovers reputation through Queen Caroline affair: increased circulation of the *Register*; *Rural Rides* (1830); parliamentary reform campaign 1830–2; MP for Oldham 1832–5.

'Orator' Henry Hunt (1773–1835), born of Wiltshire gentry; loyalist until he reads Cobbett and supports Burdett from 1805; 1812 defeated as 'people's candidate' in Bristol; Burdettite in City and Westminster politics until Watson and Thistlewood persuade him to address Spa Fields meetings December 1816; his evidence helps free Watson, Preston, and Thistlewood in 1817 treason trial; advises non-violent mass meetings for constitutional reform henceforth; on Peterloo platform August 1819, after which Watsonites give him triumphal entry to London, but he repudiates Watsonite violence; sentenced to thirty months' imprisonment for 'sedition' (at Peterloo) in March 1820.

Francis Place (1771–1854), radical tailor; LCS until 1797; prospers in wartime; active in Westminster politics as Burdettite until 1812, and again 1818–20.

John Thelwall (1764–1834), reformer, lecturer, poet; joins LCS 1793; imprisoned May–October 1793; tried for treason at Old Bailey and acquitted; returns to cause of parliamentary reform and edits the *Champion* 1818–22.

Alderman Matthew Wood (1768–1843); a consistent reformer; City alderman 1807, sheriff of London 1809, lord mayor 1816, MP for City of London 1817–43. In May 1820 calls in parliament for George Edwards's prosecution; champions Queen Caroline thereafter.

Historiographical Note

In the last four decades of the last century a dozen or more historians thoroughly surveyed England's radical cultures from the era of the French revolution through to the Chartist 1840s. Inspired in part by E. P. Thompson's *Making of the English Working Class* (1963), most of them were interested in the supposed onward march of labour or the supposed 'making' of working-class consciousness and militancy. None had much interest in the Cato Street conspiracy because it failed both projects. Also, as was the way then, the histories that encased the territory – of mentalities, images, song, topography, women, families, material culture – were under-valued.

Thus Thompson's *English Working Class* gave Cato Street no more than ten of its 958 pages, and this without examining home office papers and spy reports. John Belchem's exhaustive biography of *'Orator' Hunt: Henry Hunt and English Working-Class Radicalism* (1985) touched on Cato Street incidentally. Iain McCalman's *Radical Underworld: Prophets, Revolutionaries and Pornographers in London, 1795–1840* (1988) brilliantly excavated a scurrilous blackguard tradition of radical and utopian argument among London's disaffected plebeians, but it too mentioned the conspiracy briefly. So did Malcolm Chase's *The People's Farm: English Radical Agrarianism, 1775–1840* (1988) and David Worrall's *Radical Culture: Discourse, Resistance and Surveillance, 1790–1820* (Detroit, 1992); this last described radicalism's 'cultural settings' but gave the Cato Street story thirteen pages. Others also touched the subject lightly: I. J. Prothero, *Artisans and Politics in Early Nineteenth-Century London:*

John Gast and His Times (1979), 89–133; J. A. Hone, *For the Cause of Truth: Radicalism in London 1796–1821* (Oxford, 1982); J. A. Epstein, *Radical Expression: Political Language, Ritual and Symbol in England, 1790–1850* (Oxford, 1994).

By the later 1990s interest in the radical and labour history of this era was waning. Chase's single-year study of *1820: Disorder and Stability in the United Kingdom* (2013) returned to it, but again it gave Cato Street no more than eight core pages before attending more keenly to George IV's efforts to divorce Caroline. J. Gardner's *Poetry and Popular Protest: Peterloo, Cato Street and the Queen Caroline Controversy* (2011) addressed the literary responses to Peterloo and Cato Street but was derivative and under-informed on the conspirators. The conference essays in J. McElligott and M. Conboy (eds), *The Cato Street Conspiracy: Plotting, Counter-intelligence and the Revolutionary Tradition in Britain and Ireland* (Manchester, 2020) are concerned, the editors say, with 'broader issues' than the conspiracy, and particularly with 'the comparisons and contrasts between the underexplored British insurrectionary tradition and the history of Irish violence'.

Robert Poole's fine *Peterloo: The English Uprising* (Oxford, 2019), M. Bush's path-breaking *The Casualties of Peterloo* (Manchester, 2005), J. Riding's *Peterloo: The Story of the Manchester Massacre* (2018), and P. B. Ellis's and S. Mac A'Ghobhainn's *The Radical Rising: The Scottish Insurrection of 1820* (2016) have bypassed Cato Street more understandably. C. Parolin's *Radical Spaces: Venues of Popular Politics in London, 1790–c. 1845* (Canberra, 2010) and K. Navickas's *Protest and the Politics of Space and Place, 1789–1848* (Manchester, 2016) share the present book's interest in place, but Parolin astonishingly gives the Cato Street conspiracy no more than a footnote, while Navickas is mainly concerned with the northern industrial towns over sixty years. The popular narratives of the conspiracy published half a century ago avoid complexities, contexts, and footnotes: J. Stanhope, *The Cato Street Conspiracy* (1962); D. Johnson, *Regency Revolution: The Case of Arthur Thistlewood* (1974).

Of rare quality in the *Oxford Dictionary of National Biography* (*ODNB*) are M. Chase's seventeen biographies of radicals in this period (Cato

Street men included), C. Emsley's brief biographies of earlier radicals, and Dickinson's on Spence. Valuable too are the biographies in J. O. Baylen and N. J. Gossman, *Biographical Dictionary of Modern British Radicals* (3 vols, Brighton, 1979) (*BDMBR*), particularly Emsley's on Thistlewood (I, 471–5).

Trial Reports

In the notes, trial reports etc. are referenced by short title or abbreviation (on left).

1820: THE CATO STREET TRIALS

Howell   [references in notes are to columns, not pages] The quasi-official *Complete Collection of State Trials and Proceedings for High Treason and Other Crimes and Misdemeanours from the Earliest Period to the Present Times*, was initiated by William Cobbett and edited by T. B. Howell. The Cato Street trials are reported in vol. xxxiii (1826), cols. 681–1566. They transcribe verbatim everything said at the 1820 trials in some 350,000 words. They were taken in shorthand by Thomas Curson Hansard, whom the court employed for the purpose and for which he was paid £285.

Gurney   [references in notes are to volumes and columns] Howell's ambition was matched by the shorthand writer William Brodie Gurney's transcription of the *Trials of Arthur Thistlewood ... and Others, for High Treason* (2 vols, 1820). Transcriptions in Howell and Gurney differ slightly in phrasing though not substance. Gurney was the shorthand writer to both houses of parliament and brother of the prosecuting counsel in the Cato Street trials. His volumes were printed by Luke Hansard, T. C. Hansard's brother. Their publication was advertised in the *Morning Chronicle* as early as 3 May 1820, two days after the executions.

Sherwood, Neely and Jones	The publishers Sherwood, Neely and Jones issued a brief volume, *The Trials of Arthur Thistlewood and Others* (1820), 'taken in short hand according to the method invented by John Byrom'. It reports Thistlewood's trial in full, but the trials of Ings, Brunt, Tidd, and Davidson are abbreviated.
Fairburn, *Trials* (1820)	John Fairburn's *The Trials of A. Thistlewood, J. Ings. J. T. Brunt, W. Davidson, and R. Tidd … To which is added a Copious Acount of the Execution* (1820), aimed at a popular readership by selling for two shillings. Its abbreviated reports contain valuable circumstantial details about the proceedings.
Authentic History	G. T. Wilkinson's *An Authentic History of the Cato-Street Conspiracy; with the Trials at Large of the Conspirators, for High Treason and Murder* (1820) competently narrates the history of the 1820 arrests, trials, executions, and ensuing protests about the role of the spy Edwards. First issued in sixpenny parts from 18 May onwards and then as a complete volume, it contains precised or paraphrased trial transcriptions along with newspaper material and short biographies. Wilkinson was a practised crime reporter who edited *The New Newgate Calendar Improved* (6 vols, *c.* 1809–20).
Kelleher, *Lives*	*The Lives of … the Leaders of the Cato Street Conspiracy collected from the Most Authentic Sources, with Original Letters etc.* (P. Kelleher, Guardian Office, Strand, 1820) summarises contemporary understandings and fictions but is unreliable in detail.
OBSP	The online trial reports in the *Old Bailey Sessions Papers* (and in sundry *Newgate Calendars*) are abbreviated and paraphrased and are not used in this book.

1817: THE TREASON TRIALS FOR THE SPA FIELDS
INSURRECTION OF 2 DECEMBER 1816

Howell (1817)

T. B. Howell, *A Complete Collection of State Trials and Proceedings for High Treason and other Crimes and Misdemeanors from the Earliest Period to the Present Time* (1824), vol. XXXII, cols. 1–673.

Fairburn (1817)

John Fairburn's Edition of the Whole Proceedings on the Trial of James Watson, Senior, for High Treason: ..., *to which is Added the Arraignment and Discharge of Arthur Thistlewood, Thomas Preston, and John Hooper, Tried, in the Court of King's Bench* ... *June 9, 1817 and Following Days* (1817). This is Fairburn's 'cheap edition', in 24 parts at a penny-halfpenny per part. It claimed to contain 'full one-half more matter' than any other publication but at half the price, and to give the 'whole of the evidence ... entire'. It contains a useful index.

Trials at Large (1817)

The Trials at Large of Arthur Thistlewood, Gent., James Watson, the Elder, Surgeon, Thomas Preston, Cordwainer, John Hooper, Labourer, for High-treason ..., *June 9, 1817* ... *Taken in Shorthand by a Gentleman of the Bar* ... (J. Lewis, Clerkenwell, 1817). The 1817 proceedings are transcribed verbatim but the 'least interesting' evidence was summarised. 'Not one word' was omitted of the spy Castle's evidence (109, note). Another edition from Sherwood & Co. was entitled *The Trials at Bar of Arthur Thistlewood* ... *etc.* Its publication (for 7 shillings) was advertised in the *Times* on 9 July 1817.

MANUSCRIPT SOURCES

National Archives, Kew, London
  Home Office Papers

HO 40.3.3: 873–914

HO 40.3.4: 915–28 (Spa Fields, 1816–17)

HO 40.7.1 (precis of London disturbances, June–Sept. 1817)

HO 40.7.5: 1–2102 (precis of London disturbances, June 1818-Jan 1819)

HO 40.10.5: 155–70 (Moggridge's interrogation, 1817)

HO 42.136–202 (HO 42.155–, for 1816–17)

HO 42.199: 535–635 (spy reports, Nov. 1819 – Mar. 1820)

HO 44.1–6 (after 23 February 1820)

Treasury Solicitor's Papers: TS 11.695

Treasury Solicitor's Account Ledger: AO. 3. 1104

Newgate Prison Registers: PCOM 2/22–3

University of Southampton Library

Wellington Papers, MS61 WP1/660, fos 1–6

Notes

CHAPTER 1   THE CATO STREET CONSPIRACY: WHAT HAPPENED

1. Howell 751–2.
2. HO 42.199: 634.
3. *Trials at Large* (1817), 230.
4. Howell 786.
5. HO 42.199: 557.
6. Howell 749, 983, 1490; TS 11.198.
7. Others attending would be Vansittart, chancellor of the exchequer, Robinson, president of the board of trade, Bathurst, secretary for war and colonies, Wellesley Pole, master of the mint, Melville, first lord of the admiralty, Lord Mulgrave, minister without portfolio, and Westmorland, lord privy seal.
8. John Scott, 'Ode to the Drum', in Thompson, *Tribute to Liberty*, 61.
9. Cf. Williams's print, *The British Atlas, or John Bull supporting the Peace Establishment* (Sidebotham, 1816, reissued 1818), BM 1868,0808.8321.
10. The mansion was later renumbered 44. For furnishings and decor see *Survey of London: Volume 39(1)*, 86–9, and *Volume 40(2)*, 117–66.
11. Pellew, *Sidmouth*, iii, 318.
12. TS 11.198; Howell 723, 781–2.
13. Gurney ii, 401; HO 44.1.158: 186; HO 44.4.36; HO 44.4.34: 102–3.
14. Howell 885; *Authentic History* 173; HO 44.4: 37; HO 42.199: 626. Gee's Court was a narrow crevice of seventeen back-to-back dwellings off Oxford Street, a half-mile north of Grosvenor Square. Its footprint survives.
15. *Republican*, 28 April 1820.
16. Howell 545, 786, 1389, 1510.
17. Howell 727, 998.
18. Howell 1559; HO 13.36: 97–8.
19. Smith, *Napoleonic Wars Data Book*; Cookson, *British Armed Nation*, 95–100.
20. *ODNB*; Redding, *Recollections*, i, 346–7.
21. HO 42.199: 545.
22. Kelleher, *Lives* (1820), 32; *Authentic History* 51.
23. Howell 1288–9; HO 44.4: 205; HO 44.5: 483.
24. Fairburn (1817), 160 (Castle's evidence).
25. HO 44.4: 362–4; *Trials at Large* (1817), 266.
26. HO 44.4: 9–11.
27. Howell (1817), 38, 242, 327; TS 11.197: 208.
28. Prothero, *Artisans and Politics*, 123.
29. Howell 1391; Rede, *Canning*, 399–400.

30. Howell 1391; Gurney I, 580–2; Rede, *Canning*, 399–400; HO 44.4.96: 306–16.
31. HO 42.199: 626.
32. Gurney II, 438; Howell 1252.
33. *Morning Chronicle*, 30 May and 12 December 1805.
34. *Morning Post*, 1 April 1823; T. Smith, *Account of the Parish of St. Mary-le-Bone* (1833), 217.
35. Howell 805–8, 1146, 1396.
36. TS 11.198.

CHAPTER 2   ARRESTS AND REACTIONS

1. HO 44.4.44.
2. *Times*, 25 February 1820.
3. HO 44.4.115.
4. HO 44.4.90.
5. TS 11.198; *Authentic History* 41.
6. *Gentleman's Magazine*, 90(1) (1820), 269.
7. The names that fill this chapter are sorted in 'The People Listed' at the back of the book.
8. *Morning Chronicle*, 24, 25, 26 February 1820.
9. Howell 825; Alison, *Castlereagh and Stewart*, III, 112n.; *Morning Chronicle*, 7 March 1820; *Authentic History* 73; HO 42.199: 618, 621.
10. Howell 776–8.
11. HO 44.4: 201; Howell 1169.
12. Howell 762.
13. *Morning Chronicle*, 7 March 1820; *Authentic History* 83.
14. S. T. Coleridge, 'The Devil's Walk', *Morning Post*, 6 September 1799.
15. HO 44.5: 497; *Morning Chronicle*, 25 February and 3 March 1820; *Authentic History* 58–60.
16. HO 44.6: 132.
17. HO 42.199: 634; HO 44.6: 132, 229.
18. HO 44.6: 25.
19. HO 44.4: 253.
20. Fairburn, *Cato-Street Conspiracy*, 34; Bayley, *Tower of London*, II, 653; Dixon, *London Prisons*, 41, 46; Thornbury, *Old and New London*, II, 60–76.
21. HO 42.16: 508. On Wright, *OBSP*, ref. no. t18230910–3; and HO 17.39.135 (Criminal Petitions, I.); *Annual Register* (1820), 60.
22. Pellew, *Sidmouth*, III, 320.
23. *Morning Chronicle*, 26 February 1820.
24. J. Bew, *Castlereagh: A Life* (2012), 475.
25. *Times*, 2 March 1820; *Observer*, 3 March 1820.
26. For Géricault see Chapter 18.
27. BM 1887, 0722.251: taken from Williams's inaccurate print, *The Hay-Loft Plot of Thistlewood* (February 1820).
28. Grosvenor, *Lady Wharncliffe*, I, 265.
29. Byron to Southey in his *The Two Foscari* (1821); M. Kelsall, *Byron's Politics* (Brighton, 1987), 83–6.

30. Byron to J. C. Hobhouse, 29 March 1820, in Marchand (ed.), *Byron's Letters*, VII, 62–3; Gardner, *Poetry and Protest*, ch. 7.

31. Grierson (ed.), *Letters of Scott*, VI, 177; McMaster, *Scott and Society*, 137.

32. Southey (ed.), *Life of Southey*, V, 25–6.

33. Hare (ed.), *Two Noble Lives*, I, 95–6.

34. Quennell (ed.), *Princess Lieven to Metternich*, 15–17. The princess told Metternich that the Russian embassy at 36 Harley Street was expected to 'come down' in twenty years' time. But today (renumbered) it stands full of plush dentists and the richest of Harley Street's Georgian interiors and plasterwork.

35. Rush, *Residence at Court*, 223, 225.

36. Pellew, *Sidmouth*, III, 312; Greville, *Memoirs*, I, 24 February 1820.

37. Alison, *Castlereagh and Stewart*, III, 111–112n.

38. Aspinall, *Henry Hobhouse*, 16; *Diary of Lord Colchester*, III, 121, 124; Chase, *1820*, 138.

39. HO 44.6: 88.

40. HO 46.6: 32, 38; *Authentic History* 92–6, 112–13.

41. Treasury Solicitor's Account Ledger: AO. 3. 1104. For their briefs the attorney general and solicitor general each got £331, along with hefty payments for 'advice'. One official was paid £130 for the effort of 'passing the pardons under the great seal' of the spy Edwards and of the crown witnesses Dwyer, Monument, and Adams. Thomas Hansard got £285 for taking and transcribing shorthand notes of the trials, and another £48 for printing the chief justice's charge, the indictments, and the witness and jury lists.

42. *Quarterly Review*, 55 (1836), 474; Thornbury, *Old and New London*, II, 469.

43. *Authentic History* 393.

44. *Times*, 25 February 1820.

45. HO 44.6.243; *Authentic History* 434.

46. HO 44.5.35: 79–80.

47. HO 42.199: 564; HO 42.197: 506. Years later Preston's family told a missionary who attended his deathbed that Edwards had warned Preston not to go to Cato Street: Vanderkiste, *Notes and Narratives*, 156–8.

48. HO 44.6.27: 78–9; *Authentic History* 51–36, 67–70; *Morning Chronicle*, 29 February 1820.

49. HO 44.3.31: 33–4; HO 44.3.32: 78–9; HO 44.4: 295–7; Prothero, 'Thomas Preston', *ODNB*. Preston allowed the missionary Vanderkiste to serve him the sacrament on his deathbed – though only to shut him up, the missionary thought (*Notes and Narratives*, 156–8). Far away in New South Wales, the transported John Shaw Strange read this in the *Bathurst Free Press*, 14 January 1857, and wrote to the editor that far from being the wicked heathen the missionary described, Preston was 'a strictly honest man in all his dealings, sober, industrious, a kind father and a faithful friend; possessing, moreover, too powerful a mind to be ensnared and sacrificed like myself and others, by the notorious villain, Edwards the spy, and his employers'.

50. *Morning Chronicle*, 29 February 1820.

51. *Times*, 20 November 1820; *Morning Chronicle*, 18 September 1819, 18 November 1820, and 6 and 7 January 1821. Sidmouth to the king, Poole, *Peterloo*, 385; Palin's debt, HO 44.3.54: 56; list of weapons, HO 44.5.53: 190–1.

CHAPTER 3   INTERPRETING THE CONSPIRACY

1. Masterman, *From the Abyss*, 24–5.
2. McElligott and Conboy (eds), *Cato Street Conspiracy*.
3. Chase (ed.), *Davenport*, 58.
4. Poole writes (*Peterloo*, 385) that Cato Street's 'lurid details have captured the historical headlines' and eclipsed Peterloo's. Not so, when his book, like others, gives Cato Street a half-page summary and dismisses it for its unimportance.
5. McCarthy, *Story of the Nations*, 94, 97.
6. White, *Waterloo to Peterloo*, 199; Stanhope, *Cato Street Conspiracy*, 28, 57; Gardner, *Poetry and Popular Protest*, 129.
7. J. C. D. Clark, *English Society 1668–1832* (Cambridge, 2000), 446; Hilton, *Mad, Bad, and Dangerous People*, 252.
8. *Republican*, 12 May 1820.
9. *Bristol Mercury*, 23 January 1841.
10. Cobbett, *History of Regency and George IV*, 399–400.
11. Thompson, *English Working Class*, 709.
12. P. P. Howe (ed.), *The Complete Works of William Hazlitt* (1930–4), xx, 136.
13. *Morning Post*, 18 August 1819.
14. *Republican*, 3 (1820), 44–5.
15. Cobbett, *History of Regency and George IV*, 399–400.
16. G. Borrow, *The Romany Rye* (2 vols, 1858), ii, 349, 354–5 (writing this in 1854, Borrow exaggerated Ings's role and wrote that seven were hanged, among other inaccuracies); Thompson, *English Working Class*, 700.
17. Prothero, *Artisans and Politics*, 128.
18. Hazlitt, *Political Essays*, xxv.
19. *Examiner*, 5 March 1820.
20. *Republican*, 28 April 1820.
21. HO 44.6: 105.
22. Holland, *Memoirs of Whig Party*, 280; Bamford and Wellington (eds), *Journal of Mrs. Arbuthnot*, i, 7.
23. *Cobbett's Weekly Political Register*, 6 May 1820.
24. Greig (ed.), *Farington Diary*, iii, 166.
25. *Morning Post*, 18 August 1819.

CHAPTER 4   WHAT THEY WERE UP AGAINST

1. John Thelwall, *Champion*, 7 May 1820, cited by Scrivener, *Seditious Allegories*, 201.
2. G. Best, 'Thompson's *Making of the English Working Class*', *Historical Journal*, 8 (2) (1965), 271–81.
3. *Times*, 19 April, 26 and 27 August, 16 September 1816.
4. Turner, *Old Boys*, 55.
5. Hackwood, *William Hone*, 231–2.
6. Thorne, *House of Commons, 1790–1820*, i, 46.
7. Daniell, *Meteorological Essays*, 288–9, 400–1; Howell 743.

8. *Morning Post*, 3 January 1820.
9. *Morning Post*, 19 and 20 January, 1 March 1820; *Times*, 18 January 1820.
10. Southey (ed.), *Life of Southey*, IV, 360.
11. Thompson, *English Working Class*, 671–2.
12. Phipps (ed.), *Ward Memoirs*, II, 16–44.
13. Hibbert (ed.), *Gronow Reminiscences*, 223–4.
14. Wooler, *Lecture on Heads*, 18.
15. Quennell (ed.), *Princess Lieven to Metternich*, 15–18; Vane, *Papers of Viscount Castlereagh*, IV, 174; Tuite, *Byron and Celebrity*, 130–1.
16. Bloom and Bloom (eds), *Piozzi Letters*, VI, 303.
17. *Republican*, 28 April 1820.
18. Martineau, *History of England 1816–1846*, I, 243.
19. *Morning Chronicle*, 14 September 1819.
20. *Cobbett's Weekly Political Register*, 13 May 1820.
21. Gatrell, *Hanging Tree*, 616–19.
22. While only 9 people were executed in all Prussia in 1818 and 5 in 1822, in no year of the 1820s did English and Welsh executions fall below the 50 of 1825. There were 107 in 1820, 114 in 1821, and 74 in 1829. Burglary, housebreaking, robbery, and murder were the leading hanging crimes. A few wealthy forgers and sodomites were hanged, but marginalised people made up the vast majority. Most were aged under twenty-one, and in London and major towns most were recent immigrants. Add to these the 162,000 convicts transported between 1787 and 1868, some 3,600 of whom were shipped off for 'political' crimes. Twice as many went from Ireland as from England, Scotland, and Wales. Gatrell, *Hanging Tree*, 616–19.
23. Anon., 'Schoolmaster's Experience in Newgate', *Fraser's Magazine*, 5 (1832), 736.
24. Gathorne Hardy (ed.), *Gathorne Hardy*, I, 22.
25. *Trial of David Tyrie, for High Treason* (1782). Tyrie was a naval clerk executed on Southsea Common, Portsmouth, for passing information to the French. After his burial sailors dug up his quartered body and carried away bits of it 'to shew their messmates on board'. This breach of decorum was one reason why he was the last treason convict to be dismembered.
26. C. Emsley, 'An Aspect of "Pitt's Terror": Prosecutions for Sedition during the 1790s', *Social History*, 6(2) (1981), 155–84.
27. Thale (ed.), *London Corresponding Society*, xii, xxiv; M. T. Davis, 'London Corresponding Society (*act.* 1792–1799)', *ODNB*.
28. Thale (ed.), *London Corresponding Society*, 428; Thale (ed.), *Francis Place*, 177.
29. Evans, *Christian Policy*, iii–v.
30. Emsley, 'Pitt's Terror'.
31. J. A. Cannon, 'Tierney, George (1761–1830)', *History of Parliament* (www.historyofparliament.org); *Annual Register* (30 November 1819), 131.
32. *Times*, 19 June 1817; K. McKenzie, 'Exit Pursued by a Bear: Oliver the Spy and the Imperial Context of British Political History', *History Australia*, vol. 13(1), 2016, 80–94.
33. HC Deb (1817), vol. 36, cols. 975–96, 1016, 1084, 1006; Porter, *Plots and Paranoia*, 41–65.

34. McCalman, *Radical Underworld*, 264 n. 66. Spy keys are in HO 40.9: 4 and HO 40.10: 83.
35. HC Deb, 9 May 1820, vol. 1, cc. 243 and 262.
36. HC Deb, 18 February 1817, vol. 35, cc. 411–20.
37. *Journal of the House of Commons*, 73 (1818), appendix, 77.
38. *Annual Register* (1819), 117–18.
39. Cookson, *British Armed Nation 1793–1815*, 95, 99–100; Smith, *Napoleonic Wars Data Book*.
40. Wellington, *Correspondence and Memoranda*, I, 127–9.
41. Douet, *British Barracks 1600–1914; Survey of London: Volume 45*, 64–8.
42. Hilton, *Mad, Bad, and Dangerous People*, 252.
43. Gatrell, *City of Laughter*, 75; Patterson, *Burdett*, I, 263.
44. Hunt, *Memoirs*, III, 596–7.
45. HO 42.197: 394 (18 October).
46. *A Trifling Mistake in … Erskine's Recent Preface* (1819), 48–50 (my italics).
47. Smith, *Whig Principles*, 349.
48. Bruce, *Life of Napier*, 139–40.

CHAPTER 5 WHAT THEY BELIEVED

1. D. Mitch, 'Education and Skill of the British Labour Force', in Floud and Johnson (eds), *Cambridge Economic History*, I, 344.
2. HO 44.5: 507.
3. Preston, *Life and Opinions*, 13, 14, 36.
4. Colvin, *Keats' Letters*, 299.
5. *Black Dwarf*, 30 December 1818; Belchem, *Hunt*, 122; Marshall, *Wreath of Freedom*, 13.
6. HO 42.199: 246.
7. HO 44.5.85: 425–30; Worrall, *Radical Culture*, 194–6; McCalman, *Radical Underworld*, 146–7.
8. For Cooper's citation from Burns see p. 356.
9. D. T. Andrew (ed.), *London Debating Societies: 1776–1799* (1994), 351–71, British History Online (www.british-history.ac.uk/london-record-soc/vol30/pp351-371).
10. The LCS's presence was relatively thin in the walled City, Southwark, the proletarian East End, and the genteel West End: Barrell, *Spirit of Despotism*, map 1.9, 50–1.
11. HO 40.3.3: 42–3.
12. Bamford, *Life of a Radical*, II, 25–6.
13. McCalman, *Radical Underworld*, 197, 89–90.
14. HO 42.42.145: 332–5.
15. HO 40.9: 613–14.
16. TS 11.205.
17. HO 44.4: 69.
18. HO 44.5: 376.

19. From 'The Rights of Man, Or, Things as they were Intended to be by Divine Providence. Written by a Spencean Philanthropist', *Medusa, or The Penny Magazine*, 1 March 1819.

20. M. Chase, '"The Real Rights of Man": Thomas Spence, Paine and Chartism', in Bonnett and Armstrong (eds), *Spence*, 13–25; Dickinson (ed.), *Political Works of Spence*, 'Introduction'.

21. Chase (ed.), *Davenport*, 16.

22. T. Spence, *Pigs' Meat* (1795), III, 220–9.

23. F. Place, 'Collection for a Memoir of Thomas Spence', BM Add. MSS 27,808, iii.

24. *Cobbett's Weekly Political Register*, 14 December 1816; Kent and Ewen (eds), *Writings of Hone*, 366–7.

25. HC Deb, vol. 35, col. 134 (29 January 1817).

26. TS 11.199.

27. TS 11.45.167; McCalman, *Horrors of Slavery*, 122.

28. Thompson, *English Working Class*, 162.

29. Gatrell, *City of Laughter*, 38; HO 40.136; *Cobbett's Weekly Political Register*, 14 December 1816.

30. 'Spence's Plan', in *Spence's Songs* (1807).

31. John Barrell gives a fine account of the tokens in 'Radicalism, Visual Culture and Spectacle in the 1790s', *Romanticism on the Net*, 46 (May 2007). See also R. H. Thompson, 'The Dies of Thomas Spence (1750–1815)', *British Numismatics Journal*, 38 (1969–70), 152–4, 162; Fitzwilliam Museum, 'The Propaganda Coins of Thomas Spence and His Contemporaries' (online exhibition catalogue, www.fitzmuseum.cam.ac.uk/dept/coins/exhibitions/spence/index.html, accessed 9 September 2021); Wood, *Radical Satire and Print Culture*, 68–82.

32. Gatrell, *City of Laughter*, 485.

33. Gatrell, *City of Laughter*, 520–1.

34. Hone, *Three Trials*, 107, 125–6, 163.

35. McCalman, *Horrors of Slavery*, 122.

36. Davenport, *Thomas Spence*, 5.

37. McCalman, *Radical Underworld*, 2, 31.

38. HO 40.7: 906–7; HO 40.7: 2036–7, cited by Fryer, *Staying Power*, 222.

39. *Hampshire Chronicle*, 27 July 1818.

CHAPTER 6 FANTASY, MYTH, AND SONG

1. *Cobbett's Weekly Political Register*, 6 May 1820.

2. Palmer, *Sound of History*, 16–17.

3. J. Le Goff, 'Mentalities: A History of Ambiguities', in Le Goff and Nora (eds), *Constructing the Past*, 169.

4. Preston, *Life and Opinions*, 36, 25–6; cf. McCalman, *Radical Underworld*, 144–6.

5. HO 42.199: 591 (11 January 1820).

6. HO 42.199: 547.

7. Preston, *Life and Opinions*, 25–6.

8. *Black Dwarf*, 15 September 1819 (punctuation simplified).

9. Chase (ed.), *Davenport*, 49.
10. HO 42.197 (18 October 1819); HO 42.199: 482.
11. HO 44.5: 225–6.
12. 'A New Song: Burke's Address to "The Swinish Multitude!"', in Thompson, *Tribute to Liberty*, 3–4.
13. Thompson, *Tribute to Liberty*, 18, 33.
14. HO 40.10: 264.
15. Chase (ed.), *Davenport*, 7.
16. McCalman, *Radical Underworld*, 140–1.
17. Richmond, *Condition of... Scotland*, 183.
18. HO 42.143: 307–8; HO 42.197: 393; HO 40.9: 613–14.
19. Howell 1288–93 and 1554–8.
20. Howell 1319, 1221; *Authentic History* 293.
21. *Republican*, 28 April 1820; *Authentic History* 76. In May Adams denied his statements were made under duress: HO 44.6.72: 231–4.
22. Howell 994–5.
23. *North Briton*, 1–100 (1769), 453, 469, etc.; *Observations upon ... Mr. Wilkes. Addressed to Free-Born Englishmen* (1763), 34–5.
24. Spence in *Rights of Infants* (1797).
25. 'The Berry-Bush, or True Antient Liberty', in Marshall, *Wreath of Freedom*, 5.
26. HO 42.197: 394.
27. Marshall, *Wreath of Freedom*, 34.
28. Defoe had first used the term in his ironically entitled verses, 'The True Born Englishman' (1700): 'scarce one [English] family is left alive, / Which does not from some foreigner derive'.
29. R. H. Thompson, 'The Dies of Thomas Spence (1750–1815)', *British Numismatics Journal*, 38 (1969–70), 152–4; J. Barrell, 'Radicalism, Visual Culture and Spectacle in the 1790s', *Romanticism on the Net*, 46 (May 2007).
30. *Cobbett's Weekly Political Register*, 6 May 1820, 459 (also 331, 387, 465, 485, 615, 765; and *Rural Rides* (1830), 133–4).
31. *Telegraph*, 20 March 2020.
32. HO 42.199: 628 (1817).
33. White, *London in the Nineteenth Century*, 131.
34. Howell 785; HO 42.199: 612.
35. *Morning Post*, 21 August 1819.
36. Thompson, *Tribute to Liberty*; E. Rüdebusch, *Irland im Zeitalter der Revolution* (1989), 232; J. Kirk, *Cultures of Radicalism in Britain and Ireland* (2015), 150; Jenny Farrell, '"Of no Court Tyrants we're Afraid": The Literature of the United Irishmen', *Culture Matters*, 15 May 2018 (www.culturematters.org.uk, accessed 9 September 2021).
37. *A New Loyal Song, 1793.* A version of this was published in 1820 in *The Wreath of Freedom* and republished in the Chartist *Northern Star* as late as 1849: P. Pickering in Watt, Scott and Spedding (eds), *Cheap Print and Popular Song*, 123.
38. Sibly, *Trial of Thomas Hardy*, ii, 33–4. For variants: P. Scott, 'The Early History of "Why should we idly waste our Prime"', *Burns Chronicle*, 128 (2018), 38–49.
39. *Black Dwarf*, 1 September 1819; HO 42.199: 233A.

CHAPTER 7 REBELLION'S HABITATS

1. HO 42.136: 691; A. Smith, 'Arthur Thistlewood: A Regency Republican', *History Today*, 3(12) (December 1953).
2. *La jeune femme et ses trois enfants*, BM Prints and Drawings, 1888,0619.19.
3. Brown, *Sixty Years' Gleanings*, 30; *Examiner*, 8 December 1816.
4. Thale (ed.), *Francis Place*, 107.
5. Hunt, *Memoirs*, III, 326.
6. E. Casey, *The Fate of Place: A Philosophical History* (Berkeley, Calif., 1998), ix.
7. Coleridge, *Table Talk*, 24 July 1830, I, 181.
8. Now obliterated under the junction of Shaftesbury Avenue and Charing Cross Road.
9. HO 42.199: 550 (7 December 1819).
10. HO 44.4.87: 291–2.
11. Fairburn (1817), 214; *Trials at Large* (1817), 244–5.
12. Hunt, *Memoirs*, III, 329–30.
13. HO 42.199: 595; Diprose, *St Clement Danes*, I, 222; Thornbury, *Old and New London*, III, 36–44; Strype, *Survey*, IV, ch. 7, 118.
14. Howell 747.
15. Several thousand probably died in the flames. The year before, bubonic plague killed 75,000–100,000 Londoners out of 460,000. The Great Fire did destroy most rats, but they soon recolonised the City and never ceased to flourish.
16. McKellar, *Birth of Modern London*, 71.
17. Hawksmoor cited by McKellar, *Birth of Modern London*, 30; J. Fielding, *An Enquiry into the Causes of the Late Increase of Robbers* (1751), 116–17; De Quincey, *Confessions of an English Opium Eater* (1986 edn), 81.
18. Only six pre-Fire domestic buildings survive today (much restored): Prince Henry's Room, 17 Fleet Street; a house at 229 Strand; the Old Curiosity Shop, Portsmouth Street; 44 Cloth Fair; 74–5 Long Lane; and Barnard's Inn, Holborn.
19. Thornbury, *Old and New London*, III, 10–15.
20. Diprose, *St Clement Danes*, I, 107, 275, 180; Thornbury, *Old and New London*, III, 15–25.
21. Gatrell, *City of Laughter*, 6–7; Schwarz, *London in the Age of Industrialisation*, 51; Rudé, *Hanoverian London*, 57–8.
22. L. Schwarz and J. Boulton, 'The Preindustrial Urban Environment and the Pattern of Disease in Eighteenth-Century Westminster', Economic History Society conference, 2008 (https://research.ncl.ac.uk/pauperlives/esrcpre sentations.htm, accessed 20 September 2021).
23. Wilson, *Dissenting Churches*, III, 474; Ivimey, *English Baptists*, 387; Thornbury, *Old and New London*, I, 92–104.
24. Speck, *Paine*, 119.
25. *Morning Chronicle*, 4 December 1816.
26. Howell (1817), 31–2; Prothero, *Artisans and Politics*, 11; *Trials at Large* (1817), 39, 62–3, 180, 236–7, 246; Hunt, *Memoirs*, III, 329–30.
27. 'Dean Street' (pencil drawing, 1890), London Metropolitan Archives, q3829176.

28. HO 42.199: 595.
29. Hazlitt, 'On Coffee-House Politicians' and 'On Vulgarity and Affectation', *Table Talk* (1821); Hackwood, *Hone*, 236.
30. Strype, *Survey*, iii, 12, 227; Thornbury, *Old and New London*, i, 92–104.
31. Gatrell, *Hanging Tree*, 353–66.
32. HO 42.197: 381; *Authentic History*, 56–7; HO 42.199: 535–57.
33. Crowther fancied that the house had been Jack Sheppard's in the 1720s. This was an invention in Harrison Ainsworth's novel *Jack Sheppard* (1839–40); that wondrous thief had no connection with the White Lion, only with Wych Street.
34. C. E. H. Chadwyck-Healey, 'The White Lion Inn, Wych Street', *Notes & Queries*, 6th series, 1 (3 April 1880), 269–70.
35. HO 42.197: 500–6.
36. *Authentic History* 56–7.
37. Price, 'A New Song' (*c.* 1810), Bodleian Ballads, Roud no. V34307 (http://ballads.bodleian.ox.ac.uk/search/printer/Price, accessed 20 September 2021).
38. *Morning Post*, 4 March 1816; *Examiner*, 5 September 1819; HO 44.4: 40–1.
39. D. Worrall, 'Artisan Melodrama and the Plebeian Public Sphere: The Political Culture of Drury Lane and its Environs, 1797–1830', *Studies in Romanticism*, 39(2) (2000), 221.
40. Diprose, *St Clement Danes*, i, 112.
41. Gatrell, *Hanging Tree*, 152–3.
42. Norman, *London Vanished and Vanishing*, 164–5 (with 1904 watercolour of White Hart Yard).
43. HO 42.199: 559, 595; HO 42.42.145: 332–5.
44. Howell 1005, 1010, 1007, 1221.
45. *Authentic History* 27.
46. *OBSP*, ref. nos. t17890114–62 and t17930220–52.
47. Dickens, *All the Year Round*: 'Brooke Street, Holborn', 24 June 1871, and 'Old Stories Retold', 10 November 1866.
48. 1841 Census, Middlesex, St Andrew Holborn (Above the Bars), St Andrew Eastern, District 16.

CHAPTER 8 A TERRORIST IN THE MAKING: 1774–1816

1. Howell 1245.
2. Howell's report replaced inflammatory passages in Thistlewood's speech by dots (...), but they are fully reported in Gurney ii, 625–32, cited here.
3. Sadler, *Crabb Robinson Diary*, ii, 50.
4. Fairburn, *Trials* (1820), 120; *Authentic History* 350.
5. *Republican*, 28 April 1820.
6. 'The odds of a lone-actor terrorist having a mental illness is 13.49 times higher than the odds of a group actor having a mental illness': Nafees Hamid, 'What Makes a Terrorist?', *New York Review of Books*, 23 August 2017. E. P. Thompson thought that the contemporary to whom the clinical terms 'psychopath' and 'neurotic' best applied was Castlereagh.

7. In 1817 Humphrey published a stipple engraving of the Spa Fields prisoners in profile after a lost drawing by Scharf; Scharf's 1817 Thistlewood portrait was published in lithograph during the 1820 trials.

8. Anon., 'The Late Mr. A. Wivell, Portrait Painter', *Art Journal* (1849).

9. Redding, *Recollections*, 346–7.

10. *Morning Post*, 11 February 1818.

11. *Authentic History* 5–6, 22–3.

12. Hare (ed.), *Two Noble Lives*, I, 94; Jennings, *Croker Papers*, I, 163; Dowden, *Journal of Thomas Moore*, III, 121.

13. HO 44.5.85: 425–30 (27 March 1820).

14. J. Barrell, 'Radicalism, Visual Culture and Spectacle in the 1790s', *Romanticism on the Net*, 46 (May 2007), para 27. Cf. R. Newton, *Promenade in the State Side of Newgate* (BM) and *Soulagement en Prison* (Lewis Walpole Library, Yale University); 'On the Improper Conduct of the Jailer of Newgate', 1794, *Diary of Thomas Lloyd kept in Newgate Prison, 1794–6* (Digitial Library @ Villanova University).

15. *Republican*, 28 April 1820.

16. Kelleher published the short-lived weekly *Guardian* 'on principles of attachment to our present establishment in Church and State'. On Cato Street: 'a more monstrous design could not have been entertained unless by demons' – etc.

17. These stories were uncritically accepted by Prothero, *Artisans and Politics*, 89–90, and by the several historians who then echo Prothero (e.g. Gardner, *Poetry and Popular Protest*, 118).

18. Howell 802; *Authentic History* 173.

19. HO 42.199: 475–6; HO 79.3.9.

20. HO .5.55: 200, 341, 361–2, 383–5, 393–4 (11 March 1820); HO 44.4.95: 304–5 for informant W. Goodenough; for Banks see Addington Papers, Devon County Archives, 152M.C1820.OH29; M. T. Thistlewood, *The Family History of the Thistlewoods in England and Overseas* (2001, privately published; Cambridge University Library, 2003.8.3377). Cf. J. Venn (ed.), *Alumni Cantabrigienses* (Cambridge, 2011), II, 586; J. C. Walter, *Records of Woodhall Spa and Neighbourhood* (Horncastle, 1899), 160, 180. (The Thistlewood entries in *ODNB* and *BDMBR* incorrectly name William Thistlewood as Arthur's father.)

21. Hall, *In Miserable Slavery*, ix; Burnard, *Mastery, Tyranny, and Desire*; Legacies of British Slave-Ownership Database, University College London (www .ucl.ac.uk/lbs/, accessed 20 September 2021).

22. HO 42.145: 332–5; Thale, *London Corresponding Society*, 428.

23. *Times*, 2 May 1820.

24. He was named Marmeduke Thistlewood Thornelly; 'Julian' was prefixed later. The birth date in the Horncastle parish records is confirmed by family historian Clare Bevan. I thank her warmly for this and other information. Thistlewood had an earlier bastardy order issued against him for a daughter whom he left to her fate: Thistlewood, 'Family History of the Thistlewoods', 5.

25. *Sporting Magazine* (February 1813), 204; *Times*, 20 February 1815; *Examiner*, 26 February 1815; HO 42.136: 691.

26. Haynes, *Our Friends – the Enemies*, 175–6.

27. McCalman, *Radical Underworld*, 23–4.

28. Kelleher, *Lives*, 3.

29. Redding, *Recollections*, I, 346–7. Alexander Astly is not to be confused with John Ashley, a Belfast republican banished after the United Irish rebellion of 1798, or Philip Ashley, founder of the Olympic theatre in Wych Street, or his son John, who died in Paris of debt and drink in 1821.

30. Bew, *Castlereagh*, 112.

31. *Morning Chronicle*, 8 February 1811; *Leeds Mercury*, 16 March 1811.

32. Patterson, *Burdett*, I, 254.

33. *Republican*, 28 April 1820; McCalman, *Radical Underworld*, 33.

34. Thale, *Francis Place*, 178n.; Thale, *London Corresponding Society*, 402. The blood money rumour turned on a misreading of Arthur's brother's *qui tam* prosecution in 1815 to regain the money which Arthur had lost in gambling: W. P. Taunton (ed.), *Reports of Cases . . . at Common Pleas*, VI (1818), 141.

35. Howell 737–8, 862; Gurney I, 283; Belchem, 'Hunt', *ODNB*.

36. Hunt, *Memoirs*, II, 75.

37. HO 42.136: 691–709. A half of England today is owned by 25,000 aristocrats, gentry, corporations, oligarchs, and City bankers – under one per cent of the population. An equitable redistribution would give every man, woman and child just over half an acre: *Guardian*, 18 April 2019.

38. Howell 774.

CHAPTER 9   THE SPA FIELDS INSURRECTION: 1816–17

1. *Trials at Large* (1817), 256; Fairburn (1817), col. 42.

2. *Morning Post*, 21 August 1817.

3. Bamford, *Life of a Radical*, I, 24; *Trial by Jury: . . . Dinner . . . to celebrate the Acquittal of the State Prisoners* (1817), 9.

4. TS 11.200: 869, cited by Belchem, 'Watson', *ODNB*.

5. In context the 'he' might refer to the big brother, 'young' Watson: HO 42.143.307–8.

6. HO 44.5: 242.

7. Birth date from *Times*, 19 February 1817; Knapp and Baldwin, *Newgate Calendar* (1828), IV, 211.

8. *Trials at Large* (1817), 241; Howell (1817), 363–4.

9. *Times*, 11 December 1816.

10. HO 44.4: 367–96 (Castle's statement).

11. Fairburn (1817), 255–6.

12. Epstein, *Radical Expression*, 81.

13. Fairburn (1817), 53–7.

14. HO 44.4: 362–4.

15. Howell (1817), col. 396.

16. Howell (1817), col. 236.

17. Fairburn (1817), cols. 142–3.

18. *Times*, 19 June 1817.

19. *Observer*, 8 December 1816; HO 40.8.1: 35; HO 42.170; and HO 42.155.

20. Hunt, *Memoirs*, III, 241.
21. Bamford, *Life of a Radical*, II, 19.
22. Belchem, *Hunt*, 59n., 63–9, 118–19.
23. HO 44.4: 391–4. A paper found on Watson senior after the riots listed: 'Committee S. – Sir F. Burdett, Lord Cochrane, Mr. A. Thistlewood, Mr. J. Watson, Mr. Gale Jones, Major Cartwright, Mr. T. J. Evans, H. Hunt Esqr., Mr. Hardy, Mr. R. O. O'Connor, Mr. Blandford' (TS 11.199 and 202).
24. Thornbury, *Old and New London*, II, 298–306.
25. By May 1817 new buildings were going up, and a year later Spa Fields was 'either covered with heaps of brick earth, excavated for laying foundations, or occupied by immense heaps of bricks, manufactured or preparing for the kiln': *Survey of London: Volume 47*, 239–63.
26. *Times*, 16 November 1816.
27. TS 11.201.870.533. Phrases in this poster were repeated in Watson's speech: *Times*, 3 December 1816. On the virgins in white, *Trials at Large* (1817), 47, 179 (Castle's evidence).
28. Angelo, *Reminiscences*, I, 472.
29. This account draws on the *Observer*'s 'Complete and Well Digested Narrative of the Riots: and also the Police Examinations of such of the Rioters as are in Custody . . .', 8 December 1816; the spy Castle's narrative HO 44.4: 362–402; Dowling's report in HO 40.3.2: 28–33; Dowling letter, 6 December, HO 42.156: 212–15; Howell 570; and Hone's *Meeting in Spa Fields*. Hone's account, up to the crowd's departure for the City, followed *Morning Courier*, 4 December.
30. Hunt, *Memoirs*, III, 370–1, 544.
31. In early February 1817, Southey's juvenile drama *Wat Tyler* was pirated by Hone and others subsequently, to expose the now tory poet laureate's apostasy.
32. Howell (1817), col. 95.
33. HO 42.156: 176–7.
34. See note 29 above for sources.
35. TS 11.202.870: 358.
36. HO 44.4: 362–402 (Castle).
37. *Morning Chronicle*, 21 December 1816.
38. *OBSP*, ref. nos t18161204–59 and t18190707–156.
39. Bamford, *Life of a Radical*, II, 26.
40. *Trials at Large* (1817), 197.
41. Fairburn (1817), 60; HO 42.167: 15–16.
42. *Times*, 3 December 1816; Fairburn (1817), 157.
43. Hunt, *Memoirs*, III, 374–5.
44. Belchem, *Hunt*, 58–9, 64–5.
45. *OBSP*, 15 January 1817, ref. no. t18170115–64.
46. *Black Dwarf*, 19 March 1817.
47. HC Deb, vol. 35, c. 754.
48. R. Poole, 'French Revolution or Peasants' Revolt? Petitioners and Rebels in England from the Blanketeers to the Chartists', *Labour History Review*, 74(1) (2009), 7, 15.

49. Fairburn (1817), 134–6; *Morning Post*, 4 December 1816.
50. Moggridge's statement, 29 April – 3 May 1817: HO 40.10: 158.
51. *Examiner*, 4 May 1817.
52. HO 42.167: 504.
53. *Observer*, 12 October 1823; T. M. Madden (ed.), *The Memoirs . . . of Richard Robert Madden* (1892), 89.
54. *Trials at Large* (1817), 20–1, 132–3; *Times*, 29 April 1817.
55. HO 40.9: 2, Oliver's narrative; HO 40.10: 83 for secret list of spies, including Moggridge; *Times*, 11 September 1819; HO 44.4: 223–4.
56. Romilly, *Memoirs*, III, 298.
57. *Examiner*, 494 (15 June 1817), 380–4.
58. Hunt, *Memoirs*, III, 503.
59. *Examiner*, 9 November 1817; Shelley, *Prose Works* (1912), 379.
60. Howell (1817), 421–2; *Trials at Large* (1817), 268, 92. In July, three weeks after his own release from imprisonment in Tothill Fields for sheltering young Watson, the engraver William Holl celebrated the four prisoners' release by engraving their group profile from Scharf's drawings. It sold well from Humphrey's printshop in St James's Street.
61. Sadler, *Crabb Robinson Diary*, II, 56.
62. *Times*, 17 and 18 June 1817; Fairburn (1817), 358; *Trial by Jury. Speeches . . . at a Dinner . . . to celebrate the Acquittal of the State Prisoners* (1817), 12–13.
63. Hooper's death and funeral: HO 40.7: 2089; *Gentleman's Magazine*, 87(2) (December 1817), 633; *Morning Post*, 12 January 1818.
64. Gatrell, *City of Laughter*, 526.

CHAPTER 10   THISTLEWOOD UNHINGED: 1818–19

1. TS 11.198.
2. *Republican*, 28 April 1820.
3. *Morning Chronicle*, 8 September 1817; HO 40.7: 1929; HO 42.142: 170; Worrall, *Radical Culture*, 113–24.
4. 'C's' report: HO 40.9: 613–14.
5. Thale, *London Corresponding Society*, 402.
6. HO 40.10: 158 (Moggridge, 2–3 May 1817).
7. *Examiner*, 4 May 1817; *Morning Post*, 30 April and 5 May 1818.
8. HO 42.167: 406, 370. For letters to Sidmouth in June: HO 42.167: 22–3, 38–9.
9. McCalman, *Radical Underworld*, 108.
10. HO 42.156: 108.
11. *Examiner*, 8 February 1818; *Times*, 9 February 1818; Pellew, *Sidmouth*, III, 207–8; *Morning Chronicle*, 15 and 29 May 1818.
12. HO 42.177: 631–2.
13. Thistlewood suspected that John Hunt had betrayed him in April 1817, though he retracted his accusation in his Crown and Anchor speech on 31 July 1817: *Trial by Jury: . . . Dinner . . . to celebrate the Acquittal of the State Prisoners* (1817), 13.
14. On 12 October 1819 the spy 'B.C.' reported that to raise funds Thistlewood had 'frequent interviews with a person in the king's Bench named Ascomb,

state side [i.e. a political prisoner], formerly a considerable [merchant?] in Yorkshire' (HO 42.197: 386; cf. HO 44.5.30: 70–1, where the report is that Thistlewood visited a 'fellow prisoner Hascomb'). I am unable to identify the man. A 'Robert Askam offered [the HO] information about Thistlewood' on 25 February 1820 (HO 44.4.43: 177). A report of 10 March concerns 'the involvement of Richard Dickson Askan and his son with Thistlewood prior to the conspiracy' (HO 44.5.51: 124–31: Covid-19 closures have prevented my consulting this). McCalman was wrong to think 'Ascomb' was John Ascham, a pornographer and printer of 71 Chancery Lane who published one of Wedderburn's anti-slave pamphlets in 1831 and a pirated edition of Shelley's *Poems* in 1834 ('George Cannon', *ODNB*; McCalman, *Radical Underworld*, 205).

15. Belchem, *Hunt*, 85.
16. *Times* and *Morning Chronicle*, 23 July 1819.
17. HO 42.199: 9.
18. HO 42.197: 507–8.
19. HO 44.5: 260, 264.
20. *Morning Post*, 7 July 1819.
21. *Times*, 22 July 1819. The *Times*'s references to Hunt, Cobbett, etc. were so sarcastic that at Smithfield its reporters were hissed at. But by September Hunt regarded it as 'one of the most respectable papers for certainty of information': *Times*, 14 September 1819. The *Examiner* reported the meeting at half the *Times*'s length.
22. HO 42.190; Hunt *Memoirs*, iii, 597.
23. Belchem, *Hunt*, 103–5.
24. A spy reported that Gast was 'very violent' at White Lion meetings, but he kept clear of the later conspiracy: HO 42.197: 503.
25. *Morning Chronicle*, 23 July 1819.
26. *Examiner*, 25 July 1819.

CHAPTER 11 PETERLOO IN LONDON: 1819–20

1. Poole, *Peterloo*, 2 (citing Boyd Hilton in *Times*, 27 August 2018); Prentice, *Historical Sketches*, 166.
2. 'Manchester Tyranny', in Marshall, *Wreath of Freedom*, 27.
3. Howell 1548, 1556, 1558.
4. Howell 1551.
5. Howell 985.
6. Poole, *Peterloo*, 363.
7. Pellew, *Sidmouth*, iii, 253–61; Bamford, *Life of a Radical*, i, 221.
8. New, *Henry Brougham*, iii, 193.
9. Prentice, *Historical Sketches*, 31.
10. Poole, *Peterloo*, 205, 252.
11. Poole, *Peterloo*, 249.
12. Weller, *Wellington at Waterloo*, 178–9; Strachan, *From Waterloo to Balaclava*, 117.
13. Harmer's letter to the *Times*, 1 October 1819.
14. *London Gazette*, 6 October 1818.

15. Bruton, *Three Accounts of Peterloo*, 15.
16. Pellew, *Sidmouth*, iii, 253–61.
17. TS 11.1056.
18. Hunt, *Memoirs*, iii, 617.
19. Bush, *Casualties of Peterloo*; Poole, *Peterloo*, 153, 352; *Report of the Metropolitan and Central Committee*, 20.
20. Campbell, *Life of Carlile*, ch. 3.
21. Bamford, *Life of a Radical*, i, 222–3.
22. *Report of the Metropolitan and Central Committee*, 20–1, 24–5.
23. Prentice, *Historical Sketches*, 171.
24. Manchester University Library, English MS 172 (www.library.manchester .ac.uk/search-resources/, accessed 20 September 2021).
25. Poole, *Peterloo*, 352, 298.
26. *Manchester Meeting, Redford vs Birley*, 20, 60–4.
27. W. Axon, *Annals of Manchester* (1886), 208.
28. *Report of Metropolitan and Central Committee*, 67; HO 79.3.341: 512–14 and 543–7; Hunt, *Memoirs*, iii, 637–8.
29. *Examiner*, 22 August 1820.
30. *Morning Chronicle*, 29 November 1819.
31. *Examiner*, 22 August 1819; *Times*, 1 October 1819.
32. Belchem, *Hunt*, 121.
33. Worrall, *Radical Culture*, 186; *Morning Chronicle*, 2 September 1819.
34. *Examiner*, 29 August 1819.
35. *Times*, 11 September 1819; Parolin, *Radical Spaces*, 159–61.
36. *Morning Post*, 20 August 1819.
37. *Times*, 14 September 1819.
38. *Times*, 11 September 1819. The following draws on the loyalist *Times*, liberal-whig *Morning Chronicle* (both 14 September 1819), radical *Black Dwarf* (15 September) and *Examiner* (which largely repeats the *Times*: 19 September). Hunt's modern biographer, excellent on the minutiae of radical quarrels and on the quarrelsome dinner after the Triumph, gave Hunt's Entry only a passing sentence: Belchem, *Hunt*, 123.
39. *Morning Post*, 25, 30 June 1807.
40. Worrall, *Radical Culture*, 201.
41. HO 42.202: 334–5.
42. *Black Dwarf*, 15 September 1819.
43. *Republican*, 3 March 1820.
44. J. Gardner, 'Cobbett's Return to England in 1819', in J. Grande (ed.), *William Cobbett, Romanticism and the Enlightenment* (2015), 61–76.
45. MacKenzie, *Spy System in Glasgow*, 183.
46. HO 42.199: 512–15; HO 42.194 and 195; Belchem, *Hunt*, 124–5.
47. HO 42.199: 59–64.
48. HO 42.197: 391.
49. HO 42.199: 37; HO 42.197: 381.
50. Pellew, *Sidmouth*, iii, 311; *Morning Post*, 21 October 1819.
51. *Morning Post*, 30 October 1819; *Morning Chronicle*, 2 November 1819.
52. *Black Dwarf*, 3 November 1819.

53. HO 42.199: 205.
54. HO 42.199: 548, 591; *Morning Chronicle* and *Morning Post*, 9 December 1819.
55. HO 44.5.56: 1–6.

CHAPTER 12 EDWARDS THE SPY: 1819–20

1. HC Deb, 2 May 1820, vol. 1, c. 55.
2. Knight, *Passages of a Working Life*, I, 228–9.
3. HC Deb, 9 May 1820, vol. 1, cc. 243, 262.
4. HC Deb, 9 May 1820, vol. 1, c. 242; Aylmer, *Memoirs of Edwards*; Howell 1546.
5. HO 40.7.4:2100 (27 January).
6. Edwards on 11 March had to swear to his reports in readiness for the prosecutions: precised in HO 44.5: 1–317.
7. Howell 1546.
8. *Republican*, 8 October 1819.
9. *Republican*, 28 April 1820; Holyoake, *Carlile*, 16–19.
10. *Republican*, 3 March 1820.
11. HO 42.199 (26 January).
12. *Republican*, 28 April 1820.
13. HC Deb, 9 May 1820, vol. 1, c. 244; HO 44.5.82: 413–20.
14. HO 44.5.112: 507; Howell 1074–7.
15. HO 42.199: 579.
16. HO 44.6: 51, 60.
17. *Examiner*, 26 August 1821; HO 44.9.63: 164–7; Belchem, 'Watson, James', *ODNB*.
18. HO 42.199: 568 (22 December in Scotch Arms).
19. HO 42.199: 591 (11 January 1820).
20. Preston followed suit. When a shoemaker from 'White Capel' (Whitechapel) asked him for the half pint of gin that he owed him to settle their bet that it 'would be all up' in nine days' time, Preston could say little more than that 'it wouldn't be long now'. HO 42.199: 546, 569, 572, 574.
21. HO 42.199: 584–5 (2 January).
22. HO 42.199: 545, 589–90.
23. HO 42.199: 513, 455, 536.
24. G. Pentland, '"Betrayed by Infamous Spies"? The Commemoration of Scotland's "Radical War" of 1820', *Past & Present*, 201(1) (2008). Historiographically, this cruel tragedy has been as flippantly dismissed as Cato Street has: 'a damp squib', Allan Massie opines comfortably in *The Scotsman*, 9 April 2016, reviewing P. B. Ellis and S. Mac A'Ghobhainn's powerful *The Radical Rising: The Scottish Insurrection of 1820* (2016).
25. HO 42.199: 567, 559, 568.
26. HO 42.199: 581, 583.
27. HO 42.199: 563, 583, 552.
28. HO 42.199: 557–8.
29. HO 42.199: 594–608.
30. HO 42.199: 605–18.
31. HO 42.199: 620, 625–6, 634.

32. HO 42.199: 622, 634–5.
33. HO 44.4: 295–7.
34. HO 42.6: 337.
35. HO 44.6: 160, 251, 255, 309, 319.
36. Brown, *Sixty Years' Gleanings*, 238–9.
37. HC Deb, 21 April – 26 June 1820, i, 249; *Cobbett's Weekly Political Register*, 13 May 1820.
38. HC Deb, 9 May 1820, vol. 1, c. 268; HO 44.4: 155; *Authentic History* 416–34.
39. HO 44.4: 152, 249; HO 44.6: 243, 257, 261–2, 311, 315.
40. Oliver designed St George's church in the frontier town of Grahamstown (where the present writer first went to university): HO 44.4: 3 and HO 42.199: 581; P. Pickering, 'Betrayal and Exile: A Forgotten Chartist Experience', in Davis and Pickering, *Unrespectable Radicals?*, 201–2; K. McKenzie, 'Exit Pursued by a Bear: Oliver the Spy and the Imperial Context of British Political History', *History Australia*, 13(1) (2016), 83; Healey, 'George Edwards' and Chase, 'W. J. Richards, [Oliver the Spy]', both *ODNB*.
41. Lamb, *The Three Graves*, in *The Champion*, 13–14 May 1820. In *London Magazine* (May 1825) Lamb subtitled the reprint, 'Written during the time, now happily almost forgotten, of the spy system'.

CHAPTER 13 CONSPIRATORS AND OTHERS

1. *Morning Chronicle*, 23 October 1819.
2. Place Papers, xxxviii, BL Add. MSS 27826, fo. 172; A. Griffiths, *The Chronicles of Newgate* (1884), 148–50.
3. HO 42.152: 11–15.
4. HO 42.199: 512–15; HO 40.3.2: 28–33; HO 42.156: 212–15.
5. McCalman, *Radical Underworld*, 132–3.
6. TS 11.204; Bamford and Wellington (eds), *Journal of Mrs. Arbuthnot*, i, 7. A month after release, Hobhouse won his seat at the Westminster election and was returned as Burdett's colleague.
7. Bodleian Ballads, Roud no. V3055, Oxford.
8. Fairburn (1817), 156; HO 47.197.2: 500ff.
9. *Morning Chronicle*, 24, 25 February 1820; *Authentic History* 14; HO 44.5.85: 425–30.
10. Therry, *Reminiscences*, 98; *Examiner*, 7 March 1863, 149.
11. Howell 1558; *Morning Post*, 15 July 1819.
12. Kelleher, *Lives*, 32.
13. HO 42.199: 574.
14. Kelleher, *Lives*, 31–3; *Authentic History* 28, 398–9.
15. HO 44.4: 40.
16. HO 44.4.87: 291–2.
17. Howell 792.
18. Howell 997–8.
19. *Times*, 19 February 1817.
20. On teeth etc., *Times*, 19 February 1817. On Thelwall and Gale Jones, Greig (ed.), *Farington Diary*, i, 118–19. On Watson's daughter: *ODNB*, citing TS

11.200: 869. On Evans's dropsy, McCalman, *Radical Underworld*. On Adams, Ings, Brunt, et al.: *Authentic History* 300; Kelleher, *Lives*, 23; Howell 1289; *ODNB* and *BDMBR*, entries by Chase, Dickinson, Davis, and Emsley. On Harrison: G. Parsons, 'The Cato Street Conspirators in New South Wales', *Labour History*, 8 (May 1965), 3–5.

21. Brown, *Sixty Years' Gleanings*, 143, 262–3.
22. HO 42.199: 589.
23. Gurney II, 608; Howell 1436–8.
24. HO 44.6.50: 137–8 (Brunt's poems); HO 44.6.104: 332 (wall inscriptions in Tower); cf. *Authentic History* 415.
25. Here I follow B. Keegan, 'Cobbling Verse: Shoemaker Poets of the Long Eighteenth Century', *Eighteenth Century*, 42(3) (2001), 196–8; E. J. Hobsbawm and J. W. Scott, 'Radical Shoemakers', *Past & Present*, 89 (1980), 86–114; R. A. Church, 'Labour Supply and Innovation 1800–1860: The Boot and Shoe Industry', in R. Davenport-Hines (ed.), *Capital, Entrepreneurs and Profits* (1990), 91–2; D. Goodway, *London Chartism, 1838–1848* (Cambridge, 1982), 154–62; Tiffany, *Infidel Poetics*, 187–90. Cf. Robert Bloomfield, *Poems* (1809 edn), I, xxi; W. E. Winks, *Lives of Illustrious Shoemakers* (1883), 232.
26. Brown, *Sixty Years' Gleanings*, 33.
27. *Memoirs of Thomas Hardy* (1832), 13–14.
28. M. Thale, 'London Debating Societies in the 1790s', *Historical Journal*, 32(1) (March 1989), 81.
29. *The Literary Panorama, and National Register*, III, 1808.
30. *A Collection of Addresses Transmitted by Certain English Clubs and Societies* (1793).
31. Thale, *London Corresponding Society*, 27–8; Howell 1076, 1171, 1302, 1552; HC Deb, 9 May 1820, vol. 1, CC. 242, 244, 246.
32. Howell 1067.
33. *Trials at Large* (1817), 229 (Castle's interrogation).
34. Chase (ed.), *Davenport*, 18–19; Brown, *Sixty Years' Gleanings*, 45–8.
35. Howell 842.
36. Kelleher, *Lives*, 31–4.
37. *Authentic History* 414.
38. Howell 972.
39. Howell 1288–91, 1550.
40. *Republican*, 28 April 1820.
41. Howell 773–80, 1288–93, 1554–8.

CHAPTER 14 WIVES, MARRIAGES, CHILDREN

1. HO 42.199: 136–7; HO 42.193: 501.
2. HO 44.5.45: 114.
3. Gatrell, *Hanging Tree*, 88.
4. Southey, *Letters from England*, p. 373; *Memoirs of Despard*, 47.
5. HO 44.6.85: 271–2; depicted in *Illustrated London News*, 29 December 1888.
6. *Authentic History* 101; HO 44.6: 269, 271.
7. HO 44.6: 269; *Times*, 1 May 1820.
8. HO 44.6: 243.

9. *Morning Post*, 8 March 1820; HO 42.199: 590; civil death registers.
10. Howell 1288–91; 'Curable Patients Book', vol. 1 (1816–22), London Metropolitan Archives, H64.B01.008. On Brunt's son and Edwards: Brown, *Sixty Years' Gleanings*, 238–9.
11. *Observer*, 7 May 1820; *The Examiner*, 7 May 1820.
12. Therry, *Reminiscences*, 96–9; 1828 census (and other records on Strange), www.ancestry.co.uk . Cf. G. Parsons, 'The Cato Street Conspirators in New South Wales', *Labour History*, 8 (May 1965), 3–5; K. McKenzie, 'Exit Pursued by a Bear: Oliver the Spy and the Imperial Context of British Political History', *History Australia*, 13(1) (2016), 83; K. Hannon (esp. on Bradburn), 'The Fate of the Transported Cato Street Conspirators', in McElligott and Conboy (eds), *Cato Street Conspiracy*, 153–68 (Hannon wrongly states that Cooper was unmarried); Pickering, 'Betrayal and Exile', in Davis and Pickering, *Unrespectable Radicals?*, 201–2.
13. HO 42.193: 501.
14. *Republican*, 11 February 1820.
15. McCalman, *Radical Underworld*, 105–6.
16. HO 44.4.362–8 (undated); Fairburn (1817), 160.
17. HO 42.199.585.
18. HO 44.5: 230; HO 42.199 (25 January 1820).
19. *Authentic History* 73.
20. Bamford, *Life of a Radical*, ii, 159–60.
21. *Stamford Mercury*, 24 March 1820; 'Sir Nathaniel Conant', *ODNB*.
22. HO 44.6: 146.
23. *Times*, 22 April 1820; *Yorkshire Gazette*, 5 August 1820.
24. *Era*, 20 April 1856.
25. Cited here is the letter from Thistlewood's granddaughter and Julian's daughter, Miss Sophie Thornley Thistlewood (b. 1839), to the widow of George Thistlewood in Lincolnshire: *Nottingham Evening Post*, 22 November 1907. My thanks to Clare Bevan for alerting me to this.
26. George's descent from Julian is proved by his Paris marriage banns, issued in 1889 for Marie Stub and Georges [*sic*] William Thornley Thistlewood, son of Julian and Adèle Victoire Petit: 'Archives de Paris et sa région: Publications des bans de mariages 1860–1930' (www.ancestry.co.uk) (my thanks again to Clare Bevan). Cf. also Museum of Osny, 'Thornley à Osny' (n.d.) (https://en.calameo.com/read/003564072c077f6ed5cb6, accessed 20 September 2021).
27. Kelleher, *Lives*, 35.
28. *Republican*, 28 April 1820, 221–3.
29. Howell 1108–10.
30. HO 42.199: 561; Howell 727, 998.
31. Howell 1451.
32. Howell 1110.
33. *Morning Chronicle*, 3 May 1820, republished in *Authentic History*.
34. *Authentic History* 405–7; Gurney i, 657–61.

CHAPTER 15   MEN OF COLOUR: WEDDERBURN AND DAVIDSON

1. Dabydeen thought that early eighteenth-century blacks were sufficiently assimilated to find 'pleasure, companionship, and a degree of protection' in lower white society: *Hogarth's Blacks*, 37, 39. McCalman suggested that London's radical underworld provided 'a haven from racial discrimination' since Wedderburn 'recorded no instances of prejudice in his deprived and ethnically diverse milieu': 'Anti-Slavery and Ultra-Radicalism in Early Nineteenth-Century England: The Case of Robert Wedderburn', *Slavery and Abolition*, 7(2) (1986), 103. Cf. Linebaugh and Rediker, *Many–Headed Hydra*; Myers, *Reconstructing the Black Past*, 131; Walvin, *England, Slaves and Freedom*, ch. 4. On eighteenth-century racist assumptions see Fryer, *Staying Power*, ch. 7.

2. E. Long, *The History of Jamaica* (1774), ii, 476; P. Thicknesse, *A Year's Journey through France and Part of Spain* (2 vols, 1778), ii, 102–5, 108–11; *Cobbett's Weekly Political Register* (1804), 935, cited by Fryer, *Staying Power*, 238; on Carlile, Hanley, *Beyond Slavery*, 231.

3. *Cobbett's Parliamentary History*, vol. xix (1814), 306.

4. HO 42.199: 604.

5. *Hull Packet and Advertiser*, 3 March 1823.

6. *Morning Post*, 22 August 1817; *Suffolk Chronicle*, 23 August 1817; Hanley, *Beyond Slavery*, 220.

7. Gatrell, *City of Laughter*, 480–2.

8. Hanley, *Beyond Slavery*, ch. 8, n 54, 203–39.

9. Middlesex Sessions Papers, Justices' Working Documents, October 1795 and PCOM 2.0194072 (www.digitalpanopiticon.org, version 1.2.1, accessed 20 September 2021).

10. McCalman, *Radical Underworld*, 54.

11. *Survey of London: Volumes 31 and 32(2)*, 219–29; McCalman, *Radical Underworld*, 132; *Examiner*, 26 September 1819.

12. *Morning Chronicle*, 21 August 1819; HO 42.199: 134 (21 November).

13. HO 42.197: 395.

14. Worrall, *Radical Culture*, 180–1.

15. HO 42.199: 136–7 and 422.

16. *Morning Post*, 27 January 1820; *Times*, 26 February and 10 May 1820.

17. HO 44.4: 322; HO 44.5: 51; HO 44.5: 494–5; *Republican*, 3 March 1820.

18. HO 42.199: 545.

19. Howell 1461–2.

20. Cf. P. Vernon and A. Osborne, *100 Great Black Britons* (2020), 214–20; H. Mackey's biography in *BDMBR* i, 113–14, and Livesay, *Children of Uncertain Fortune*, 362–6. Like everyone else, these accept highly questionable accounts of his ancestry and career and pass over their awkward moments.

21. Howell 1460.

22. F. Cundall, *Historic Jamaica* (1915), xix–xx; *Cobbett's Political Register*, 6 May 1820. The *Jamaica Almanac* for 1787 lists a single Peter Davidson as one of many magistrates and parochial officers in St Mary's precinct, Middlesex County, Jamaica; while a Donald Davidson of Lilyfield in the parish of St Ann is listed as owner of 101 slaves in 1817. Other Davidson

references are scattered throughout this source, but none is in notable office (www.jamaicanfamilysearch.com, accessed 20 September 2021). If William was illegitimate, he might have been named after his mother, but not if the father acknowledged the boy. William might have been the son of a plantation attorney, but that was a humbler matter. For information my thanks to Guy Grannum, Caribbean specialist and Head of Systems at the National Archives, Kew.

23. *Authentic History* 317; Howell 1440.
24. Thornbury, *Old and New London*, v, 204–24.
25. *Authentic History* 95.
26. *Authentic History* 410–11.
27. Kelleher, *Lives*, 20–1, 12–13.
28. *Authentic History* 412.
29. Worrall, *Radical Culture*, 193.
30. HO 44.5.73: 391–2.
31. Howell 1549.
32. *Authentic History* 14.
33. *Authentic History* 14, 408–10; Howell 1461; Prothero, *Artisans and Politics*, 124–7; HO 42.199.
34. HO 42.199: 547.
35. HO 42.199: 571.
36. HO 42.197 (spy report 14 November 1819).
37. HO 42.197.500–7; HO 42.199–200; Fryer, *Staying Power*, 218.
38. HO 42.197.503; HO 44.4.317; 44.5.38; HO 44.1.157: 185; HO 44.4.33: 100–1; HO 44.4.97: 317–19; Gurney II, 506.
39. Howell 1550.
40. *Authentic History* 412–14; Sherwood, Neely and Jones, 196; *Times*, 2 May 1820.

CHAPTER 16   TRIALS AND VERDICTS

1. Addington Papers, 4 April 1820: Devon County Archives, 152M.C1820. OH33.
2. *Authentic History* 98–100.
3. Howell 358; Gatrell, *Hanging Tree*, 536.
4. *OBSP*, 12 April 1820; *Morning Chronicle*, 17 April 1820.
5. *Morning Chronicle*, 18 April 1820.
6. *Times*, 20 April 1820.
7. Chancellor, *Diary of Philipp von Neumann*, I, 18–21, and von Neumann's unpublished diary transcript, Cambridge University Library, GB 12 MS Add. 8350, vol. 1, 40–1.
8. Howell 851, 893.
9. Except by Gatrell: *Hanging Tree*, 435–9. Prothero, *Artisans and Politics*, 131; *Annual Register* (1820), 163.
10. Howell 851.
11. As it was, it irked the home office that the jury refused to convict the conspirators on every count of the charges: Aspinall, *Henry Hobhouse*, 22.

12. *Cobbett's Political Register*, 6 May 1820.
13. Scrivener, *Seditious Allegories*, 199–200.
14. Thelwall in Scrivener, *Seditious Allegories*, 199; *Republican*, 28 April 1820.
15. Hunt, *Memoirs*, iii, 375; *Cobbett's Political Register*, 6 May 1820.
16. Howell 872.
17. Adolphus's speech: Howell 850–94; precised in *Authentic History* 195–250.
18. *Authentic History* 227.
19. Howell 872.
20. Howell 871; *Authentic History* 220; HO 42.199: 624, 634.
21. Howell 740–1, 867.
22. *Authentic History* 279–80; HO 42.199: 609. Edwards's reports failed to mention this plan because he had been watching Wellington's and Ellenborough's houses when Harrison proposed it.
23. *Authentic History* 279–80; Howell 870.
24. Howell 1561.
25. *Authentic History* 239–50.
26. Wellington Papers, University of Southampton Library, MS61 WP1/660, fos 1–6. Copies are also in the Liverpool Papers in the British Library. Henderson, *Recollections of . . . John Adolphus*, 113.
27. *Authentic History* 415.
28. *Cobbett's Political Register*, 6 May 1820; Howell 1562.
29. Aspinall, *Henry Hobhouse*, 22; HO 44.6: 88 (26 April).
30. HO 44.6: 208.
31. HC Deb, 25 April 1814, vol. 27, cc. 538–41. In 1814 the hanging, drawing, and quartering of traitors was abolished in favour of hanging until dead, followed by decapitation and quartering, the parts 'to be disposed of as His Majesty and his Successors shall think fit'.
32. On the following, Gatrell, *Hanging Tree*, ch. 18.
33. Aspinall, *Henry Hobhouse*, 17, 22; *Authentic History* 352.

CHAPTER 17   MAY DAY AT NEWGATE

1. *Cobbett's Political Register*, 6 May 1820; *Newgate Monthly Magazine*, 1(3) (1824–5), 141; Wakefield, *Punishment of Death*, 228–35, 247–58.
2. *Memoirs of Despard*, 77; *Trial of Bellingham*, 25; Shelley, 'We Pity the Plumage, but Forget the Dying Bird' (1817); *Trial of James Wilson*, 48.
3. HO 44.6.34: 103–4; *Black Dwarf*, 3 May 1820; *Morning Chronicle*, 1 May 1820.
4. Raikes, *Journal*, iv, 305–7.
5. Gatrell, *Hanging Tree*, 616.
6. Kelleher, *Lives*, 43.
7. Gatrell, *Hanging Tree*, ch. 2; Quennell (ed.), *Princess Lieven to Metternich*, 33.
8. Thackeray, *Fraser's Magazine*, 22 (1840), 150–8; Nicholson, *Autobiography*, 8–9.
9. Marchand, *Byron*, ii, 694.
10. *Bristol Mercury*, 8 May 1820.
11. Fairburn, *Trials* (1820), 134–6; McCalman, *Radical Underworld*, 147; Raikes, *Journal*, iv, 305–7.
12. *Theatrical Journal*, 11(550) (1850), 201.

13. Bamford and Wellington (eds), *Journal of Mrs. Arbuthnot*, I, 15–16.
14. Detailed accounts of the executions are numerous. I follow *Examiner*, 7 May 1820; *Morning Chronicle* (and others), 2 May 1820; Fairburn, *Trials* (1820), 137–8.
15. *Authentic History* 399.
16. *Examiner*, 7 May 1820, embellished in *Authentic History*, 383–4.
17. According to Raikes, the executioner mislaid the axe. He and Lord Alvanley were horrified when an assistant burst into the sheriff's room and took a large knife from the cupboard to replace it (*Diary*, IV, 306). I find no further reference to the axe until a passing mention in H. Mayhew and J. Binny, *The Criminal Prisons of London* (1862), 595. The *Illustrated London News* (29 December 1888) depicted Newgate's 'chain cupboard', which held the axe 'formerly carried before prisoners at execution, another version being that it was made for the Cato-street Conspirators but not used': by then, clearly, its Cato Street provenance was doubted. The Museum of London now exhibits a pristine axe which it claims was made for the Cato Street executions, but offers no evidence of its provenance.
18. Since no hangman trusted himself to remove Despard's head with an axe in 1803, a surgeon had to hack at the neck with a dissecting knife, but he 'missed the particular joint aimed at, and was haggling at it, till one of the executioners took the head between his hands, and twisted it round several times, and even then it was with difficulty separated from the body'. *Memoirs of Despard*, 12.
19. C. Hindley, *Life and Times of James Catnach* (1878), 92; *Cobbett's Political Register*, 6 May 1820.
20. HO 44.6: 135–6, 217–18.
21. HO 44.4: 295–7.
22. HO 44.6.73: 235–42.
23. HO 44.6: 90 and 289; Worrall, *Radical Culture*, 200.
24. *Authentic History* v.
25. Bloom and Bloom (eds), *Piozzi Letters*, VI, 95, 386–7; Bamford and Wellington (eds), *Journal of Mrs. Arbuthnot*, I, 15–16; Quennell (ed.), *Princess Lieven to Metternich*, 15, 33; Robinson (ed.), *Letters of Princess Lieven 1812–1834*, 47.
26. Bamford, *Life of a Radical*, II, 160–1.

18 EPILOGUE: GÉRICAULT GOES TO CATO STREET

1. Théodore Géricault, *Scéne de pendaison à Londres* (or *La pendaison d'Arthur Thistlewood et de ses complices*), 1820, pencil and sepia wash, 40.8 × 32.2 cm. (*Musée des Beaux-Arts de Rouen*, inv. 882.9.1); Clément, *Géricault: Étude biographique et critique*, 358; Eitner, *Géricault*, 350 (n. 59); Anon., *La folie d'une monde* (Musée des fine arts de Lyon, 2006), 10; Bazin, *Géricault: Étude critique, documents et catalogue raisonné*, VII, 19–22.
2. For these reasons I wrongly assumed in my *Hanging Tree*, 178n.55, that Géricault depicted another execution entirely.

3. N. Athanassoglou-Kallmyer, 'Géricault's Severed Heads and Limbs: The Politics and Aesthetics of the Scaffold', *Art Bulletin*, 74(4) (1992), 604, 610; Miles, *Medusa*, 212.

4. C. Sells, 'New Light on Géricault, His Travels, and His Friends, 1816–1823', *Apollo*, 73 (1986), 393–4.

5. The work commented on the corruption and incompetence that had resulted in the wreck of the French frigate *La Méduse* off West Africa in 1816. The ship had had too few lifeboats. After the commander and officers made sure they were themselves safely in one, they cut adrift 149 men and one woman whom they were towing on an improvised escape raft. Of these, 135 perished during twelve nightmarish days and nights of cannibalism, insanity, and murder.

6. C. Sells, 'Two Letters from Géricault to Madame Horace Vernet', *Burlington Magazine*, 131(1032) (1989), 217; C. Sells, '"Raft of the Medusa": Géricault's Later Projects', *Burlington Magazine*, 128(1001) (1986), 563–9.

7. The exhibition ran from 12 June to 30 December 1820: Eitner, *Géricault*, 211. In early 1821 Bullock shipped the *Medusa* to Dublin for further viewing (not a success). *Literary Gazette and Journal*, 1 July 1820, 427; *New Monthly Magazine* (September 1820), 317; *Times*, 22 June 1820; Sells, 'New Light on Géricault', 393–4.

8. *Arthur Thistlewood, chef de la conspiration* (BM 1887, 0722.251). It was taken from Charles Williams's inaccurate print, *The Hay-Loft Plot of Thistlewood and his 24 Conspirators* (February 1820).

9. Eitner, *Géricault*, 156–7.

10. B. Prendeville, 'The Features of Insanity, as seen by Géricault and by Büchner', *Oxford Art Journal*, 18(1) (1995), 100.

11. Miles, *Medusa*, 199.

12. L. Eitner, 'Erotic Drawings by Géricault', *Master Drawings*, 34(4) (Winter 1996), 375.

13. Eitner, *Géricault*, 204, 221.

14. Wilkie's Cato Street drawings (now lost) are listed in auction records: Tromans, *Wilkie*, 46.

15. Greig (ed.), *Farington Diary*, VIII, 242, 252–3.

16. *Le Conservateur littéraire* (4 vols, Paris, reprinted *c.* 1922–38), 2(1) (May 1820), 292–3.

17. Gatrell, '146 Artists and Engravers of Covent Garden', *First Bohemians*, 386–7, 389–404.

18. *La jeune femme et ses trois enfants*, BM Prints and Drawings, 1888, 0619.19.

19. Eitner, *Géricault*, 216 and 349n.35; S. Lodge, 'Géricault in England', *Burlington Magazine*, 107(753) (December 1965), 617. 'Elmore' is recorded at several addresses. What survives of the 1821 census schedules for Marylebone lists an 'Elmore' at 46 Duke Street and (with family included) at 3 John Street. The latter household comprised two males, one aged twenty to thirty (Géricault?!), the other thirty to forty, four females aged twenty to thirty and another aged forty to fifty (servants?).

20. *Authentic History* 173.

21. J. W. Carleton (ed.), *Sporting Review* (July 1859), 7.

22. See p. XXX above. Bazin, *Géricault*, vii, 20–3. Géricault also reworked an old master painting in Elmore's possession: N. Lesure and L. Marty de Cambiaire, *The Martyrdom of Saint Hippolytus: A Painting by Pierre Subleyras Reworked by Théodore Géricault* (2013), 22–5.
23. *Authentic History* 6, 22, 104.
24. Eitner, *Géricault*, 225; Lodge, 'Géricault in England', 617; Bazin, *Géricault*, vii, 19–20.
25. [739] Gatrell, *First Bohemians*, 328–9; Gatrell, *Hanging Tree*, 180, 191.
26. Although Goya's 'black' paintings, his study of a madhouse, and his etchings of the *Disasters of War* are all coeval with the British regency and share Géricault's unflinching vision and may exceed it in their clarity, they too were unknown outside closed circles in Madrid until the second half of the nineteenth century.
27. R. Hughes, *Goya* (2003), 308; R. Hughes, 'The Unflinching Eye', *Guardian*, 4 October 2003.

THE PEOPLE LISTED

1. Some ages are disputed. For Cato Street I follow *ODNB* when baptismal date is given, otherwise Newgate prison registers: PCOM 2/22–3. *ODNB* states that Brunt was born in Union Street, off Oxford Street, London, but the registers say he was born in Retford.
2. HO 42.197: 506.
3. HO 44.4: 203.

Bibliography

PRIMARY WORKS AND MEMOIRS

Alison, A., *The Lives of Lord Castlereagh and Sir Charles Stewart* (3 vols, 1861)

Anon., *Memoirs of the Life of Colonel E. M. Despard, with His Trial at Large* (Manchester, 1803)

Anon., *The Trial of J. Bellingham* (1812)

Anon., *The Trial of James Wilson for High Treason* (Glasgow, 1834)

Aspinall, A., *The Diary of Henry Hobhouse, 1820–1827* (1947)

Aylmer, E., *Memoirs of George Edwards* (1820)

Bamford, F. and Wellington, duke of (eds), *The Journal of Mrs. Arbuthnot, 1820–1832* (2 vols, 1950)

Bamford, S., *Passages in the Life of a Radical* (2 vols, 1844)

Bayley, J., *History and Antiquities of the Tower of London* (2 vols, 1825)

Bloom, E. A. and L. D. (eds), *The Piozzi Letters, Volume 6, 1817–1821* (2002)

Bonnett, A. and Armstrong, K. (eds), *Thomas Spence: The Poor Man's Revolutionary* (2014)

Brown, John, *Sixty Years' Gleanings from Life's Harvest: A Genuine Autobiography* (1859)

Bruce, W. N., *The Life of General Sir Charles Napier, G.C.B.* (2nd edn, 1885)

Campbell, T. C., *The Battle of the Press: as Told in the . . . Life of Richard Carlile* (1899)

Chancellor, E. B. (ed.), *The Diary of Philipp von Neumann* (2 vols, 1928)

Chase, M. (ed.), *The Life and Literary Pursuits of Allen Davenport . . . Written by Himself, 1846* (1994)

Cobbett, W., *The History of the Regency and Reign of King George the Fourth* (1830)

Colchester, Lord, *The Diary and Correspondence of Charles Abbot, Lord Colchester* (3 vols, 1861)

Colvin, S., *The Letters of John Keats to His Family and Friends* (1925)

Daniell, J. F., *Meteorological Essays and Observations* (1827)

Davenport, A., *The Life, Writings and Principles of Thomas Spence* (1836)

Diprose, J., *Some Account of the Parish of St Clement Danes Past and Present* (2 vols, 1868)

Dixon, W. Hepworth, *The London Prisons* (1850)

Dowden, W. S. (ed.), *The Journal of Thomas Moore* (5 vols, 1986)

Evans, T., *Christian Policy, the Salvation of the Empire* (1816)

Fairburn, J., *Narrative of the Cato-Street Conspiracy, Being an Impartial Account of the Attack in the Stable, . . . the Apprehension of the Prisoners, . . .* (1820)

Gathorne Hardy, A. E. (ed.), *Gathorne Hardy, First Earl of Cranbrook* (2 vols, 1910)

Greig, J., (ed.), *The Farington Diary* (8 vols, 1922–8)

Greville, C., *The Greville Memoirs: A Journal of the Reigns of King George IV and King William IV* (3 vols, 1874)

Grierson, H. (ed.), *The Letters of Sir Walter Scott* (12 vols, 1932–7)

Grosvenor, C., *The First Lady Wharncliffe and Her Family (1779–1856)* (2 vols, 1927)

Hare, A. J. C. (ed.), *The Story of Two Noble Lives: Memorials of Charlotte, Countess Canning, and Louisa, Marchioness of Waterford* (3 vols, 1893)

Hazlitt, W., *Political Essays, with Sketches of Public Characters* (1819)

Hazlitt, W., *Table Talk* (1821)

Henderson, C. E., *Recollections of the Public Career and Private Life of the Late John Adolphus* (1871)

Hibbert, C. (ed.), *Captain Gronow: His Reminiscences of Regency and Victorian Life, 1810–1860* (1991)

Holland, Baron, *Further Memoirs of the Whig Party: 1807–1821* (1905)

Holyoake, G. J., *The Life and Character of Richard Carlile* (1849)

Hone, W., *The Meeting in Spa Fields. Hone's authentic . . . account . . . of all the proceedings on . . . December 2d, . . . 1816* (1816)

Hone, W., *The Three Trials of William Hone* (1817; reprint 1876)

Hunt, H., *Memoirs of Henry Hunt, Esq., Written by Himself in H.M. Gaol at Ilchester* (3 vols, 1820–2)

Ivimey, J., *The History of the English Baptists* (1830)

Jennings, L. (ed.), *The Croker Papers: Correspondence and Diaries of John Wilson Croker, 1809 to 1830* (3 vols, Cambridge, 2012)

Johnstone's London Commercial Guide and Street Directory, 1818

Kent, D. A. and Ewen, D. R. (eds), *Regency Radical: Selected Writings of William Hone* (2003)

Knight, C., *Passages of a Working Life during Half a Century* (3 vols, 1863–4)

McCarthy, J., *The Story of the Nations: Modern England* (1898)

McCalman, I. (ed.), *The Horrors of Slavery (1824) and other Writings by Robert Wedderburn* (1991)

MacKenzie, P., *An Exposure of the Spy System Pursued in Glasgow . . . 1816–17* (Glasgow, 1833)

Manchester Meeting, 16th of August, 1819. Report of the Trial, Redford against Birley and others for an Assault . . . (Manchester, 1822)

Marshall, J., *Wreath of Freedom, or, Patriot's Song Book: Being a Collection of Songs in Favour of Public Liberty* (Newcastle, 1820)

Marchand, L. A., *Byron: A Biography* (3 vols, 1957)

Marchand, L. A. (ed.), *'Between Two Worlds': Byron's Letters and Journals* (Cambridge, Mass., 1977)

Martineau, H., *The History of England during the Thirty Years' Peace, 1816–1846* (2 vols, 1849–50)

Masterman, C., *From the Abyss: Of its Inhabitants, by One of Them* (1902)

Nicholson, R., *The Lord Chief Baron Nicholson: An Autobiography* (1860)

Pellew, A. G., *Life and Correspondence of Henry Addington, first Viscount Sidmouth* (3 vols, 1847)

Phipps, E. (ed.), *Memoirs of the Political and Literary Life of Robert Plumer Ward* (2 vols, 1850)

Prentice, A., *Historical Sketches and Personal Recollections of Manchester* (1851)

Preston, T., *The Life and Opinions of Thomas Preston, Patriot and Shoemaker* (1817)

Quennell, P. (ed.), *The Private Letters of Princess Lieven to Prince Metternich, 1820–1826* (1938)

Raikes, T., *A Portion of the Journal Kept by Thomas Raikes, Esq., from 1831–1847* (4 vols, 1856–7)

Redding, C., *Fifty Years' Recollections, Literary and Personal* (3 vols, 1858)

Rede, L. T., *Memoir of . . . George Canning* (1827)

Report of the Metropolitan and Central Committee . . . for the Relief of the Manchester Sufferers (1820)

Richmond, A., *Narrative of the Condition of the Manufacturing Population and . . . State Trials in Scotland* (1824)

Robinson, L. G. (ed.), *Letters of Dorothea, Princess Lieven, during her Residence in London 1812–1834* (1902)

Romilly, S., *Memoirs of the Life of Sir Samuel Romilly, Written by Himself* (edited by his sons, 3 vols, 1840)

Rush, R., *Residence at the Court of London from 1819 to 1825* (1833)

Sadler, T. (ed.), *The Diary, Reminiscences, and Correspondence of H. Crabb Robinson* (3 vols, 1869)

Sibly, M., *The Genuine Trial of Thomas Hardy, for High Treason* (2 vols, 1795)

Southey, C. C. (ed.), *The Life and Correspondence of Robert Southey* (6 vols, 1850)

Strype, T. J., *A Survey of the Cities of London and Westminster* (1720; online edition, www.dhi.ac.uk)

Thale, M. (ed.), *The Autobiography of Francis Place* (Cambridge, 1972)

Thale, M. (ed.), *Selections from the Papers of the London Corresponding Society 1792–1799* (Cambridge, 1983)

Therry, R., *Reminiscences of Thirty Years' Residence in New South Wales and Victoria* (1863)

Thornbury, W., *Old and New London* (3 vols, 1878)

Thompson, R., *Tribute to Liberty: Or, A Collection of Select Songs, together with . . . Toasts and Sentiments. Sacred to the Rights of Man* (1793–5)

Trial by Jury. . . . Report of the Speeches of Messrs. Hunt, Watson, Thistlewood, Preston, . . . at the Crown and Anchor Tavern, July 21, 1817, at a Dinner given to celebrate the Acquittal of the State Prisoners (1817)

Vanderkiste, R. W., *Notes and Narratives of a Six Years' Mission . . . among the Dens of London* (1852)

Vane, C. W., *The Despatches and Other Papers of Viscount Castlereagh* (4 vols, 1853)

Wakefield, E. G., *Facts relating to the Punishment of Death in the Metropolis* (1831), in M. F. Lloyd Prichard (ed.), *Collected Works of Edward Gibbon Wakefield* (1968)

Wellington, duke of, *Despatches, Correspondence and Memoranda of Field Marshal Arthur Duke of Wellington* (8 vols, 1867–80)

Wheatley, H. B., and Cunningham P., *London Past and Present: Its History, Associations, and Traditions* (1891; Cambridge, 2011)

Wilkinson, G. T., *An Authentic History of the Cato-Street Conspiracy; with the Trials at Large of the Conspirators, for High Treason and Murder* (1820)

Wilson, W., *Dissenting Churches and Meeting Houses in London* (3 vols, 1810)

Wooler, T. J., *A Political Lecture on Heads, by the Black Dwarf* (January 1820)

SECONDARY WORKS

Barrell, J., *The Spirit of Despotism: Invasions of Privacy in the 1790s* (Oxford, 2006)

Bazin, G., *Théodore Géricault: Étude critique, documents et catalogue raisonné* (8 vols, Paris, c. 1987–97)

Belchem, J., *'Orator' Hunt: Henry Hunt and English Working Class Radicalism* (Oxford, 1985)

Bruton, F. A. (ed.), *Three Accounts of Peterloo by Eyewitnesses* (Manchester, 1921)

Burnard, T., *Mastery, Tyranny, and Desire: Thomas Thistlewood and His Slaves in the Anglo-Jamaican World* (Chapel Hill, NC, 2009).

Bush, M., *The Casualties of Peterloo* (Manchester, 2005)

Chase, M., *1820: Disorder and Stability in the United Kingdom* (Manchester, 2013)

Chase, M., *The People's Farm: English Radical Agrarianism, 1775–1840* (1988)

Clément, C., *Géricault: Étude biographique et critique, avec le catalogue raisonné de l'œuvre du maître* (Paris, 1868)

Cookson, J. E., *The British Armed Nation, 1793–1815* (Oxford, 1997)

Dabydeen, D., *Hogarth's Blacks: Images of Blacks in Eighteenth-Century English Art* (1985)

Davis, M. T. and Pickering, P., *Unrespectable Radicals?: Popular Politics in the Age of Reform* (2013)

Dickinson, H. T. (ed.), *The Political Works of Thomas Spence* (Newcastle upon Tyne, 1982)

Douet, J., *British Barracks 1600–1914: Their Architecture and Role in Society* (1998)

Eitner, L., *Géricault: His Life and Work* (1983)

Epstein, J. A., *Radical Expression: Political Language, Ritual and Symbol in England, 1790–1850* (Oxford, 1994)

Floud, R., and Johnson, P. (eds), *Cambridge Economic History of Modern Britain* (3 vols, Cambridge, 2004)

Fryer, P., *Staying Power: The History of Black People in Britain* (1984)

Gardner, J., *Poetry and Popular Protest: Peterloo, Cato Street and the Queen Caroline Controversy* (2011)

Gatrell, V., *City of Laughter: Sex and Satire in Eighteenth-Century London* (2006)

Gatrell, V., *The First Bohemians: Life and Art in London's Golden Age* (2013)

Gatrell, V., *The Hanging Tree: Execution and the English People, 1770–1868* (Oxford, 1994)

Goodway, D., *London Chartism, 1838–1848* (Cambridge, 1982)

Hackwood, F. W., *William Hone: His Life and Times* (1912)

Hall, D., *In Miserable Slavery: Thomas Thistlewood in Jamaica, 1750–86* (1989)

Hanley, R., *Beyond Slavery and Abolition: Black British Writing, 1770–1830* (Cambridge, 2018)

Haynes, C., *Our Friends – the Enemies: The Occupation of France after Napoleon* (Cambridge, Mass., 2018)

Hilton, B., *A Mad, Bad, and Dangerous People? England 1783–1846* (Oxford, 2008)

Hone, J. A., *For the Cause of Truth: Radicalism in London 1796–1821* (Oxford, 1982)

Johnson, D., *Regency Revolution: The Case of Arthur Thistlewood* (1974)

Linebaugh, P., and Rediker, M., *The Many-Headed Hydra: The Hidden History of the Revolutionary Atlantic* (2000)

Livesay, D., *Children of Uncertain Fortune: Mixed-Race Jamaicans in Britain and the Atlantic Family, 1733–1833* (Chapel Hill, NC, 2018)

McCalman, I., *Radical Underworld: Prophets, Revolutionaries, and Pornographers in London, 1795–1840* (1988)

McElligott, J. and Conboy, M. (eds), *The Cato Street Conspiracy: Plotting, Counter-intelligence and the Revolutionary Tradition in Britain and Ireland* (Manchester, 2020)

McKellar, E., *The Birth of Modern London: The Development and Design of the City 1660–1720* (Manchester, 1999)

McMaster, G., *Scott and Society* (Cambridge, 1981)

Miles, J., *Medusa: The Shipwreck, the Scandal, the Masterpiece* (2012)

Myers, N., *Reconstructing the Black Past: Blacks in Britain, c. 1780–1830* (1996)

New, C. W., *The Life of Henry Brougham to 1830* (Oxford, 1961)

Norman, P., *London Vanished and Vanishing* (1904)

Palmer, R., *The Sound of History: Songs and Social Comment* (Oxford, 1988)

Parolin, C., *Radical Spaces: Venues of Popular Politics in London, 1790–c. 1845* (Canberra, 2010)

Patterson, M. W., *Sir Francis Burdett and His Times (1770–1844)* (2 vols, 1931)

Poole, R., *Peterloo: The English Uprising* (Oxford, 2019)

Poole, S., *The Politics of Regicide in England, 1760–1850: Troublesome Subjects* (Manchester, 2000)

Porter, B., *Plots and Paranoia: A History of Political Espionage in Britain 1790–1988* (1989)

Prothero, I., *Artisans and Politics in Early Nineteenth-Century London: John Gast and His Times* (1979)

Rudé, G., *Hanoverian London 1714–1808* (1971)

Schwarz, L. D., *London in the Age of Industrialisation: Entrepreneurs, Labour Force and Living Conditions, 1700–1850* (Cambridge, 1992)

Scrivener, M., *Seditious Allegories: John Thelwall and Jacobin Writing* (University Park, Pa., 2010)

Smith, Digby, *The Greenhill Napoleonic Wars Data Book* (1998)

Smith, E. A., *Whig Principles and Party Politics: Earl Fitzwilliam and the Whig Party 1748–1833* (Manchester, 1975)

Speck, W. A., *A Political Biography of Thomas Paine* (2015)

Stanhope, J., *The Cato Street Conspiracy* (1962)

Strachan, H., *From Waterloo to Balaclava: Tactics, Technology, and the British Army 1815–1854* (1985)

Survey of London: Volume 45, Knightsbridge (ed. J. Greenacombe, 2000)

Survey of London: Volume 47, Northern Clerkenwell and Pentonville (ed. P. Temple, 2008)

Survey of London: Volumes 31 and 32(2), St James, Westminster (ed. F. H. W. Sheppard, 1963)

Survey of London: Volumes 39(1) and 40(2), Grosvenor Estate, Mayfair (ed. F. H. W. Sheppard, 1977, 1980)

Thompson, E. P., *Making of the English Working Class* (1963)

Thorne, R. G., *The House of Commons, 1790–1820* (1986)

Tiffany, D., *Infidel Poetics: Riddles, Nightlife, Substance* (Chicago, 2009)

Tromans, N., *David Wilkie: The People's Painter* (Edinburgh, 2007)

Tuite, C., *Lord Byron and Scandalous Celebrity* (Cambridge, 2015)

Turner, D., *The Old Boys: The Decline and Rise of the Public School* (2015)

Walvin, J., *England, Slaves and Freedom, 1776–1838* (1986)

Watt, P., Scott, D. B. and Spedding, P. (eds), *Cheap Print and Popular Song in the Nineteenth Century* (Cambridge, 2017)

Weller, J., *Wellington at Waterloo* (1991)

White, J., *London in the Nineteenth Century: 'A Human Awful Wonder of God'* (2007)

White, R. J., *Waterloo to Peterloo* (1957)

Wood, M., *Radical Satire and Print Culture, 1790–1822* (Oxford, 1994)

Worrall, D., *Radical Culture: Discourse, Resistance and Surveillance, 1790–1820* (Detroit, 1992)

Worrall, D., *The Politics of Romantic Theatricality, 1787–1832: The Road to the Stage* (2007)

Index

References such as '178–9' indicate (not necessarily continuous) discussion of a topic across a range of pages. Wherever possible in the case of topics with many references, these have either been divided into sub-topics or only the most significant discussions of the topic are listed. Because the entire work is about the 'Cato Street Conspiracy', the use of this term (and certain others which occur constantly throughout the book) as an entry point has been restricted. Information will be found under the corresponding detailed topics.